PUBLICATIONS
OF THE
ARMY RECORDS SOCIETY
VOL. 9

ROBERTS IN INDIA

The Military Papers of Field Marshal Lord Roberts
1876–1893

The Army Records Society was founded in 1984 in order to publish original records describing the development, organisation, administration and activities of the British Army from early times.

Any person wishing to become a Member of the Society is requested to apply to the Hon. Secretary, c/o the National Army Museum, Royal Hospital Road, London, SW3 4HT. The annual subscription entitles the Member to receive a copy of each volume issued by the Society in that year, and to purchase back volumes at reduced prices. Current subscription details, whether for individuals living within the British Isles, for individuals living overseas, or for institutions, will be furnished on request.

The Council of the Army Records Society wish it to be clearly understood that they are not answerable for opinions or observations that may appear in the Society's publications. For these the responsibility rests entirely with the Editors of the several works.

Roberts (centre right, with riding switch) and Heads of Departments at Kabul 1880. Macpherson facing him, Hugh Gough in between, Macgregor standing behind Roberts, Massy seated third from right.

(*NAM* 6,181)

ROBERTS IN INDIA

The Military Papers of Field Marshal Lord Roberts
1876–1893

Edited by
BRIAN ROBSON

Published by
ALAN SUTTON
for the
ARMY RECORDS SOCIETY
1993

First Published in the United Kingdom in 1993
Alan Sutton Publishing Ltd · Phoenix Mill · Far Thrupp · Stroud
Gloucestershire

First published in the United States of America in 1993
Alan Sutton Publishing Inc · 83 Washington Street · Dover NH 03820

British Library Cataloguing in Publication Data

Roberts in India
I. Robson, Brian
954.03092

ISBN 0-7509-0401-1

Library of Congress Cataloguing in Publication Data applied for

Typeset in Ehrhardt
Typesetting and origination by
Alan Sutton Publishing Limited.
Printed in Great Britain by
The Bath Press, Avon.

Contents

Maps

Editorial Acknowledgements

The vast bulk of the extant papers of Lord Roberts is in the National Army Museum, London, together with other relevant collections such as that of Field Marshal Sir Frederick Haines. This volume would not have been possible without the massive assistance, generously given, of Dr Alan Guy, Dr Peter Boyden and the staff of the Reading Room of the Museum. It is the model of what an archive ought to be. I am grateful also to the Council of the Museum for permission to reproduce papers and photographs in its possession.

I am grateful in only slightly lesser degree to Dr R.J. Bingle and the staff of the India Office Library and Records, to Lady de Bellaigue, Registrar of the Royal Archives at Windsor, to the Librarian of the Royal Commonwealth Society of London, to the Librarian of the William R. Perkins Library of Duke University, North Carolina, to the staff of the Centre for Kentish Studies at Maidstone, and to Mr Stephen Wood and the Department of Armed Forces History of the National Museums of Scotland, Edinburgh.

Documents in the Royal Archives are reproduced here by the gracious permission of Her Majesty the Queen. Material in the Crown copyright is reproduced with the permission of Her Majesty's Stationery Office. Other material is reproduced with the kind permission of the Council of the Royal Commonwealth Society, the Kent County Council and the Trustees of the William R. Perkins Library.

Among individuals, I am indebted to Lieutenant-Colonel I.A.J. Edwards-Stuart, Mrs Edwina Hancox and Lady Black for help in trying to trace papers of their ancestor, Lord Roberts; to Mrs David Guthrie-James for assistance in trying to trace papers used by her late husband in compiling his biography of Lord Roberts; to Miss Patricia Methven, Archivist of King's College, London, for her help in locating Roberts material world-wide; and to Mr John Andrews, lately Chief Librarian, and Mrs Judith Blackshaw, of the Ministry of Defence Central Library, London.

I owe a particular debt to Dr Ian Beckett, of the Department of War Studies at the Royal Military College Sandhurst and Honorary Secretary of the Society, for his wise guidance and help; and very particularly to my old friend and colleague, Mr Anthony Bennell, for much practical help and scholarly advice, willingly given. Mrs Sue Atkins typed successive drafts with skill and patience, while Mr Pat Shipp read the final draft with great care and extraordinary accuracy.

As always, I owe a deep debt to my wife who has acquiesced without complaint in the heavy expenditure of resources and companionship which this volume has entailed.

Hove   Brian Robson
May 1992

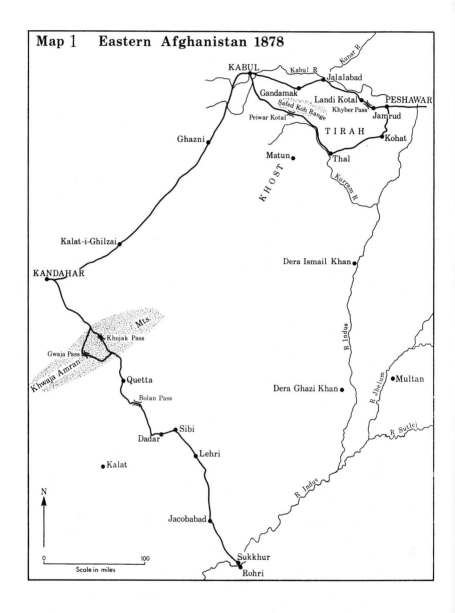

Map 1   Eastern Afghanistan 1878

KABUL   Kabul R.   Kunar R.
Jalalabad
Gandamak   Landi Kotal   PESHAWAR
Safed Koh Range   Khyber Pass   Jamrud
Peiwar Kotal
T I R A H   Kohat
Ghazni
Matun   Thal
K H O S T   Kurram R.

Kalat-i-Ghilzai
Dera Ismail Khan
KANDAHAR

Mts.
Khojak Pass
Gwaja Pass
Khwaja Amran
Quetta   Dera Ghazi Khan   Multan
Bolan Pass
R. Indus   R. Jhelum

Sibi
Dadar   Lehri   R. Sutlej
Kalat

N

Jacobabad   R. Indus

0   100   Sukkhur
Scale in miles   Rohri

Introduction

It can plausibly be argued that, despite the monumental aberrations of two world wars, the British Imperial army reached its zenith in the last quarter of the nineteenth century. That period is dominated by two soldiers – Garnet Wolseley and Frederick Sleigh Roberts.

Almost exact contemporaries, their careers followed different paths for forty years. Wolseley, from an impoverished background, had sought fame and position in the cannon's mouth – in Burma, the Crimea, the Indian Mutiny, China, Canada, Ashanti, South Africa. By 1876, at the age of forty-three, he was a substantive major general, twice knighted. He was closely identified with the reforms of the Liberal War Minister, Edward Cardwell, and was widely regarded as the hope of the future, soon to be immortalised by W.S. Gilbert as 'the very model of a modern major general'.[1]

Roberts, the son of an East India Company general, had served with distinction in the Mutiny, but thereafter had pursued his career within the department of the Quartermaster-General in India. By 1876, he was a substantive colonel (and local, or temporary, major-general) but he was virtually unknown outside the Bengal Army and had never commanded troops. Within nine years, he was Commander-in-Chief in India and Wolseley's rival for the highest posts in the British Army. It is that meteoric rise which is, in a sense, the theme of this volume.

A volume of papers is not a biography and the papers here have been selected, not to provide a connected career narrative, but to illustrate the main issues and events of this phase of Roberts' career, to give something of the flavour of late Victorian military life in India, and to provide signposts for other historians.

Frederick Sleigh Roberts was born on 30 September 1832 at Cawnpore, where his father, Abraham Roberts, was commanding the 1st Bengal European Regiment. (He was christened Sleigh in honour of the garrison commander, Major-General William Sleigh, an old friend of his father). Abraham Roberts was the son of a Rector of Waterford and his second wife, Isabella (Frederick's mother) was the daughter of Abraham Bunbury, of Kilfeacle, Co. Tipperary. Frederick was thus born into that

Anglo-Irish squirearchy which has produced such a disproportionate number of British generals. Abraham Roberts had served as a brigadier during the First Afghan War but had been replaced as a result of differences with the political authorities at Kabul. He held one further command – that of the Punjab Division and, when that was divided, of the Peshawar Division.

Fred, as he always signed himself, was educated at Eton and the East India Company's military college at Addiscombe. He was commissioned into the Bengal Artillery, the most prestigious branch of the old Bengal Army, and reached India in 1852. He was posted to a battery at Peshawar, where he acted as ADC to his father. In 1856, with the aid of parental influence, he was appointed acting Deputy Assistant Quartermaster-General at Peshawar. Thus, by one of those strokes of luck which punctuated his career, he was in a key place when the Mutiny broke out in May 1857. He was appointed to the staff of the Punjab Moveable Column, under John Nicholson, which played a major role in the siege and capture of Delhi. Subsequently, he served under the Commander-in-Chief, Sir Colin Campbell, at the final relief of Lucknow. When the Mutiny ended, he had won the VC and had become known as a promising officer to the leading military figures in India, from the Commander-in-Chief downwards.[2] With the absorption of the Bengal Artillery into the Royal Artillery, he had become a British Army officer and eligible for posts in that army.[3]

After home leave, he resumed his career in the Quartermaster-General's Department. Apart from relatively brief participations in the Ambeyla expedition of 1863, the Abyssinian expedition of 1867/8 and the Lushai expedition of 1871/2, he was to serve in staff posts for the next nineteen years. It will seem odd to a modern career officer that Roberts should deliberately have eschewed regimental duty and the pleasures of command but there was calculation in the decision. The Quartermaster-General's Department was not then concerned primarily with logistics but with operational planning and intelligence; it was the nearest thing to a General Staff. In the small world of official India, it was at the centre of military and political affairs, and Roberts rubbed shoulders with the great and good. By 1874, he was acting Quartermaster-General, becoming substantive on his promotion to full colonel in January 1876.

Fully to understand the papers in this volume it is necessary to understand the civil and military structures of India at this time. At the head of the government of India stood the Viceroy and Governor-General (a title held since 1858). He was normally a second-rank British political figure, sometimes a diplomat like Lytton. (After 1807, only one Indian civil servant became Viceroy – John Lawrence, Viceroy from 1864 to 1868). The Viceroy was assisted by an Executive (or Supreme) Council – legally, the Government of India was 'the Governor-General in Council'. In 1876, there were six Ordinary Members of Council (including a Law Member and a Military Member) and one Extraordinary Member (the Commander-in-Chief in India). The Ordinary Members were normally Indian civil servants except for the Military Member who was a soldier, and the Law Member who was normally a lawyer from England. Each Ordinary Member took charge of one of the seven departments of the Government (Foreign, Home, Finance, Legislative, Public Works, Military, and Agriculture and Revenue); the Viceroy himself took charge of the Foreign Department. Each Department was headed by a Secretary to the Government; the Secretary to the Government in the Foreign Department was colloquially known as 'the Foreign Secretary'. In the winter months (October to March), the Government resided in Calcutta, moving to Simla for the summer.

The Viceroy and the Government of India were subject to the control of the Secretary of State for India, on behalf of the Cabinet. The Secretary of State had his own Department (the India Office) and his own Council (the Council of India), composed of retired Indian officials and generals; in formal matters, the Secretary of State acted as 'the Secretary of State in Council'.

There was no unified Indian Civil Service until 1893; officials were appointed to one of the three Presidency civil services (Bengal, Madras and Bombay). By 1876, nevertheless, the term 'Indian Civil Service' was coming into use as a convenient piece of shorthand. The highest ranks formed the Covenanted Civil Service. It was open to Indians but the obstacles placed in their way ensured that by 1876 there was only a tiny handful. Indians formed a much larger proportion of the Uncovenanted Service which provided the junior ranks of the administration.

British India was divided into the three Presidencies, each under a Governor, assisted by a Council and a Presidency government modelled on the Central Government, except that external affairs were reserved to the Centre. (In Bengal, the Viceroy had been the Governor but because of pressure of work, the administration was in the hands of a Lieutenant-Governor). Bengal, the largest of the Presidencies, was divided into a number of provinces, each under a Lieutenant-Governor; the provinces were divided into divisions and districts under Commissioners and Deputy Commissioners. Madras and Bombay were not divided into provinces but otherwise followed much the same pattern,[4] except that Commissioners and Deputy Commissioners were usually called Collectors and Deputy Collectors.

Alongside British India were the hundreds of native states, bound by treaty to the British Government but exercising varying degrees of internal autonomy. They varied in size and importance, from states such as Hyderabad and Mysore, which covered major areas of the sub-continent, to petty rajadoms of a few square miles. Their external affairs were in the hands of the Central Government which exercised a general oversight of their internal affairs through Residents (in the larger states) and Agents, who might supervise a number of states, as in Rajputana.[5]

The military administration paralleled the civil. The regular troops were divided into three Presidency armies, each with its own Commander-in-Chief and administration; the Commander-in-Chief of the Bengal Army, the largest, was also 'the Commander-in-Chief in the East Indies' i.e. Commander-in-Chief in India. As such, he exercised a large measure of operational control of all three armies, as well as of senior appointments, but the Madras and Bombay Commanders-in-Chief controlled a major part of personnel and logistic administration, including regimental appointments and promotions, dress and equipment. Each army included British Army regiments, serving in India for periods of upwards of fifteen years and refreshed each year by drafts of men from home. These regiments were paid for by the Indian Government and came under the day-to-day control of the Indian military authorities, but personnel matters such as promotions and matters of internal administration, as well as equipment, remained under the direct control of the Commander-in-Chief at the Horse Guards in London. In 1876, the Presidency armies numbered some 120 regiments of native infantry and 50 regiments of British infantry, 30 regiments of native and 9 of British cavalry, with 6 batteries of native artillery and 86 British, totalling some 65,000 British and 130,000 native troops. There were other substantial forces at the disposal of the Government, notably the Punjab Frontier Force (under the direct control of the Lieutenant-Governor of the Punjab), and the Hyderabad Contingent (which came directly under the Viceroy). There were a number of local regiments, such as the Central India Horse, permanently based in the same place in peace but available for service elsewhere in event of war. Finally, many of the native states maintained sizeable bodies of troops, some of which did useful service in the Second Afghan War.

The most notable feature of the military organisation was the division of responsibility between the Commander-in-Chief India and the Military Member. The latter was the official channel of communication between the Viceroy and the C-in-C, and controlled the military budget as well as the logistical departments. Given his financial powers, there was in practice little except purely operational matters in which he was not entitled to be consulted and to exercise a power of veto. It was a system reminiscent of the division between the Admiralty and the Navy Board in eighteenth century England. It was a recipe for friction, confusion and delay, made worse by the fact that the Military Member was invariably junior in rank to the C-in-C but an Ordinary Member of Council whereas the C-in-C was only an Extraordinary Member, and by the fact that Army Headquarters was based at Simla while the Military Department alternated between Simla and Calcutta. The majority of British officers in the native regiments were members of their Presidency Staff Corps, in effect a General List from which regimental and staff appointments were made. Some older officers opted to stay on their original regimental lists. All senior appointments, with very minor exceptions, could be held by either British Army or Indian Service officers.[6]

By 1876 the great phase of British expansion in India was over and, while internal security remained a preoccupation, the issue which dominated military thinking was the expansion of Russia in Central Asia and the possibility of an Anglo-Russian war. In 1830, the Russian frontier to the north had been a thousand miles from Kabul, separated by a belt of independent khanates. By 1876, the khanates – Kokand, Samarcand, Bokkhara and Khiva – had been swallowed up and the effective Russian frontier lay along the Oxus, less than two hundred miles from Kabul and three hundred or so from Peshawar. A strategic railway was being pushed eastwards from the Caspian to link up the Central Asian cities and to increase the striking power of the Russian Governor-General of Turkestan, at Tashkent.

The possibility of a Russian invasion of India had been present in official minds in London and Calcutta, since the beginning of the nineteenth century.[7] It had been a major cause of the First Afghan War in 1838. In the 1860s, Clarendon, as Foreign Secretary, had attempted to set up a buffer zone between the two expanding empires in Central Asia. The failure of that attempt left Afghanistan as the *de facto* buffer, but attempts by the British to bind the Amir and to accept a British presence in his country had come to nothing, to be succeeded by a pragmatic policy of 'masterly inactivity'.[8]

The Conservative election victory of 1874 produced a decisive change.

Disraeli and Salisbury, the new Secretary of State for India, determined to force the Amir to accept a British Resident in order to combat what they saw as an increasing pro-Russian orientation. Northbrook, the Liberal Viceroy, could not accept the policy and, when he resigned early in 1876, Robert Bulwer Lytton was appointed to carry out the policy.[9] He found in India a group of younger officers and officials, notably Roberts, George Colley (Lytton's Military Secretary) and Cavagnari (the Deputy Commissioner of Peshawar) keen to pursue a 'forward policy'. It led directly to the Second Afghan War in November 1878, and indirectly to Roberts' ascent.

The war changed little. The British gained a number of valuable strategic modifications to their frontier with Afghanistan, but the bitterness left by the war meant that no British representative could be based in Afghanistan and no reliance could be placed upon Afghan support in event of a Russian invasion. The Russians were left undisturbed to complete their occupation of Central Asia up to the Persian and Afghan borders.

Whether the Russian Government ever seriously contemplated an invasion of India may be doubted. It would be surprising if the Russian General Staff had not drawn up contingency plans, and no doubt individual officers, such as Skobolev, were ready to take the matter to a trial. For their part, statesmen on both sides were quick to see that the situation in Central Asia offered a means of exerting pressure in the wider diplomatic manoeuvring, without proceeding to the test of war.

The Indian authorities were bound to take the threat seriously. The continuing Russian expansion, the extension of the Central Asian railway, the difficulties over delimiting the Russo-Afghan frontier and (in the late 1880s) Russian penetration over the Pamirs, all led people like Roberts and Macgregor to conclude that a war with Russia was inevitable. Between 1877 and 1893, Roberts produced more than twenty major papers on the subject and sought tirelessly to bring home the gravity of the situation to politicians and the public in England. The strategic thought in these papers shows a good deal of continuity but there is a perceptible shift in tone. The earlier papers are essentially offensive in attitude, looking for ways of attacking Russia via Herat or directly across the Oxus into Russian Turkestan. But the papers from roughly 1883 onwards are more defensive in character. There is no longer an assumption that India's own resources would enable it to act against Russia but a clear recognition that, after allowing for the necessary internal security forces, the forces left over would not suffice even for the active defence which was the basis of Roberts' strategy. That strategy had crystallised by 1885 into the occupation of the Kandahar-Ghazni-Kabul line for active defensive purposes and as the springboard for an offensive, given the necessary resources, via Herat. It emphasised the importance of Kandahar as against Kabul, a re-echoing of Roberts' belief at the end of the Second Afghan War that Kandahar should have been retained.

Roberts' strategy required a massive reinforcement from home.[10] That conflicted directly with the ideas of Wolseley, hitherto the dominant strategic voice in England, whose plans for war with Russia envisaged an attack via the Black Sea or Asia Minor, requiring all the troops that could be spared. Although many influential people, including Salisbury, Prime Minister from 1886 to 1892, and Brackenbury, the Director of Military Intelligence at the War Office and a leading protagonist of Wolseley's views, came to share Roberts' views, ministers were never prepared to commit themselves to the reinforcement of India.[11]

Nothing perhaps is more interesting in Roberts' papers than the evidence of the low esteem in which he and other Indian officers, such as Stewart, held a majority of the native troops. Roberts' career, exclusively in the Bengal Army, and his experiences in the Mutiny and Second Afghan War made him a strong protagonist of the theory of the so-called 'martial races' of North India – Sikhs, Punjabis, Dogras, Pathans, Gurkhas. In his unusually long tour as C-in-C India, he was able to manipulate the racial composition of the native regiments accordingly. By 1893, the proportion of the martial races in the infantry had risen from a quarter in 1881 to a half. A major concern was to retrieve the cuts in strength made as an economy after the Second Afghan War. By raising new regiments and by increasing unit establishments in both British and native units, the cuts had been made up when Roberts left India. Significantly, he had abandoned the post-Mutiny principle of keeping the native troops armed with inferior weapons to those of the British when the native infantry were re-equipped with Martini-Henrys in the 1890s. Of some significance also was the decision to equip and train some of the troops of the native states to broadly regular standards. Roberts, however, never believed that the native regiments (with a handful of exceptions) were capable of meeting European troops, a view which underlay his insistence on the need for massive British reinforcements in event of a Russian war.

Reform at the unit level was matched by reform of the higher levels of administration and organisation, the recommendations of the Eden Commission providing the agenda. What could be regarded as the key issue – the abolition of the Presidency armies and their replacement by four Army Corps, including one for the Punjab – was frustrated by the stubborn opposition of the Duke of Cambridge.[12] The other key issue – the relationship between the Military Member and the C-in-C – similarly went unresolved until Kitchener's arrival in 1902. Roberts' contribution was to introduce a system of common files, a step so obvious as to highlight the essential folly of the basic system. The threat of war over the Pendjeh incident of 1885 had led to the *ad hoc* organisation of two army corps. When he became C-in-C, Roberts was able to build on that by setting up a Defence Mobilisation Committee and earmarking in peacetime a field army of two army corps and a reserve division. As in the British Army, the correct solution to the higher organisation of the Indian Army lay in the creation of a true General Staff, as foreshadowed in the Eden Commission report, but it was not a solution which appealed to the Duke of Cambridge. Roberts' views were equivocal; ironically, when it was introduced into the British Army in 1904, following the Esher report, it was Roberts, as C-in-C, who found himself the main victim. The Indian Army had to wait for a General Staff until the debacle in Mesopotamia in the First World War had demonstrated the unworkability of the Kitchener system.[13]

The last major strand of Roberts' reforms was the large-scale improvement of the communications infrastructure of the North West Frontier. Railways and roads were the key to his forward defence strategy, and the most important single element was the extension of the railway up the Bolan Pass to Quetta and then on to Kandahar. The cost and effort emphasised the importance of the Kandahar strategy, but although the railhead reached the border during Roberts' time as C-in-C, the extension to Kandahar remained a political impossibility. At the northern end of the frontier, the railway was pushed across the Indus to Peshawar but it took the Third Afghan War in 1919 to provide the impetus to push the railway through the Khyber.[14] In the centre, the Zhob expedition of 1890 and the opening up of the Gomal Pass provided access to Ghazni. These, and extensive improvements to roads, acted as a force multiplier to the field army which Roberts had organised.

Historians have made much of the rivalry between Roberts and Wolseley, but it is possible that the differences have been exaggerated at the expense of the agreements.[15] At the personal level, relations seem always to have been courteous if not close – indeed, the two men appear to have met only once before 1881, when Wolseley took over from Roberts on the staff of Hope Grant's division after the relief of Lucknow.

Correspondence between the two is notable for its paucity. The two major issues which seemed most to divide them – short service and the strategy for a war with Russia – were linked. Wolseley's interest in short service engagements derived largely from his perception of the need for large reserves for a European campaign. Roberts, by contrast, was concerned with a campaign in India and Afghanistan where conditions did not favour very large armies but put an emphasis upon seasoned and acclimatised troops. (It is worth noting that Wolseley's experience lay in campaigns of relatively short duration). But from the start, in his Mansion House speech of February 1881, Roberts had argued for both a short service and a long-service army, and the changes in enlistment introduced in July 1881 had gone a long way to bridging the differences between the two views. By 1893, Roberts was in favour of three-year initial engagements. From the beginning, he had seen that the key to recruiting lay, not in manipulating lengths of engagement or physical standards, but in improving the actual conditions of service to match the improvements in social conditions and expectations outside. But Wolseley had, if anything, an even longer pedigree as the soldier's friend, and agreed with Roberts on the need to promote men on merit, rather than seniority, and upon the need for a General Staff.[16]

Ambition was another common bond. Wolseley's was more obviously displayed, but Roberts' ambition was obvious to observers such as Macgregor and Edwin Norman: and whereas Wolseley scarcely bothered to hide his contempt for politicians and journalists, Roberts was at pains to cultivate them. Politicians, for their part, undoubtedly saw advantage in discreetly fostering the rivalry,[17] and, in turn, the perception of an apparent rivalry encouraged officers to congregate in one camp or the other. What might have happened if Roberts had become Quartermaster-General in 1882, in harness with Wolseley as Adjutant-General, is one of the more intriguing questions of this period.

No volume on Roberts can in the end evade the question of the mass executions at Kabul, because they affect our perception of the man and because they affected the subsequent course of Anglo-Afghan relations. There is, first, the justification and, second, the scale. Every military commander has the right and the duty to ensure the personal safety of his men, and, in the Second Afghan War, Stewart, Bright, Maude, Hume and Tytler all executed civilians for attacks on their troops or camp followers.[18] Although Roberts, on Lytton's advice, used the same argument as part of his subsequent justification for what happened at Kabul, the matter rests essentially on a different footing. Roberts arrived in Kabul with clear and vigorous orders to punish those guilty of the attack on Cavagnari and his Mission. New ground had nevertheless been introduced in Roberts' proclamation of 12 October 1879, issued the same day as he formally took possession of Kabul. In that proclamation, the death penalty was extended to those who had led the opposition to the British advance. The case for that rested on the sophistry that the British were there as the allies of the Amir and that all who opposed the British were rebels against the Amir.[19] Lytton, who was not consulted, saw the weakness of that argument and advised Roberts not to use it in his defence.[20] Roberts in due course claimed that no man had been hanged simply for fighting against the British and the official list of those executed contains no one hanged on that charge. Magregor, Roberts' Chief of Staff and one of those closest to the work of the Military Commission, was not persuaded.[21] Nor, it would seem, were other officers, because the material on which the charges made by Harrison and other journalists were based, was clearly provided by officers serving at Kabul.

The proceedings of the Commission were arbitrary in the extreme and Roberts himself regarded them as equivalent to a drumhead court martial.[22] The witnesses were examined in private by Mahomed Hiyat Khan, a Punjab official, since none of the three-man tribunal spoke Pashtu, and their depositions only submitted, so that the accused were not able to cross-examine the witnesses. There was in these circumstances a strong suspicion that some witnesses had used the opportunity to pay off old grudges. Significantly, although Lytton had expected retribution to fall on the prominent figures who he believed lay behind the massacre, no evidence could be found against any of them; with the exception of the Kotwal (Chief Constable) of Kabul, the men executed were ordinary rank and file. Given the inherent difficulty of identifying accurately the active members of a mob of several thousands, the emotional pressure to exact vengeance, and the arbitrary nature of the proceedings, there must be doubt as to whether those executed were all guilty of the charges levelled against them or whether Roberts was justified in claiming that men were not executed for the simple crime of opposing his advance.

The return submitted by Roberts and placed before the House of Commons contained 87 names, covering all men executed up to 26 December 1879. The figure of 87 was amended from an original figure of 97, which was stated to have included an element of double counting. Writing in January 1880, Lytton claimed that a further 10 men had been executed since 26 December and this would seem to have been based upon a press report from Kabul.[23] The figure of 87 is clearly not the sum total of all of those executed in or around Kabul, although it may be the total of those condemned by the Commission. It does not include the eight men that Hensman records as having been shot without trial on 13 December 1879,[24] nor the four headmen shot on 3 January 1880. Since the records of the Commission and the notebooks in which Roberts apparently entered the verdicts appear not to exist, the true total is impossible to determine.[25] Roberts' surviving papers contain nothing of significance on the subject and his autobiography relegates the matter to a single footnote. The executions alienated Afghan support, strengthened public opposition in England to the war and contributed to the Liberal election victory of 1880, and damaged Roberts' reputation for political sagacity. One is tempted to see in them an echo of the grim days of the Mutiny only twenty years before.

The circumstances of Roberts' last two years in India were not entirely happy. At the end of 1889, as his tenure of command was coming to an end, he was offered the post of Adjutant-General, the most senior post in the British Army after that of Commander-in-Chief, in succession to Wolseley. He accepted without hesitation, subject only to Cabinet and Royal approval [256, 257]. The obvious solution to the problem of his successor was a straight swap between him and Wolseley, but the latter was no longer interested in India; his sights were fixed on the Aldershot command as a means of securing the command in the event of a European war. The Queen and the Duke of Cambridge wanted the Duke of Connaught appointed to India, as a stepping stone to succeeding the Duke of Cambridge. The appearance at the beginning of 1890 of the report of Hartington's Royal Commission acted as a solvent to these plans. The report recommended the abolition of the post of Commander-in-Chief and its replacement by a post of Chief of Staff responsible to the Secretary of State.[26]

The Queen's furious opposition, stimulated by the Duke of Cambridge,[27] forced the Cabinet to abandon this proposal, at least until the Duke of Cambridge retired, but it determined it not to have another Royal C-in-C. As Wolseley put it bluntly to the Queen's Private Secretary, 'Behind all this matter is the Duke of Cambridge. Hartington, and all the Secretaries of State here in my time, have suffered so much at his hands, have had all needful reforms in the Army so blocked by him that one and all are determined never to have another Prince who might prove equally immovable and irremovable'.[28] In turn, this meant the exclusion of the Duke of Connaught from the India command. Roberts was therefore asked to extend for a further two years, to April 1893, even though it involved almost certainly the permanent loss of the Adjutant-Generalship [262].[29] Since the Cabinet were subsequently unable even to secure Roberts the home leave which he had requested,[30] he was justified in feeling that he had been shabbily treated [263]. When he left India, there was no active post available for him. When the Duke of Cambridge was finally persuaded to go in 1895, he was succeeded by Wolseley and Roberts took the vacant command in Ireland, from which he was rescued by the Second Boer War. He succeeded Wolseley in 1901, at the age of 68, but it was not a particularly fruitful tenure and it came to a somewhat unhappy conclusion in 1904 when the post was finally abolished. Thereafter, he espoused the cause of universal National Service for home defence. He died in November 1914 while visiting Indian troops in France and was buried beside Wolseley in the crypt of St Paul's.

Sources and Editorial Method

The great bulk of Roberts' papers covering the period of this volume were deposited in the Army Museum's Ogilby Trust in 1955 by General Sir Euan Miller, Roberts' godson and the residuary legatee of Roberts' surviving child, Edwina. They were transferred to the National Army Museum in 1971. The papers had been used by David James for his 1954 biography in which he recorded the fact that, by agreement with Edwina, Countess Roberts, he had destroyed those papers 'of no permanent value'. There is no precise record of what was destroyed but, from a comparison between the present archive and references in James' book, it would appear that much, and perhaps all, of Roberts' personal correspondence with his wife and family, together with some material about his early life, has thus disappeared. Other papers, including letters of appointment and warrants, were deposited by General Miller in the Museum in 1955.

From the beginning of the Second Afghan War, Roberts appears to have set out deliberately to keep all his papers (there are few papers before 1878), almost as if he realised at that point that he was going to become a major figure. The surviving papers are very voluminous, running to some 236 volumes, but they are sparse in places; there is, for example, remarkably little about the executions at Kabul, the most controversial episode in his career. Much of the official correspondence was printed on the Government Printing press in Calcutta at the end of Roberts' time as Commander-in-Chief India, and bound up in twelve red leather volumes. (The numbering indicates that there should have been thirteen volumes but Volume I, which would have covered the period before 1878, is missing both from the set in the National Army Museum which was Roberts' own, and from that in the India Office Library and Records). Where a comparison is possible between the originals and the printed versions, it can be seen that the printed versions differ only by the insertion of some paragraphing and minor punctuation, and in the standardisation of place names such as Kabul. Nevertheless, wherever possible, the originals have been used here.

Where a word is indecipherable or missing, it is indicated in square brackets. Significant editorial omissions are indicated by asterisks, minor ones by three points. Opening and closing salutations have been omitted, and dates and addresses at the beginning of each document are given in a simplified, standardised form.

Telegrams present a special problem. They occur in three forms:

(a) a small number exist on the original telegraphic form or 'flimsy'; these are described in the text as 'Telegram';

(b) an equal number exist as manuscript copies, often a decipherment of an originally enciphered version; these are described as 'Manuscript telegram';

(c) the bulk are in printed form and are described as 'Printed telegram'.

In the front pages of his diary for 1878 (RP 92/18), Roberts set down a number of simple cyphers, noted in some cases as 'HQ Cypher'. These are letter transposition cyphers. Those occurring in Second Afghan War telegrams are numerical cyphers, as will be seen from some telegrams reproduced here. I have found no keys to these.

The other main sources of material relating to Roberts in this period are the papers of his Indian contemporaries in the India Office Library and details, together with other relevant collections used, are listed in the Bibliography.

Abbreviations

BL	Papers in the British Library.
Childers MSS	Papers of Hugh Childers MP, formerly in the library of the Royal Commonwealth Society.
Duke University	Papers in the William R. Perkins Library of Duke University, North Carolina.
HP	Papers of Field Marshal Sir Frederick Paul Haines in the National Army Museum, London, accession no. 8108–9.
IOR	Papers in the India Office Library and Records, London.
JSAHR	*Journal of the Society for Army Historical Research.*
LP	Papers of Robert, 1st Earl of Lytton, in the India Office Library and Records, reference no. MSS Eur E218.
Ly P	Papers of Sir Alfred Lyall in the India Office Library and Records, reference no. MSS Eur F132.
NAM	National Army Museum, London
PH	Passed higher examination in Hindustani.
RA	Papers in the Royal Archives, Windsor.
RP	Papers of Lord Roberts in the NAM, accession no. 7101–23.
Stanhope MSS	Papers of Edward Stanhope MP in the Centre for Kentish Studies, Maidstone, reference no. U 1590/0305.

Glossary

Amir	the title used by the rulers of Afghanistan (from the Arabic meaning 'leader').
Badragga	a tribal escort to provide safe conduct.
Barakzais	a branch of the Duranis(qv) which had been the ruling family in Afghanistan since 1826.
Batta	a special monetary allowance given to soldiers on active service.
Boh	a local chief.
Crore	100 lakhs(qv) or 10,000,000.
Dacoit	a bandit or armed robber, usually part of a gang.
Daffadar	a sergeant in a cavalry regiment.
Duranis	one of the two great divisions of the Afghan people, originally called Abdalis but renamed after Ahmed Shah Durani, the founder of modern Afghanistan. ('Duran' is the Persian word for pearl.)
Durbar	an audience or levee; also a council of state.
Ghilzais	the other great division of the Afghan people.
Gomashta	a native agent or contractor.
Havildar	a sergeant in an infantry regiment.
Jemadar	the lowest rank of native commissioned officer.
Jirga	a tribal gathering.
Khan	a Muslim honorific, roughly equivalent to 'Esquire'.
Kotal	a mountain pass or col.
Kotwal	a head police officer.
Malik	a tribal elder.
Mullah	a Muslim priest.
Mustaufi	Chief Financial Adviser or Minister.
Naik	a corporal in the infantry.
Pal	a small one- or two-man tent.
Risaldar	the equivalent of a jemadar in the cavalry.
Risaldar Major	the senior native commissioned officer in the cavalry.
Ryot	a tenant farmer or cultivator
Sangar	a breastwork or shelter built of stones.

Sayyid (or Said)	a Muslim religious leader claiming descent from the Prophet's son, Husain.
Sepoy	the common term for an infantry soldier.
Serai	a resthouse for travellers cf caravanserai.
Shahzada	literally 'son of the king', or prince, but used more normally to denote royal descent.
Sirdar	a notable or prominent man.
Sowar	literally 'a horseman' but used normally to mean a cavalry trooper.
Subadar	a native commissioned officer next in rank above a jemadar.
Subadar Major	the senior native commissioned officer in the infantry.
Tehsildar	the official in charge of a Tehsil or subdivision of a District.
Vakil	an agent; also an Indian attorney or pleader.
Wazir	a Chief Minister.
Yabu (or yaboo)	a native pony.

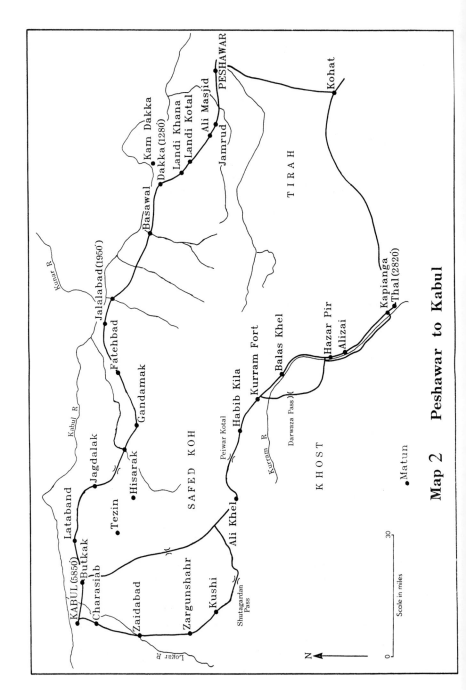

Map 2   Peshawar to Kabul

I

January 1876 to August 1879

The Second Afghan War, First Phase

At the beginning of 1876, Roberts travelled down to Bombay to say farewell to the retiring Commander-in-Chief, Lord Napier of Magdala. He was there when the new Viceroy, Lord Lytton, arrived and he at once proceeded to pay his respects:

> Lord Lytton received me on board the steamer which had brought him from Suez in a most friendly fashion. He told me that he had been greatly interested during the voyage reading a paper by me detailing the steps that would have to be taken in India in the event of a Russian Army crossing the Oxus and invading Afghanistan.[1]

> This Paper had been prepared by Lord Napier's order and he had sent the copy Lord Lytton was reading to the Secretary of State for India.

> From that moment Lord Lytton was my friend. The 'Forward Policy' which I advocated was the policy that appealed to him. . . .[2]

Lytton, a minor diplomat and poet, the son of the novelist, Edward Bulwer-Lytton, was a somewhat curious choice for Viceroy, but Disraeli and Salisbury, the Secretary of State for India, had a new and aggressive policy to forward and they needed (as Disraeli put it to the Queen) a man of 'ambition, imagination, some vanity, and much will'. In 1830, the moving edge of the Russian frontier had been a thousand miles from Kabul; by 1876, it lay effectively along the Oxus, the northern boundary of Afghanistan, less than two hundred miles from Kabul and only some two hundred and fifty miles from Peshawar. Kaufman, the Governor-

General of Russian Turkestan, corresponded regularly with the Amir, Sher Ali, whom many in India and London believed to have become strongly anti-British. Lytton's remit was to re-establish British influence in Afghanistan and to prevent the country falling under the sway of Russia; as a first, vital step, the Amir was to be required to accept a resident British officer as envoy (although not necessarily at Kabul itself).[3]

Salisbury had failed to persuade Lord Northbrook, the Liberal Viceroy, or his Council, that the new policy was right or that the premises on which it was based were correct. The impasse was resolved by Northbrook's resignation, thus paving the way for Lytton's appointment. Although he had no Indian experience, Lytton quickly came to share Salisbury's views and he found in India a group of younger officers and officials, including Roberts, who were not only of the same mind, but went further in espousing the concept of a 'Scientific Frontier' – a concept based upon the belief that against an inevitable war with Russia, India could be defended only along the line of the Hindu Kush and that it was necessary therefore for India to secure in advance the essential entry points into Afghanistan and to extend its authority over the transborder tribes. Lytton tended to despise senior officials as unimaginative and obstructionist and it was among these more junior officials that he found the intellectual and emotional support he required. In turn, Roberts, as Quartermaster-General and responsible for operational planning and intelligence, was in a position to push the new policy in military circles. An observer wrote subsequently that

'The Viceroy's real counsellors, in private as in political matters, were his Private Secretary, Colonel George Pomeroy Colley, the Quarter-Master-General, Major-General Frederick Roberts; and the Deputy Commissioner of Peshawar, Major Louis Cavagnari; but though the military theories of the former agreed perfectly with the ambitious schemes of the two latter and though all alike concurred in fostering the Viceroy's ignorant contempt for the danger he was preparing to run – Roberts . . . was in a far better position than a recent arrival in India like Colley or a political officer like Cavagnari, for judging of the fitness of the Indian Army for the task which they were seeking to impose on it, and to that extent must be held the more responsible of the three.'[4]

Over a period of some two years Lytton tried and failed to persuade Sher Ali to accept a resident British officer and closer relations with

Britain. In parallel, Lytton took up the question of the organisation of the trans-Indus districts along the frontier with Afghanistan, a subject already raised by Salisbury with Northbrook. Lytton proposed that all of British India west of the Indus, including Sind, should form a new province under a Chief Commissioner responsible directly to the Government of India and charged also with relations with Kabul; as part of the plan, the Punjab and Sind Frontier Forces would be amalgamated.[5] Salisbury had, apparently, intended to appoint Sir Lewis Pelly as Chief Commissioner, but Lytton wished to have Wolseley, who initially accepted and then withdrew.[6] Lytton then offered the post to Roberts who accepted early in 1878. Pending resolution of the details of the plan and receipt of the Secretary of State's approval, Lytton proposed that Roberts should take command of the Punjab Frontier Force in order to familiarise himself with the geography and problems of the frontier. Although it meant coming down in rank from local major-general to brigadier-general, Roberts accepted and took up command in March 1878, embarking immediately upon an extended tour of all the stations and regiments of his new command, arriving back in Simla in May, where Lytton wished to consult him on the detailed arrangement of the new province.

In the early summer of 1878, the Russians were preparing, unwittingly, to redeem the failure of Lytton's Afghan policy. With the Anglo-Russian crisis over the Near East and Turkey reaching its climax, the Russians decided to exert pressure in Europe by sending a mission to Kabul while at the same time despatching three columns of troops from Central Asia towards Afghanistan.[7] When the Amir refused to accept a similar, hastily organised British mission, his officers turning it back in the Khyber, war followed almost inevitably in November 1878.[8]

At the end of September 1878, with war approaching, Lytton, against the wishes of the Commander-in-Chief (Sir Frederick Haines), had secured Roberts' appointment as commander of the Kurram Column, one of the three columns which, under Haines' plans were to invade Afghanistan.[9] Roberts' column was the smallest of the three but it was of high quality, and Roberts did not scruple to use his influence at Simla to strengthen his force and to secure to himself full political powers [8, 9, 10, 11]. His formal instructions reached him at the end of October [5, 13] and he was ready to move when the ultimatum to Sher Ali expired on 20 November [14].

The Anglo-Indian armies which invaded Afghanistan were, in many respects, distinctly old-fashioned. The artillery was muzzle-loading, and of relatively short range, there was no regular system of transport, the brigades and divisions were organised *ad hoc,* and among the Indian Army officers at least there was no organised system of staff training – officers 'learned on the job'. The British infantry regiments were still absorbing the effects of the short-service engagement system introduced by Cardwell. Some regiments, such as the 92nd, still contained a high proportion of the older, long-service men; others, such as the recently arrived 2/8th, were full of young, short-service men. Many officers believed that the short-service men were inferior in stamina and physique to the long-service soldiers, and less effective; in Indian conditions, where the climate, drink and boredom ensured the survival of the fittest, they were probably right.

The war would be the first major test of the post-Mutiny Indian armies. Apart from a handful of light field and mountain batteries, all artillery was in British hands and the same reasoning had led to the native regiments being equipped with the inferior Snider rifle, a weapon of which the Amir possessed considerable quantities himself. But the most significant of the post-Mutiny reforms were those which had reduced the number of British officers in the regiments, and placed the command of companies and troops in the hands of native officers, and shifted the primary areas of recruitment of the Bengal Army from Bengal and Oudh to the Punjab. In consequence, many of the sepoys were not only of the same religion, but even from the same tribal background, as their Afghan opponents. The first clashes were awaited therefore with something more than the usual excitement. In one respect at least the Anglo-Indian troops had made a major advance since the First Afghan War; a body of experience and doctrine had been amassed on the tactics of mountain warfare and many regiments, particularly those of the Punjab Frontier Force, were experienced practitioners.[10]

Roberts had no formal Intelligence staff and his information about his opponents was limited to what could be picked up from the local tribesmen [16, 17] and casual visitors such as Wali Mahomed (see Section 1, Note 25). Few army officers spoke Pushtu, the common language of Eastern Afghanistan, and the Quartermaster-General's Department had no field organisation or doctrine. In the field, intelligence matters rested largely in the hands of the political officers whose knowledge, nevertheless, scarcely extended beyond the frontier.

Roberts encountered no opposition in occupying the Kurram Valley and won a smart victory on 2 December when he seized the Peiwar Kotal, the pass leading out of the valley at its north-western end, which gave him a jumping-off point for a possible advance on Kabul [15, 16, 17]. His victory was marred only by treachery among some of his Pathan sepoys [20, 21]. The speed and cleanness of Roberts' success stood out in sharp contrast to the somewhat fumbling success of Sir Sam Browne, commanding the Khyber column, in seizing the Afghan fort of Ali Masjid, at the entrance to the Khyber Pass. Almost overnight, Roberts acquired a public reputation as a fighting general.

The political side of his command proved slightly more difficult to master [19, 22, 24, 25]; and a subsequent expedition to Khost revealed something of the fickleness of the Press as well as leaving Roberts with the beginning of a reputation for harshness [27, 28, 31, 32, 36, 37, 38, 39, 41, 50, 53, 55].[11]

At the end of May 1879, the first phase of the war came to an end with the signature of the Treaty of Gandamak by Sher Ali's successor, Yakub Khan [56, 63].[12] Cavagnari, who had negotiated the treaty, was appointed the first envoy to Kabul and Roberts received him in July when he passed through on his way to Kabul [70, 71]. It was for Roberts a gloomy occasion:

> 'my staff and I dined that evening with the Mission. After dinner, I was asked to propose the health of Cavagnari and those with him, but somehow I did not feel equal to the task; I was so thoroughly depressed and my mind was filled with such gloomy forebodings as to the fate of these fine fellows, that I could not utter a word. Like so many others, I thought that peace had been signed too quickly, before, in fact, we had instilled that awe of us into the Afghan nation which would have been the only reliable guarantee for the safety of the mission.'[13]

Roberts then repaired to Simla for the summer, where he had been selected to sit as a member of a commission under Sir Ashley Eden, the Lieutenant-Governor of Bengal, to look into the future organisation of the Army in India [66, 68].[14] Roberts had been promoted to substantive Major-General in December 1878 and received the KCB for his part in the campaign. While at Simla he remained in command of his Force, now garrisoning the Kurram which had been placed under British administration by the Treaty [69, 72].[15] It was intended to withdraw the bulk of them in the autumn when the risk of sickness had diminished.

The last document in this Section [73] reflects Lytton's intention to take up the re-organisation of the administration of the frontier districts again, now that the war appeared to be over. In accordance with the amended proposals forwarded by the Secretary of State, the frontier was to be divided into two Divisions and Roberts was to be the Commissioner of the Northern Division, covering the Pathan tribes. The Southern Division, covering the Baluch tribes, Sind and Khelat, was to be under Sandeman.[16]

A word needs to be said about Roberts' correspondence while in the Kurram. Political and strategic direction was provided to him via the Foreign Department of the Government of India; copies of all such letters and telegrams, both to and from Roberts, were copied to the Viceroy, the Quartermaster-General (for the C-in-C) and, in the early stages, to the Lieutenant-Governor of the Punjab. On purely military matters, such as discipline or supplies, Roberts corresponded with Army Headquarters although the volume of such correspondence is surprisingly low. In addition, Roberts directly corresponded with both the Viceroy and the Foreign Secretary, Alfred Lyall, by letter and telegram, both semi- officially and personally; the context normally shows the nature of the correspondence. Telegrams between the Kurram and Simla or Calcutta normally took a matter of hours, letters to Simla a matter of three or four days, and a week to Calcutta. Letters to and from England about a month, depending on when they caught the mail steamer at Bombay (for homeward mail) or Brindisi (for outward mail).

1
Napier of Magdala to Duke of Cambridge

[Manuscript copy]   Calcutta
                                           21 May 1874

In a previous letter, your Royal Highness asked what officer I thought of proposing for the Quarter Master Generalship.[1]

It is an appointment requiring such special qualifications and information regarding India that I have been unable to name any officer who could approach Lieut. Colonel Roberts in fitness for it.

It is embarrassing to have an officer in that high appointment who is dependent upon his Deputy, so that I have thought it better to do nothing at present, leaving Lieut. Colonel Roberts officiating for a few months, when we may expect him then to be full Colonel. I should then send his name forward instead of at present opening the question regarding his rank.

The appointment could not be better filled.

IOR MSS Eur F 114/21/14

2
Viceroy (Lytton) to Commander-in-Chief (Haines)

[Holograph]   23 November 1876
                                           Peshawar

Will it be convenient to you to join me, with General Roberts, at 1½ p.m. for a conference on frontier matters? To admit of this arrangement I propose lunching at 1 p.m. punctually, and shall be glad if you and Genl Roberts can lunch with us. I have asked the Lᵗ Govnʳ[2] to meet us for the same purpose at the same hour. These are the subjects I propose to discuss.

1. Peshawar Cantonment and all questions connected with it, such as the Barracks, the Fort and the Chenab Sanatorium. With the exception of the Fort, all these questions appear to me to turn on the primary one. Is it or is it not expedient to keep large bodies of British troops permanently stationed beyond the Indus?

2. Kohat. The blockade – utility or necessity of the Pass – situation of the Fort – Road to Rawal Pindi etc., etc.

3. Thal – Force at – road to intermediate posts –

4. Khelat. Occupation of: strength & distribution of garrison Reinforcement of Quetta. Troops whence drawn whom under Amalgamation of Sind & Punjab forces etc.

5. Military preparations for war with Russia etc.

As all these questions have more or less reference to political & military considerations in dealing with which I may hereafter require the assistance of my Private & Military Secretaries,[3] I hope you will not object to their being present at our discussion of them. For a different though similar reason I should be glad of your assent to the presence of Sir L. Pelly[4] who was Ld Salisbury's authority for expecting the new frontier Gov^t if I decide on separating it from those of Bombay & the Punjab, and who is just now in rather a false position owing to the suspension of the Cabul Mission. His attendance will be a compliment to him which he will appreciate, and I think it can do no harm.

I will have Cavagnari, Johnston, & Genl Taylor in attendance to answer questions if necessary. I forgot to mention Mr Thornton who ought also I think to be present. – I enclose Norman's Memorandum.[5] I have been jotting down some questions on points of detail in regard to military preparations which I should wish to submit to you privately by and by. But probably they are all anticipated in the Mem^o to which you referred last night, and for a copy of which I shall be very grateful whenever it is completed.

HP 1/ff36–38

3
Roberts to Sir Edwin Johnson (Military Member)

[Holograph]   Hyderabad, Sind
11 March 1877

As Owen Burne will doubtless shew you a memorandum by Macgregor[6] on 'Armenia as a seat of war', and as you may not have time to read it very carefully, I write to prevent you committing yourself too hurriedly to Macgregor's views. He may of course be correct in advocating the Bussora[7]-Bagdad-Bitees route as the best for a force from India to take if required for operations in Armenia – but I studied the subject a year ago when it seemed possible we might be called upon to assist the Turks in Asia Minor or Armenia, and the conclusion I came to was that the route was an extremely difficult one for the advance of an army, and would only be adopted under exceptionable circumstances.

Macgregor is I think too sanguine about the <u>capability</u> of the Tigris for transport purposes. As far as Bagdad, 500 miles from Bussorah, arrangements could no doubt be made to convey an army with its stores, with a certain number of transport animals – from Bagdad to Suzeereh,[8] the point where Macgregor would begin his march is upwards of 400 but he believes that the Tigris for this distance 'could be utilised to any extent to bring up stores', he admits obstacles exist which he thinks could be removed, but this is a point which should positively be determined. Chesney[9] went 50 miles above in 1836, and reported the river to be shoaly, channel irregular and very different from that portion between Bagdad and Bussora. So far as I know no European has been up the river further than Chesney, and this makes me sceptical as to its capabilities – there is a great caravan trade between Bagdad and Armenia, and Georgia, and if the river Tigris was navigable, or could be made so, it seems almost certain it would have been.

The way in which a force from India could best assist operations in Armenia would depend on a variety of circumstances, but I believe that the most convenient plan would be to send it by sea thro' the Suez Canal and land it either at Alexandretta or on the southern shore of the Black Sea. However an opinion on this point could not be given without knowing the object of the campaign and the task that would be required of an Indian Contingent.

There is one thing I would like to urge on you, and that is not to favour any proposal for the employment of Indian troops out of India except under the command of an officer who will be able to ensure their being properly treated – unless this is insisted on the troops will probably be treated as the Turks were in the Crimea, or made coolies of as the West Indian regiment was in Ashantee, and instead of returning to India happy and contented as was the case after China and Abyssinia the troops will be disappointed with foreign service and there will be considerable difficulty in getting others then to leave the country again. I can explain myself better when we meet but I can't resist writing this now as letters from England lead me to believe that India will possibly be called upon to furnish a contingent in the event of war between England Russia. It is a point for consideration whether we could not be made more use of nearer our own base, India, but here again the pros and cons must be fully known before an opinion can be offered.

RP 162/5

4
MEMORANDUM TO CONSIDER THE MEASURES WHICH SHOULD BE ADOPTED IN INDIA IN THE EVENT OF ENGLAND JOINING TURKEY IN THE WAR AGAINST RUSSIA

Paper by Roberts as Quartermaster-General, India

[Printed copy]   Simla
                                                 4 June 1877

In the event of England joining Turkey in the war against Russia, what could India do?

The reply to this question depends on so many conditions that certain hypotheses must be accepted before any conclusions can be arrived at.

These conditions may be thus enumerated:-

1st – That England does not intend Russia to gain possession of Turkish Armenia, and thus secure command of the head-waters of the Tigris and Euphrates.

2nd – That England is determined to protect Egypt and keep open the passage of the Suez Canal.

3rd – That England will not permit the occupation of Constantinople, or the dismemberment of the Turkish Empire in Europe.

4th – That the action of Persia is extremely doubtful, but it is more than probable she is secretly allied to Russia.

5th – That all intercourse with Afghanistan is broken off, and that the Amir is known to be hostile, and has been endeavouring to rouse the tribes on the North-West Frontier against us.

6th – That no increase to the British force in India can be expected beyond what would be required to place corps on a war footing.

7th – That any operations in Europe would probably be undertaken by the Army from England and the Mediterranean.

Under such circumstances, the part that India could take in the war would be limited to one or more of the following measures:-

1st – To sending a Native contingent to Egypt.

2nd – To sending a force up the Tigris either for operations eastwards against Persia, or northwards *via* Bagdad and Mosul towards Armenia, or north-eastwards *via* Kermanshah and Tabriz towards Georgia.

3rd – To sending a force to Syria, thence to advance *via* Diabekir towardes Armenia or Georgia.

4th – To landing a force on the south or east coast of the Black Sea for a similar purpose.

5th – To sending a force into Persia by way of the Persian Gulf.

6th – To sending a force to Herat in view to a possible movement westward towards the Caspian, or northwards towards Merv.

7th – To sending a force into Turkestan for the purpose of driving the Russians from the Khanates.

8th – To sending officers to Turkish Arabia and Armenia to assist the Turkish Armies, and towards Central Asia in view to raising the Turkomans and other tribes in the neighbourhood of the Khanates.

* * *

It is evident, therefore, that an expedition from India, *via* the Persian Gulf and the Tigris valley towards Armenia or Georgia could only be accomplished with considerable difficulty and loss of time; the equipment of the army would require a vast amount of costly preparation, and though it is within the bounds of possibility that such an expedition could be carried out successfully, it is one that does not commend itself and which should only be undertaken in an extraordinary emergency.

If an advance on Armenia or Georgia, *via* Asia Minor, be considered, the reasons why the troops destined for the work should be sent from England instead of India are even stronger than those urged in the case of Egypt.

* * *

Operations in Southern Persia could be easy compared to any of the lines we have hitherto considered.

(a) It is nearer our base.

(b) A small, well equipped force would probably suffice to bring the Persians to terms without proceeding farther inland than Shiraz or Shuster.

On the other hand –

(a) A force operating in Southern Persia could have no direct influence on a war between Russia and England, and would afford no material assistance to Turkey.

(b) The force would be locked up in a tract of country which could probably be brought to terms by a few men-of-war.

The present attitude of Persia is evidently due to the promptings of Russia, who naturally wishes to see us drawn off from her lines of advance in Asia, and to prevent us taking any action in Armenia, Georgia, the north of Persia, or Afghanistan.

Having committed us to the southern shores of Persia, Russia would endeavour to induce the Persians to besiege Herat, assisting them with officers and material. A Persian garrison in Herat would, under existing circumstances, be tantamount to a Russian occupation. It seems necessary, therefore, that we should avoid all military complications with Southern Persia, and trust to our fleet to keep the shores of the Persian Gulf quiet, while we devote our whole strength to checkmating the advances of Russia on the north of Persia, the north-west frontier of Afghanistan, and in Central Asia.

The points which will determine the nature, extent, and direction of such a campaign are –

(a) The force Russia could bring against us, supposing it was decided to operate in the Khanates.

(b) In what manner would the tribes of the Khanates receive a British army, and what assurances could we give them that they would be protected from the wrath of Russia at the termination of the war.

(c) What objects would be gained by an advance to Herat, and thence possibly towards Merv and the Caspian.

(d) What opposition might be expected in this direction.

(e) What action are we prepared to take with regard to Afghanistan.

(f) Would it not be advantageous to regain our lost influence in Persia and maintain her frontier in the direction of the Elbourz mountains and Atrek Valley.

(g) Our relations with the frontier tribes.

(h) The practicability of the several routes by which an army could advance.

(i) What would the strength of the force be.

These questions must be carefully enquired into before any plan for a campaign can be decided upon.

* * *

To save Afghanistan from Russia, and herself from eventual attack by Russia in a position strategically weak, it is absolutely necessary for India to be in possession of Herat, and of some position such as Balkh covering the passes through which the line of communication from Samarkand to India *via* Kabul leads.

From such a position England might view without anxiety the extension of Russian power in Central Asia. Her right would be protected by the impassable range of mountains lying between Kashgar and the Pamir; the Hindu Kush, covered by a force at Balkh, would be her centre; and Herat, her left, which, while checking the further advance of the Russians from the west, would enable her to regain lost influence in Persia, give her absolute control over Afghanistan, and bring her in alliance with the Turkoman tribes.

To carry this out, it is essential that Afghanistan and Kashmir should be made to understand that their and our interests are identical. As regards Kashmir there will probably be little difficulty. Afghanistan may be already committed to Russia, or may not be prepared to receive us as allies, in which case an occupation of that country, temporary or permanent as the future may determine, may be found necessary.

Afghanistan, therefore, is the point to which our thoughts and energies must be directed. After all that has recently occurred, it is a question whether it would be politic to make any overtures to the present Ruler, or whether it would not be wiser to leave matters as they are until the time for an advance arrives. It will perhaps be acknowledged that the time for advancing is rapidly approaching, and that without reference to the hopes or fears of the Amir. Meanwhile the army should be equipped, and when everything is ready, Sher Ali should be informed of our determination.

If he decide to cast his lot in with ours, matters will be simplified; should he prefer a Russian alliance, then we must take such steps as seem best to ensure Afghanistan giving us the least amount of trouble.

The question as to the best line of advance cannot be determined independently of Afghanistan; were she friendly, it would no doubt be possible to make Tashkend the objective *via* the Oxus and the Khanates.

* * *

If Afghanistan could be induced to join heartily with us, it would no doubt be possible for a portion of the force to reach the Oxus or even the Khanates in less time than that given above.

Should the contrary be the case, it is impossible to say how long it would take to reach Tashkend, and it would be difficult to decide on the strength and composition of the army to accomplish such an undertaking. The force would have to be large enough to occupy Afghanistan, to keep open communication for upwards of 1,000 miles, and to be able to meet on Russian territory an army the strength of which it is not possible to calculate but which is known to be considerable. During the greater part of the winter, the several detachments on the line of advance could hope for no support from each other, and the main army would have no line of retreat open to it.

Any operations, therefore, in the direction of Central Asia, seem to be prohibited, unless we can previously be assured of the friendship of the Afghans, and of the neutrality, if not the active assistance, of the tribes in the Khanates.

An advance towards Herat does not present the same difficulties. From Quetta, our frontier post, Herat is distant about 530 miles; as far as Kandahar, 144 miles, the Kojak pass is the chief obstacle; but as a British army crossed this pass 40 years ago, after having marched from Ferozepore, upwards of 750 miles, it is not likely to cause delay now that operations will commence within 50 miles of its summit.

* * *

The roads from Persia, Seistan, the Caspian Sea, Merv, Khiva, Bokhara, Kandahar, Maimana, Balkh and Kabul, all meet at Herat: hence its position is of great strategical importance, and this is attested by the fact that from the 12th to the 17th centuries it has been on seven occasions demolished and rebuilt.

The advantages of an advance towards Herat are –

1st · – Its proximity to our base.

2nd – The comparative easiness of the route, and the fact that it can be adopted at any season of the year.

3rd – The belief that Kandahar could be occupied without much opposition.

4th – The possibility of protecting the flank from attack from Kabul, by the occupation of Kalat-i-Gilzai, 90 miles on the Kandahar-Ghuzni-Kabul road.

5th – The fact that a moderate-sized army would suffice for the occupation of Herat, irrespective of the attitude of Aghanistan, for keeping open the communication with our base, and for placing a force in the field at Herat, sufficient to cope with anything that could be brought against it under existing circumstances.

6th – The occupation of Herat would bring Afghanistan to terms.

7th – It would reassure the Turkomans, and place them in immediate connection with us.

8th – It would in all probability regain our lost influence in Persia.

9th – It would effectively check the advance of Russia towards India from the southern shores of the Caspian, and the lower valley of the Oxus.

10th – It would enable us to raise a force of Afghans, Turkomans, and Persians sufficient to drive the Russians from the southern and eastern shores of the Caspian, and by rousing the Circassians to make her position on the western shores extremely dangerous.

A force assembled at Quetta by 1st November could reach Kandahar on the 20th November, and Herat by the middle or end of the following January.

* * *

In the first instance, 10,000 men would be required for Kandahar and Kalat-i-Gilzai and for maintaining communication between these places and Quetta. For Herat and the road from Kandahar, 10,000 more men would be necessary, leaving 10,000 men available for any move beyond Herat.

Additional heavy guns should accompany the army to be placed in position at Kalat-i-Gilzai, Kandahar, Herat, and elsewhere.

These operations would fall mainly on the Bengal and Bombay Armies. Should a contingent be sent to Egypt or Asia Minor simultaneously with them, Madras and Bombay would have to provide the troops.

RP 95/1; also RP 100/1

[Roberts added a note to the paper in 1890:

'This paper was written nearly *13* years ago. Since then our position and that of Russia in Central Asia have changed considerably. Notwithstanding this, there is much in this paper which still holds good. F.R. 8–1–90.'

A further holograph note was added to Roberts' copy of the relevant printed text of his papers (RP 95/1)

'Since this was written, 25 years ago, matters have materially changed and nothing we could now do would prevent Russia from occupying Herat, from which place her frontier post is not further distant (about 60 miles) than we at Chaman from Kandahar. R. 23 Aug: 1902']

5
H.K. BURNE[10] TO ALL SPECIAL NEWSPAPER CORRESPONDENTS

[Printed copy]   Simla,
No 376K   16 October, 1878

In conveying to you the authority of the Government of India to join the Quetta/Kohat Column under the command of Major-General M.A. Biddulph C.B.[11]/F. Roberts, C.B., V.C. I am desired to forward, for your information and guidance, copy of the rules which have been laid down on the subject of your relations with the military authorities.

2. You should apply to the Quarter Master General of the Army for the necessary passes, and for orders for the supply of camp equipage, and the Commissary-General will be instructed to supply carriage, rations, and forage for one horse, on the same terms as allowed to other officers under present regulations.

[Annexed]

Rules for the guidance of Special Correspondents with Columns in the Field.

1. All Special Correspondents with columns are subject to the orders of the Officer Commanding, under the provisions of the Indian Articles of War, Act No. V of 1869, *(d)*, Application of Articles.

2. Whilst any restriction or supervision over correspondence will be avoided, the Government of India relies on the gentlemen of the Press not writing or communicating any news for publication which may be useful to the enemy, or furnishing any particulars prejudicial to the British interest.

3. Officers commanding columns, if they think it necessary, are empowered to require any telegraphic messages, which gentlemen of the press propose to send, to be submitted for inspection before despatch.

4. Gentlemen of the Press should distinctly understand that, in the event of their infringing any of these rules, or any rule which it may be hereafter considered necessary to lay down, they will be liable to be removed from camp.

5. Gentlemen of the Press will be allowed carriage and camp equipage from Government to the extent, and on the same terms as regards payment, as sanctioned to all officers under present regulations. (The scale allowed to each officer consists of 80lbs. of camp equipage and 80lbs. of baggage).

6. Rations for self, for servants, and for a horse, as allowed to a

Staff Officer, will be sanctioned from the Commissariat on payment.

7. Passes will be issued to such Correspondents as have been approved by the Government of India.

HP 38/p. 510

6
Adjutant-General India to Major-General M. Biddulph

[Printed copy]
Simla
18 October 1878

No. 100

The Chief this morning drew my attention to the *Pioneer* of the 16th October, containing a correspondent's letter, dated Mooltan, 12th October, in which your Field Force orders of the 8th October are set forth. In addition to the above is matter connected with the payment of telegrams and other matters which you have referred to His Excellency.

Sir Frederick Haines believes he is aware of the author of the above; however this may be, he desires that you will communicate to your staff that His Excellency, in nominating officers for staff employ in the field, believes that he entrusts them with duties which should occupy every minute of their time, and that the last thing expected from them is to become newspaper correspondents. The press of this country has been well supported by Government, and has its own agents. Should therefore it come to His Excellency's knowledge that officers are employing themselves otherwise than in their legitimate duties and using material for correspondence of which they could only have become possessed through their official positions, they shall assuredly be relieved.

[Copied to Roberts on 21 October 1878]

HP 38/p. 510

7
Adjutant-General India to Roberts

[Printed copy]   Simla
                                                  22 October 1878

No. 138–K

I am directed by the Commander-in-Chief to inform you that, with the sanction of Government, you have been appointed to the command of a column of troops as per margin [Not printed but see Document 14]

2. Your first endeavour will be to get this force together in the Upper Miranzai valley and to establish an entrenched post at Thal.

3. This post should be of such dimensions as to cover two guns, a regiment of native infantry, and a wing of cavalry, to be detailed from the troops of the column and at Kohat. The object of this detachment is to maintain your communications, and to afford a convenient half-way depot for sick and stores, provision of shelter for which should be provided.

4. His Excellency cannot too forcibly impress upon you the necessity of securing in your interests the services of the Chiefs and Khans of influence of the tribes bordering on your route and the district of Kuram.

5. In communication with the Civil authorities, it would be very desirable to cause one of those chiefs to accompany you, and to secure the services of as many of the chiefs of Turis [indecipherable] as may be available.

6. It will be for you to consider, with the information at your disposal, the nature of operations most likely to secure the objects of Government. The positions respectively of Kuram, Khost and Dawar, all south of the Safed-Koh, held by or more or less subordinate to the Kabul Government, must be accepted as within the zone of your operations.

7. Your first object will be to engage any of the troops belonging to

the Amir of Kabul in occupation of Kuram, to drive them and the ruler from the valley, and to take possession of the same, as also of Khost; and to communicate to the inhabitants of Dawar that the British has replaced Afghan supremacy from date of notification, but to leave any practical application of such supremacy for future adjustment at a convenient time.

8. It is difficult to define the limit to which your action should immediately extend in the direction of Kabul. Without question the Kuram district must be held to extend to the watershed of the Kuram river, embracing the Hariab valley and Mangal country up to the Shutargardan and Zurmat passes.

9. In the first instance, however, it may be desirable to command the Paiwar pass and the road as far as the village of Ali Khel or hamlet of Rokian, near to the junction of the direct road from Kabul by the Gharigi road with the Shutargardan route, and which marks the boundary between Jaji and Ghilzai lands.

10. Every endeavour should be made to gain over the Ahmadzai faction of the Ghilzai tribe, who hold the lands on the watershed on this line to Kabul, and whose tents and herds seek shelter in the winter months in the Kuram district.

11. Discipline demands that the officers, soldiers, and followers confine themselves to the roads; and that the latter especially be prohibited from wandering into villages or destroying crops.

12. Every encouragement should be given to the people to supply your bazars, and at every camp a place not only be allotted for such trade, but a British and a native non-commissioned officer of the Provost Marshal's establishment be told off to protect them and to prevent disputes.

13. The considerate and friendly demeanour of all towards the people will do more than anything else to secure their good-will and assistance. The Jajis and Turis of Kuram, having nothing in common with the 'powers that be' at Kabul or with the Afghan tribes, may be expected gladly to espouse our cause.

14. Although the most direct route from Kohat to Kuram is through the Zaimukht country, policy immediately demands that its adoption be positively prohibited.

15. On first arriving at Kuram, the position of Muhammad Azim's

fort in the centre of the valley, and which has hitherto been the seat of Government, would appear to present the most desirable location for the establishment of your headquarters; and, should such appear to you desirable, it would be well to concentrate there your depot and supplies, and without delay secure all available shelter.

16. The matter of supply is a most important one, and every endeavour must be made to rapidly collect some two or three months in advance of the daily demands of the force.

17. Too great stress cannot be placed upon your limiting baggage, while at the same time ensuring that every soldier and follower is fully provided with all articles of warm clothing as sanctioned, and that your stores of ammunition and food are continually maintained.

18. The protection and care of your carriage is a matter of great importance. The former must be secured by prohibiting grazing of camels without escort, and the latter by constant inspections.

19. Grass-cutters when beyond our present border will, whilst engaged at their calling, require protection. Much, however, of your supply of provender for maintenance of horses and cattle will have to be secured from the villagers; but, in obtaining this, parties must not be permitted to act indiscriminately, but invariably act under the immediate orders of an officer, British or Native.

20. With these orders for your general guidance, the Commander-in-Chief, with the full authority of Government, must leave the matter to your discretion and judgment, in which His Excellency has the fullest confidence.

21. Should affairs in Kuram appear to justify such a measure, it will be for you to distribute your force, so as to expose it as little as possible to the inclemency of the winter. Such consideration would justify the retention of any portion of it at Thal or elsewhere as circumstances on the spot may appear desirable.

NAM 1878–80(581) – *The Second Afghan War* (abridged and re-edited official history) Vol. 1, pp. 117–19.

8
Roberts to Adjutant-General India

[Printed telegram]   Simla
                                                         25 October 1878

Confidential

When giving me final orders, please have it clearly stated that, while every deference is to be paid to opinions of politicals, the General in Command is alone responsible.

RP 101/IV

9
Roberts to General MacLagan,[12] Chief Engineer of the Punjab.

[Printed copy]   Kohat,
                                                         25 October 1878

From the enclosed memorandum you will see that the Bullock train travelling between Rawal Pindi and Kohat is getting slower and slower; not a mile an hour, the state of the road being the chief cause. I hope you will be able to help us. If an Assistant Engineer could go into camp and march up and down the road as far as Kushalgurh, matters would doubtless mend; besides the road, the water supply and accommodation for man and beast of the several halting-places require carefully looking after. Now everything is in our favour, but once the bad weather begins and the roads get heavy, our communication with Rawal Pindi will be seriously interrupted. Excuse my being pressing about these roads; they are most important, and I fear if we lose the next three or four weeks our commissariat will be greatly inconvenienced; we cannot expect the fine weather to last longer than that. Mr Scott[13] I believe goes over the road frequently, but travelling 50 or 60 miles a day in a mail cart cannot do much good. There is a broken bridge between

23

Kushalgurh and Kohat which should be repaired. Captain Harvey[14] is now sending revised plans and estimates, and calculates that after receipt of orders to commence, it would take him four months at least to finish the job; he could repair the bridge with timber in less than a month and I hope you will sanction this being done. I will write to you officially to-morrow. I am anxious also to have the road to Thull put into good order before rain falls.

RP 101/V

10
Roberts to Colonel Sibley[15]

[Printed telegram]   Kohat,
                                          25 October 1878

Burlton telegraphs that 1,000 Kohat camels have been diverted by order of the Commissary General. Please see to this. Unless your orders are carried out, this force will never be equipped.

RP 101/VI

11
Roberts to Colonel George Colley, Private Secretary to the Viceroy

[Printed copy]   Kohat,
                                          27 October 1878

Very many thanks for sending me the cypher telegram received this evening. I am sorry the Cabinet would not be guided by the Viceroy; to insist on an ultimatum being now sent to the Amir seems unnecessary to all who know Asiatics; it will be attributed to fear on our part, and will certainly be misunderstood by Sher Ali. I shall continue my preparations and on the 20th proximo shall be at Thull ready to advance with my column, and be prepared to reach the Afghan position between the Peiwar and Shutar Gardan passes by the 30th idem. There will be plenty of time before the snow falls for us to turn the Afghans out, and our doing so will have the best possible effect on the Ghilzais and other tribes, who will hesitate about joining us if they find that the Afghans are allowed to remain in the position they have taken up until snow forces them to retire.

I only require two things – first, elephants and cradles for the Royal Horse Artillery Battery, second, to be allowed to take on the 72nd Highlanders. My force is not strong enough, now that the Guides and the 4th Goorkhas have been taken away, to warrant my attacking a strong position without a British regiment in reserve, and it would be almost impossible to reach the Afghans before snow falls, if I had to take horsed guns over the Peiwar. With elephants it would be easy enough, but knowing how little consideration is shewn to this column, I am afraid I shall not get my own way, either as regards the British regiment, or the elephants, unless I am helped. I will send in my report as to how I would propose to carry on operations to-morrow. I deciphered your message owing to Waterfield[16] being here. Could I not be entrusted with the key book, as Waterfield and I may not be always together?

RP 101/VII

12
Roberts to Colley

[Printed telegram]   Kohat
                                                29 October 1878

Clear the line. Personal. I regret much to say that I could not advance from Thull with the column complete and a month's provisions before 15th November unless I am considerably assisted with supplies, clothing for followers, and carriage from Peshawar and Rawal Pindi. If I am, I could make a start about the 10th November, but to enable me to move off on 15th even the Commissariat must be ordered to forward on without delay all stocks and stores now *en route*. The column would have been almost ready now had not orders from Simla directed all carriage and sup-

25

plies to Peshawar. If absolutely necessary a move could be made about 5th November to the foot of the Peiwar Kotal with one Brigade and one Battery, and by halting every two or three days to send back for supplies. Followers however would be without clothing and the equipment of the column would not be satisfactory. As explained in a letter which you will receive tomorrow, for anything like a rapid advance to and over the Peiwar, elephants for Horse Artillery are essential, they with their gear are available at Peshawar, but I have hitherto failed to obtain sanction for them to be sent here.

RP 101/VIII

13
Memorandum from Foreign Department

[Manuscript copy, marked 'The accompanying extract of a Memo from the Secy Gov[t] of India Foreign Dept[t]. dtd.7th inst., forwarded to Major Genl. Roberts VC, CB for information. By order. S. Black.[17] Colonel Mil. Sec. Punjab Gov 12 November 1878'.]

Very Confidential   Simla
No. 2507P   7 November 1878

. . . Her Majesty's Gov[t] having decided that an ultimatum shall be sent to the Amir, demanding an apology, and the acceptance of a permanent British Mission in Afghan territory; and that failing receipt of a satisfactory reply by the 20th Nove., the Amir shall be treated as a declared enemy of the British Government, the following orders will be issued in the Foreign & Military Departments.

1. The troops will be held in readiness to cross the Frontier at all points on the 21st instant.

* * *

Kurram Column

8. The operations of the Kurram Column will include the occupation of Kurram Valley, the Paiwar Kotal and the expulsion of any

garrisons the Amir may have established in the Upper Kurram Valley, or on this side of the Shutur Garden Pass. In no case will any troops be pushed beyond the range of mountains dividing the watershed of the Kurram and Kabul Rivers. The Officer Commanding the Column will also push his reconnaissances, as opportunity may offer, into the Khost Valley, and will, if military circumstances will permit, dislodge the Amir's administration from that tract, so as to prevent the Amir drawing either supplies or revenue from it. He will also explore the roads leading to the country beyond.

9. The Officer Commanding the Column will have the chief direction of political, as well as military affairs, within the limits of his command, beyond the British Border, and a Political officer will be attached to him. On military matters he will correspond with the Commander-in-Chief, and on political matters, with the Gov^t of India in the Foreign Department.

10. Upon entering the Amir's territory, the Officer Commanding will ascertain & determine what measures, if any, are necessary, for carrying on the ordinary civil administration of the country which his troops will occupy. His object will be to preserve order, while withdrawing from the Amir's civil officers all authority, except such as may be left to mere local officials, and he will at once prohibit and intercept the collection of any revenue for the Amir's treasury. He will, at the same time, spare no effort to obtain the good will of the inhabitants of the country within which he operates, and of the neighbouring tribes; & he will protect them as far as possible from being molested, or from suffering hardship from the passage of the troops through their lands. He will endeavour to settle a friendly understanding with the Ghilzais & other tribes in the vicinity, or at least to secure their neutrality, explaining that the British Gov^t desires to avoid all interference with their internal affairs, and that the military operations are directed against the army of the Amir alone. He will take steps for keeping himself well informed regarding the course of events, & the state of feeling in the interior of Afghanistan, especially in the Kabul Valley & at the Capital. But he is not authorised to entertain any negotiations with the Amir

or the Kabul Sirdars, and any such overtures, if they are made, will be referred to the political authorities in the Khyber Pass, or at Peshawar.

RP 154/3

14
Roberts to Quartermaster-General India

[Typed copy]   Camp Thull
                                                    20 November 1878

No. 183

I have the honour to report my arrival at this place.

2. The disposition of the troops under my command is at present as follows:-

At Thull.

F.A., R.H.A.[18]   5th P.I.
No. 1 Mountain Battery.   5th Goorkhas.
Squadron 10th Hussars.   21st P.N.I.
Wing 5th P.C.   23rd Pioneers
12th Bengal Cavalry.   29th P.N.I.
2/8th Foot.   7th Co. Sappers & Miners

At Gandiour. (9 miles from Thull)

No. 2 Mountain Battery.   Wing 72nd Highlanders.
Half G/3 R.A.   2nd P.I.

At Kohat.

Half G/3 R.A.   Wing 72nd Highlanders
About 140, 2/8th Foot.   Wing 5th P.C.
                                    28th P.N.I.

3. The troops at Gandiour will move on to Thull when the troops now here cross the frontier.

4. The following corps have been detailed to form the first column to cross the border as soon as orders may be received:-

F.A., R.H.A.	2/8th Foot
No. 1 Mountain Battery	5th P.I.
Squadron 10th Hussars.	23rd Pioneers.
12th B.C.	29th P.N.I.
7th Co. (Bengal) Sappers & Miners.	

5. The second column to follow the next day will consist of:

Half G/3 R.A.	5th Goorkhas
Wing 72nd Highlanders.	2nd P.I.

6. The garrison at Thull will be composed as follows:-

No. 2 Mountain Battery
Wing 5th P.C.
21st P.N.I.

7. The first days operations I propose to confine to crossing the river and seizing the small fort of Kapiganj which will form a convenient depot for my commissariat stores, and will possess the advantage of being on the right side of the river for sending on supplies to the Force when it is in occupation of the upper part of the Koorum valley.

8. A crib bridge has now been completed over the river, but it is liable to be injured or swept away if the river should be in flood, and it is therefore desirable to have the main Commissariat depot on the further or right bank.

9. When Kapiganj has been occupied, it is my intention to place in it the chief part of the Thull garrison, leaving only a small detach-

ment on the left bank of the river for the protection of any stores which might arrive and be unable to cross, and of the depot hospital.

10. I propose also to occupy on the first day of the advance the small fort of Ahmadi Shamu, about 6 miles beyond Kapiganj. A detachment* under the command of Colonel J.H. Gordon,[19] 29th P.N.I., will be employed on this service.

11. The health of the troops is improving and may now be considered generally good, except the 2/8th Foot, regarding which regiment I shall submit a separate report to the Adjutant General.

Detachment
Squad. 10th Hrs.
12th B.C.
19th P.N.I.
No. 1 Mn. Batty

RP 154/3

15
Alfred Lyall, Foreign Secretary India, to Roberts

[Holograph]   Lahore
                                    26 November 1878

So far as we have heard, your entry into the Kuram valley has been unopposed, and I even conjecture that you will meet with a friendly reception. You will be able quietly to replace the Amir's authorities, and to arrange for keeping good order in the open districts.

The Viceroy considers that your occupation gives an excellent opportunity for closely looking into all local facts & circumstances which may bear upon the question if it arrives (and it may arrive soon) whether we should, for political and military purposes, take possession of any part of the country now under your military occupation, and, if so, in what way and to what extent we should hold it. You should understand (and I am writing confidentially) that the Govt. of India may at any time have to state definitely the precise objects of their operations, and to lay down the terms & conditions upon which they will be prepared to conclude fresh arrangements with Afghanistan.

In short, we may at any time be asked what we want – and it may be safely predicted that we are likely to require, for one thing, a rectification of our frontier. The question therefore which might be carefully considered beforehand is whether there are any points or districts which it will be desirable to hold permanently for the protection and tranquillity of our frontier, and for the retention of which we might stipulate whenever negotiations were opened, or whenever our military operations drew to a close for any other reason.

Such a question depends obviously on many local circumstances & considerations; upon the situation of any particular tract, upon the class & character of its inhabitants, upon its defensibility, and the like. Will you, accordingly, have the kindness to consult Waterfield on the subject and instruct him to submit, through you, a report discussing the advisability & practicability upon political grounds, of retaining in our hands certain portions of the Kurram Valley, & possibly of the Khost valley. What we want are materials for judging and decision in the event of it becoming necessary to decide upon the question of occupying this part of Afghanistan.

Annexation is not necessarily contemplated; it might be sufficient to establish a protectorate, or to administer certain districts politically through our frontier officers. Whether a strong garrison would be indispensable is mainly a military question, connected with our military frontier arrangements – but it is of course inseparable from the political question.

LyP 24/1

16
Roberts to Foreign Department

[Manuscript copy]   HQ Kurum Column, Kurum
27 November 1878

No. 1

I have the honour to report, for the information of the
Government of India, that on the 21st November I crossed the
River Koorum and encamped with the First Brigade of the troops
under my command at Kapianga. Here there is a fortified post
established by the Amir of Kabul for the collection of tolls, and
held generally by irregular troops numbering about 120 men. The
post was evacuated on the night of the 20th; three men only posted
as sentries on the river bank being captured by our troops. Of
these men one was a Turi and two were Ghilzais.[20] They represented that they had been forcibly detained in the post and had
seized the opportunity of our arrival to effect their escape. I
thought it better to release these men, retaining their arms, which
were the property of the Kabul Government.

On the same day I drew up a brief proclamation in the spirit of
the instructions conveyed to me by the Government, stating that
the force under my command had advanced with no intention of
punishing the subjects of the Amir; that all supplies would be
promptly paid for, and that the inhabitants of the country
through which we might pass would receive no injury at our
hands. I stated that payment of revenue to the Amir or the ren-
dering of any assistance to his troops must be discontinued, and
that arrangements would shortly be made to secure a proper
administration of the country and the welfare of its inhabitants
under British rule. I stated also that our Government had no
intention of interfering with the internal affairs of tribes independent of the Amir, or of invading their country or molesting
them in any way.

Copies of this proclamation were sent on the same day to the
Turis of the Upper and Lower Kurum valley and to Khost; also to

the Daur Waziris and to the following tribes:- The Jajis, Chakmanis, Mongals and Makhbals.[21]

On 23rd November I proceeded to Hazir Pir Ziarat, the inhabitants of the villages on the road invariably evincing a most friendly disposition. On the next day I called together the leading men of Bali Amin and the neighbouring villages in the Lower Kurum valley, and a few men from Khost who had come down to meet me. I represented that they were most of them aware of the nature of administration in the territory already under British rule, and that a similar administration would prevail in the country newly annexed by the British Government. I had every reason to believe that the prospect of being placed under our rule was sincerely welcome to both the Turis and Bangashes[22] of the Kurum valley. I was confirmed in this belief on reaching the Upper Kurum valley, and approaching Mahomed Azim's fort, the late H[d]Quarters of the Dawrani administration in the valley. All the influential men of the neighbourhood, including a number of Shia Sayids,[23] met me on the road and accompanied me to the encamping ground. They tendered their services in affording any information as to the different roads by which we might advance or in exerting their influence with the neighbouring tribes. One of the Sayids volunteered to go and bring in the leading men of the Jagis and Chakmanis. I took advantage of his offer, and he appeared next day accompanied by some fifteen men of these tribes, and bringing a letter from others saying that they were willing to help us and to take charge of the road over the Paiwar Kotal and Shutar Gurdan Pass on payment of an annual subsidy. Those present also agreed to give assistance to our troops on their advance towards the Shutar Gurdan Pass.

Malik Shah Newaz Khan, a Manitowal Zaimusht,[24] appeared in camp yesterday. He is a man of considerable influence with his tribe; has been for many years in receipt of a subsidy from the Amir of Kabul, and was deputed a short time ago by Sirdar Wali Mahomed Khan[25] to summon the Zaimusht and Ali Sherzai Jirgahs[26] to Kabul. He expressed himself favourably disposed towards the British Government, and willing to give his assistance as far as he was able.

33

Arrangements have been made for the collection of wood, grass and other articles required by the troops and not procurable from the Commissariat Department, and it is hoped that in a short time a market will be established in the vicinity of the camp for the supply of these articles to the troops on payment.

I have also directed the Comm^t authorities to arrange for the presentation of 1000 maunds of barley and wheat to the inhabitants of the valley, who are absolutely without seed corn for the spring harvest. The civil authorites at Kohat will be requested to refund this amount of grain to the Comm^t stores from which it will be drawn, and it is hoped that these arrangements made for the welfare of the inhabitants of the Kurum valley will meet with the approval of the Government of India.

RP 154–3/4

17
Roberts to Colley

[Printed copy]   Camp Alikhel
                                          10 December 1878

Private

Villiers[27] showed me your letter of the 30th ultimo in which you propose writing to me about the composition of a force for an advance in the spring from Kuram towards Kabul and for a possible move onwards towards Bamian, Balkh and even farther. I intended writing to you on this very subject as soon as I returned to Kuram for there are many things in my present column which require changing before I should feel satisfied to start on such an expedition.

In the first place, the column should consist, as regards natives, of as many Hindoos, and as few Mahomedans as possible. Villiers has doubtless told you how nearly the turning movement on the night of the 1st instant came to an untimely end, in consequence of the determination of the Pathans of the 29th Native Infantry not to make the business a surprise. I detected the lagging and was fortunately near the front when two shots were fired by men of the Pathan company; we were not loaded, all around us was silent, so that the sole object of loading and firing must have been to give the enemy warning of our approach. It was too dark to examine the men's rifles, indeed there was not time to do so; I therefore halted the regiment, and moved the 5th Goorkhas and a company of the 72nd behind them to prevent their altogether slinking away, until I saw we were near the Kotal, when I sent back word to General Thelwall[28] to send them on too: we were not a moment too soon, but you may fancy my anxiety when I discovered the tricks the 29th were up to. I am having the whole matter enquired into, and will then report it officially to the Adjutant General. I could never go into action with the regiment again: and as soon as an opportunity offers I intend to send it back to Thull. Some of the Sikhs behaved well in the after part of the day, but I am grievously disappointed both with the regiment and its Commanding Officer.

Without doubt, Pathans consider Sher Ali as their big man, and it requires a very good regiment, and a very good Commanding Officer, such as the 5th Punjab Infantry under Major McQueen[29] to be of use in a war of this sort.

To cross the Shutar Gardan and the Hindu Kush, I should like to have with me –

2 Complete Brigades numbering	4,200	Infantry
1 Regiment of Pioneers	700	
2 Companies of Sappers	200	
1 Squadron of British Cavalry	120	
3 Regiments of Native Cavalry	1,200	
Total	6,420	

With 1 Battery R.H.A.	6	Guns
1 Field Battery	6	
2 Mountain Batteries	12	
Total	24	

and 2 Gatling guns.

The present Punjab Mountain Batteries should be increased from 4 to 6 guns each, and I would strongly recommend that the 320 lbs. weight gun, to be carried in two pieces,[30] should take the place of the present 200 lb. gun, if the result of its trial is as satisfactory as I am told it is. There would be just time to have two complete batteries sent out if a telegram were despatched now. The Spanish Government have already adopted the gun, and we shall probably never require it more than we do now. Meanwhile orders might be issued to enlist gunners and drivers and to purchase sufficient mules.

Seeing the distance the column might have to travel, and the possibility of meeting Russian troops, it is very necessary that every regiment should be efficient in all respects. Four of mine are all I could wish, *viz.*, the 72nd Highlands, 5th Punjab Infantry, 5th Goorkhas, and 23rd Pioneers, but none of the other regiments of Infantry are corps to take over the Shutar Gardan, except perhaps the 28th, which I have only seen as yet on the parade ground. The 2nd Punjab Infantry is good in its way, but the Pathan element is very strong in it; the 21st have also a great many Pathans; the 8th Foot may do fairly well two or three years hence, but it is now in bad order, has no interior economy, and is composed of young lads. My second British corps should be a seasoned one like the 92nd Highlanders, and for the Native Infantry I would select the 44th from Assam, and either the 3rd or 4th Sikhs, their present Mahomedan companies being replaced by Sikhs, or else the 28th Native Infantry (which has a good Commanding Officer) if treated in the same way. Assam seems a long way to send for a regiment, but it is worth doing so under existing circumstances; the 44th is a good fighting corps, and is composed almost entirely of a hardy class of Goorkhas. For cavalry I only require one more regiment added to those now at my disposal to complete the Brigade, and I would name the 14th Bengal Lancers as being well mounted, and all or nearly all Hindoos of a good fighting class; this would give me the Squadron 10th Hussars, 12th Bengal Cavalry, 14th Bengal Lancers, and 5th Punjab Cavalry: not too many I think for a country of so vast an extent as that between the Hindu Kush and the Oxus. I must then have two good Brigadier-Generals; Cobbe[31] is a nice plucky old fellow who would command a Brigade of a Division of an army when not likely to be separated with considerable credit, but he is not fit for a Brigade likely to have to act independently; he has not sufficient self-reliance, nor is he physically fit for the hardships of such a campaign as we are now contemplating. Thelwall is, I am satisfied, no soldier in the field; he is admirable in looking after troops or camps or making peaceful arrangements, and I would name him as the best man I know to command in Kuram; he would soon get things into order and would be much more in his element than he is against an artful, skilful enemy on the hill side. Of all men for a commander I would prefer Jenkins,[32] and if you will throw the Guides Cavalry and Infantry into my column in addition to the troops I have named, I would back myself to reach Tashkend before this time next year. Macgregor would be my second choice for a Brigadier-General, and if it is not considered essential that one of the Brigade Commandants should be of the British service, I would say give me Jenkins and Macgregor; if one must be of the home service, then Jenkins and Buchanan,[33] the ex-Colonel of the 9th Foot who went home a few months ago. For the Cavalry, Artillery and Engineers I have Commanders who suit me admirably, but unless I have really good men for the Infantry Brigades, I shall be dreadfully hampered. For a column likely to go so far from its base and having to maintain a long line of communications, Government should be liberal with the Commissariat and Medical Establishments. Not only will more officers be required but more subordinates. Even here I have at times been obliged to dispose my troops to suit the power of the Commissariat Officer to feed them. More gomashtas and victualling sergeants are required in the one department; more apothecaries, native doctors, dressers, sweepers, &c., in the other. Then I should require a fair supply of really good tools, and to have the troops, British and Native, properly equipped with boots, shoes and warm clothing before we start. I can think of nothing else to make the column complete: if the Viceroy will entrust me with the troops I have named above, including the Guides Corps, and give me two trusty generals, I do not think His Excellency will be disappointed in any plans he may have formed for the column to carry out.

I will add a few words on what is required to be done in Kuram. As soon as I have visited Khost I shall be able to speak with more certainty, but my present opinion is that the people between the Kuram at Thull and the Shutar Gardan will never give much trouble: we have tumbled down the Amir's Government, such as it was, and must now replace it. I have already applied for two or three Pushtoo-speaking Police Officers of the stamp of Captain Tucker and three or four Tehsildars, but I would strongly recommend that Major Macaulay be sent from Dera Ismail Khan to settle the country, and that he be assisted by Captain Warburton.[34] Both speak Pushtoo fluently, both are energetic and get on well with natives; in a short time it would be quite possible to leave Captain Warburton in charge with an Assistant under him; but at first a man like Major Macaulay is required.

Mr Christie[35] is not at all the man for a newly conquered Province; he has no energy nor resource, and would be of far more use at Kohat or Bunnoo than he is here. When we move on in the spring, I would leave General Thelwall in command here, and place at his disposal –

1 Regiment of British Infantry, so long as there may be disturbances with Kabul.

2 Regiments of Native Infantry.

1 Wing of Native Cavalry.

4 Mountain guns.

With this force he could control the whole country from Thull to the Shutar Gardan, including Khost and Daur, and maintain the communications in strength.

RP 101/XV

18
Roberts to Viceroy

[Printed]
State telegram – Precedence.   Kuram
                                                14 December 1878

We marched yesterday to Kariah on the Kuram: *en route* the baggage was attacked by a band of marauders belonging to the

Monguls who live on the left bank of the Kuram river. Owing to the great steadiness of the 5th Goorkhas who were on rear guard, the baggage was all saved, and the Monguls suffered severely; the ground, however, was extremely difficult and all in favor of the attackers who caused us considerable loss: killed – 3 Goorkhas; wounded – Captain Goad, Transport Train, and Captain Powell,[36] 5th Goorkhas; 11 Goorkhas, 1 72nd and 1 Gunner No. 1 Mountain Battery. The officers are both very severely wounded, one Goorkha is badly wounded, the remainder more or less slightly. The attack was quite unprovoked as we were not near the Mongul country. The tribe were probably induced to trouble us by some refugees from the Amir's army, as a few men in uniform were seen, and one Enfield rifle was picked up. Some of the 72nd Highlanders did admirable service with the Henry-Martini Rifle. The conduct of the 5th Goorkhas is beyond praise.

RP 101/XVIII

19
Foreign Secretary India to Roberts

[Manuscript copy] Camp   Lahore
                                                16 December 1878

No. 240 C.P.

I am directed to acknowledge receipt of your letter No. 1 dated the 27th November, reporting to the Government of India the measures taken by you on entering the Kuram valley, for the occupation and political administration of that country.
2. His Excellency the Viceroy and Governor General is pleased to approve generally these proceedings. It is observed, however, that your letter mentions an address delivered by you to the headmen and others of the neighbourhood of Hazir Pir Ziarat, in which they are informed that an administration similar to that in British India, will prevail in the country newly annexed to the British Government. And you add that the prospect of being placed

under our rule was sincerely welcome to several tribes in the valley.

3. His Excellency the Viceroy apprehends that the use of the word annexed may be accidental; at any rate the persons to whom it was used are not likely to appreciate political distinctions of phrase. Nevertheless I am to remark for your information that it is not desirable to proclaim, in any part of Afghanistan, the annexation, actual or proximate, of any territory to British India.

4. It is the intention of the Government of India to detach certain tracts upon our border from the Amir's authority, and to place them under political superintendence, and under a protectorate which will be completely efficacious as against any power in Afghanistan. You can therefore give assurance of complete permanent protection, whenever this is necessary to be given; though of course you will do this with caution, and will refer for orders whenever you feel any doubt as to the range over which this protectorate should hereafter extend. But it does not fall within the present policy of the Government to declare the annexation of any territory.

RP 154-3

20
Roberts to Adjutant-General India

[Printed copy]   HQ Kuram Field Force, Kuram
No. 132–D   16 December 1878

I have the honour to report for the information of His Excellency the Commander-in-Chief the following circumstances in connection with the 29th Native Infantry.

2. In consequence of the excellent character I had received of the 29th Native Infantry and the high reputation of their Commanding Officer, I selected the regiment to lead the advance on the Spingawi Kotal during the night of the 1st December 1878, placing under Colonel Gordon's command the 5th Goorkhas in addition to his own regiment.

3. We had calculated that starting from camp at 9 p.m., there would be about four hours to spare in the middle of the night during which time the men would rest. The road certainly proved extremely bad, and the distance was perhaps longer than was expected, but neither of these facts was sufficient to account for the slow progress the column was making. Wishing to ascertain the cause of delay, I proceeded to the head of the column and was at once struck by the very straggling manner in which the leading regiment was marching. I called Colonel Gordon's attention to this circumstance, and desired him to close up his men, and to call upon them to push on more quickly; while I was talking with Colonel Gordon, a shot was fired from one of the Pathan companies, followed in about two minutes by a second shot; the Sikh companies of the regiment immediately closed up, and Colonel Gordon's orderly, a Sikh, whispered in his ear that there was treachery amongst the Pathans.

4. The position was an extremely anxious one; it was impossible to say how far we were from the Spingawi Kotal, or whether the shots could be heard by the enemy: it was also impossible to ascertain who had fired the shots without delaying the advance, and this I was loth to do in the uncertainty as to the distance still to be traversed. Unwilling as I was to take any step which could discredit a regiment bearing so high a character as the 29th, I felt that our enterprise had been already imperilled by the conduct of the Pathans, and that the occasion was not one for hesitation, for unless we could reach the Spingawi while it was still dark, the turning movement, instead of being a success, would in all probability have ended in a disaster.

5. I accordingly took Colonel Gordon on one side and said that sorry as I was to pass his regiment by, the conduct of some of his men admitted of no other course; he entirely agreed with the necessity of the measure, and suggested that a company of the 72nd Highlanders should be brought to the front in addition to the 5th Goorkhas.

6. Orders were given to this effect and by dint of pressing on we were enabled to arrive at the Kotal just as the first streaks of dawn were appearing. Had we been one quarter of an hour

later, the enemy must have discovered us, when the result of the turning movement would have been very different from what it was.

7. During the action on the heights between the Spingawi and Peiwar Kotals many of the Pathans and other Mahomedans of the 29th shewed considerable reluctance to go forward, though some Sikhs of the regiment under Major Channer, V.C., and Lieutenant Picot,[37] showed a gallant example, and as may be seen by their list of casualties, suffered heavily.

8. On the evening of the 2nd instant no less than 34 sepoys of the 29th were missing; it was afterwards ascertained that 16 of these, Sikhs, having lost their way, had found themselves near the 5th Punjab Infantry and remained with that regiment throughout the action; the remaining 18, all Pathans, returned direct to their camp below the Peiwar Kotal.

9. This circumstance was not known to me until two or three days after the action, when I sent for Colonel Gordon to enquire whether he had been able to ascertain who had fired the shots in the Spingawi Pass, and whether he did not think the Pathan Native officers must have known who the culprits were.

10. Colonel Gordon then told me that one man had confessed to firing the second shot and that he suspected the Jemadar of the Pathan company was aware at the time who fired both shots. Colonel Gordon also informed me of the fact that a number of men were missing the day of the fight, and that he had sent 14 Pathans back to Kuram to be discharged with ignominy, keeping four of the seniors to be tried by Court Martial. I pointed out to Colonel Gordon that it was his duty to have reported the absence of men from their colours during an action, that he had no power to discharge men while on service, and that as the behaviour of the Pathans of his regiment had been so unsatisfactory, I saw nothing for it but to convene a Court of Enquiry.

11. As I was on the point of starting for the Shutar Gardan when Colonel Gordon told me of the desertion of these men, I directed Brigadier-General Thelwall to convene a Court of Enquiry of which he was to be President; he apparently misunderstood the orders and assembled a Regimental Court, which went so little

into the subject that I have been obliged to assemble a second Court of Enquiry which is now sitting. The proceedings will be forwarded without delay. I have no doubt but that the complicity of one or more Native officers will be proved, and in the event of this being the case, and trial by General Court Martial being necessitated of any or all the men now under confinement, I have the honour to request that you will favor me by telegraph with the Commander-in-Chief's wishes, should the Court find the prisoners guilty and sentence them to death.

12. As soon as the Court Martial has finished its proceedings, it is my intention to order the 29th Regiment Native Infantry to Thull, there to await His Excellency's further instructions.

RP 101/XX

21
Roberts to Adjutant-General India

[Printed copy]   Camp Kuram
No. 146–D   24 December 1878

In continuation of my letter No. 132–D., dated the 16th December 1878, I have the honour to report for the information of His Excellency the Commander-in-Chief that the Court of Enquiry in the case of some sepoys of the 29th Punjab Native Infantry closed its proceedings on 18th December 1878.

2. A careful perusal of these proceedings satisfied me that the two sepoys who discharged their rifles on the night of 1st to 2nd December 1878, the Jemadar of E. Company who failed to report their criminalty, and the 18 men who absented themselves from their colours during the action of the 2nd December, should all be brought to trial without delay.

3. Acting under the authority conveyed to me by warrants and by the order of the Governor-General in Council, I ordered a General Court Martial composed of European Officers in accordance with the 75th and 96th Indian Articles of War, to assemble on Friday, 20th December.

4. The two prisoners, Hazrut Shah and Mir Abaz, were arraigned upon the alternative charges of "Having unlawfully loaded and discharged their rifles with intent to convey intelligence to the enemy" and of "Having committed the same act without such intent."

Hazrut Shah was found guilty of the graver charge and was sentenced to death by hanging, and Mir Abaz, convicted on the minor count only, was awarded two years imprisonment with hard labour. The Court admitting the possibility that he, a much younger soldier, might have loaded and discharged his rifle without intending treachery in the excitement of the momentary confusion arising from the first shot.

5. Jemadar Razan Shah was also charged alternatively and was found guilty of "Having become aware of Hazrut Shah's treachery and failing to report it".

The evidence proved that the Jemadar, though assured at the time of Hazrut Shah's guilt, made no report until 5th December, and it may be inferred that he would not have spoken even then had he not learned that he was implicated by the evidence of a wounded sepoy, 'Lance Naik Fazel Ahmed'; he therefore richly merited his sentence of seven years' transportation. The eighteen men who absented themselves from their regiment during the action of 2nd December were all convicted, and, except the two youngest who were awarded imprisonment for two years and one year respectively, were awarded transportation – five for 14, ten for 10, and one for 7 years.

6. These awards, though severe, are not in my opinion heavier than is demanded by the gravity of the crime of which the prisoners were found guilty, and the Court Martial appears to have exercised a careful discretion in apportioning their sentences to the position and length of service of the offenders.

7. The proceedings of the Court Martial terminated yesterday the 23rd December and under authority of my warrants I confirmed the sentences passed on all the prisoners, and being unwilling to delay longer than was absolutely necessary the departure of the 5th Punjab Infantry escorting the sick and wounded to Kohat, I ordered a parade of all the troops at Kuram, at 11 o'clock this

morning, when each charge, finding, and sentence was read in English and Urdoo, and the sentence passed on Sepoy Hazrut Shah was carried into effect.

8. After witnessing the execution the remaining prisoners were handed over to the 5th Punjab Infantry and were marched from the parade ground to the first halting place on the road to Kohat where they will be delivered to the officer in charge of the civil jail.

9. The serious misconduct of so many sepoys before the enemy, the recent desertions of trans-frontiermen with their rifles from more than one regiment, and various other indications have all pointed to the necessity for a stern example; and deeply as I regret to have been obliged to adopt such stringent punitive measures, I feel assured that they will have the most salutary effect upon the minds of all Pathans or others whose fidelity and sense of duty may have been momentarily shaken by the appeals of their co-religionists.

10. Your telegram dated 23rd December arrived this evening at 8 p.m., and I am gratified to find that my action with regard to the prisoners was such as the Commander-in-Chief would have approved, had it been possible to await His Excellency's orders. This however appeared unadvisable in view of the uncertainty of our telegraphic communication and of the immediate necessity for moving the sick and wounded and a large portion of the force now at Kuram.

11. I append the original proceedings of the Court of Enquiry, and extracts showing the charge, finding, and sentence in each trial: also a copy of an order which I have caused to be read at the Head of every Native Regiment in Urdoo, and where necessary in Pushtoo.

12. I am much indebted to Lieutenant Wilson,[38] 12th Bengal Cavalry, for the very able assistance he has afforded me as Officiating Deputy Judge Advocate.

RP 101/XXIII

22
Speech by Roberts to Kurram Valley Chiefs

[Printed copy]
Kuram Camp
26 December 1878

. . . Generally, I am satisfied with the reception I have met with in the valley; it was natural you should hesitate to believe we intended to afford you permanent protection so long as any vestige of the Amir's authority was before your eyes; you have seen the last trace of that authority swept away, and I have assembled you here today to tell you that neither Sher Ali Khan nor any other Amir of Kabul will ever again be permitted to reign over Kuram. Depend upon it you will never have cause to regret exchanging the Durani for British rule. I am not prepared to state what form of Government it may please the Viceroy and Governor-General to establish, but it will be such a Government as is best suited to your habits and customs. You have a right to expect protection of life and property, peace and prosperity, and I think you will all admit that you have a better chance of enjoying these advantages under the British than under the Duranis.

* * *

I can only repeat the assurance I have already given, that from Thull to the Shutar Gardan, not a village, nay, not a yard of land, will be allowed again to come under the control of the Amir of Kabul; neither will the British Government ever again permit the Kabul Government to interfere in any way with the independent tribes bordering on British territory.

PP (HoC) (1878/9), LVI – Afghanistan No. 4 (C2251);

(copy in IOR L/MIL/14/39)

23
Roberts to Viceroy

[Printed telegram]   Hazar Pir
State telegram – Precedence   30 December 1878

As already reported I do not anticipate opposition in Khost, but I think it right to bring to Your Excellency's notice that my force is extremely weak for the occupation of the strategic points it is necessary for the present to hold in the Kuram valley and for protection of my long line of communication, *viz.*, 130 miles from Kohat to Zabberdast Killa and 40 miles from Hazar Pir to Khost.

Independent tribes border the whole line; and as the country is still unsettled, it is necessary to give adequate protection to convoys, especially as several more or less successful attempts have lately been made to cut up camp followers and carry off camels. Until some levies can be organized, the preservation of the telegraph line requires the maintenance of a number of military posts. The infantry I am taking to Khost consists of 200 of the 72nd Highlanders, the 21st and 28th Native Infantry. It will probably be necessary to leave some troops in Khost, and I shall then be without the means of forming even a small column, which is not desirable. For the above reasons I am of opinion that another regiment of British Infantry, one of Native Infantry, and if possible one of Native Cavalry, should be sent to Kohat, and placed at my disposal.

RP 101/XXV

24
Alfred Lyall, Foreign Secretary India, to Roberts

[Holograph]   Calcutta
                                                3 January 1879

I enclose a cutting from the Times of India[39] which announces "an important political declaration" said to have been made by you, to

47

the effect that the Kurram valley belongs henceforward to the Empress of India. I am rather afraid that the declaration, if it was made, is at least premature; and that if it is telegraphed to England we may have to answer questions about our instructions to which we are not yet prepared with a very precise reply. We have told the Secretary of State that we do not propose to make any territorial annexations from Afghanistan to British India; and we still hope that there may be no necessity for modifying this statement. I myself am very much disinclined to annex any new country; though I am entirely in favour of holding under political management any tracts from which it may be essential for the security of our frontier, to exclude the Amir. But my letter of the 16th. Decr. last (240) to your address, which I hope you received, contained an authoritative exposition of the views of the Government regarding annexation. This letter ought to have reached you about the time which the Darbar at Kurram, reported by the newspaper, was held.

Will you kindly let me hear whether it reached you, and tell me whether the political instructions which it conveyed are sufficiently clear.

I believe that the Gov^t of India will not desire any considerable extension even of protected territory, and will be quite satisfied with a protectorate over the tribes and tracts which it is really necessary to control, in order to keep in our hands the passes; so that we may enter whenever we like, and that the commercial channels may remain open. I fancy that our frontier will be rectified on this principle; though I assume that we shall wait on other very important political engagements to be undertaken by Kabul, for the permanent exclusion of the Russians. But I am writing rather conjecturally since all depends on whether Sher Ali comes back upon some terms which we may see fit to impose, or whether his place is taken by some other Amir who might sincerely accept the English alliance. For, of course, we should make our conditions of peace easier to a friend than to an enemy who had reluctantly surrendered.

I see that Lumsden in a letter to you of the 8th October (para 7) gave you some political instructions which I ought to have asked him to cancel – I do not know why he told you to establish British 'supremacy', whatever that may mean, in Daur; he did not tell you to do so in Kurram and Khost.

We have all been very jubilant over your success in the field, which has given the greatest pleasure to all your friends.

LyP 24/4

25
Enclosure – extract from the *Bombay Gazette* 30 December 1878

[Manuscript copy]

On Thursday afternoon General Roberts held a Durbar at the headquarters camp at Kuram. The principal Khans, Maliks and headmen of the Kuram Valley & the country extending over the Peiwar, and as far as AliKhel, were there, those who had done good service received handsome turbans and robes of honour, those who had been remiss were admonished. At the conclusion of the ceremony General Roberts made an important, political declaration, to the effect that henceforth the Queen of England and Empress of India must be looked to by the tribes and not the Ameer, whose rule had passed away for ever from the Kuram valley. It was difficult to say what is the precise form the British Gov^t in Kuram would take, but the great fact was clear that the Amir's rule had been destroyed.

Those who assisted would be loyally remembered by the British Government. He warned those not disposed to assist, but to make mischief, that the British Gov^t was powerful enough and determined to punish them.

LyP 24/16

49

26
Viceroy to Roberts

[Manuscript telegram]   Calcutta
                                                6 January 1879

Newspapers talk of numbers deserting from your force camp followers being cut off and killed and reprisals. Please keep me fully
informed on these points and let me know precisely how many
desertions have occurred so far how many camp followers have
been killed and what reprisals have been made. I think the policy
of running a telegraph line thro an unsettled country is always
questionable. It is an almost irresistible temptation to mischief & if
it is subject [?to] frequent interruptions and entails large numbers
of men & posts for its maintenance I should suggest its discon-
tinuation.

RP 37/6

27
Roberts to Viceroy

[Printed telegram]   Matun, Khost
State telegram   7 January 1879

The Force reached Matun, Khost cantonment, yesterday. The
Deputy Governor met the column half-way. There was a good
deal of uneasiness in the valley yesterday and several reports were
received of an intended attack on our camp. All necessary precautions were taken and an urgent summons was sent to the chief
Maliks who were warned that severe punishment would follow any
trouble given to us by the people of the valley; this had the desired
effect and before midnight the principal men arrived in camp. I
have received so many urgent telegrams from Peiwar Kotal and
Kuram relative to expected attacks by Monguls, and there is so
much general uneasiness that I have decided to leave Khost tomorrow and march towards Kuram, where I can be on the 10th if

necessary. I am sorry to be obliged to hurry away from Khost, but it is wise to concentrate my troops, which are at present a good deal scattered. An application from Bannu reached me during the night for assistance from Thull, but there are no more troops there than are required for the safety of that place.

RP 101/XXVIII

28
Roberts to Viceroy

[Printed telegram]   Khost
State telegram – Precedence   8 January 1879

The enemy collected in considerable strength yesterday almost surrounding our camp; a night attack was evidently intended, so I thought it advisable to take the initiative and about noon moved out in three small columns. The result was most successful; the enemy lost severely and were completely beaten, never attempting to follow up the troops when a retirement took place. The Mountain Batteries under Captains Swinley and Morgan[40] made excellent practice. The Cavalry under Colonel Hugh Gough[41] was admirably handled and did great execution: forty sabres 5th Punjab Cavalry under Major Stewart charged a large body of the enemy and killed between twenty or thirty, while the skirmishes of the 10th Hussars under Major Bulkeley and 5th Punjab Cavalry under Major Williams[42] drove off a large number of the enemy who had got into broken ground, shooting several. We captured nearly 100 prisoners, 500 head of cattle, some sheep and large quantities of grain. Our loss was small: one Duffadar, 5th Punjab Cavalry, and one sepoy 21st Native Infantry killed, four of 5th Punjab Cavalry wounded. Yesterday's success will no doubt have a salutary effect all over Kuram and Khost, and possibly also on the Bannu frontier, as the Kabul Khel Waziri Jirga who are with us saw how easily large numbers of undisciplined men could be defeated by a few British troops. It is very desirable now not to leave this until our relations with the people are placed on a satisfactory footing. I have determined therefore to halt for the present, more especially as Colonel Thelwall reports that the Monguls have apparently abandoned their intention of attacking the Peiwar Kotal on ascertaining the strength of its defences. Snow has fallen on the Safed Koh.

RP 101/XXX

29
Roberts to Viceroy

[Printed telegram]   Khost
State telegram   9 January 1879

Your Excellency's telegram of 6th instant received last night. The statement given in the newspapers regarding desertions taking place and camp followers being killed are greatly exaggerated. I only know of five desertions, all trans-border men: three in 5th Punjab Infantry, one at Thull before we crossed the frontier, one in camp under Peiwar Kotal, and one at Kuram after our return from the Shutar Gardan, and two in 29th Native Infantry, both I believe at Kuram. Twenty-two followers have been killed to date, seven in action, three at Thull, one at Hazar Pir, seven in Darwazgai Pass and four here yesterday, murdered while buying grain in a village professing to be friendly. The victims were nearly all camel men or grass-cutters and with the exception of those killed in action and here, lost their lives from inattention to orders framed expressly for their safety. The only punishments inflicted for these outrages have been the hanging of four men and flogging of one, all caught red handed; arrangements have at the same time been made with the nearest tribes, which it is hoped will render the communications safer in future. The telegraph line has, considering all things, been very little interfered with, certainly not so often on this as on the other side of Kuram at Thull; and since it was understood that it could not be cut with impunity, one village having been heavily fined, it has scarcely ever been interrupted. No posts are maintained expressly for telegraph, all existing ones would be required for postal service, irrespective of the telegraph line. Your Excellency may rest assured that every care is taken to secure the safety of the camp followers, and that no undue severity has been or will be exercised in our dealings with the people. The result of our short sojourn in Khost is more satisfactory than I could have hoped, and the punishment inflicted here on 7th instant was not more than the occasion deserved, and the safety of this force necessitated. Everything is quieting down now and I hope we shall have no more trouble. Had I been less prompt it might have been different.

RP 101/XXXI

30
Roberts to Viceroy

[Printed telegram]   Khost
State telegram   10 January 1879

Affairs are settling down and the people are becoming reassured; nearly all the principal Maliks have tendered their submission and expressed regret for the past. The post is brought in regularly from Hazar Pir, and I am hopeful that for some time at any rate Khost will give no further cause for anxiety. Looking moreover to its somewhat isolated position and the well-known influence of its many Moollas, I do not think it would be wise to leave here for the present a smaller force than one regiment of Native Infantry, two troops of Cavalry and two Mountain guns: and this I propose doing, placing two months' provisions in the fort and raising a few levies to keep open communications with Hazar Pir. Colonel Waterfield agrees with me that there are no men in the valley of any position to undertake responsibility, that a representative of the civil power would be helpless here at present wihout a military force, and that the district without some administration would rapidly fall into anarchy and confusion; moreover to abandon the valley now would certainly be considered as a sign of weakness not only by the people of Khost but by all the country, and would do away in a great measure with the good effect of the fight on 7th: this I feel sure Government does not wish, and I trust that my proposals for the occupation of the valley will be approved of. Leaving troops here may necessitate the recall of the 5th Punjab Infantry from Kohat and bringing on some of the 14th Bengal Lancers from Thull to occupy Hazar Pir in strength, and to afford me the means of forming a small movable column. All well. Troops healthy. Weather fine but cloudy.

RP 101/XXXII

31
Roberts to Lyall

[Holograph]   Camp in Khost
                                               14 January 1879

I enclose the copy which reached me of your telegram of the 4th Instant, together with the decipher; the telegram was either mutilated *en route*, or your cypher is not quite the same as Thornton gave me. Kindly see to this, as it is desirable there should be no mistakes in such messages.

I enclose the last letter I received from Wali Mahomed Khan, and now send my reply, which I hope will be approved of. Your letter of the 8th Inst. with extract from Bombay paper reached me yesterday, ere this you will have received a copy of my speech to the Turis and Jajis at Koorum on 26th Ult. I think I did not exceed the instructions contained in your letter No. 240 of 16th December last. Nothing was said about annexation, nor about the "Queen of England and Empress of India." The people were promised protection in such a form as the Viceroy might hereafter determine. Everything is settling down most satisfactorily, and I am sanguine that, if we have to advance in the spring, the Shutar Gardan road will be open to us. Captain Rennick[43] is doing well at Alikhel and is by degrees getting hold of the Gilzais, he is evidently a man of nerve, and by a bold front and tact broke up a combination of Jajis and Mungols who gave out their intention of attacking the Kotal. Rennick remained at Alikhel with less than 40 men and endeavoured to reassure General Thelwall, who with some 1200 men and three guns is strongly entrenched at the Kotal, and could defy all the Mungols in the country; but I am afraid the General is not a man of nerve: he sent me several urgent telegrams which showed that he was afraid of the result, and called on Koorum for assistance; Koorum in its turn called on Hazar Pir and Darwazgai; and as the officers in Command of these places considered the position on the Kotal must be dangerous, they moved forward. The communications were of course interrupted, and I made up my mind on the 6th that it would be better for me to retrace my steps, and settle matters in the rear. I had done all that seemed necessary before leaving Koorum, the strength of each position was carefully considered, and I had no anxiety, but I cannot control gentlemen's nerves; and some people are not satisfied unless they have as many disciplined and well armed men as the enemy, an unorganized and undisciplined rabble. The assemblage of so many men in Khost on the 7th of course put a movement towards Hazar Pir or Koorum out of the question; my business was to settle with the people here first, and this I think we did effectually on the 7th; the enemy acknowledges to having nearly 100 killed and a great many wounded, and I have taken care to let them know that our loss was only two killed and five wounded; then we punished them severely otherwise by burning every village from which we were fired at and appropriating all the grain, &c., we found inside.

I hope the Viceroy does not think I am exercising undue severity. I can assure His Excellency I am not; my force is not very large, and it is necessary to let the people understand that it can hit hard; this they do now, and are evidently prepared to accept the situation; prompt tratment is in the end the most merciful, and my experience of Asiatics is that they must be taught to fear you before they will make friends.

The sound of our guns on the 7th was heard as far as Thull, and must have reached Daur also, and I am in hopes that the news of the victory will have put a stop to the proposed raids in the Bannu district. The people here are becoming quite reassured: having been punished, they are now treated as kindly as possible. Waterfield is getting hold of them by degrees; our communications are open, the post comes in daily, the telegraph line is not interrupted, and offers have been received from the Turis to help us with 2,000 or 3,000 men if we require assistance; everything indeed is much more settled than we could have hoped for.

LyP 24/5; printed copy in RP101/XXXIII

32
Roberts to Quartermaster-General India

[Printed telegram]   Camp in Khost
State telegram   17 January 1879

Your telegrams of 13th and 16th and mine of 30th Ultimo and 10th Instant. Considering the smallness of my force and possibility of an early advance on Kabul, I have come to the conclusion that it would not be expedient to leave troops in Khost. I propose remaining here till towards the end of January, by which time I hope the country will be sufficiently settled to admit of our placing a Native gentleman in civil charge and protecting him with some levies now being raised. Troops would require certain supplies being sent, and I have not the means of protecting constant convoys. I was obliged to move a wing 2nd Bengal Infantry to Thull, as the men of the 29th had only one night in bed, but I did not do so until after the arrival of 5th Punjab Infantry at Kohat which made the garrison of that place larger than it has been for some months past. In consequence of the length of my communications and smallness of my force, both escorts with convoys and garrisons of posts have been necessarily so weak as to cause me considerable anxiety; indeed as I telegraphed on 7th, I thought it would have been necessary for me to retire from Khost to reinforce Koorum and Peiwar. It would doubtless be better to leave a garrison here; but as too small a one would only court attack, it seems to me more prudent to trust to the effects of the punishment the people have already received, and to form a suitable movable column at Hazar Pir ready to return to the valley if necessary. If possible a regiment of Native Infantry, a Mountain Battery and some Cavalry should be placed at Alikhel; this would have the best possible effect on the tribes bordering the Shutar Gardan route. A regiment of British Infantry is required at Kuram to enable the Goorkhas to take their share of escort duty, which will become heavier as supplies have to be pushed farther foward. I would not move a regiment across the frontier until actually necessary in order not to delay the collection of supplies, but it would be satisfactory to feel that another regiment of British Infantry was at my disposal. The troops now with me, minus the 23rd Pioneers which will be employed road making and a Mountain Battery available for Alikhel, would be conveniently placed at Hazar Pir. Thull should not be left without a complete regiment of Native Infantry, so long as convoys start every few days. I trust these views will meet with His Excellency's approval and that in addition to another British Infantry Regiment, the 14th Bengal Lancers may be available should I require more help. Grass abounds in Khost, and the valley is admirably suited for cavalry. If I had had more cavalry on the 7th, the enemy would have suffered very great loss. I will take care not to withdraw the 5th Punjab Infantry from Kohat without sending back the wing 2nd Bengal Native Infantry; the former corps is sickly and will be improved by rest at Kohat. Proposed disposition of troops follows by post.

RP 101/XXXVII

33
Colonel O.T. Burne, India Office, to Roberts

[Manuscript telegram]   Calcutta
                                          19 January 1879

Personal and Secret

Cabinet anxious to terminate hostilities and minimise territorial acquisitions. They seem prepared to recognise necessity for permanent occupation of Peiwar but would probably prefer treating it as military occupation rather than annexation and increase of British territory. Please bear this in mind in reporting on proposed administration. We hope you can do without Khost and reduce area of occupation as much as possible.

RP 37/5

34
Napier of Magdala to Roberts

[Manuscript, with holograph   Gibraltar
signature]   21 January 1879

I must send you a line to convey my most sincere and hearty congratulations on your admirable success. Every thing has been done excellently.

Never mind a word the wretched correspondents have written to England; every one does you justice. There is in your Camp the correspondent of the Standard[44] whose productions are particularly unjust and offensive and the cause is evidently your having curtailed his first telegram. It is a pity that we are harassed in the Field by such Pests, but their falsehoods only live for a short time.

I always tell everyone that you are not a bit lucky but that your success is the natural result of good ability, good courage and an unfailing determination to see everything in war that was possible and to study everything that could fit you for your present position.

RP 49/7

35
Roberts to Lyall

[Printed copy]   Camp in Khost
     23 January 1879

I sent you a cypher telegram yesterday regarding the feelings of the tribes in this part of the world; they are uneasy and cannot make up their minds that we are masters of the situation. Several sections have come in as I have reported from time to time, and if I could stay here, I believe nearly all would submit; but I am most anxious to return to Kuram; being off the line locks up carriage which could be usefully employed in the collection of supplies, besides which the troops could be working on the roads.

The Shahzada[45] arrived yesterday, and I intend to march back towards Hazar Pir on the 28th. With levies I am hopeful we shall be able to hold this place; the Khostwals themselves will not give trouble unless great pressure is put on them from Afghanistan or by Moollas; indeed, I think they will assist the Shahzada to maintain order. We are associating the chief men of the valley with him to this end; it is of course possible there may be a combination, and the Shahzada may find it too hot for him, in which case he must leave the valley. He can reach Hazar Pir from Matun with his traps in one long day, and about his own personal safety I have no anxiety. Khost can always be re-taken without trouble; but as holding it strengthens our position in Kuram materially, I hope we shall be able to keep it.

I do not know what arrangements have been made for the Native Contingent,[46] but it strikes me that this valley and Kuram would be the very place for it. There will be no trouble eventually in administering this tract of country, and with a Brigade of troops about the Peiwar Kotal, the Contingent would more than suffice for its protection, when an advance is made on Kabul. The climate would suit the Contingent and there would be no difficulty about getting supplies for them in Khost. I hope Khost will be retained, not 'annexed': that is a bad word: merely occupied. The revenue the Amir received from the whole province was about $1\frac{1}{2}$ lakhs: this might be paid to him: in a few years it would be doubled and we should be in a position which would give us great power over the hill tribes on the Derajat frontier. You will understand this from the sketch. I am quite certain that there would be no peace in Kuram without holding Khost as well.

RP 101/XXXIX

36
Roberts to Lyall

[Holograph]
Camp Hazar Pir
2 February 1879

My telegram of 30th Ultimo will have informed you that we have left Khost to its fate for the present. On entering the valley I reported that it could not be held without placing a tolerably strong garrison at Matun; after the little engagement on the 7th Ult. affairs seemed to be settling down and I thought it just possible a Native Gentleman like the Shahzada Sultan Jan might be able to carry on for a time but first impressions proved to be correct for the Mongols, Jadrancves and the other hill tribes assembled the moment we marched away. Fearing something of the sort, I purposely halted 10 miles off, and as it became apparent that the Shahzada would have no place we determined to bring him away while we could do so without trouble. Accordingly we marched back to Matun with something under 1000 men and 4 guns, cleared all the property out of the Fort, and brought away the Shahzada, having previously assembled the principal Maliks of Khost to whom we made the place over.

There was a great collection of hill men, between 4000 and 5000 at least, who endeavoured to muster up courage to attack us, but two weak squadrons of Cavalry skilfully handled by Hugh Gough were sufficient to keep them in check.

It would no doubt have been more satisfactory to have held Khost but I could not do so with my present force, and as the Shahzada was not acceptable there was nothing for it but to leave the valley. We can return when we like, the road is easy, and as regards the people of the valley, no serious opposition need be expected, or could be made, they are entirely in the hands of the Moollas who are of course averse to British rule but even the Moollas could scarcely work up the Khostwals were it not for the hope of being assisted by the independent hill tribes, who are within easy hail, and in whom there is a strong fanatical feeling.

This letter should reach you on the 9th Inst. and you could perhaps send me a telegram a day or two later telling me whether I am empowered to treat with the Gilzai and Logar chiefs. I need scarcely point out how their being with us or not affects any advance into Cabul from Koorum, with them on our side a force from AliKhel could reach Cabul in 10 or 12 days, and would probably arrive at or near the Capital without having lost a man in action. With them against us it would be very different; once an advance is decided upon the quicker the business is over the better; the people of Cabul are all expecting us, the tribes en route are somewhat perplexed at the great delay, but as soon as a British force is in possession of Cabul the whole country would to a certain extent settle down.

LyP 24/pp. 39–41;
printed copy in RP 101/XLV

37
Roberts to O.T. Burne

[Printed telegram]   Hazar Pir
Cypher telegram   4 February 1879

Personal. Can you help me to get rid of Mr Macpherson, *The Standard* correspondent? He was guilty a short time ago of adding to a telegram after I had countersigned it, and his letters are misleading to the public; they are absolutely false, manufactured I presume, because I refused to countersign telegrams equally false. Notwithstanding his objectionable style and manner, I endeavoured to help him in every way. Now communication is next to impossible, and his expressed determination is to vilify everything that is done; it is not in the interests of the public service that he should be allowed to remain. *The Standard* shall not be inconvenienced, as an officer will act as correspondent until a successor to Mr Macpherson can be appointed. I am only too anxious that an independent and qualified correspondent should be with the column; there is nothing to conceal. Assist me, for I really cannot let him remain in my camp, or march about with me.

RP 101/XLVI

38
O.T. Burne to Roberts

[Manuscript copy in Roberts' hand]   Calcutta
Cypher telegram   [Undated but
                                            probably
                                            5 February 1879]

Personal. You have it in your own power to dismiss correspondents who misbehave and I was about to telegraph you about Macpherson. Report officially that you have dismissed him and we will cancel passes.

RP 37/17

39
Major H. Collett,[47] AQMG to Roberts, to Maurice Macpherson

[Manuscript copy in Roberts' hand]   Head Quarters, Kuram
                                            6 February 1879

I am directed by Major-General Roberts, C.B., V.C., Commanding the Kurrum Field Force, to acquaint you that he does not consider it desirable you should any longer perform the duties of Press Correspondent with this column, and to request that you will be good enough to make your arrangements for proceeding towards Thull at an early date.

2. A convoy will leave this for Thull to-morrow, and as there may not be another opportunity of travelling in that direction for some time to come, you may possibly find it convenient to accompany this convoy.

3. Major-General Roberts has not taken this very serious step without due consideration, nor without deep regret; no one is more anxious than he is to have all matters connected with this column made public: it is due to the Home and Indian Governments and also to the people of England that the corres-

pondents of the Press should have every opportunity of giving faithful and accurate accounts of all that goes on while an army is in the Field; this the Major-General took especial pains from the first to arrange for, and it was his wish to treat you with every confidence and to give you such information as it was in his power to afford.

4. There is not, nor should there be, anything to conceal in the conduct of a column situated as the Kurrum Field Force is – it is only necessary that the operations should be truthfully reported; and that any gentleman who does not wish to confine himself to the mere recording of fact, but also to criticise the manner in which the operations have been conducted, should be fully informed of all that is being done and of the many and varied reasons which may have led to certain lines of action.

5. Why you have not been able to obtain such accurate and necessary information, the Major-General thinks you yourself are perhaps best able to explain; that you have not been in possession of facts is evident from the very inaccurate accounts that have appeared from time to time in the columns of *The Standard* and the alarming nature of your further comments upon them. The effect of such communications has been to keep the English Public in a state of constant apprehension regarding this Force, the safety of which has never been for one moment imperilled.

6. Major-General Roberts has frequently pointed out to you the inaccuracy of your information on occasions of your submitting telegrams for his countersignature; that you have not trusted him is evident from the tenor of your postal letters over which he can of course have no control; nor can the Major-General feel that he has any control over your telegrams, since it was brought to his notice that you had been guilty of adding to a telegram after it had been approved of and countersigned by him.

7. One of the many evil results of incorrect statements founded on information derived from irresponsible sources is to weaken the confidence of a Force in its Commander, and thus to impair that willing and hearty co–operation by all ranks without which no military operations can be successful.

8. Under these circumstances the Major-General considered he

was only acting in the interests of the public service by obtaining from the Government of India the necessary sanction for your withdrawal from this force.

RP 160/2; printed copy in RP 101/XLIX

40
Roberts to O.T. Burne

[Printed copy]   Kuram
Cypher telegram.   6 February 1879

I have dismissed Mr Macpherson, and reported officially having done so. Please inform *The Standard* and furnish Pretyman with necessary passes until some other correspondent may be appointed. Mr Boyle asked Pretyman to write for *The Standard*.[48]

RP 101/XLVIII

41
Roberts to Major-General Martin Dillon[49]

[Manuscript copy]   Koorum
                                       7 February 1879

I have two letters of yours to answer, 3rd and 10th January. Many thanks for them and for your kind congratulations notwithstanding the special correspondent's statements. I think you and others will give the Koorum Column credit when the true accounts of what has happened are before you. Unfortunately *The Standard* representative proved to be an unmitigated cad, picked up by Mr Boyle in the streets of Bombay; knowing the mischief such men can do, I endeavoured to keep in with him, and gave him every assistance; he complained to me more than once of the scant civility he received from officers, and I was able to make his life more bearable; personally of course I have never had a word with him, and I was certainly considerably surprised when I read his extremely inaccurate account of the reconnaissance on the 28th November. I had refused to sign a telegram he submitted the following morning, in which he talked about disaster, retreat, panic, &c.; and this caused him to think apparently that the liberty and independence of the Correspondent was being interfered with – the fact is there never was the slightest grounds for Mr Macpherson's misrepresentations. My original intention was to ascertain if the enemy were still below the Peiwar Kotal, and, if I could catch him in difficulty with his guns to attack him; it was impossible to find out from the people of the country where the Afghans were, but it was reported by many that they could not get their guns up the hill to the Kotal; this proved not to be the case, our reconnaisance disclosed their position exactly, and before it became dark the leading regiments were withdrawn without difficulty, and without being followed up by a single man. General Thelwall had selected a position for our camp about two miles in advance of the site I had fixed upon, and as soon as it became known that the position was within range of the enemy's guns, the one in rear had to be made use of; no tents had been pitched, indeed, I believe when the enemy opened fire none of the camp equipage had passed the place where we finally encamped. No troops could have behaved more steadily even in the withdrawal, so I think I was justified in refusing to sign the correspondent's telegram in which such words as disaster, retreat, panic, occurred. As regards the men being "tired and hungry," I presume soldiers are often both on service, but our commissariat was well up, and before 10 p.m., every man in camp had fed – there is nothing to boast of, for nothing had been done but the most ordinary manoeuvre, but I may say that it was thoroughly successful, it gave me information about the position which was very valuable, and decided me not to attempt an attack from our left. During the few days following the reconnaissance Mr Macpherson was laid up and consequently could not take any part in the fight of the 2nd December, fortunately so perhaps for him and me, his nerves were evidently a good deal shaken by the few and very distant shots which were fired on the 28th November, and I am afraid that the really heavy fire on the 2nd December would have upset him altogether, and might have resulted in telegrams and letters even more startling than have already appeared. You will see from the enclosed letter that I have taken the very strong measure of requesting Mr Macpherson to proceed to the rear, and I hope you will agree that I have done right, one of his telegrams, altered after I had countersigned it, was brought to me by the Telegraph Master. I sent for Mr Macpherson who confessed to having made the alteration or addition; he did not seem to think he had done anything wrong, but promised not to do so again, a promise I fear he has not kept for several telegrams have since then been published by *The Standard* which I never saw before dispatch. I trouble you with this long story in the hopes you will do me the favour to interview the Editor of *the Standard* and explain matters to him; shew him the letter that has been sent to Mr Macpherson and this letter also if you think proper – and assure him that any qualified correspondent he may depute to this column will be received with every courtesy and kindness, and afforded every assistance: my wish is that the London papers should be informed of all that is going on, and until a successor to Mr Macpherson arrives I will take care that a weekly letter is sent to *the Standard*, and that anything of interest or importance is telegraphed without delay.

We are now anxiously looking out for the opening of Parliament, when no doubt the future policy of Government with regard to Afghanistan will be made public – the general impression is that the war is over for the present, as a soldier, I should regret this, but I am satisfied it is the wisest thing to do; it may be somewhat unusual to declare peace while your enemy declines to come to terms, but an advance on Cabul now would involve us in a series of difficulties – Yacoob Khan would fly as soon as he found that his army would not, or could not, opppose us, we should then have to place Wali Mahomed, or some other puppet on the throne; and unless we happened to fix on some one who would be received favourably by the people of Afghanistan, it would be a case of Shooja Shah and Dost Mahomed Khan over again. With all his faults and dislike to us, Sher Ali is the man best fitted to rule the Afghans, next to him probably Yacoob Khan – by advancing now we should certainly drive the latter off to Herat and might possibly bring on complications there with the Persians, by holding hard, Yacoob Khan may be able to make himself tolerably secure on the throne, and it is within the bounds of possibility that Sher Ali might return. Should either give us trouble hereafter, we can reach Cabul in ten days or a fortnight from our present positions. I quite think that there cannot be permanent peace until we have occupied Cabul, and advanced perhaps further; but for the present I would stay as we are, and see what turns up.

I don't know who could have told you that I have recommended more officers being attached to Native regiments, my opinion is that the regiments are now as good as they can be, and that if more officers were given, we should very soon return to the unsatisfactory state regiments were in before the Mutiny; the pay would not be sufficient to attract the good men it does now. Several officers in each regiment would weary for want of sufficient employment, the best would by degrees be taken away for staff employ, and would not be replaced, and in a very few years the regiment would deteriorate. What I do advocate is that, on a declaration of war, two young officers should be sent to do duty with the depot, but beyond this I would not go, at the close of the campaign they could easily be absorbed, officers always go home in large numbers when a war is over.

It is quite a pleasure to command troops now there really is no trouble, week after week goes by without a single crime, and from the day we crossed the frontier I have not heard of an instance of an inhabitant of the country being maltreated, or of a village being entered without leave.

We are all in grief at the loss of the 10th Hussars' Squadron, which has been ordered to join regimental Head Quarters at Jelalabad; Both officers and men desired to remain, and I much wish it could have been so. On two occasions in Khost they were opposed to really absurd odds; they dismounted as quietly and steadily as if they were on parade and caused the enemy very severe loss by the fire of their admirable weapon, the Martini-Henry Carbine. To shew you how much I appreciated the Xth. I annex a copy of a short order I issued on their departure [not printed]. The 72nd Highlanders are good all round, it would please you to see them turn out for a guard of honour every man as clean and neat as if he were on the barrack square, and when work or fighting has to be done, you could not wish for men more willing and keen. Crime, I may say, is unknown. The 2/8th has the makings of a good regiment but the men are young and suffered so much from sickness that I have never had more than a wing with me, that wing is in rude health now, one per cent. only being in hospital on the Peiwar Kotal notwithstanding the extreme cold. The two Batteries of Artillery F/A, R.H.A., under Colonel Stirling, and G/3 under Major Parry[50] are, as the Artillery always are, in first rate order; no sickness, no crime. Of the native regiments, I give the palm to the Goorkhas, they simply do not know what fear is. But all the Corps in the column are good. The behaviour of some Pathans in the 29th N.I. was unfortunate, and I much regretted having to sentence one man to death and several others to transportation, but prompt action was necessary, or the infection would have spread. Moollahs abound in Kurram and Khost and the people are very fanatical. . .

RP 160/1; printed copy in RP 101/L

42
Annual Confidential Reports

[Holograph on printed Form]   Head Quarters Camp Kuram
No. 409   12 February 1879

Brigadier General A.H. Cobbe, – Commg Brigade – Is an officer of considerable regimental experience; he has only recently been appointed to the command of a brigade, and as he was wounded shortly after he took the field I have not had much opportunity of judging of his qualities as a Commander; my impression is that Brigadier General Cobbe would carry out any work entrusted to him as the Commander of a brigade with care and exactness, but that he is scarcely possessed of sufficient self reliance to warrant his being placed in an independent command on active service.

Brigadier General J.B. Thelwall, C.B. – Cmg Brigade – Is an officer who has seen a great deal of field service and has considerable varied regimental experience having served in H.M. 24th Foot for some 14 years, and commanded the 21st P.N.I. since it was raised in 1857 – Brigadier General Thelwall has great method and has much useful information regarding soldiers, both British and Native, understanding well how to arrange for their comfort and well being. His health is indifferent and this has probably produced a nervous timidity, which, in my opinion, unfits him for being a leader of troops in the field or for any position of great responsibility on active service.

Lt. Colonel Alex. Lindsay[51] – Comg. Royal Artillery – Is a very painstaking, careful officer, he has good judgement and thoroughly understands his duty as Commanding Officer of Royal Artillery in the field.

Lieut Colonel A.E. Perkins[52] – Comg. Royal Engineers – Is an unusually intelligent, energetic gallant officer with considerable experience of war; his health unfortunately is not good, but nevertheless he carried on his duty as Commanding Royal Engineer in a thoroughly satisfactory manner.

Colonel Hugh Gough, CB. VC. – Commanding Cavalry – Is a most efficient leader of cavalry, a good fearless rider, bold, decisive and possessed of good judgement. Colonel Gough has had several opportunities of shewing his skill as a commander of cavalry during the last few months, and, on each occasion, he has greatly distinguished himself.

RP 148

43
Draft confidential reports on Commanding Officers

[Holograph draft]   HQ Camp Kuram
                     [not dated but clearly
                     February 1879]

Colonel Drew[53] is an officer in whom I have no confidence; his battalion is not in good order, and he himself has neither the firmness nor energy required for the efficient command of a young regiment.

Ag Lieutenant Colonel Currie[54] has an excellent regiment, the discipline of which he has well maintained, without, however, I am afraid, securing the esteem and respect of his officers and men. As a Pioneer Corps, I do not think the regiment is as efficient as it was some years ago, owing to Colonel Currie not taking such an interest in the work as his predecessor did. Col. Currie has some good qualities as a soldier, and has seen a good deal of service but I should nevertheless hesitate before placing him in any position requiring great coolness & resolution.

Colonel Gordon[55] is an active and intelligent officer, and for several months, has conducted the command of the troops at Thull to my entire satisfaction. His regiment has proved the least reliable in the field of the corps which have been under my command, this I am inclined to attribute in some measure to a want of discrimination on Colonel Gordon's part in the selection of his Native Commissioned and Non Comd officers, and to the proper classes from which recruits should be entertained.

RP 148

44
Lyall to Roberts

[Manuscript copy]
Calcutta
14 February 1879

I telegraphed to you yesterday the views of the Government regarding your suggestion about corresponding with Yakub Khan. Lord Lytton makes rather a point of keeping in Cavagnari's hands all dealings with Kabul or with people whose business and aims are purely political, and connected with some final relations between us and the Afghan state. This seems safest, as the work is at best a tangled skein; but I doubt myself whether Yakub Khan has either the will or the power to negotiate with us to any solid end. Nor do I expect much from any such negotiations while Sher Ali is still at large in the country, and at war with us. We have postponed, for the moment, the proclamation we were going to issue, placing the Khyber, Kurram, Pishin and Sibi, under our protectorate – because there was an idea that if it came out just as the news of that desperate disaster at the Cape has appeared, people might fancy us in a hurry to draw in our horns and wind up, by reason of the Cape check.[56]

You will think me very sensitive about newspaper correspondents, when you see that this letter incloses some more cuttings,[*] but I cannot help feeling a little nervous about Rennick as your diplomatist – I fear he will let you in some day. See the inclosed account of Wali Mahomed, and of his interview with Rennick, at which the correspondent appears to have assisted confidentially [not printed]. It seems rather rash of Rennick to let all this rather undignified talk of his doings get about.

[*]From "Englishman" of 14 Feby 1879 being letter from Special Correspondent Kohat Column of 6 Feby 1879.

LyP 24/ff45–46

45
Roberts to Lyall

[Printed copy]   Head Quarters, Kuram
                                                    14 February 1879

I received your cypher telegram about Rennick going to see
Padshah Khan[57] last evening. I quite see the necessity of all diplomatic communications with Yakub Khan being in one man's hands;
but it struck me that if no one from Jellalabad direction could influence Yakub Khan, Padshah Khan might possibly be able to do so.
Yakub evidently sets great store on keeping in with him. You need
not be anxious about my not keeping Rennick under; I know all
about him and will not give him too much tether; he is well suited
for his particular place and gets on in an extraordinary way with the
Natives. I enclose Padshah Khan's last letter to Rennick. I will keep
up friendly understanding with him and the Logar Chiefs, and get
him to meet me on the road should an advance be decided upon. It
is of course most desirable to give Sher Ali or Yakub Khan every
possible chance of coming to terms; I see no other such satisfactory
termination to the present business; but if Conolly's[58] information is
correct (see his enclosed letter) [not printed], Russia is evidently
doing all in her power to prolong hostilities. This is but natural.

RP 101/LI

46
O.T. Burne to Roberts

[Manuscript telegram]   Calcutta
                                                    21 February 1879

Personal. Supposing demonstration or advance on Cabul becomes
necessary to upset Yacoob. Your force cooperating with Browne.
Have you sufficient force available and what is earliest date at
which it could be undertaken.

RP 37/7

47
Roberts to Colley

[Printed copy]   Kohat
Cypher State telegram   22 February 1879

Personal. To advance on Kabul I ought to have two Brigades of
Infantry besides Pioneers, two complete regiments of Native
Cavalry and the squadron 9th Lancers and Artillery now with my
Column including G–3 at Kohat; then a Brigade of Infantry with
a Battery of Artillery should be left at Peiwar Kotal and Alikhel.
That portion of the Native Contingent now with Watson[59] would
suffice for Thull and Kuram and intervening country, one or two
companies of British Infantry from the regiment at the Kotal
being placed in Kuram Fort, and so long as Thull is the main
depôt I would recommend a wing of Native Infantry being there;
this could not be provided from Kohat unless the garrison of that
place is somewhat increased. An additional Battery would be
required for the Peiwar Kotal, and one for Kohat if it be considered necessary to leave Artillery there. The two Brigades should
consist of 72nd and 92nd Highlanders, 28th Native Infantry, 2nd
and 5th Punjab Infantry, 5th Goorkhas, and 23rd Pioneers. This
would leave for the Kotal 8th Foot, 21st and 29th Native Infantry.
If some assistance be afforded in camels or mules to push supplies
on to Kuram, I could start on or about 15th March.

RP 101/LII

48
Roberts to Colley

[Printed copy]   Kohat
                                                  25 February 1879

I am much obliged for your letter of the 19th instant. My telegram
of the 22nd will have informed you that, in the event of an advance
to Kabul, the only addition necessary to the troops now here and

onwards towards the Peiwar Kotal would be a wing of native Infantry for Thull, a Battery of Artillery for the Kotal and Alikhel, and any Artillery Government might think necessary for Kohat. With the 92nd and G–3 complete, I shall have all I want now that operations are not contemplated to the north of the Hindu Kush: 2 Brigades of Infantry with the Pioneer Regiment, 1 Brigade of Cavalry, 1 Battery Horse Artillery, 1 of Field Artillery and 8 Mountain guns. For the Kotal position there would be a regiment of British Infantry, two of Native Infantry, and there should be a Battery of Field Artillery. The Native Contingent will suffice for Thull, Kuram and intervening country, assisted by a wing of Native Infantry at Thull, and by one or two companies of British Infantry in the Kuram Fort. I do not think it would be advisable to have less troops between Kohat and the Shutar Gardan than what I have named. Could it have been possible to have gone on to Kabul immediately after the capture of the Peiwar Kotal, the tribes surrounding Kuram, Hariob and the Shutar Gardan need scarcely have been considered; but it is different now. Emissaries from Kabul have been busy with the hill people the last few months. We shall have a certain amount of opposition now during our progress up to the Shutar Gardan, and for a few days there may be some trouble in the neighbourhood of the Peiwar Kotal and Alikhel, but all this will subside once we have reached Kabul. The tribes have recovered from the effects of the victory of the 2nd December, and could not now resist attacking a large convoy passing up the Hazar Darakht defile. The occupation of Kabul will make them understand that we cannot be denied, but nothing short of that will prevent them troubling us until they themselves have been taught a lesson.

I have been keeping all the troops that could possibly be spared from the immediate front as near the base as possible; this has materially assisted the commissariat, and has enabled a certain amount of supplies to be collected at Kuram. The 5th Punjab Infantry, as you know, I sent back to Kohat, and the Squadron IXth Lancers I halted there, but it is time they should be moved forward and that the columns for the advance should be assembled near Peiwar. The Monguls and the other tribes are becoming restless, communication with Kabul is more frequent, and if Yakub Khan gives any sign of taking the field either in the direction of Kushi or Jellalabad, we shall have to be on the alert. Unless he comes to terms without a fight, we may expect to hear of his troops assembling soon after the 10th proximo. The following arrangements would have to be made before I can march beyond Alikhel:-

1. 92nd Highlanders and 1/2 G–3 Royal Artillery to march from Kohat to Alikhel, distance 140 miles.
2. Wing 8th Foot to march from Kohat to Peiwar Kotal, distance 130 miles.
3. A Battery of Field Artillery to be brought from Rawal Pindi to Peiwar Kotal, distance 230 miles.
4. A battery of Artillery to be brought from Rawal Pindi to Kohat, if it be considered desirable to have Artillery at Kohat, distance 100 miles.
5. 14th Bengal Lancers to withdraw a squadron now at Michni and Shubkudr to Kohat, distance 60 miles, and then to march to Alikhel, 140 miles further.
6. A wing of Native Infantry to be brought from Rawal Pindi to Thull, distance 160 miles.

These movements would take several days, and no time should be lost in commencing them, once it has been decided to go to Kabul.

I read Hamley's[60] lecture, and was sorry I could not agree with so great an authority: he seemed to me to have omitted all consideration of the political part of the question. I also differ with his military reasoning, and am at a loss to understand how he could advocate giving up the command of the Passes and being satisfied with holding only the eastern debouches. In my opinion we should occupy Dakka: the country up to the Shutar Gardan: Quetta and the Pishin Valley; these points will give us command over all the roads leading from India to Afghanistan. It would be a mistake I think to cross the Shutar Gardan and go as far as Kushi. The Shutar Gardan is a limit everyone understands: the occupation of Kushi would certainly result in our having to go to Kabul ere long, and for many months the force there would be so cut off from supports, that it might have to hold its own against an Afghan army.

I cannot tell you how grateful I am to the Viceroy for his kind action in regard to Mr Macpherson: I never expected so much support and was prepared to brave *The Civil and Military* and any number of other papers rather than have such a firebrand in the camp. His Excellency's assistance quite prevents Mr Macpherson's dismissal being attributed to personal feeling on my part (except perhaps by Colonel Cory).[61] I do not propose of course to take any notice of the letter from Mr Macpherson to Major Collett, published in *The Civil and Military Gazette* unless desired to do so officially: it is as truthful as his communications to *The Standard*.

I know no one so well fitted to be Quarter Master General as Macgregor; associated with him as Deputy, I should like to see a man like Elles or East.[62] Both have passed P.H., both have experience of India, and either would do admirably as a future Quarter Master General.

It is very kind of you to send us condensed Reuters. We are all naturally anxious for news from Europe and the Cape.

I am in here for a few days to take a general look round. On the 1st I return to Kuram, and will remain there and thereabouts unless summoned to meet the Chief at Thull or here. Should we move onwards, I hope Lyall will send me a good Political Officer. Waterfield will not be able to stir for some time and Christie will be required at Kuram, besides he is not quite the man for such a position . . .

RP 101/LIII

49
Roberts to Lyall

[Holograph]   Kohat
                                    26 February 1879

Thanks for yours of the 20th instant. I have just telegraphed to you that Rennick reports Yacoob Khan has taken the Amirship and that he is supported by the Ghilzais, Kohistanis, &c. This seems to be very likely, and I believe the Ghilzais will force him to come to terms with us, the best thing that could happen both for him and us. Indeed this seems to be the only satisfactory solution to our difficulties. If Yacoob Khan holds out, an advance on Cabul is inevitable; it may suit us to issue a proclamation saying we have got all we require and will await the turn of events, but we shall be misunderstood by our own people, by the border tribes and by the Afghan nation; one and all will attribute our action to fear, partly of the Afghans and partly of Russia; and the result will be that Yacoob Khan will receive support from many who are now holding aloof; Russia will be aggrandised in their eyes, and we shall have trouble all along the frontier; indeed, it is quite possible Yacoob Khan may take the initiative and attack us. An advance on Cabul would settle all this, and unless Yacoob Khan comes to terms, I strongly recommend no other course being adopted. Yacoob Khan would probably fly after his troops were defeated, but we should no doubt get him back in time.

I had intended writing to you before on this subject, but from your former letter it seemed to me that Government had determined not to advance now, but to issue a proclamation such as was done to end the Burmese War in 1852–53, and I did not wish to suggest difficulties; but as you now ask for my views, I have no hesitation in giving them.

I trust most sincerely that Yacoob Khan will make peace, and I believe he will; if he does not, depend upon it the longer an advance on Cabul is put off, the more difficult it will be. Three months ago it would have been a mere walk over the passes; now we shall have a certain amount of opposition, and a year or so hence we shall have to meet a large army, probably organised and officered by Russians; meanwhile there will be no peace on the frontier.

LyP 24/ff53–54; printed copy in RP 101/LIV

50
Roberts to Dillon

[Manuscript copy]   Kuram
                                         7 March 1879

Many thanks for your kind letter of 7th Ult. just received. I'll not fail to look after Captain Wynter, in the meantime it will be satisfactory to you to know that he is considered by Major Palmer,[63] the head of the Transport with this column, as his ablest assistant.

I am told that Hozier[64] writes the military articles in *The "Standard"*, he has been down on me twice, and I believe mainly from want of proper information:-

1st – the passage of the Mangior defile.
2nd – the Expedition to Khost.

I should not attempt to explain matters to Hozier, but as you remark in your letter under reply "while you are strongly commended generally, a class find fault with you for not having sent your baggage before you on the occasion of Goad's death". I should like to tell you what really happened. No doubt, from the account given in the columns of *the Standard*, it would appear that I had not taken proper precautions.

As soon as I had decided on returning to Kuram by a different route from the one I advanced by, I got rid of all my sick and heavy baggage, sending everything I could from Alikhel *via* Paiwar, keeping only two days' provisions, kits, tents, and ammunition.

The troops with me were 4 weak companies 72nd Highlanders, a Mountain Battery (4 guns), 23rd Pioneers and 5th Goorkhas. I enclose a copy of the report submitted from which you will see that I was not taken by surprise, that I occupied the Kotal which commanded the entrance to the pass as soon as I was near enough to do so; and that I started very early (2 a.m.) so as to make sure of clearing the pass before dark, however long and difficult it might prove.

The carriage consisted of mules and camels, chiefly the former, the mules I started off first, and arrived on the Kotal myself just as the last of them had crossed, and as the first of the camels was reaching the top of the ascent. Four companies of the Pioneers formed the advance guard – two more were distributed amongst the mules, and the remaining two followed the mules. At this time there was no sign of any enemy, and it was not until I had gone three-fourths of the way through the pass that I saw a few men, and came across two followers of the Pioneers, one killed, the other wounded; I had given Colonel Currie Comg the Pioneers orders not to push on too fast, but to keep the rear mules within a short distance of the leading camels; it proved, however, impossible to do this, the mules walked twice as fast over the rough stony ground as the camels did, and halting them in the narrow pass caused great confusion. The mules carried our tents, kits, and ammunition, the camels two days' supplies, so I thought it better to let 6 companies of the Pioneers push on in charge of the mules, while 2 companies crowned the first height that could be crowned with orders not to come down till the rear guard had passed.

Up to this time I had not heard the sound of a shot, nor had I received any report that the Goorkhas had been attacked. It was then considerably past noon, the days were short, and wishing to see the Artillery clear of the defile before dark, I sent word to bring on the Battery in charge of the 4 companies 72nd, leaving the usual baggage guards of that regiment with their camels. This left the Goorkhas alone, but they had very few camels to protect, and with my small force I don't know that a better distribution could have been made. The Kotal was held till the last, and at the first practicable place in the pass the heights were crowned. Not an article of baggage was lost, and considering the very difficult nature of the country our casualties were very small.

With regard to Khost, my instructions were to reconnoitre the country and to remove the Durani Government. As soon as affairs in Kurum were settled, I made arrangements for going to Khost. I had previously represented the weakness of the Column for such extended operations, and before entering Khost I telegraphed to the Quarter Master General pointing out that I had not sufficient troops to occupy Khost, and that I should have to retire without being able, I feared, to make arrangements for the administration of the valley. When I had reconnoitred the whole place and had every yard carefully surveyed we retired, we did so unmolested, and we could return to-morrow unopposed. I have no wish to enlighten Hozier or the public on these points, but I am anxious that you and Lord Napier should know that I did not neglect ordinary military precautions while passing through the Mangior defile, and that I was not rash as regards Khost. My force has been, I think, from the first too small, but I considered it was not for me to make difficulties, but to do the best with the means at my disposal, feeling sure that the Commander-in-Chief and Government would fully appreciate the position I was placed in.

RP 160/2; printed copy
in RP 101/LV

51
Roberts to Lieutenant-Colonel Tyndall,[65]
2nd Punjab Infantry

[Holograph]   Camp Thull
                                                 14 March 1879

I am afraid it will be a great disappointment to you all that your regiment is not one of those detailed by the Chief for this Column should it advance across the Shutrgardan; His Excellency has named two of his own regiments,[66] the 21st and 28st and two of the Frontier Force 5th Goorkhas and 5th Punjab Infantry. I don't think we could expect more than this, but I fear your disappointment will not be less keen.

I am very sorry not to have you with me. I like the regiment and I don't know any corps on the frontier that has a better set of officers.

NAM 5704-23

52
Roberts to Lyall

[Printed copy]   Camp, via Kohat
                                          19 March 1879

Many thanks for your cypher telegram despatched yesterday. I am
delighted to hear that negotiations will not be pressed until the
snow melts; I was afraid it might be found necessary to advance at
once, and that, this column could not do.

I hope Yakub Khan will come to terms now that Sher Ali is
dead; he is the only man I believe the Afghans will accept as their
ruler; if this is the case, of course it is undesirable to force him to
vacate the throne; at the same time, if he is unreasonable, I see
nothing else for it; the only hope then would be, that he would
return when he was tired of being a fugitive.

In my letter of the 14th instant, I said "A Political would perhaps
not be necessary"; the reason was I could not name a man to you
for the position. I think I have found one now in Colonel T.
Gordon;[67] you know him as well as I do, and if we advance, I
should much like to have him with me as Political; both Conolly
and Rennick would work well under him. I have ascertained from
General Lumsden that the Commander-in-Chief will not make
any objection to Gordon leaving the Head Quarters Staff. If the
arrangement seems to you a feasible one, will you kindly send me a
telegram that I may talk over matters with Gordon before he
leaves this part of the country with the Chief.

RP 101/LX

53
Roberts to W.B. Lindsay, Private Secretary to the
Under Secretary of State for India[68]

[Printed copy]   Head Quarters, Kuram Field Force
                                          21 March 1879

I have the pleasure to acknowledge the receipt of your letter of 21st
ultimo, forwarding *The Standard* correspondent's accounts regard-

ing the recent operations of the Kuram column in Khost, and the report from *The Times* of Mr Anderson's[69] question on the same subject and Mr Stanhope's reply thereto. Will you convey to Mr Stanhope my best thanks for thinking of me in this matter, and for the very nice way in which he answered Mr Anderson's question in the House of Commons.

You will no doubt have heard before this reaches you that I found it necessary to recommend to the Government of India that Mr Macpherson, the special correspondent, should be dismissed from my camp in consequence of the generally untruthful and alarmist character of his accounts to *The Standard*.

I do not think it would be desirable for me to make any other public or official contradiction of Mr Macpherson's statements; whatever I might write would be subject to an insolent rejoinder, and would afford amusement and pleasure to those people who think that the liberty of the Press has been interfered with by the ejection of a correspondent from a military camp.

For Mr Stanhope's satisfaction, however, I enclose a short account by the three officers who had principally to deal with the prisoners, *viz.*, the officer commanding the regiment in whose charge the prisoners were placed, the medical officer who attended to the wounded, and the Assistant Adjutant General of the Kuram Field Force. [not printed]

Mr Stanhope will observe from these statements that the firing by the guard upon the prisoners was a military necessity, partly to prevent their escape, and partly to prevent the success of their attempt to overpower the guard. He will remark too that as soon as the resistance was quelled, immediate attention was given to the wounded, and to the removal of the dead. With reference to that part of Mr Anderson's question regarding villages being burnt, and the Dragoons[70] being ordered to take no prisoners, I would explain that the people of Khost were distinctly warned that if we were attacked, every village from which we were fired upon would be destroyed. Our position was an anxious and difficult one: a very small force in an enemy's country without any hope of support. We were safe so long as it was understood that we could not be molested with impunity, and I had no option but to make an example when I found we were literally surrounded by the enemy, whose numbers and boldness would have rapidly increased had they seen any signs of weakness or fear on our side. My wish was to make friends not enemies of the Khost people; and I was as merciful as it was possible to be under the circumstances.

The cavalry which made the final charge numbered less than 40 sabres; the enemy were certainly ten times as many; no commander could, I feel sure, in such a contingency have had anything to say to prisoners. The business of the cavalry was to drive off the enemy with as little loss as possible to themselves. This was done, the number of the enemy killed being between *30* and *40*, not *300* and *400*, as I believe was telegraphed to England in the first instance.

Mr Stanhope is of course at liberty to make any use of this letter and enclosures he may think desirable.

RP 101/LXI

54
Roberts to Lyall

[Printed copy]   Camp Spinak
Private   28 March 1879

Looking to the possibility of an early advance on Kabul, I am desirous of placing my views before you as to the management of the Kuram Valley, until the time comes when some definite form of government may be determined on.

If Watson is likely to remain here, nothing is required but to place him in military and political charge; it would be impossible to find a man better fitted for the work; but I gather from him that his stay is uncertain, and my present instructions are to make over the command of the troops to him in the event of my having to cross over the Shutar Gardan; but nothing has been said to me about political charge.

Waterfield is very anxious to carry on the work, but it seems to me out of the question his attempting it. The Doctors say it will be some months before he can get about, and that it will be still longer before he will regain the complete use of his leg. What you require is some one who will be for ever in the saddle, who will get a thorough insight into the people, and who is not tied down by regulations. I am satisfied that after a few years good personal government Kuram will be a valuable acquisition. The people are ready to welcome our rule, and the more I see of them the more I like them. Whoever comes here should be prepared to stay; a man is wanted such as Harry Lumsden was in Eusofzai, or Coke in Kohat; but the difficulty is to find the right person. If Waterfield were in health, he would probably be considered of too high rank to superintend Kuram for any length of time, and, unless I am mistaken, he is better fitted for a Province in which rules and regulations are in full force than for a newly occupied country, where the people require to be won over by personal influence and constant intercourse. Christie is evidently more inclined for indoor than out-of-door work; and though he is doing well in a quiet way, probably years would pass before he even once visited the whole of the valley.

If we advance, I hope to be accompanied by T. Gordon; but when peace is made and Watson withdraws, I think Gordon would be the best man to administer Kuram, with Conolly and perhaps Rennick under him. It is essential that officers sent here should be able to converse with the inhabitants; none of the above mentioned speak Pushtoo, but all are good Persian scholars, and would no doubt quickly acquire the language of the country. Meanwhile I should advise attaching Conolly to Watson; he would gradually become *au fait* with what is going on, and be of great assistance to Gordon, or whoever might relieve Watson. Waterfield will feel having to go away, but I have partially prepared him for it; a nice letter from you putting it down to his accident would soothe him. So long as Watson remains here, Christie might perhaps do so too, and carry out some rough settlement; but when the permanent administration is being organised, I would remove him to some place requiring less bodily activity. I have marked this 'Private', but of course you can shew it to the Viceroy; I would not like my views about Waterfield to be known elsewhere, he is such an old friend, and has so many admirable qualities that I am unwilling to say a word against him officially, but I cannot help seeing he is not the man for this place under existing circumstances.

RP 101/LXIII

55
Roberts to Colonel C.C. Johnson,[71] Officiating Quartermaster-General India

[Printed copy]   Camp Peiwar
No. 439   1 April 1879

I have read in the London "Times" of Tuesday, 18th February, a report of the Parliamentary debates of the previous evening, during which Mr Anderson asked the Under Secretary of State for India regarding the truth of certain newspaper reports which had been published about my proceedings in Khost on the 7th and 8th January. I beg the favour of being permitted to state, for the satisfaction of his Excellency the Commander- in-Chief and of the Government of India, what really occurred on that occasion.

2. Mr Anderson quotes newspaper accounts to the following effect:-

(a) That I caused "numerous villages" to be "looted" and burned.
(b) That before the cavalry charged the enemy, I ordered them to take no prisoners.
(c) That "some 90 prisoners" who had been taken were tied together by ropes; that on their making some attempt to escape, they were set upon and many of them were slaughtered "in their bonds"; and that "the dead, the living, the dying and the wounded were still tied together and all were lying huddled up in one confused mass of bodies".

3. The first statement – that I caused numerous villages to be looted and burned – is correct. The exact number so treated was

eleven; and I considered their punishment in this manner both deserved and necessary;

* * *

9. I considered it necessary to put into effect my threat of the previous evening, "that summary and severe retribution would be exacted from all who had given admittance to the Mangals or other persons having hostile intentions towards us". The warning thus given had been conspicuously disregarded; our unarmed camp-followers had been cruelly murdered in villages within half a mile of our camp, our baggage animals at graze had been carried off, and our troops had been fired upon from the very villages which had been expressly told what punishment they might expect to receive for treacherous conduct to us.

10. I therefore gave orders for certain villages which had harboured the enemy, and from which hostile shots had been fired, to be plundered and burned. This was an act of retributive justice which I considered necessary for the safety of the troops under my command; and I submit that both the circumstances of the time and the subsequent result fully justified the action which I judged it necessary and prudent to take. The punishment was not inflicted without consideration and discrimination.

11. Regarding the cavalry being ordered to "make no prisoners" the facts are these . . . I ordered Major J.C. Stewart, 5th Punjab Cavalry, who had with him about 40 sabres, to charge them. He said, "Am I to make prisoners, Sir?" I replied, "No, do not stay to do that, your party is too small. Disperse them as best you can". By this order, I meant him to understand that he was to kill as many of the enemy as he could, but that he was to keep his men together, and not let them scatter, or encumber themselves with prisoners. The result of the charge was that between 30 and 40 of the enemy were killed. This was the number given in the

official telegram, but a "nought" got added during its transmission.

* * *

12. With reference to Mr Anderson's third statement. . . The native officer in command of the guard was placed in a difficult position. He was responsible that the prisoners did not escape. One man had already succeeded in doing so; some were struggling with the sepoys of the guard for the possession of their rifles; one had tried to seize the officer's sword, and had been pistolled by him; and all were attempting to free themselves from the ropes with which they were fastened. The piquets all round were firing; and it appeared probable that a night attack on our camp, with the intention of releasing the prisoners, was in actual progress.

13. Under these circumstances I consider that the native officer was absolutely free from blame in issuing the order which he did to kill the prisoners who were attempting to escape.

* * *

14. The statement that, "the dead, the living, the dying and the wounded were lying huddled up in one confused mass of bodies" is a distortion of the truth. This state of things undoubtedly existed immediately after the prisoners had been killed; but it existed for a few minutes only and was unavoidable. . . The newspaper correspondent leaves his readers to infer that nothing was done to relieve the sufferings of the wounded, or to distinguish the living from the dead; but this is inaccurate, and his letter appears to have been written with the view of presenting a vivid and thrilling, rather than a true, account of what happened.

[Subsequently printed and presented to House of Commons, dated 16 June 1879 (Parliamentary Papers (HoC) 1878/9, LVI];
RP 101/LXIV; IOR L/MIL/17/14/35

56
Viceroy to Roberts

[Manuscript telegram]   Lahore
                                              2 April 1879

Personal. Assuming that it is desirable to put pressure on Yakub in
aid of negotiations what demonstration short of occupation of
Kushi can you make. When snow melts do you anticipate difficulty in feeding force at Kushi if required to advance there.
Explain fully by telegram and letter your views on present military
situation on two suppositions. First that we desire to treat with
Yakub but may have to apply further pressure. Second that he may
decline to treat and we decide to upset him.

RP 37/9

57
Roberts to Viceroy

[Printed telegram]   Alikhel
                                             3 April 1879

Personal. Your Excellency's telegram of yesterday. By 18th instant I
shall have the column ordered for advance massed at Alikhel also a
portion of General Watson's force with the road made fit for horsed
guns as far as Rokian, where some supplies will be collected. I cannot,
I fear, make any further demonstration in aid of negotiations. The
Hazar Darakht defile commences within a few miles of Alikhel, and it
would not be prudent to enter it unless prepared to push over the
crest of the Shutar Gardan as far as Kushi. Our leaving Alikhel will be
the signal for a general rising of all the independent tribes, and my
hope of overcoming successfully the considerable opposition we are
certain to encounter is by a rapid advance into the Logar valley. No
force could halt between Alikhel and Kushi, no forage is procurable,
and there is not a position that could be occupied for any length of
time. To advance a certain distance from Alikhel and then retire

would have the worst possible effect all over the frontier. The Turis will be loyal as long as we are supreme; the Jajis are not well disposed and will turn against us if they see the slightest chance of success; the independent tribes will undoubtedly oppose our passage over the Shutar Gardan. Wheat is said to be scarce this year in Logar, but other grain would no doubt be forthcoming; and after we have been a few days in the valley I do not anticipate great difficulty in feeding my force from the resources of the country. The military situation is so mixed up with the political that Your Excellency will, I am sure, forgive me if I consider both together and give my opinion freely. My impression is that Yakub Khan will not treat now until he has tried the fortunes of war, and that he has come to this determination partly on account of a feeling that he will strengthen his position in Afghanistan by making a show of resistance, and probably owing to Wali Mahomed Khan being in a British Camp. The recent combination in his favor proves, I think, that he has correctly felt the pulse of the people as regards military resistance and a want of confidence in Wali Mahomed; and his desire to negotiate through Padshah Khan and his selecting to accompany that portion of his army destined to operate in the Shutar Gardan direction also prove, I think, his unwillingness to have anything to say to the column which Wali Mahomed accompanies. Were the position of Yakub and Wali Mahomed reversed, I believe that the Afghans would espouse the cause of the latter, or of almost any one in preference to that of a Ruler chosen by us. As matters now stand, I think no lasting or satisfactory peace is possible with any one but Yakub; the Afghans seem determined to support him. I hear that Abdoolla Jan's[72] mother has recognised him, and that Abdoolla Karim, a Kohistani Chief, has given him his daughter in marriage, and promised to aid with a large number of fighting men. If Yakub still declines to treat, I recommend an advance on Kabul by the Khyber and Kuram columns; nothing short of this will settle matters or make the Afghans and frontier tribes understand that we are all-powerful and cannot be denied. I would strongly urge every inducement being given to Yakub not to flee when his troops are beaten, and I think I could ensure his not doing so.

RP 101/LXV

58
Roberts to Lyall

[Printed copy]   Camp Kuram
                                                 8 April 1879

Your letter of the 1st instant. Many thanks for the information you have sent me from time to time. You must have your hands full, and I do not expect to hear from you except when there is important news to communicate.

I think you are wrong in attributing the attitude of the tribes to the fact of the Government having corresponded with Yakub Khan. They would have sided with any ruler of Kabul against us. Religion has much more to do with the present combination against us than I think you give it credit for. Moollas are busy all over the hills, and nothing short of their being convinced of our strength will keep the people quiet. I cannot hope that Yakub Khan will consent to receive a mission, for I have but little faith in its being successful, while every day's delay makes him stronger and increases his prospects of help from Balkh and Herat.

As I have telegraphed to you to-day, I can be ready by the 20th instant, but I would prefer the advance being delayed till the end of the month; the season is unusually late, and though the snow is melting rapidly, it still continues on the northern slopes of the hills. Fairly warm nights and a bright moon are great advantages, and unless there are good reasons for an earlier move, I would name the 1st of May. It is important to keep the exact date absolutely secret; no one but Sir Sam Browne and myself need know it. A good start on this side especially will save me much opposition; hillmen can remain away from their homes only as long as their food lasts; they will be chary to assemble before actually necessary, and I hope to give them the slip through the Hazar Darakht defile, provided our plans are not disclosed.

I see you still contemplate the possibility of having to break off with Yakub; my advice is not to do if it can be avoided; the tribes will fight against us whether you proclaim Yakub as an enemy or not; and unless I am very much mistaken, it would be difficult to find any one else with whom satisfactory terms could be made, or who would be able to hold his own in Kabul without active support. Yakub Khan will, I believe, eventually be our ally; he has a difficult part to play now; but as soon as he has shewn his people that we are not to be resisted, I am hopeful that he will agree to our demands and that the majority of the nation will stand by him. You cannot expect peace and quiet in Afghanistan for some years; what has happened after the death of each successive Amir will happen again; but from all I can learn Yakub Khan has a better chance of becoming the ultimate ruler than any other member of the Barakzai family.

I wish you could find time to visit this part of the country. I think you would agree with me about Khost; to leave it in the hands of the Afghans would cause great trouble in Kuram.

Pray do not think I am annoyed at your repeated warnings regarding Rennick; I am extremely obliged to you for putting me on my guard; I see his peculiarities and am aware he cannot be trusted too far. I have already forbidden him to send letters to Padshah Khan or any one else in Kabul without my seeing them first. I have made everything quite right with Waterfield both about Gordon and Watson; it would be difficult to have any dealings with Waterfield except as 'quite right', for a nicer fellow never lived. His leg, I am glad to say, is getting on well, but it will be some time before he will have the use of it.

RP 101/LXVII

59
Roberts to Lyall

[Printed copy]   Kuram
                                                16 April 1879

Herewith the letter [not printed] the Moola brought to the Jaji Maliks, and about which I telegraphed to you today.

The Moola seems very confident that Yakub Khan will give in. I certainly did not think he would; but no doubt he feels that it is difficult to trust those about him. Padshah Khan will come over to us as soon as we are on the Shutar Gardan, and, if the Moolla is correct, Daood Shah[73] intends doing the same on the other side of the Safed Koh. I hope the campaign will end thus for the Viceroy's sake, as I can quite understand His Excellency desiring an early peace; but I would have liked to have taken a force over the Shutar Gardan just to show the people that nothing can stop British troops, and because I believe that without doing so the Afghans and independent tribes will never understand our action.

RP 101/LXVIII

60
Roberts to Colonel Allen Johnson, Military Secretary at the India Office, London

[Printed copy]   Kuram
                                             18 April 1879

I am much obliged to Lord Cranbrook[74] for giving me an opportunity of explaining about the statement which appeared in *The Standard* of the 17th March last, relative to military correspondents in my camp.

The enclosed memorandum gives an account of the real state of the case. I trust His Lordship will consider it satisfactory.

MEMORANDUM

On Mr Macpherson receiving his dismissal from my camp, I gave him to understand that, in the interests of *The Standard* newspaper, I would appoint some officer in this force to carry on the duties of correspondent until such time as an accredited successor should arrive. My selection for the moment fell upon Captain Pretyman, my Aide-de-Camp, for the following reasons:-

1st. At the time of the assault of the Peiwar Kotal, when Mr Macpherson was on the sick list, and unable to witness the operations, he requested Captain Pretyman to write a telegram and letters to *The Standard*, describing the action of the 2nd December and subsequent operations. On my consenting to this arrangement, Captain Pretyman performed this service for Mr Macpherson. The telegram and two letters appeared in due time in the columns of *The Standard*, and under the head of "from our special correspondent." On more than one occasion later on Mr Macpherson requested Captain Pretyman to write military letters descriptive of the operations of this column. All of these were written and signed by Captain Pretyman. *2nd.* Mr Boyle, the special correspondent of *The Standard* with the Kandahar Column, had requested Captain Pretyman, with whom he travelled from London to Bombay in October last, to write any military letters descriptive of the operations of the Kuram column, which he might feel disposed to send to *The Standard*. Bearing in mind these facts, I naturally came to the conclusion that Captain Pretyman was the officer especially designated by circumstances to fulfil the duties of correspondent to *The Standard* during the interim which might elapse before Mr Macpherson's successor should arrive. Within 24 hours of my making the offer to Captain Pretyman, Mr Macpherson, on leaving the Camp, signified to me his wish that another officer, *viz.*, Captain Woodthorpe, R.E.,[75] should take up the duties of correspondent. I immediately sent for that officer, and asked him to act: an arrangement which was more acceptable, for obvious reasons both to myself and to my Aide-de-Camp. Captain Woodthorpe then sent telegrams and letters to *The Standard*, until relieved of his duty very shortly afterwards by order of His Excellency the Commander-in-Chief. With regard to the military correspondents of other London papers, neither of the officers representing the *Times* and *Daily Telegraph* belonged to the Head Quarter Staff of the Kuram column.

RP 101/LXIX

61
Roberts to Colley

[Printed copy]   Kuram
Cypher State telegram – Precedence.   27 April 1879

Personal. Macgregor writes that the advance of a complete division from Gandamak seems hopeless for want of carriage, and suggests that this column should co-operate with the Khyber force to admit of a force of sufficient strength approaching Kabul by the Butkak route. Instead therefore of two separate and disconnected advances *via* Kushi and Jagdallak, one advance might be made with a force strong enough to go on alone to Kabul, if necessary; about 7,000 men should suffice for this purpose. The presence, however, of a smaller number, say 4,000 within 30 miles of Kabul would probably bring matters to an issue, and if His Excellency desires further pressure on Yakub to assist negotiations, I am prepared to advance with a picked force of about 4,000 men *via* Hisarak and the Lakari Pass to Tezin. The day I leave Hisarak for Tezin, a Brigade 3,000 strong belonging to the Khyber column should advance to Hisarak as a support; once at Tezin there should be no difficulty about supplies. The troops left behind by me could make the road from the Hariob valley to Hisarak; the brigade there could continue it on to Tezin. Our communications both by Gandamak and Peiwar would be complete. I have ascertained the nature of the road from Hariob to Hisarak, and there is nothing to stop lightly equipped troops, and by moving rapidly and secretly little or no opposition may be expected. I could start about 1st May, reaching Tezin on 4th or 5th day. On receipt of approval to these proposals, I would name the date for the brigade of the Khyber column to be at Hisarak. As these movements will require very careful arrangements, I should not feel justified in recommending them to His Excellency unless I were allowed to retain unfettered command of my own division as well as of the brigade of the Khyber column in support. Undoubtedly Ghilzais are combining. An early advance on Tezin would take them by surprise, and in all probability bring several influential men over to our side. One advantage of these proposals is that existing transport will suffice to meet my and General Watson's demands.

RP 101/LXXII

62
Viceroy to Roberts

[Manuscript telegram]   Simla
                                                         6 May 1879

Clear the line. Secretary of State telegraphs. Times insists speech of General Roberts to Durbar of Jajis stating terms demanded by British Government do not include location of troops at Kandahar Herat Balk. Only desires to secure a frontier by which it may have the power to enter Cabul whenever wanted. Do you know who reported to Times and can you obtain copy of report sent. Telegraph substance of speech as accurately as possible.

RP 37/12

63
Roberts to Lyall

[Holograph]   Camp Kuram
                                                    12 May 1879

I am so delighted at the successful result of the campaign, to have Yakub Khan in a British camp is indeed a triumph, infinitely better than our sending a mission to Cabul.[76] I certainly did not think the end was so near, or that Yakub Khan would agree to our terms without further pressure; if he did not intend to accept all and every one he would not have left Cabul so there can be no doubt but that our quarrel with the Amir is over.

The Viceroy must be well satisfied and what a help it will be to the Ministry. I congratulate you most heartily. It would have been very satisfactory to have taken my splendid division across the

Shutagardan but I quite understand the necessity of ending the War as soon as possible, and as regards Russia, indeed Europe generally, nothing could be better than the present state of affairs; it shews that Yakub Khan feels he could not secure the Amirship while at enmity with us, and that he must be dependent on us for the future; this is just what is wanted.

I am very sorry that anything I may have said to the Jajis should embarrass Lord Lytton. I trust however this will not be the case and that His Excellency will not be in any way troubled by my allusion to the nonlocation of troops at Kandahar, Herat etc.

Waterfield is much better. I am trying to persuade him to return with me to Alikhel, the change would do him good. The climate of this valley is nearly perfection, you can have almost any temperature you wish. I have selected a capital site for a permanent station, and am only waiting to hear peace proclaimed to commence building. I hope you will pay Kuram a visit in the Spring?

How well Creagh[77] seems to have behaved at Kam Daka. I am glad he had a chance.

When it is decided that troops are not to go over the Shutagardan there are one or two places in this valley that should be visited. I would have gone there ere this, but I was afraid of being out of the way when called upon to advance. One spot is [? "Suiya"][78] up the Kuram river, the Mongols who live there and the Ahmed Khel Jajis inhabiting the country between [? "Suiya"] and Ali Khel have been the leaders in several attacks on our followers – only last Saturday they fired on our woodcutters, and on Woodthorpe while surveying on a hill above Alikhel. The whole thing would only last 2 or 3 days and would avoid our being troubled afterwards.

Another tribe the Moosazais near Ibrahimzai and Sadha have given a good deal of trouble on our line of communication. Before, however, entering their country I would propose to build a small fort near the mouth of their chief pass, and learning more than is known now of the tribe. The fact of the post being constructed would probably bring them to terms or induce them to attack us, which would doubtless produce the same result – should this measure not succeed then a visit into the hills would be necessary.

You will let me know when replying to this what the Viceroy's wishes are. Khost I imagine will be left alone, but I think it would be as well to explore the country as far as Suiya. The road onwards passes through "Kosein"[79] and "Gurdez", and I am under the impression that this will be the easiest line eventually between India and Afghanistan – it will come out at Ghuznie.

LyP 24/ff. 67–69

64
Lytton to Roberts

[Holograph]   Simla
                                                18 May 1879

I cannot adequately say how reluctant I have been to express dis-approval of any incident in the generally admirable management of your difficult task in the Kuram, nor how great was the pain it gave me to address to you any communication in this sense . . .

Your previous speech, made some months ago, which publicly announced that the restoration of Cabul jurisdiction in the Kuram Valley would, in no circumstances, be permitted by the British Gov[t] caused me considerable embarrassment. The Cabinet had not, at that time, come to any decision on the conditions of peace with Cabul and it was more especially anxious to remain uncommitted about territorial conditions. Your announcement about the Kuram burst like a bomb upon them, and unluck-ily they read it for the first time in the English newspaper, just when a certain section of the Cabinet had got it into their heads that (like Frere)[80] I was bent on forcing the hand of H.M. Gov[t]. Lord Cranbrook immediately telegraphed me to enquire on what authority you had made this public announcement . . . with some difficulty I succeeded in inducing him to give to your statement that qualified support which it received from him when he was questioned about it in Parl[t]. But it put the Cabinet in a very bad humour with me, at a time when it was very desirable that I should, if possible, possess their fullest confidence; and it also

bequeathed to us a practical embarrassment in our present negotiations with Yakub . . .

When Lord Cranbrook complained to me of these premature
assurances I told him that (although unwilling to disavow them
publicly) I would privately point out to you the embarrassment in
which they had placed us, and ask you to be more cautious for the
future in your public utterances.

. . . you may imagine my surprise when I received from Lord
Cranbrook a few weeks ago another telegram calling my attention to your last Durbar speech, as reported in the London
Times, and asking me on what authority it proclaimed the
restoration of Jellalabad and Kandahar, as also our intention of
permanently menacing Cabul from a position enabling us to
enter it whenever we please. Here again I had reluctantly to reply
that you had no authority from me for the speech of which I
heard for the first time through Lord Cranbrook himself. And
here again the announcement publicly made by you was most
embarrassing for it was made just as the Ameer was on his way to
Gundamuck to open there negotiations for peace, and therefore
just at a time when it was especially desirable that we should not
prematurely disclose our hand, and that the ultimate restoration
of Candahar and Jellalabad should appear as very important concessions to HH. resulting from the negotiations about to open,
and entirely dependent upon concessions we must first demand
from him.

Your proclamation vitally affected our relations with Cabul. But
the management of those relations had been confided exclusively
to Major Cavagnari, and they were being conducted with as much
secrecy as possible, under very critical and anxious conditions,
from Jellalabad. If the Gov^t of India had been authorised by the
Queen's Gov^t to make such a public declaration, urbe et orbe, as to
the fundamental bases of our Afghan policy at such a time, the
very last authority through whom that declaration could be properly made would have been any one of its General Officers commanding in the field. In these circumstances, it was practically
impossible for me to contest the conclusions of H.M.G. that your
language, if publicly challenged, must be officially disavowed; and

I had no choice but to put on official record some evidence that it was unauthorised and disapproved by the Govt^t of India.

Hence the official note that you will have rec^d from the Foreign Dept^t. That Note however has not been circulated. No Member of my Council has seen it. I do not think that any of them know it has been written; nor do I think its existence is known even in the Dep^t itself for I have told Lyall to lock it up in a box for the present; and it will never be produced unless absolutely required for the defence of the Gov^t in case of a Parliamentary attack . . .

RP 37/14

65
Roberts to Foreign Department, Simla

[Printed copy]   Alikhel
State telegram [Cypher in italics]   18 May 1879

Clear the line. It would be preferable to *retain in our hands* all the *country* up to the *crest of the Shutar Gardan*, but I see no cogent reason against *British administration* being limited by *Karaktiga*, sixteen miles *beyond Alikhel* and six miles short of the *Shutar Gardan. Karaktiga* is the *boundary* between the *Jajis* and *Ghilzais*; it is politically important to have *complete hold* of the *Jajis* who are *Sunis*, not *Shiahs*. This we should not have by *stopping short* at *Alikhel*. The *Shamoo Khel* is the most *powerful section* of the *Jajis*; they occupy from *Kermana south of Alikhel* to *Rokian* and *Drekula*, and have always held *Jajithana*, the principal post in the *Hazar Darakht, two miles* this side of *Karaktiga. Alikhel* in fact *juts* into the heart of the *Shamoo Khel* country, part of which would be *under British* and *part under Afghan rule*. At *Karaktiga* the pass leading from the *Monguls, Jadrans* and *Ghilzais* joins *Hazar Darakht*. I propose building a thana there to command *this important pass*. This thana would *clearly define the boundary between British and Afghan administration*. During an ordinary winter it would be *scarcely possible to keep troops at Alikhel*, and yet I do not see how we can *leave it unoccupied* unless the *whole of* the *Jaji coun-*

try is under *our control*. One section, *the Ahmed Khel*, still hold aloof; and if the *Amir has power* over any portion of the *Jajis*, much trouble will ensue. The *Amir* well knows *what power* limiting our *administration to Alikhel would give him*. Complete control over the *Jaji tribe means eventually influence over Mongul* and other *independent tribes*. In my opinion *it is essential for the peace of Kuram that the Amir* should have *nothing whatever to do with the Jaji tribe*.

RP 101/LXXVIII

66
Roberts to Colley

[Printed copy]   Camp Kuram
Private   27 May 1879

I am much obliged for your letter of the 21st instant. Shortly after its receipt I heard from Gandamak that the treaty had been signed, so no doubt I shall soon get orders regarding the withdrawal of the Punjab Contingent; the weather is hot for marching, but wet, not heat, is to be feared; and if it is true that cholera is disappearing from the Punjab, the troops will, I hope, reach their destinations without suffering. An amnesty will, I believe, have a good effect; the last section of the Jaji tribe submitted about a week ago, and in a few months I quite believe that the Monguls and other tribes on this border, who have the power of troubling us, will come in; the people generally are infinitely better disposed than could have been expected; they have seen our strength, and will soon understand it will be to their advantage to be on good terms with us.

Much as I should have liked to have taken my division over the Shutar Gardan, I am greatly delighted that peace has been so speedily and satisfactorily concluded. Please offer my sincere congratulations to His Excellency, and say how relieved I am that all has ended so well.

This is good news about the committee to enquire into our military system.[81] I have often wished for one to be convened, and am only sorry that other work stands in the way of my being a member of it, for nothing would delight me more than going into the many interesting questions which will be brought forward. His Excellency would, I think, find General Donald Stewart the most satisfactory President, but perhaps he also could not be taken for long from his present position. The work of such a committee is, however, so important, that if possible the best men should serve on it. Stewart knows Native troops better than any other officer of the Bengal Army: he is thoroughly practical and independent, and has great experience. Bernard and Bradford[82] will ably represent the civil and political administration, and there is no one I would rather see in my place on such a committee than Macgregor. The Chief will probably name Lumsden, Sir N. Chamberlain, and Jebb, and the Bombay Commander-in-Chief Burrows.[83] Baker[84] is, I think, a better selection that either East or Elles, though both, the latter especially, are good officers. As you say, a good committee ought to do lasting good to the Indian Army.

I shall be very glad to take a run up to Simla when affairs have settled here. Please thank His Excellency for thinking of me. My wish for some time past has been to go home on short leave; it is more than ten years since I last left England, but I fancy I shall not be able to get away this year at any rate.

RP 101/LXXXI

67
Roberts to Macgregor

[Holograph]   Camp Karea
                                                   13 June 1879

I have been looking out for a letter from you in continuation of your telegram about Stewart and Strahan[85] being unable to make out their journey over the Lakarai Pass. If we had communicated with each other earlier the business could have been managed but it took me a couple of days to get hold of the Bukherkhel maliks.[86] As I telegraphed to you I crossed the Lakarai on Sunday 1st June and waited till late in the afternoon on the other side expecting Stewart and Strahan. The road is difficult, that could of course be improved, but so far as I could see the country on the other side is very confined, not the kind of place one would like to take an army through – steep hills and narrow valleys. Since that time I have been reconnoitring to the South of the Shutagardan and have come to the conclusion that the easiest route from India to Afghanistan is by the Kuram Valley, Kosein and Gurdeze and then over the Altamur pass to Cabul or direct to Ghuznee. We were just above Kosein a few days ago, and fixed the position of Gurdez approximately. There is one bit between the Western end of the Kuram Valley and Suriya I have not seen yet but hope to go there tomorrow – and will then send Woodthorpe up to the top of a high hill overlooking the Mangol country. The greater part of the Mangols have come in, I expect the remainder in a day or two. It is very amusing creeping over the country by degrees and making the people lift their own purdah. I have a small compact force at hand, but generally trust to a Badragga[87] after going a few miles – in some instances the men have shewn us how they had intended opposing our advance. It is strange but after they have once submitted, they seem to have as much pleasure in showing us over their country as we have in looking at it.

Cholera about is unfortunate, I fear the Contingent will catch it – one or two cases were reported in this valley lately. Our troops are very healthy, and so they ought to be for the climate is splendid. I wish you had been as lucky.

* * *

Duke University 7–1–61 ALS

68
Roberts to Viceroy

[Printed copy]   Camp Shalozan
Private   18 June 1879

I beg to thank Your Excellency for your very kind letter of 11th instant, regarding my appointment as one of the Military

Members of the Mixed Commission of Enquiry into Army Expenditure and Organisation.[88]

I feel much flattered at having been selected to share in such important work: no one is more sensible than I am of the urgent necessity which exists for some radical change in present arrangements; and a mixed commission, such as Your Lordship has ordered, is, I believe, the only way by which a subject of such moment to the future of India could be intelligently and impartially considered.

General Stewart would have been a tower of strength to such a commission; he has great experience, and is thoroughly independent, but it is evident he could not now be spared from Kandahar. Sir Ashley Eden will make an excellent President, and there are doubtless many advantages in having a civilian instead of a military man in that position.

It is not necessary for me to assure Your Excellency that I will endeavour to the utmost of my ability to assist the commission in arriving at some satisfactory conclusion, and that Your Lordship's wishes and hopes as regards the future of the Indian Army, and with which I sympathize most completely, will have my cordial and loyal support.

I do not think that the interests of the Public Service will in any way suffer by my absenting myself for a time from Kuram; everything has settled down more expeditiously and more satisfactorily than I had any reason to expect. The tribes on this side of the Shutar Gardan seem clearly to understand that peace has been definitely made with the Amir, and that Kuram will in future be administered by the British. Even the Monguls, Makhbils, Musazais and other independent tribes have sent in their headmen to see me, and expressed their wish to live on good terms with us.

Within the last few days there has been a steady influx of traders from the Kabul direction, and the Ghilzais speak of instructions having been received from Yakub Khan concerning road arrangements, and of "Sahibs" coming from India. Those who have recently left Kabul itself describe the attitude of the Afghans as being generally well disposed towards the Amir, and that never during Sher Ali's life was the city so quiet, or the people so contented as at present.

I understand that General Cobbe is likely to be transferred to the Agra Brigade; this will leave General Forbes[89] senior officer in Kuram; he is well fitted to command the troops during my absence, and I would suggest that he be placed in political and military charge with Major McQueen attached to him as Political Officer. It would be unnecessary, I think, to appoint special officers in lieu of Generals Cobbe and Forbes. Colonel J. Gordon, the Senior Officer of the Indian Service in Kuram, could take the former's place in command of the troops from Thull to the Peiwar Kotal, and Lieutenant-Colonel Parker,[90] 92nd Highlanders, could command the troops in advance of the Kotal. This arrangement would cause the supersession of Colonel Drew of the 8th Foot, but I believe he contemplates an early exchange, and would probably be glad to take leave; in my opinion he is not fit to command any position of importance. General Forbes and Major McQueen are quite able to administer Kuram, and I should have no anxiety in leaving the valley with these two officers at the head of affairs.

In a letter addressed to Mr Lyall, dated 9th instant, I recommended that two young officers should be appointed as Assistants to Major McQueen, viz., Captain Kennedy and Lieutanant Neville Chamberlain.[91] Mr Christie, the present Political Assistant, is desirous of returning to the Punjab; I would allow him to do so, and would also release Captain Rennick as soon as he can be provided for in a regiment: the good front he showed at Alikhel last winter entitles him to some consideration, but I have no wish to retain his services in Kuram. Should my suggestions be approved of, I would ask Your Excellency to allow me to receive early information by telegram if possible, so that no time may be lost in introducing those officers to whom the care of Kuram may be entrusted, to the work before them.

I am writing to General Fraser regarding the Public Works Department requirements of the valley.[92] Material abounds, and with energetic officers the inexpensive kind of huts I propose to build should not take long.

The chief want is a good road from Rawal Pindi via Kohat and Thull.

RP 101/XCI

69
Roberts to Lyall

[Printed copy]   Camp Peiwar
                                                  30 June 1879

I am having a statement of our monthly expenditure prepared, and hope to send it to you in a few days. I have endeavoured in every way to keep down expenses, and have dispensed with the services, as occasion offered, of people who accompanied us across the frontier, and who were no longer required in Kuram.

We must talk over the administration of Kuram when we meet: meanwhile I understand it is your wish that Christie should remain here: you have also sanctioned Conolly's services being retained while Hyat Khan[93] is on leave; these two, with the Shahzada, will be able to carry on the work, but please tell me whether, when I go away, I am to make the chief political authority over to Christie, or to General Massy,[94] who will, I presume, be the officer in command of the troops during my absence. General Massy is without any frontier experience, and with but little knowledge of Natives, and would probably not care to undertake political work. I would recommend Major McQueen being placed in political charge, if there is any chance of his being made Superintendent of Kuram eventually; otherwise it would perhaps be better to leave it in Christie's hands. I will, of course, retain political authority while here, but I should like to know what your wishes are when I leave, so that I may take measures accordingly. General Massy reports that he will join me on the 10th July, and it will be very convenient if you would send me a telegram on the subject before that date. I should like to remain in Kuram until Cavagnari has crossed the Shutar Gardan; after that I should not be sorry to have a few days to myself at Simla before the Army Commission meets. A short rest would be very acceptable.

I do not know what your authority is for concluding that Hyat Khan has had too much of his own way: I can assure you it is not the case, and Gordon will tell you the same. Hyat Khan has been of great use to me as an Interpreter, as a man who knows the character of most of the principal Natives on this frontier, as a Mahomedan loyal to the British Government, and as being active and intelligent; but he has not been left in any single instance to deal with the tribes according to his own ideas or fancies, and were you to pay Kuram a visit, I think you would be satisfied that the political authority and management are in my hands alone. So long as Waterfield was able, he came about with me; Christie from the commencement remained at Kuram to carry on the civil and judicial work. I had, therefore, to choose between Hyat Khan and the Shahzada; for many reasons I selected the former: he is unfortunately not a very brave man, and this would prevent his ever satisfactorily filling any position where his courage and coolness might be seriously tried, but he has many qualities which rendered him well fitted for the work I required of him.

The summary settlement is sufficiently advanced to admit of the Shahzada carrying it on during Hyat Khan's absence, and before the latter's leave expires, I hope I shall have an opportunity of talking over the future of Kuram with you. I do not think there will be any difficulty about assuming control of Kuram as its boundaries are now defined, and I do not anticipate any dispute or friction with the Kabul authorities on this head. The Amir naturally tries to make all his people believe that our occupation of Kuram is only temporary; the construction of roads, cantonments, &c., will do more than anything to prove to them this is not the case. Rennick returns to regimental duty to-morrow; he did really good service at Alikhel last winter, and for this I should like to see him rewarded in some way, but I never wish to have him under me again; he is a man I could not work with.

RP 101/XCIV

70
Roberts to Viceroy

[Printed telegram]   Alikhel
                                                          20 July 1879

Kushdil Khan[95] came to our camp at Karatiga yesterday to meet Major Cavagnari, escorted by a regiment of cavalry and some irregular infantry. As Major Cavagnari left the British camp, a salute of 15 guns was fired by our Mountain Battery. The Embassy then proceeded to Kasim Khel, where tents were pitched for their reception. After partaking of tea and refreshments, we rode to the crest of the Shutar Gardan escorted by the Amir's troops. On our return we found lunch prepared for fity officers. Shortly afterwards we took leave of Major Cavagnari and his party, also of Kushdil Khan, who, however, insisted on accompanying us some distance. Everything was done by the Afghan officials to honour the British Embassy, and the reception of myself and officers was most cordial. The Amir has insisted upon the Embassy, their escort and followers being his guests during the march to Kabul; at each stage tents have been pitched for their use. As Major Cavagnari has passed through, the Kuram is all quiet, I propose availing myself of Your Excellency's permission to visit Simla. I shall leave Kuram on the 22nd instant.

RP 101/XCVIII

71
Roberts to Foreign Secretary India

[Printed telegram]   Kurram
                                                 21 July 1879

The satisfactory and cordial reception of Embassy by the Amir's officials on the Shuturgandan has had a most beneficial effect all over Kurram. Some people doubted peace had been made, others thought it was only temporarily, and many believed the meeting of our envoy with the Kabul authorities would be the signal for an outbreak. Some few of the local men I took with me up the Hazardarakht were so convinced there would be a disturbance that they hesitated to go as far as Kharatiga when the time for the meeting arrived. All are satisfied now, and the large majority are I believe really glad that peace has been concluded.

Arrangements have been made for safety and despatch of letters and telegrams between Ali Khel and Kabul. Post now takes about 86 hours.

PP (HoC) (1880), LIII – *Afghanistan (1880) No. 1 (C 2457)*, 4, enc. 6.

72
Roberts to Viceroy

[Printed copy]   Simla
                                                      9 August 1879

Sir Robert Egerton[96] is, I think, right in his opinion that the Amir should not be placed by us in a position of recognised authority over the Waziris, or other independent tribes. At the same time as the raid on Tank[97] was clearly committed at the instigation of the late Amir, I see no objection to the tribe being informed by the present Amir that they cannot expect any assistance from him, now that he has made peace with the British, and that if they are willing to surrender to our terms, we will do what we can to lessen the severity of those terms. Sir Louis Cavagnari is sure to manage the business without committing the Govenment, and it will be very satisfactory if matters can thus be arranged, for it is certainly not desirable to have any frontier expeditions just when peace with Afghanistan has been concluded. Should the Amir show no inclination to communicate with the Waziris, or should his representation to them not be accepted, an expedition seems inevitable. I would be inclined to let matters rest until 1st September, when I would tell the Waziris that, if they did not submit before the end of the month, punitive measures would be adopted. I have returned the files, which accompanied your Excellency's note of the 7th instant, to Mr Batten,[98] and have asked him to let me know when it would be convenient to Your Excellency to see me, should you desire to speak to me on this subject.

RP 101/CI

73
Roberts to Massy

[Printed copy]
Simla
1 September 1879

I am very glad you think the new station and road will progress satisfactorily under Miller and Spratt.[99] I will try and get two more assistants sent to Kuram, so that each Executive Engineer may have three, but in the meantime if you find it necessary, Buston or Longe[100] can be employed under either Miller or Spratt; should this not be required, I should much like one or the other to finish the survey, on a large scale, of the Peiwar Kotal; Longe began it. Until this is done, no houses can be built, or we shall be committing the same mistake as was made at Simla and other hill stations, of building before the roads were laid out.

I am very glad you let Grant[101] go away; he has been anxious to leave Kuram for some time. I am afraid we shall not get a 2nd Company of Sappers up at present, but I will try and keep the 23rd Pioneers in Kuram during the winter to work.

I find the Adjutant General has returned your application about Heathcote's[102] leave; the fact is that you alone can decide the question. I have telegraphed to you that either Chapman or Broome[103] could do the work. Heathcote has not been well, and I think you will find he will do his work better in the winter if given leave now.

I do not like the idea of 25 Goorkhas being detached so far as Karatiga, nor do I like a detachment of the regiment being sent with Mr Josephs.[104] The tribes should be made responsible for the safety of the telegraph wire, and the people who have to put it up. This always seems to me to be the safest plan; a small detachment would not really deter men from attacking a post or a party, if they had determined on doing it, while any accident happening to the detachment would be troublesome.

I thought I had explained everything about the Alikhel serai to Conolly. During the winter Alikhel will be altogether abandoned by troops. The serai and any buildings we may have must be made over to the local people, who will be held responsible for their safety. In the same way the buildings at Peiwar must be made over to the Jajis (Lehwani). Conolly should be able to arrange for this, and for their holding the tower on the Kotal, in which there is a guard of the 8th Foot now. During the winter months Conolly's successor will do general work in the valley. He will make Alikhel, the safety of the Shutar Gardan road and the Hariob over to Mirak Shak[105] or whoever may be doing Mirak Shak's work, and when snow falls and the troops are withdrawn, he will leave Alikhel.

The relief will, I hope, soon be settled. So far as is known now the following troops will remain in Kuram: 67th and 72nd Foot, 1st and 14th Bengal Cavalry, 21st, 28th Native Infantry and a Punjab Frontier Force Regiment; C–4 Royal Artillery and a Battery of Royal Horse Artillery from India, with, I believe, a British Mountain Battery and No. 2 Native Mountain Battery.

What do you think of sending the 67th down to some spot near the new cantonments as soon as the weather is nice and cool and sickness has abated, and placing the 72nd at the Kotal and the 8th at Alikhel? It may be inconvenient to move any regiment just now, but I am inclined to think a change would be welcomed by all. Martial law is still in force in Kuram, and I suggest your deporting all men who commit grave offences to Kohat, and hanging or shooting all who commit murder.

RP 101/CII

II
September 1879 to October 1880

The Second Afghan War, Second Phase

Roberts was awoken in the early hours of 5 September 1879 at his house in Simla by a telegram from Conolly, the Political Officer at Ali Khel with news of the attack on Cavagnari [74]. No one, least of all Roberts, could have any serious doubt as to the outcome and at a meeting later that morning at Viceregal Lodge, the decision was taken to occupy Kabul.

Of the three forces which had invaded Afghanistan in 1878, only Roberts' force in the Kurram, some seventy miles from Kabul, was in a position to intervene speedily.[1] Even so, the responsibility thus placed on so junior a major-general was clear evidence of the reputation which Roberts had created in less than twelve months campaigning.

After a day of feverish planning [76], he left Simla on 6 September, reaching his forward base at Ali Khel on the 14th. His plan was to concentrate his force at Kushi, in the Logar plain, forty miles from Kabul, and then to move swiftly on the city.[2] His force was too small to allow him to maintain a line of communication back to the Kurram, especially with the winter snows approaching; once at Kabul, he would be isolated until he could reestablish communications via Jalalabad and the Khyber. Transport would be the key to rapid movement and this was in short supply [81, 82][3]

Roberts' military operations over the next twelve months fall into four phases:–

(1) the occupation of Kabul
(2) the attempts to quell Afghan opposition, culminating in his being besieged

(3)   preparations for a spring campaign
(4)   the relief of Kandahar and final withdrawal.

Running through these operations were the problems of exacting retribution for the massacre of the Mission and of establishing a new political organisation in Afghanistan.

He began his advance from Kushi on 30 September and ten days later, after fighting a critical action at Charasiab,[4] he entered Kabul [86]. Although his subsequent march to Kandahar attracted the greater public acclaim, Roberts always believed that his advance on Kabul was the greater achievement:

'I am delighted to see dear Mac's opinion of the advance on Kabul. I look upon it as by far the most difficult and responsible work I have had to do, and I could never understand why the British Public made so much of the march from Kabul to Kandahar. There is no comparison between the two operations in my view . . .'[5]

Vengeance and retribution were the first task of his force. To carry this out at the individual level, he set up two commissions – one, under Macgregor, to collect evidence against those responsible for the massacre of the Mission [90], the second (under Hills and then Massy) to try the accused. It was, in effect, a drum head court martial, for Lytton's private instructions [77], written under the emotional stress of Cavagnari's death, left no doubt as to what was expected.[6]

Roberts' first military duty at Kabul was to ensure the security and comfort of his force, and to establish a secure line of communication by linking up with Major-General Bright, advancing via the Khyber. The first signs of renewed Afghan opposition surfaced as he began to lay in stocks of food and forage for the winter. This opposition, led by an elderly priest, the Mushk-i-Alam ('Fragrance of the World'), grew at a rate with which Roberts' intelligence failed to keep track [97].[7] He was forced to take action at the beginning of December but in a series of actions outside Kabul he was unsuccessful in face of overwhelming numbers. On the evening of the 14th, he withdrew into his base at Sherpur, and was effectively under siege [99, 100, 101].

The siege came to an end on 23 December when he defeated an all-out attack, and reoccupied the city [111]. A casualty of these events was Massy, who Roberts blamed for the initial defeat on 11 December [112]. Massy was relieved and sent back to India but he had powerful friends, and the affair continued to harass Roberts for the remainder of his time in Afghanistan. That Massy was an incompetent cavalry brigadier was almost certainly true; but that Roberts was anxious to deflect some of the blame for his reverse is also clear [134, 146], and he went to considerable lengths to ensure that his side of the argument was heard in the right places [117, 118, 134, 146].[8]

The reoccupation of Kabul was followed by the reopening of the Military Commission. The proceedings had already disturbed public opinion in India and England, focussed in two articles in the *Fortnightly Review* by the journalist Frederick Harrison. Roberts was told to suspend action and to report the facts, which he did with a vigorous defence of his actions [102, 103, 105, 107, 109, 115, 116].[9] He was fortunate in that Parliament and the public were soon diverted by a General Election; with the change of Government, the matter of the executions drifted out of the immediate public consciousness.

Campaigning outside Kabul was not practicable in the winter months and Roberts spent the time preparing for a probable spring campaign [114, 117] and in grappling with the problem of the future government of Afghanistan. The decision to occupy Kabul had been largely a reactive one. Neither in Simla nor in London was there any clear idea as to what was to be done with Afghanistan once Kabul had been occupied. Lytton and others, including initially Roberts, were convinced that Yakub was behind the massacre [88, 89], and Macgregor's Commission spent a great deal of effort in trying to find the necessary evidence, ultimately without success [94, 95].

On the wider problem, Lytton and Roberts came to the conclusion that a policy of disintegration was the only course. Herat and perhaps Afghan Turkestan, about which the British had no up-to-date information, could be offered to Persia, Kandahar would be retained under British control with a puppet ruler, and Kabul would be left to an Afghan ruler [96]. But who? Yakub was undoubtedly the candidate favoured by the majority of leading Afghans. After Yakub the candidate with the best claim was his younger brother, Ayub Khan, Governor of Herat, but little was known of him. The only other candidate who might fill the bill was Abdurrahman Khan, a nephew and bitter opponent of the former Amir, Sher Ali, and now living under Russian protection at Samarkand [110].

To assist Roberts, Lytton sent a political adviser, Lepel Griffin [104, 106]. Roberts was not wrong in seeing this as a reflection on his conduct of political affairs hitherto[10] and, although he professed later to have been grateful for Griffin's help [131, 132], he did not cease to resent his appointment [150, 151]. A more serious threat to Roberts' position surfaced in March when he learned that the Commander-in-Chief planned to assume direct command of operations in Afghanistan, basing himself on Kabul. Roberts reacted by writing to Lytton [119, 122]. Lytton, who had no great opinion of Haines, either as strategist or commander, acted to scotch the plan [121, 123, 124].

Abdurrahman precipitated a political solution by appearing in Afghan Turkestan in February 1880. Support for him grew unexpectedly quickly, and early in April 1880, Griffin opened negotiations with him [120, 128]. Coincidentally, as part of an extended plan of operations drawn up by Haines, Stewart marched with his force from Kandahar to Kabul, being replaced at Kandahar by a force of Bombay troops.[11] Stewart's arrival at Kabul and his automatic assumption of the chief political and military command [129] was a major blow to Roberts [131] and to Griffin [133]. It led them both into a series of injudicious actions, first in attempting to get Lytton and the Indian Government to leave political matters in their hands, and secondly in threatening resignation [131, 132, 136, 137]. Stewart stood firm.

By the beginning of July 1880, the situation at Kabul was beginning to crystallise. Lytton had been replaced by Ripon, following the Conservatives' election defeat in the spring of 1880, and Griffin's negotiations with Abdurrahman had reached an advanced stage. Abdurrahman himself was approaching Kabul and Stewart was preparing to evacuate Kabul and northern Afghanistan, if necessary leaving the Afghans to sort matters out for themselves. Roberts was anxious for leave in England but he was also anxious about his future [142, 144, 145, 157].

On 28 July, with evacuation convoys already leaving Kabul, news was received that a British brigade had been totally defeated at Maiwand by Ayub and the survivors besieged in Kandahar.[12] Roberts had left Kabul on the 23rd to inspect the Khyber route:

'suddenly a presentiment, which I have never been able to explain to myself, made me retrace my steps and hurry back towards Kabul – a presentiment of coming trouble which I can only characterise as instinctive.

The feeling was justified when, about half-way between Butkhak and Kabul, I was met by Sir Donald Stewart and my Chief of the Staff, who brought me the astounding news of the total defeat . . . at Maiwand.'[13]

Roberts had no doubt that Kandahar had to be relieved from Kabul and persuaded Stewart to his point of view [148, 149].[14] Stewart wisely and generously gave the command of the relieving force to Roberts.[15] With the Griffin affair still rankling in his mind, Roberts insisted on being given full political powers in Southern Afghanistan [150, 151], pursuing the matter with a persistence which came close to irritating his friends [152, 153].

Roberts' march to Kandahar in August 1880 has entered the national folk memory. He arrived at Kandahar on 31 August, beating by a few days another relieving force under Phayre from the direction of Quetta, in what had become known irreverently as 'the race for the peerage'.[16]

Ayub was decisively defeated on 1 September 1880 [156]. Nine days later, Roberts received news that he had been appointed a GCB and Commander-in-Chief of the Madras Army [161], and after some final tidying up [166, 167, 169, 170], he resigned his command and left for India and England on 15 October.

74
Captain Conolly, Political Agent, to Roberts

[Printed telegram]   Ali Khel
                                                     4 September 1879

A man who says he is in Sir Louis Cavagnari's service has arrived in
hot haste from Kabul and solemnly states that yesterday morning
the Residence was attacked by three regiments who had mutinied
for their pay, they having guns and being joined by a portion of six
other regiments. The Embassy and escort were defending themselves when he left Kabul at noon. I hope to receive further news.

PP (HoC), 1880, LIII. *Afghanistan (1880) No. 1 (C2457)*, 21, enc. 6.
(Copy in IOR L/MIL/17/14/44)

75
Yakub Khan to Roberts

[Printed translation   Kabul
of holograph letter]   4 September 1879

Be it known to you that yesterday, Wednesday, the 15th Ramazan
[3 September] from eight in the morning until evening, thousands
of people collected for a determined attack on the person of the
Envoy and a fight and slaughter on both sides took place. At the
'Asr' [4 o'clock] prayers they set fire to the residence of the Envoy
and I with a few of my attendants and adherents am besieged from
yesterday until this day, Thursday the 16th. I have no certain
intelligence of the Envoy's condition. I know not whether he with
his attendants has been slain or some one has rescued him from
destruction. Although this event has befallen in accordance with
the divine decree, still a few evil disposed and seditious persons
who disliked and opposed the alliance and friendship between the

two Governments, are the authors of this dangerous commotion, and have stirred up the populace to bring about the ruin of this State, and the murder of the Envoy and having thus shed blood have brought the matters to such a pitch that the Afghan Government has been destroyed and ruined; this is for me a day of the utmost distress as I am confined within my house and my few attendants and adherents remain prepared to defend me and my family. All the troops and the city people, and the people of the country adjacent, have united in open revolt from my authority. I am using every effort and expedient and device in my power to suppress this outbreak, but it is to be seen with what effect.

Daud Shah, the Commander-in-Chief, whom I had sent yesterday to the assistance of the Envoy, is now lying wounded and bruised with stones, spears and blows from the butt end of guns, and is not expected to live. Those of his attendants who accompanied him have all been killed. The factories and the arsenal have been sacked, the soldiers and the people have plundered all at their pleasure. In short, my kingdom has by these events been destroyed, and after God my strong reliance is upon friendship and union with the British Government, which should communicate with, and counsel me what it considers advisable and expedient, and what it thinks proper – in accordance with the terms of perfect friendship and mutual understanding – for the extinguishing of this flame of tumult and crime, and for extricating me from this circle of fear and peril – so that I may act accordingly. Let not this remain hidden from the minds of those in charge of the British Government that so long as I live I will not let go my grasp of the skirt of friendship with and attachment to the British Government. By God's will the fact of my cordial friendship and my sincerity, and the innocence of my heart has been and will be clear and manifest as the dawn to the Government. By this affair, in which I have lost my true friend the Envoy, and through which my State was utterly destroyed and broken up, I have become greatly distracted, and am in distress and confusion as to what I should do.

PP (HoC), 1880, LIII, *Afghanistan (1880) No. 1* (C2457), 21, enc. 4.

(Copy in IOR L/MIL/17/14/44)

76
Memorandum by Roberts

[Holograph]   Simla
                               5 September 1879

(1) Send all mule and pony transport available to Kuram.

(2) Order 44th NI. from Shillong to Kuram.[1]

(3) Order 5th Goorkhas to be completed to 800 Sepoys by volunteers from 1st, 2nd and 4th Goorkhas.

(4) Have the 5th Goorkhas, the 5th Punjab Infantry, 12th Ben. Cavalry, 14th Bengal Lancers, 23rd Pioneers, and 20th NI. carefully inspected, and all sick and weakly men weeded out. Then have these regiments completed to 800 Sepoys by volunteers from Corps near Kuram. As many Sikhs, Dogras and Hindustanis as possible should volunteer.[2]

(5) Have the 12th BC. completed to 4 squadrons by transfer of one squadron from 13th Bengal Lancers at Rawalpindi; or from 5th Punjab Cavalry at Kohat.

(6) Complete the 14th Bengal Lancers. if possible, also to 4 squadrons by transfer of Jats from 3rd Ben. Cavalry, and other corps near, in which that caste may exist.

(7) Other Guide Corps to Kuram.

(8) Have 72nd and 92nd Highlanders inspected and all sick and weakly men weeded out, completing each regiment to 800 strong by volunteers from 8th and 67th Foot.

(9) Send warm clothing for British and Native soldiers to Kuram at once to be at hand when cold weather comes on.

(10) Order the new jointed gun Battery from Khyragulli to Kuram – also De Latours Battery from the Khyber.

(11) Appoint Lt. Colonel Heathcote as Head of Transport.

(12) Colonel Mignon and Captain Luckhardt from Bombay for the Commissariat.[3]

(13) Lt. Colonel Lockhart, Captain Kennedy and Lieut. Manners Smith to go with the Column in the Q.M.G. Department. Captain R.M. Stewart to go to Kuram, Major Hanna to Peshawar and Major Sanford to Simla.[4]

(14) Appoint Colonel Macgregor to command of an Infantry Brigade.

(15) And if the Viceroy will spare Colonel Baker, appoint him to command the Second Brigade.

(16) Appoint Colonel Lang RE Commg. Royal Engineers, with Major Dundas or Captain Preston as 2 in Command.[5]

(17) If Colonel Baker cannot be spared, and General Massy commands the second Brigade, I would suggest that General Macpherson, or Colonel Tytler[6] be sent to Kuram, with Colonel T. Gordon as Political Officer.

(18) If Mr Lyall can spare Mr H.M. Durand[7] I should like to have him with me as Political Secretary.

NAM 780400-76/3A

77
Lytton to Roberts

[Holograph]

Simla
9 September 1879

Very Confidential

* * *

I have purposely abstained from giving you written Political instructions in order that your action on <u>reaching</u> Kabul may be <u>perfectly unfettered</u>: and I think you will do well to take prompt advantage of this freedom of action; for I cannot guarantee its <u>prolonged duration</u>. Meanwhile, the following suggestions are merely for your consideration. If, as is probable when you enter Kabul, you find the revolted Regiments dispersed with their plunder to their own homes, or about the country, and thus out of reach of justice, I would recommend you to set a price on the head of every soldier belonging to those regiments, and to be liberal in the payment of informants charged to bring you in, without delay, from all parts of the Country persons concerned in, or connected with, the attack upon the Embassy. All such persons captured and denounced by your informants, should be promptly executed in the manner most likely to impress the population. Preliminary trials, or lengthened enquiries, in a case of this kind would be wholly out of place. The Afghans are greedy of gain, and, if denunciations prove remunerative to informants, victims will be speedily procured. It is highly probable that your informants will denounce only their personal enemies, and that some comparatively innocent persons may suffer by t his course. But that cannot be helped. If Innocence is so weak as to allow itself to be ruled and represented by Guilt, Innocence must suffer the consequences of its own weakness, when Guilt, without its aid, has been defeated. The whole Afghan Population is <u>Particeps criminis</u> in a great national crime; and every Afghan brought to death by the avenging arm of the British Power, I shall regard as one scoundrel the less in a den of scoundralism, which it is our present business to thoroughly purge with punitive fines of its Judgement Day. You cannot stop to pick and chuse Ringleaders. Every soldier of the Herat Regiments is <u>ipso facto</u> guilty; and so is every civilian, be he Priest or layman, Mullah or peasant, who joined the mob of assassins. To satisfy the conventions of English sentiment it will probably be necessary to inflict death only in execution of the verdict of some sort of judicial authority. But any such authority should be of the roughest and readiest kind, – such as a drumhead Court Martial; and its enquiry in each case limited to the question whether the executors of retribution are satisfied that it is desirable that the alleged culprit should be put to death. For, remember that it is not <u>justice</u> in the ordinary sense, but <u>retribution</u> that you have to administer on reaching Kabul. The action of your Court Martials should be quick, and the grounds of their decisions not recorded. But if protracted trials are a mistake in the circumstances you have to deal with, prolonged executions will be a still greater mistake. Avoid it. What is required is a prompt and impressive example – do not forget that there will be more clamour at home over the fall of a single head six months hence than over a hundred heads that fall <u>at once</u>. Your objects should be to strike terror, and to strike it swiftly and deeply; but to avoid a "<u>Reign of Terror</u>".

Of course the immediate and complete disarmament of Kabul is a primary essential for your own security. I would recommend an immediate proclamation that after a given time (say a week or ten days) allowed for the surrender of arms to the British Authority, all persons found in possession of any lethal weapon (knife or matchlock) within a radius (say of 20 miles) round Kabul will be shot.

* * *

I now pass to the important consideration of what should be done with the city of Kabul itself. The City of Kabul is the great national culprit, now awaiting its sentence; and I am strongly inclined to recommend the total destruction of it by fire, in order that all Afghanistan & India may plainly perceive the full flame of the candle lighted by the Kabulese as they fired the British Embassy on the evening of the 3rd of December. . . . Nevertheless I fully recognise the strong practical objections to so sweeping a measure; objections which I fear must be regarded as conclusive against it. You cannot burn Kabul, unless you do it at once; and if you burn it at once and then march back, we shall probably have no fulcrum left for further political or military action on this side the Hindu Kush. I assume then the probably permanent, and in any case lengthened, occupation of Kabul. But even on this assumption a partial destruction of the city seems to me not only possible but desirable.

* * *

In this matter you must act without reference for orders. With a view to facilitate such action I have purposely left you without written instructions, but I cannot leave you permanently, nor perhaps for any long time, without them. The public indignation at home may subside, & the public temper change, at any moment. You have for the present full powers: and you may rely on my unreserved <u>personal</u> support – after it is done – of whatever you do <u>now</u>, in the exercise of those powers, to avenge the murder of my friend – and yours. But there are some things which a Viceroy can approve and defend when they have been done, but which a Governor General in Council cannot order officially to be done.

Bear in mind, moreover, that vengeance for the precious lives we have lost, will be welcomed and applauded by the public – however terrible & far reaching it be, – if only it be <u>prompt</u>. Not otherwise. Up to the latest possible moment, the guiding principles of our Afghan policy have been – conciliation, confidence, non-intervention, and the avoidance of quarrel with the Afghan people. But that policy is no longer applicable. Confidence would now be insanity: non-intervention, cowardice. The Afghan people has addressed to the English People such a challenge as no People, with a spark of life in it, could decline: and the aim of our immediate action is not <u>Conciliation</u> but <u>Retribution</u>. The spirit of the English Nation should now be, – and I trust will be, – that of a wounded lioness raging for her slaughtered whelps. – Enough of this.

* * *

RP 37/212

<h1 style="text-align:center">78
Lyall to Roberts</h1>

[Manuscript copy]   Simla
                                    12 September 1879

Private

. . . So far as the course of affairs can be conjectured from the telegrams received from Kurram, Ali Khel, and Kandahar, it seems likely that the Amir himself did not instigate, or connive at the attack upon our embassy. His first impulse appears to have been to declare himself ruined, and to send messengers to Ali Khel and Kandahar, expressing the greatest distress and asking for advice and assistance.

Subsequently, he seems to have been persuaded that we are not likely to acquit or forgive him, and that he must be prepared for being treated as an enemy and accordingly he, or his advisers, have

122

been taking measures which look like an intention to resist us, and to stir up the tribes against us. This is natural enough; nor does it very greatly matter whether he attempts to oppose our advance; though undoubtedly he may give, through the tribes, some trouble, which we should be glad to be spared.

But it appears to me very necessary that we should know, and let the Amir know, as distinctly as possible what we are doing, and why we are doing it; that we should lay down distinctly the issues upon which our policy, and our military operations, are to proceed. If the Amir, as is but too probable, is already committed to resistance, then our course is clear, but, nevertheless, we ought to put ourselves formally in the right before the world, and especially before India and Afghanistan, by declaring our motives and our <u>immediate</u> demands. Otherwise, the Amir may maintain hereafter, and may be supported by others in maintaining, that we attacked him suddenly without offering or demanding any explanations, and that he had no recourse but to defend himself and his country as best he could. He should therefore have, at least, the opportunity of explaining or justifying his conduct in the matter of the Embassy and of showing himself desirous of making any possible reparation that we may require. If, after being given this opportunity, he fails to avail himself of it, our case against him would be so much the stronger.

For all ulterior arrangements and considerations of future policy, we must wait until we are established at Kabul . . .

LyP 24/ff71–74

79
Roberts to Yakub Khan

[Printed copy]   Ali Khel
                                  13 September 1879

. . . Whereas in accordance with your Highness' undertaking the responsibility, four British officers were sent to Kabul. After six weeks, they were ruthlessly killed in the very Bala Hissar and within the Residence and no effort was made by your Highness to protect them, and this was done by your Highness' own troops and subjects, and your helplessness and inability to carry out the treaty engagement became apparent. Moreover, it appears difficult for your Highness to establish your power even in your own capital; therefore, an English army is advancing to Kabul for this purpose to inflict retribution upon the mutineers and murderers of the said officers, and that the terms of Treaty may be concluded. The object of my Government in entering Afghanistan by the different routes is to strengthen and consolidate your Highness' Government on condition that your Highness loyally observe the friendship which has been concluded between the two Governments and in no other way is it possible to strengthen your Highness' Government.

* * *

PP (HoC), 1880, LIII, *Afghanistan (1880) No. 1* (C2457), 24, enc. 23)
(Copy in IOR L/MIL/17/14/44)

<h1 style="text-align:center">80
Viceroy to Roberts</h1>

[Manuscript telegram]   Simla
                                          15 September 1879

Keep my letter of the 9th despatched 13th strictly private to yourself. Neither shew it nor speak of it to anyone.

RP 37/23

<h1 style="text-align:center">81
Viceroy to Roberts</h1>

[Manuscript telegram]   Simla
                                          20 September 1879

Personal and secret. The last information received from you leaving no rational ground for apprehension of opposition on the part of the Amir or of the tribes on your way to Cabul and even if you encounter opposition with your strong and picked force you will give a good account of it, the Com^r in Chief would like to retard your advance till he has had developed your future communications on the Khyber. I am however of opinion that [?after arrangements made for holding] Kuram line with the force now at your disposal and reinforcements ordered for [?that] purpose you should not delay an hour in pushing on to Cabul with utmost possible expedition. Whether the force you leave behind can hold the Shutrgurdan till reinforcements arrive or has to concentrate on Alikhel seems [?to] me [?under] existing circumstance a secondary question. What I wish to impress on you is that the loss of a day may be absolute ruin to the political object for which your immediate military action is urgently required. Pray march to Cabul as soon as you can. Never mind going light. Baggage can follow. It will take a month to fully reinforce your present line and very much longer to fully establish the Khyber line.

RP 37/27

82
Roberts to Brigadier-General T. Baker, Commanding 2nd Brigade

[Holograph]   Alikhel
                                                    21 September 1879

I am sending with the 5th P.I. tomorrow Pensioned Resaldar Nakshband Khan,[8] Resaldar Behawulden Khan, and Kot Duffadar Amir Mohamed Khan – they will join you on Tuesday and stay with you till I come.

My present intention is to start from this on Thursday and overtake you at Kushi on Friday, leaving Macpherson to bring up the rear. The game is evidently to push on now. If you have to leave any treasure or ammunition on the Shutagardan, send back mules from Kushi for them they can go one day, come down the next – do all you can to clear the Shutagardan of stores also. I hope local carriage will come up for there from Kushi. If when you get into the Logar Valley you come across any of the Amir's troops, kill them all. Until we have certain proof that any soldiers actively befriended the Embassy, we must consider all as belonging to the one lot, and get rid of them whether their regiments were at Cabul or not – for soldiers caught with arms in the field trial is unnecessary, a bullet will do, if you are pressed for time, otherwise hanging, which does not waste ammunition.

All mules carrying tents and kits might be sent back for one trip to the Shutagardan. Keep <u>the ammunition mules!</u> – you may need them.

I am sending you Manners Smith as Q.M.G. – he has no experience in the department but he is very smart, and has been out with me on reconnaissance work frequently.

Try to get grass, or forage of some sort, collected at Kasem Khel – this is very important.

NAM 7804–76/10

83
Roberts to Foreign Department

[Printed telegram]   Alikhel
                                        22 September 1879

If I find the Amir's complicity in the attack on the Embassy clearly proved, or that he took no active measures to protect the Embassy after the disturbance commenced, I propose placing him in safe custody pending the Viceroy's instructions. All other Sirdars and headmen I will deal with without referring their cases for orders.

RP 101/CXXXVI

84
Viceroy to Roberts

[Manuscript telegram]   Simla
                                                        26 September 1879

Personal. In deference to strong opinions expressed in Council I
am drafting instructions to you which will be despatched in a few
days. They are however of a most general character and quite in
accordance with the views expressed in my letters to you. I think
they will strengthen without tying your hands. As soon as they
have been passed in Council I will telegraph their general purport.
Meanwhile you will advance without waiting their receipt.

RP 37/30

85
Foreign Secretary India to Roberts

[Printed telegram]   Simla
No. A–506   29 September 1879

Clear the line. Letter of instructions to guide your proceedings on
reaching Kabul despatched to you this day. Following are principal
heads. On reaching Kabul take up position securing complete
command over city; enforce surrender of fortified posts; disarm
troops and city people; take measures for collecting supplies pending connection of your communications with permanent Peshawur
base; secure personal safety of Amir with due control over his
movements; prevent withdrawal pending inquiry of persons suspected of share or complicity in attack on Embassy; and begin
close inquiry as soon as you are established at Kabul; make known
to people generally our determination to treat all classes with justice, to respect their religion, feelings and customs, while exacting
full retribution from offenders.

Punishment should be speedy and impressive without being
indiscriminate or prolonged; but take no action beyond what is

needed for safe custody or surveillance in regard to Amir or other persons whose cases may need special consideration without reference for orders of Government. Assume and exercise supreme administrative authority.

RP 154–1/1

86
Roberts to Viceroy

[Printed telegram]   Kabul
                                            13 October, 1879

Clear the line. The Bala Hissar was occupied yesterday: a very impressive sight. The Amir pleaded indisposition. His eldest son accompanied me, and all the principal Sirdars were summoned to attend to hear the Proclamation read. 67th Foot and 5th Goorkhas now occupy the lower and upper Bala Hissar respectively. Today troops march through the city. Guards will be placed at all important points; there is only one gate. General Hills[9] takes over the office of Military Governor, assisted by Nawab Ghulam Hussein Khan.[10] Three regiments with 12 guns left Ghazni a few days ago to join the Afghan troops fighting against us here: meeting the dispersed Kabul troops they fled, leaving the guns. I have sent a regiment of cavalry to bring them in. Eighty-five guns, mortars and howitzers were found in the Bala Hissar, making a total of upwards of 200 guns in our possession; vast quantity of powder, accoutrements, arms, saddlery, musical instruments, &c., also found. Snider cartridges have been made, apparently locally, in great numbers. Wounded doing well.

RP 101/CXLIII

87
Roberts to Foreign Department

[Printed telegram – 'Through   Bala Hissar
Shutar Gardan']   13 October 1879

Clear the line. Early yesterday morning the Amir walked to my camp accompanied by only two attendants and expressed his determination to resign his Amirship. He said he had intended doing so before going to Kushi, but had allowed himself to be overpersuaded. He was in very low spirits and said that his life had been a miserable one; that he would rather be a grass-cutter in the English camp than ruler of Afghanistan, and begged he might live in this camp until he could be sent to India or London or wherever the Viceroy might desire to send him. I placed a tent at his disposal, ordered breakfast to be prepared for him and begged him to think over the matter for two or three hours, and said that I would see him again at 10 o'clock, the time appointed the previous evening for His Highness to come to my camp and accompany me to the Bala Hissar. The Amir knew nothing of the proposed Proclamation and was quite ignorant of my intentions towards the Mustaufi, the Wazir, Yahia Khan and his brother.[11] At 10 o'clock I had a second interview with the Amir, who stated that he had quite decided to give up the throne of Kabul; his eldest son, and all his ministers would be in attendance. I again pointed out the serious step His Highness was taking, but finding his mind was made up I told him I would telegraph to the Viceroy for instructions; that of course he could not be forced to remain on as Amir against his will, but that I would ask him to retain the title until I could receive a reply to his telegram. The eldest son accompanied me to the Bala Hissar. The programme as telegraphed yesterday was strictly carried out and the ceremony was most impressive. After reading out the Proclamation, a copy of which I am telegraphing to you today, I dismissed all the Sirdars and native gentlemen except the Mustaufi, Wazir, Yahia and Zakariah Khan. I told these four that it was necessary to detain them until the circumstances connected with the attack on the Embassy had been throughly enquired into.

The Proclamation is being translated into Persian and will be widely circulated. At noon today the troops will march through the city, certain positions will be held by guards (there is only one gate) and General Hills will take over military control as Governor, assisted by Nawab Ghulam Hussein Khan. Your letter No. 506 of 29th September reached me late yesterday. I have anticipated your instructions almost to the letter. I trust therefore my action will be approved of.

RP 101/CLXIV

88
Viceroy to Roberts

[Manuscript telegram]   Simla
                                               15 October 1879

Personal. Your telegram of 12th to Foreign. I fully approve your proposed measures but trust you will keep Ameer under careful surveillance. Present presumption against him very strong and even if innocent uncontrolled authority cannot be restored to him. Need not scruple to dispense with his assent in arresting all suspected persons however high their position. It must be understood that you and the Ameer are for the present supreme at Cabul. Endeavour to extract from Yahia Khan native correspondence between Kashmir and Russia.[12] Who is his brother mentioned in your telegram. Never heard the name before. And who is Nek Mahomed. What is your opinion of Wullee Mahomed. Has he any party. Important to secure if possible good will of all influential Sirdars making them interested and responsible parties to any future arrangements. Your proposal Council of Regency may facilitate introduction of this principle. But any present administration should be provisional only entirely subordinate to your supreme authority and removable at will. Endeavour to take early opportunity of reducing grievances as regards taxation and privileges of

Sirdars so as to make your intervention popular. Pray get Bukhtyar Khans body examined.[13] Lord Cranbrook suggests destruction of Bala Hissar and removal (of present) capital to Candahar. What is your opinion of this proposal. How would it do to convert Cabul into [indecipherable] British Cantonment placing Afghan Gov[t] at Candahar under some southern Afghan Sirdar named by us. Endeavour to ascertain early and report total Afghan revenue and cost of Afghan administration civil and military. Secure any treasure you may find at Bala Hissar. Disarm the City as soon as you can. Beware of assassination and personal treachery. Cordial and renewed congratulations on your great success. Have written to you via Khyber. Bright[14] instructed to make all speed in opening communications with you. Try and recover Cavagnaris cipher code 21313 your attention 21314 cipher code.

RP 37/42

89
Lytton to Roberts

[Printed copy]

Simla
21 October 1879

Private and Confidential

. . . I cannot send you any instructions, either official or demi-official, in the sense of it, or in any other sense, on the situation created by the Ameer's tender of his resignation, until the proposals I have now submitted to Lord Cranbrook have been considered and decided upon by the Cabinet. This, of course, you will understand. And I feel sure that, pending the receipt of definite instructions from me, you will do nothing that could have the effect of prematurely committing either the Government or yourself, as regards the future. . . In the meanwhile, although your political position at Kabul is undoubtedly a delicate one, and the character and extent of your political authority ought, in my opinion, to be defined and proclaimed with the least possible delay, I trust that, since some delay is unfortunately unavoidable, you will be able to keep the Ameer well in hand, and the situation in statu quo till I can send you definite orders . . . I had, in accordance with a suggestion made in Council, telegraphed to you for an early and confidential expression of your own views and suggestions on the situation in which we were placed by the Ameer's resignation, with special reference to its possible effect (when known) on your military position at Kabul, and on the temper of the surrounding tribes. I should have greatly valued such information when framing the proposals now submitted to the Secretary of State but having learned, much to my vexation, that General Gordon had allowed the wire to be irreparably destroyed between Ali Khel and Shutur Gardan, I foresaw that my telegram would be long delayed in its transmission to you; and that, as the instructions which you might be anxiously awaiting must first be approved by the Cabinet, your receipt of them might be indefinitely retarded, if I awaited your reply to my telegram before submitting them to the Secretary of State for that purpose . . . My fear is that, when the Afghan people and tribes have fully realised all that is involved in the Ameer's abdication, if they find the British Government apparently taken aback and disconcerted by a fact, concerning which it behove us to show that we were the masters of the situation created by it, they may begin to form hostile combinations, likely ere long to increase our troubles . . . The present disposition of the Cabinet is . . . so far as I can yet judge, to annex the districts assigned to us by the Treaty of Gundamuk, and occupy Candahar; but to do nothing more. This policy is also, in my opinion, unsound and unsafe; and I shall spare no effort to encourage the Cabinet to a bolder course. There is little doubt in my own mind, that our hold upon at least Southern and Northern Afghanistan should now, and promptly, be made permanent and complete.

. . . Now, first, as to the Ameer's position . . . There are at present very dark suspicions against him. It is not desirable to receive with suspicion an unconvicted man, whose innocence may bye-and-bye be established. On the other hand, should he eventually be proved guilty, how embarrassing would it be to have received with honour and respect a prince shortly afterwards convicted of the foulest treachery and murder! . . .

I think your constitution of the Court of Enquiry is admirable. In MacGregor you have secured the requisite guarantee for salutary severity; in Bellew,[15] that recognised knowledge of the Afghan character which will give the public confidence in the proceedings and decisions of the Court; and in Hiyat Ali, the great political value of a Mahomedan vote.

General Vaughan[16] is about to proceed thither (Kabul) as correspondent for the Times. I will give him a letter to you; and I want you to be particularly civil to him. The Times, which reflects, I think, the present disposition of the Cabinet, has been strongly deprecating any further annexation beyond the limits of the districts assigned to us by the Gundamuk Treaty . . . General Vaughan is ready to write up any policy, of which the cue is given to him by me, or by you on my behalf. His letters to the Times from Kabul may have a considerable effect upon public opinion at home, and through it, possibly, on the attitude of the Cabinet. I want you, therefore, to keep him in good humour and up to the mark.

LP/21/pp. 93–5

90
Viceroy to Roberts

[Manuscript telegram]   Simla
                                         23 October 1879

Your telegram of 19th. I fully approve proposed employment of Ahmed Ali Jan.[17] Congratulate you on capture of criminals. Executions mentioned in your telegram are well within your full powers and of course highly approved. Hope you will be able to convict Yahia Khan and some of the others under arrest. I have reason to believe Cashmeer correspondence with Cabul goes on more actively than ever. Try to intercept it and watch arrivals and departures. Can you extract from Yahia Khan nothing about

Cashmeer. Personally I emphatically approve complete and immediate destruction of Bala Hissar. So does Commander in Chief but on this subject I cannot telegraph to you officially before tomorrow. Future treatment of Amir cannot be decided before result of your enquiries about massacre. Many of your daily telegrams missing. Lyall will inform you how many received.

RP 37/49

91
Viceroy to Roberts

[Manuscript telegram]   Simla
                                                24 October 1879

Personal. Archives and state papers of late Cabul Govt may have been concealed but cannot have been destroyed. Our possession of them most important. Try to secure them if you have not already done so. Have you exhumed and examined body of Bukhtiar Khan. This seems desirable. Have you discovered Cavagnaris body. Most important to discover and secure Treaty and correspondence between Shere Ali and Russia.[18] Destruction of Bala Hissar officially approved today.

RP 37/52

92
Lytton to Roberts

[Holograph]   Camp Naldera
                                                2 November 1879

Private & Confidential

. . . I heard the other day from your wife with great surprise and I must confess some indignation, that you have not yet received from Sir F. Haines a single word of congratulations or approval but it may be some satisfaction to you to know that, at least, in conversation, he now always refers to you in terms of the warmest enconium. Your despatch of Octr 15th to the Chief of Staff, which is the first and last of your military reports I have yet seen, has been the subject of universal praise at Military Head Quarters here; and, in my opinion, it is a model of what a military report should be. O si sic omnes! How different from the reports of poor Sir Sam Browne!

You will already have received my approval of the proposed destruction of the Bala Hissar. The sooner it is completed the better. I shall not be quite free from anxiety till all the powder in the large magazine has been removed or destroyed. I don't quite know whether I am justified by your telegram of today in assuming that you have secured the Amir's treasures; but I hope this is the case. I cannot dispose of the Amir till I have learnt the result of your enquiry into the causes & circumstances of the massacre. If you fail to convict the Sirdars & Ministers now under arrest you can certainly deport them and I will provide them with appropriately unpleasant quarters in India. But I still hope that against some of them, at least, there will be sufficient evidence for a conviction, otherwise, the result may make us look foolish. Have you no hope of extracting from Yahia Khan or any one else information about the Kashmir correspondence which seems (from what I hear) to be going on more than ever. I don't believe the Amir's assertion that he destroyed all the Russian correspondence. It is most important to lose no time in securing the Gov^t of Afghan Turkestan by some one on whom you can rely. I rather fear the Cabinet is disposed to precipitate dangerously loose and vague arrangements for the cession of Seistan and Herat to Persia; and in my judgement we ought not, in any case, to hand over Herat to Persia or otherwise dispose of it, till it has been visited by British troops next spring. In those parts of Afghanistan which we wish to influence or control, whether indirectly or otherwise, our power must be shewn & felt, before our influence or control can be effectual. But on this subject I will write to you more fully in a few days. Meanwhile any Evidence you can get out of Ayub Khan,[19] if not too expensive, may be worth having – & it is especially desirable to prevent him if possible from making premature arrangements on his own behalf, and independently of us, this winter. Lord Cranbrook still harps on the transfer of the Afghan capital to Kandahar. But it is premature to discuss this till we have settled what to do with Northern Afghanistan. General Greaves,[20] the new Adjutant General, has arrived and I am greatly pleased & encouraged by all I have yet seen of him. Lumsden had been behaving exceedingly well on the Commission and had agreed to all its recommendations till three days ago, when in consequence of strong pressure from Haines, he recanted all his previous assents and announced his intention of dissenting from the report, apparently on no other grounds than that the Duke of Cambridge will not like it. This was owing to letters from H.R.H. to Haines & Johnson – but Lord Cranbrook has given me the strongest assurances that both he and Lord Beaconsfield attach the greatest importance to the good work of the Commission which they are resolved to support and that the Duke of Cambridge's objections will be firmly disregarded unless he can support them by strong fact & argument which I know he cannot do . . . Haines and Johnson greatly overrate the power of the D. of Cambridge in this matter, for H.R.H. will not have the Cabinet with him and public opinion at home is so strong on the question of Indian Army Reform that even if there is a change of Ministry, the Liberals will take up this question just as warmly as the present Government. Colonel Allen Johnson is now officiating for Col. H.W. Burne[21] and I gather from Lord Cranbrook's letter that Sir Garnett Wolseley will certainly succeed Haines as C in C . . .

RP 37/53

93
Roberts to Military Secretary to Viceroy

[Printed telegram]   Kabul
                                             14 November 1879

On receipt of *The Civil and Military Gazette* alluded to in your telegram of 10th the correspondent, Doctor Bourke,[22] was called upon by my orders to explain his grounds for the information he had afforded the newspaper inferring that wounded Afghans had been burnt and otherwise maltreated by the 72nd Highlanders; in reply he stated his remarks referred to the 5th Goorkhas and not to the 72nd. I then assembled a Court of Enquiry, from the proceedings of which it would appear that there were some grounds for the statement, inasmuch as clothes of two Afghans were observed to be on fire. The Officer Commanding the Goorkhas asserts that his men must have thought the Afghans were dead; he denies that his men would torture the living but admits the possibility of the dead body of a Mahomedan being set fire to by his men as an act of retribution for the mutilations and indignities which their wounded and killed suffer when they fall into the hands of Mahomedans. No officer of the force except Dr Bourke has, as far as I am aware, ever seen an act of cruelty perpetrated since we crossed the frontier in November 1878. Dr Bourke was, I understand, never in action before the fight at Charasiah, and on that occasion was observed to be in a very excited state. From the evidence it would appear that when Dr Bourke reached the place where the two Afghans were lying life was extinct or practically so, and it is presumed that Dr Bourke must have considered both moribund or he would not have ordered them to be shot. Dr Bourke has been called upon to state why he took no steps to discover who the offenders were, and why he never officially reported the circumstances.

The first intimation of the act I received was through *The Civil and Military Gazette*. Proceedings of the Court, with Dr Bourke's further reply, will be forwarded to Army Head Quarters; meanwhile Dr Bourke has been ordered to furnish the Officer Commanding 72nd with a letter stating that his remarks in no way referred to that regiment. As Dr Bourke corresponds with *The Standard*, the Viceroy may think it desirable to let the public of England know the true facts of the case before his letter is published.[23]

RP 101/CXCVIII

94
Report of Macgregor Commission into massacre of Cavagnari's Mission

[Printed copy]   Kabul
                                        15 November 1879

In order to arrive at a right conclusion in regard to the cause of the late events at Kabul from the day of the massacre of the Mission to the British entry into Kabul, we think it is advisable to go back to the time of the Amir Yakub Khan's arrival at Gandamak.

2. It is to be regretted that the Commission are not in possession of copies of Major Cavagnari's correspondence with the Foreign Office at the time the negociations which led to the Treaty of Gandamak were going on, as it is likely these would show what was the feeling of the Amir in regard to the various clauses of that Treaty, and which of these he was more particularly averse to. However, in the absence of such information, the Commission would record an opinion founded on their knowledge of the Afghan character and from various sources of information which have been open to them.

3. Our opinion is that the Amir was specially averse to three of the Articles, *viz.*, Article 2, granting "a full and complete amnesty" to all his subjects who had any intercourse with the British in the late war.
    Articles 4 and 5, relating to the establishment of a British Envoy at Kabul, and "the guarantee of his personal safety and honourable treatment."
    Article 9, that relating to the assignment of territory.

4. It appears to the Commission that the evidence which they will refer to below amply supports this view, and that the dislike of the Amir to these clauses is shown indirectly, but clearly, in the general bad feeling displayed by him from the day of his return from Gandamak.

The evidence regarding his infringement of Article 2 is simply overpowering, and no further proof can be required of his infringement of Articles 4 and 5 than is afforded by the total destruction of the Embassy.

In regard to Article 9, the Commission are of opinion that no proof is required, as it is only human nature for a ruler to be averse to any cession of territory.

5. The evidences of an unfriendly feeling on the part of the Amir are abundantly set forth in the depositions taken by the Commission, and this may be summarized as follows:-

1st – The fact of the Amir's never having shown the Treaty to any one.

2nd – His infringement of Article 2.

3rd – In his having placed every possible restriction on the free intercourse between Sir Louis Cavagnari and the people of the country.

4th – In his having been aware of, if he did not instigate or encourage, a bad feeling among the Herat regiments.

5th – In his disinclination to undertake the Turkistan tour, and to going to Hindustan.

6th – In his reported destruction of Russian papers, and treatment of Russian messenger.

7th – In the general bad feeling of the Amir towards the Embassy.

6. The first of these indictments is proved by the following evidence:-

Munshi Bakhtiar Khan on the 6th July states:- "The Gandamak Treaty has not yet been shown by the Amir to any one, nor has Article 2 yet been".

These documents appear to the Commission to afford very strong circumstantial evidence that the Amir did order Nek Muhammad[24] to use his endeavours to turn the people out to fight. His plea that "there was no advantage in my having given him such an order, as whatever advantage was to be got out of it, would have accrued to him and not to me. I was in your camp, with my son and chief Ministers," is not, they think, when considered with the former acts of the Amir, sufficient to clear him. It is true that there would seem to a man of any sense but little advantage to the Amir in the assembly of the people to fight, but "nemo matalium omnibus novis sapit", and Yakub Khan's conduct no more entitles him to a reputation for wisdom than it proves his loyalty to us, and if there would be no advantage to him in collecting the people, the advantage which would have accrued to him if General Roberts had been defeated is very patent. The lessons which Nott and Pottinger[25] read them have had but little effect on the Afghan mind, and he is content to forget these and dwell on the disastrous retreat of Elphinstone's force.[26] If General Roberts therefore had been defeated, it was clearly hoped that the tribes which were at the moment of the fight at Charasia, threatening the whole of his rear and flanks, would have attacked him, and if they did not finish the business then and there, they would at least have forced him to retreat, and then the advantage which would have accrued to the Amir would have seemed to him very apparent. His share in the transaction would have been boldly avowed, and he would have shared the glory which fell on Muhammad Akbar,[27] after the massacre of the last British soldier in 1842, and which makes up to this day the [missing] of the Afghans. The Commission think the fight at Charasia was part of the same plan which dictated the apparent anxiety, for our sake, of the Ministers at Ali Khel and of the risings of the ghazis at the Shuturgardan.

The next point which the Commission should adduce in support of their opinion that Yakub Khan was privy to the fight at Charasia is afforded by the fact that until our own patrols discovered the enemy actually in position, no news whatever of impending resistance to his advance was conveyed to General Roberts, and the Commission cannot believe that Yakub Khan, whether he ordered the attack or not, did not know the people were collecting on the heights of Sang-i-Nawishta, and inasmuch as he did not give any intimation thereof, he is at least guilty after the act.

The last point which the Commission will adduce is the fact spoken to by many, that many of the Amir's most intimate friends were actually present in the fight. These men are generally called Yakubzais from their having followed his varying fortunes throughout his career.

The Commission has now nearly finished its labours.

The enquiry cannot be held to be fruitless: it has disclosed a course of conduct on the part of the Amir Muhammad Yakub Khan, which they believe is without parallel even in the treachery-stained annals of Afghanistan.

It is related in Bellew's [missing] the custom of Narranatai, or entering in, is one of the sacred laws of the Nang-i-Pukhtana.[28] By this every Pathan is expected at the sacrifice of his own life and property, if necessary, to shelter and protect any one who in extremity may flee to his threshold, and seek an asylum under his roof.

This applies even to the protector's enemies, and by some tribes the system is extended to all living creatures, man, brute, or fowl.

Now though this custom – this law – is undoubtedly more honored in its breach than its observance, there is no doubt that it is in theory at least a custom on which all Afghans pride themselves, and there is no Afghan so bold in avowal of treachery that he would deny the unspeakable baseness of the man who neglected it, and whatever their real feelings may be, there is not one man of the many examined by the Commission who did not express the strongest disgust at such a crime as the killing of a guest.

This then must all have been in the Amir's mind when he solemnly sealed a promise to protect the British Mission. He knew that in committing to his care Sir Louis Cavagnari and his comrades he was expected to protect, even at the sacrifice of his own life and property, yet how did he act?

From the moment of signing the Treaty at Gandamak he seems to have set himself to convince his people of his intention to disregard it, and by his example and his openly expressed dislike in Durbar, by his preventing intercourse between Sir Louis and his people, by his neglect to punish the seditious language of the

Herat regiments, and, in short, in every way he could, without openly breaking with us.

This conduct was just such as would have encouraged evil spirits amongst his people, to excite an attack on the Embassy; but it did not stop here. It has been made out to the satisfaction of the Commission that he must have secretly incited the soldiers to create a disturbance, which, while it would be in direct contravention of his promise, might induce the British Government to withdraw its Mission; and when the storm had been thus raised, Amir Muhammed Yakub Khan, by his gross apathy and cowardice showed beyond a doubt that the attack was to his liking, and by his refusal of all offers of assistance and his general conduct throughout the fatal 3rd September he proved he had no wish to save his guests.

Even after the destruction of the Embassy he could not shake off his hostility, leaving the noble dead to lie rotting in the sun, a prey to each passing day, he at last ordered them to be thrown into one pit, to show that even by their death his hostility was not quenched, little thinking that by endeavouring to dishonour their dead bodies he paid a silent tribute to the unflinching bravery with which they all, British, Sikh, Goorkha and Musalman, held together to the bitter end.

Not even then realizing his situation, without the courage to openly avow his deeds, he endeavoured still to deceive, while, posing himself as a suppliant to our forbearance, he secretly and persistently endeavoured to raise the ignorant people to oppose us. By these deeds, the Commission think he has forfeited all claim on the forbearance of the British Government.

The Commission do not consider it necessary to enter into any detailed discussion as to the guilt of the Amir's chief Ministers. The Wazir Mulla Shah Muhammad and Yahya Khan and the Mustaufi Habibulla were the most trusted, and it seems certain that whatever the Amir did they knew of, and therefore made themselves participators in the treacherous course he chose to pursue. Whatever may be the fate of Yakub Khan should also be theirs.

In regard to Daud Shah, the Commission refrain from gauging the exact amount of his complicity in the heinous crime it has been their endeavour to render clear. There is something to be said in his favor. He is believed to have tried to stop the outbreak. The Commission, therefore, think he may have the benefit of the doubt, more especially as, since our arrival here, he has shown a friendly spirit.

Much, very much of the atrocious crime of the murder of the British Envoy and his escort, has, the Commission think, thus been brought home to the Amir and his Ministers, but they must not refrain from placing on record that an indelible stain must always remain on the name of the whole Afghan nation; for though they have listened to many statements to the effect that such and such were ready and anxious to help, the fact remains that while the hideous crime was being slowly enacted during twelve long hours, not one Afghan struck a blow in the cause of mercy, outraged hospitality, honor or manhood . . .

RP 154–1/1

95
Roberts to Foreign Department

[Printed telegram]   Kabul
                                      16 November 1879

Clear the line. The report of the Commission on the causes and circumstances attended with the massacre of the Embassy is nearly completed; it will be copied and despatched in three or four days' time. Evidence of the Amir's guilt and complicity is as conclusive as it is possible to establish it while he remains in Afghanistan; on every point his guilt and complicity are apparent, and I believe it only requires his removal to India to produce such direct and certain proof as will convict him. It would take nearly three weeks for the Amir to reach Peshawar, so that were he to start a week or ten days hence, the Government would have ample time to read and consider the report of the Commission, which goes most fully into the case and is very ably drawn up. I think the Government would have no difficulty in deciding as to the way in which the Amir should be received and treated in British India. Yakub Khan's removal would do more than anything to settle the minds of the Afghans, and it is I think desirable he should commence his journey before heavy snow falls, which it may be expected to do in three weeks or a month at latest.[29] I would propose to keep the Ministers here under arrest, feeling tolerably confident that some conclusive proof of their guilt will be forthcoming once the people are satisfied that Yakub Khan will not be re-established as Amir and will not again be in a position to avenge himself on them.

RP 101/CXCIX

96
Roberts to Viceroy

[Manuscript telegram] Kabul
30 November 1879

Personal. General Vaughan has been talking to me about the future of Afghanistan: he seems to agree with my views and as he will probably write about them I should like to be favoured with Your Excellency's instructions as to whether they are such as you would wish advocated in the London papers. Briefly, they are to make certain of our being able to obtain possession of Herat before Russia; to occupy Kandahar in such force as will ensure our being able to do this at all seasons; to make a military road to Herat and to complete our communications by railway if possible, with India; to disintegrate Afghanistan and form tributary, or at all events dependent States; to destroy its fighting power and in future to permit only sufficient levies to be raised as will enable petty rulers to collect revenue and maintain order; to keep political control over Balkh and Badakhshan as long as possible, but to accept the fact that our eventual collision with Russia should be on and not beyond the Hindu Kush; to increase our hold over Kashmir and make its ruler much in same position towards us as the Governor of Kabul will be; to visit as much of Northern and Western Afghanistan as possible next spring and summer, and to withdraw in the autumn to Kuram and some point to be selected on the Khyber route. I will take care that General Vaughan does not write on this subject until I have received Your Excellency's instructions.

LP 218/126; printed copy in RP 101/CCVIII

97
Roberts to Foreign Secretary

[Printed telegram]

Kabul
7 December 1879

Kohistanis are assembling and inclined to give trouble. Some men under a Mullah named Mushk-i-Alam have collected again near Beni-Badam,[30] these people and the Kohistanis are too far away at present to take notice of. I am endeavouring to settle matters without proceeding to extremities. City and neighbourhood of Kabul quiet. All well.

PP (HoC), 1880, LIII, *Afghanistan (1880) No. 1* (C2457), 48, enc. 3

98
Roberts to Major-General Bright, Commanding Khyber Force

[Typed telegram]

Kabul
11 December 1879

There is great excitement here, and large numbers of the enemy have collected; we engaged them today and I hope tomorrow we shall clear them out of immediate neighbourhood of Kabul, but I am afraid of the excitement spreading along the line of communication and would wish you to reinforce Gandamak by a sufficient force to hold it in case of my having to call upon General Gough[31] to come nearer Kabul. Telegraph what troops you can send and when they will reach Gandamak; showing strength along the line will have good effect. Acknowledge receipt. You shall hear again tomorrow. If the wire is cut consider that a bad sign and push on to Gandamak, sending Gough's Brigade on towards Kabul.

RP 154–3/CCXVII;
printed copy in RP 101/CCXVII

99
Roberts to Viceroy

[Typed copy]   Kabul
                                               14 December 1879

Clear the line. We have been fighting all the morning and gained great success at first, but the enemy are coming on in such numbers that I have decided to collect my force within the Sherpur entrenchments and give up the heights above the city and Bala Hissar, as it is not possible to hold such an extended position while the enemy are so numerous; keeping up communication with the outposts would be very difficult. I have ordered Gough to push on from Gandamak as fast as he can, withdrawing the Lataband detachment as he passes by. As this excitement and combination are now sure to spread along the line of communication, I strongly recommend more troops being pushed up so as to admit of General Bright being able to keep open communication, and to enable me to clear the country should I find it impossible to do so with my present force, which seems likely looking to the overwhelming numbers and the great determination the enemy exhibit. Your Excellencies may depend on my doing all that is possible, but I foresee that I shall not be able to do all I ought unless strongly reinforced, which should be done without delay. I have ordered Arbuthnot's Brigade[32] from Jellalabad to Kabul immediately.

RP 154–3/CCXXI;
printed copy in RP 101/CCXXI

SEPTEMBER 1879 TO OCTOBER 1880

100
Roberts to Brigadier-General Charles Gough, Commanding 1st Brigade, Khyber Force

[Typed copy]   Kabul
                                                14 December 1879

March to Kabul as soon as you can and bring the Lataband
detachment with you. Hold on to all posts that are strong enough
to resist attacks; others I would withdraw, for it is very probable
the Ghilzais will rise. We have had hard fighting and have withdrawn our posts from the neighbouring hills, and the force is now
collected in Sherpur, where we shall be more than a match for the
enemy; they numbered nearly 30,000 today. I will look out for you
and assist you on the road from Butkak or Lataband if possible.
Try and keep me informed of your movements.

RP 154–3;
printed copy in RP 101/CCXXIII

101
Roberts to Charles Gough

[Typed copy]   Kabul
                                                19 December 1879

I hope you will have received a copy of the clear-the-line message I
despatched to the Viceroy and General Bright ere this reaches
you, and that you will be on your way here. It is most important
you should come without delay, and with Lataband held in front
of you I am at a loss to understand your saying you "are not strong
enough to attempt an advance on Kabul" and you "patrol the road
towards Kabul with cavalry". How can there be any enemy worth
thinking of on this side of Jagdallak so long as Lataband is occupied? I have kept Hudson[33] there on purpose to help you, but must
withdraw him if you delay longer, as his supplies are running
short. His force will be a considerable addition to yours, and if you
have only the 9th Foot, 2nd Goorkhas, and a Mountain Battery

you will be strong enough from Lataband to beat any force which the Afghans could bring against you in a country so open as this is between Kabul and a few miles of Lataband. It is impossible to overestimate the political importance of your early arrival here, and as you seem to hesitate between maintaining the line of communication safe, and advancing at once on Kabul, I must decide for you, and therefore direct you to proceed without a single day's delay after you receive this. The line of communication will soon settle itself once we [? have] reasserted our supremacy at Kabul, but that must be done without further delay, and I shall not be in a position to do it until joined by your force and Hudson's.[34]

Please acknowledge receipt, and pay any money to ensure trusty and speedy messengers being employed.

RP 154-3/CCXXXV

102
Foreign Secretary India to Roberts

[Printed telegram]   Calcutta
3 January 1880

No. 36E.P. Clear the line. Press correspondent telegraphs Kabul 30th. Commission sitting daily; ten hung today. Ends. If correct, Viceroy wishes you to telegraph grounds of sentence and offence found. Suspend further executions pending communication from here.

LP 127B/p.334

103
Roberts to Colley (Private Secretary to Viceroy)

[Printed telegraph]   Kabul
4 January 1880

Personal. Your telegram of 31st reached me last evening. I am distressed the Viceroy should think that I would adopt unnecessarily severe measures such as would embitter and prolong hostilities. My object throughout has been to make our occupation as little irksome and distasteful to the people as the safety of the force would admit. Nearly all the prisoners executed before 12th November were found guilty of having attacked, or having property belonging to, the Embassy in their possession, or bearing arms, not because they were soldiers. Between 12th November and recent disturbances nine executions took place. Seven were men convicted of having attacked the Embassy; one of having arms and threatening to use them; and one of instigating people to rise against us.

On the 26th December, the third day after the enemy had been dispersed, a general amnesty was published and all headmen were invited to come in. The charitable dispensary was re-established in the city, and it was notified to all wounded men that they would be taken care of and be at liberty to leave the hospital when they pleased. The fort of the Kohistani ringleader was destroyed because I was assured by Wali Mahomed, the Nawab,[35] Hyat Khan, and by some Kohistanis who had come in, that so long as this chief remained unpunished the people generally would not come to terms. Hastings and Durand both agreed with me that an example was necessary. Baker's Brigade marched 20 miles through Kohistan: not a shot was fired going or returning, and no one's property save the one chief's was injured. The result is that, with scarcely an exception the Kohistani headmen are now with me; those from Logar have signified their wish to come, as have Padshah Khan and other Ghilzai chiefs; all have been invited to do so. It is impossible that an army of occupation can be popular, but everything has been and will be done to make this one as little irksome as possible to the people; there has never been a complaint against a British soldier and only trivial ones against a few natives. The recent disturbances were not caused by any local feeling, nor on account of severity on our part; they were inevitable some time or another. I did not expect them so soon, but knew they must take place. I believe now the country, except possibly in the neighbourhood of Ghazni, will settle down. The city has never been so quiet or so full, nor have supplies been so plentiful. The Viceroy need have no anxiety. I only hope that His Excellency will not believe I would act in such a way as could compromise the Government, and that I shall continue to deserve and to receive his kind support, without which my position here would be very different to what it has been.

RP 101/CCLXV

104
Lyall to Roberts

[Printed copy]   Fort William, Calcutta
                                                  January 1880

His Excellency the Governor General in Council, having had under his consideration the very arduous and responsible nature of the political duties devolving on you in regard to the present administration, and future settlement, of the province of Kabul, has decided to strengthen your Staff by the appointment to it of a Political Officer of rank and experience; and for this purpose His Excellency in Council has chosen Mr Lepel Griffin,[36] C.S.I., Secretary to the Punjab Government, whose exceptional local experience and knowledge of the frontier tribes, with his administrative training and proved abilities, peculiarly qualify him for the post.

2. In communicating this appointment to you, His Excellency desires to make it clearly understood that your supreme civil and political, as well as military, authority at Kabul is in no way affected by it. Mr Lepel Griffin's position will be that of your recognised official adviser, to whom all political and administrative questions should be referred for opinion, and under whom, in subordination to you, all Political Officers now employed with your force will work. Subject to instructions from the Government of India, the ultimate decision on, and responsibility for, all action, political and military, must remain with you. It is to be understood, however, that in political and administrative

cases, and in all questions of a civil nature, whenever the opinion of the political officer has not been in accordance with your action, his opinion and your orders upon it will both be communicated at once to the Government of India in the Foreign Department . . .

HP 34/19

105
Roberts to Foreign Secretary India

[Printed telegram]   Kabul
                                             14 January 1880

Precedence Kabul fourteenth January. I am issuing proclamation announcing abolition Military Governorship and appointment Wali Muhammud to administer Kabul district, including city on our behalf. Pending final orders, I shall say nothing about other districts for the present. General Hills hands over charge today. Permanent Military Commission will also cease today . . .

LP 127B/ p.360

106
Roberts to Viceroy

[Manuscript telegram]   Kabul
                                             16 January 1880

Precedence.
Your Excellency's letter of 5th January reached me yesterday. I am indeed grateful to your Excellency for selecting so capable a political chief of the Staff as Mr Griffin. I quite recognise his exceptional ability for the position and you may depend on my working with him without friction and my not allowing personal feelings to interfere with the interests of the public service.[37] Mr Griffin will

be welcomed as the most able adviser I could have and I daresay when we know more of each other we shall be better friends than we have hitherto been. I am however very glad that your Excellency proposes to invite him to Calcutta before he starts as it is most desirable he should clearly understand the position he will occupy here and that everything should be explained to him by your Excellency.

LP 24/123;
printed copy in RP 101/CCLXXVII

107
Roberts to Colley

[Printed telegram]   Kabul
                                        20 January 1880

Personal and private. Mr Lyall has directed me to send a tabular statement showing the number of persons executed since September. Please let me know if Viceroy wishes me to do this. I understood that His Excellency considered an official statement unadvisable and that all trials should be on principle of drumhead court-martial, enquiry being limited and grounds of decision not being recorded.

The Military Commission was of this nature. My instructions to it were that all natives suspected of being soldiers or found with arms in the city or within a radius of 5 miles should be made prisoners; that all soldiers or civilians who took part in massacre of the Embassy should be executed, and that all other cases should be referred to me. If official report is desired I would suggest for His Excellency's consideration that it should be general, and in form something like my letter to Mr Stanhope, copy of which I sent to Viceroy on 16th instant.

RP 101/CCLXXIX

108
Roberts to Major-General Greaves, Adjutant-General India

[Printed copy]   Kabul
Private   23 January 1880

I was very glad to receive your letter of the 14th instant and to hear from you that the Commander-in-Chief is entirely with me. I never imagined that His Excellency had any personal feeling against me; indeed that did not seem likely or possible, for the two years I was at Head Quarters with Sir Frederick Haines I believe I had his entire confidence, and that we parted with mutual feelings of regret.

Later on things seemed to change; I knew that I was not His Excellency's selection for a command, and I did, or I imagined that I did, not receive such support and assistance as the difficulties of the operations entrusted to me required. Then I found, when I endeavoured to remedy anything that seemed to me wrong, or to offer suggestions in order to make my force efficient, I was looked upon as a man who wanted all the loaves and fishes to himself, and was told, in almost as many words, to mind my own business.[38] I am of course only alluding to private or demi-official correspondence, and which in all probability the Chief never saw or heard of. Seeing the position I had held at Head Quarters, and the terms I had been on with the officers there, I thought I was quite justified in making representations in the way I did, and in pointing out what seemed to me defects, but I received no encouragement, and in a very short time all communication between me and Head Quarters ceased, except the ordinary official correspondence.

I much regretted this, for I believed, and still think, that a great deal can be done in a demi-official way; indeed it is not possible always to write officially, besides it would have been a great pleasure to me to have kept His Excellency informed, from time to time, through Lumsden or Johnson, of all that was going on. I have a very great liking and respect for Sir Frederick

Haines, and have often wished since I left Head Quarters, now just two years ago, that matters were different to what they have been.

RP 101/CCLXXXIII

109
Viceroy to Roberts

[Manscript telegram]   Calcutta
                                        24 January 1880

Personal and secret. Most desirable that defence of Kabul executions should be placed before Public in popular and effective form as soon as possible. Griffin undertakes to write article answering Harrison[39] if furnished with necessary materials but cannot reach Kabul before end February too late for this purpose. Pray send immediately to him at Lahore full materials for proposed article which should appear without delay. All available papers and information should be placed at his disposal. He shall bring them back with him to Kabul.

RP 37/69

110
Roberts to Lyall

[Holograph]   Kabul
                                        25 January 1880

I am anxiously looking out for the "set political plan", until the intentions of Government are known people will never settle down.

With regard to your question "Who is to be the ruler of Kabul" I am sending you a cipher telegram. When we first came here, Yakub Khan certainly had not a strong party. He was by no means popular, particularly about Kabul. He had many enemies and personally I consider him anything but a strong man. The way in which he spoke to me at the time of his abdication convinced me then, and still makes me feel sure that he felt the people were against him. As against other competitors he had the Sher Ali party, and our action in regard to him has doubtless increased this party. Some misunderstood it, and thought he had not abdicated; and with the majority who, I think, knew the truth he was still looked upon as injured given the fact that we suspected him. There was no one else on the ground at the time, and a feeling thus grew up in his favour. National pride being in a great measure the active power, Yakub's faults were forgotten, and it has only been remembered that he had been sent away to India. There was no one else to put forward and Yakub Khan was looked upon as the national representative.

His popularity thus revived as suddenly as it had gone after the treaty of Gandamack, and the late letters are the result. Whether the feeling towards Yakub Khan would last is a different thing. The Mustaufi, with whom I had a long, confidential talk today, is of opinion that the Sher Ali faction is too strong to admit of any one not closely connected with Sher Ali being successful in the attempt to establish himself at Kabul. He says that he does not know much of Ayub Khan but he believes that no one but Yakub Khan or Hashin Khan would have any chance as Ruler of Kabul were we to withdraw from the country. Abdul Rahman would probably attract the soldiers, and if he or Ayub were to appear on the scene soon, they would doubtless carry the people with them so long as they remained in opposition to us.

The Mustaufi says that no one outside the Barakzai family would have any chance. He went over the principal men amongst the Gilzais, Kohistanis, Wardaks, etc. etc. – none of whom can manage even their own tribes.

Wali Mahomed will, I fear, never do, indeed during the last day or two he has given me to understand that were we to withdraw he would go a march ahead of the troops! Hashin Khan I can hardly make out, he was with me throughout the action of the 11th December and is not wanting in courage. He is certainly ambitious – sometimes I think he is less inclined than the other Sirdars to be friendly with us – it may merely be his manner, or it may be that he does not wish the Afghans to think that he is too intimate with us. Personally, I like him.

The position is no doubt a difficult one, but something must be made out of it, and the sooner the intention of Government as to the future of Afghanistan is known the better.

LyP 24/124–26

III
Roberts to O.T. Burne, India Office

[Holograph]   Kabul
                                               1 February 1880

Your letter of the 2nd January reached me yesterday – not bad, 29 days from London to Kabul? Many thanks for sending me 'Punch' and for your kind congratulations.

We had rather a rough time of it here between the 8th and 24th December but I had no anxiety as to the result. In my despatch, which I fear is in consequence somewhat lengthy, I have carefully described the position we occupy here and explained that there was all we required in abundance, such as food, water, firewood, hospital comforts, and, above all, ammunition. Sherpur is much more extensive than I could wish, but as you will see from the despatch, and the plan which accompanies it, it is not possible to reduce it. Time did not admit of my constructing shelter for the whole Force, or I should have stopped on Siah Sang, but it was all I could do to supplement the accommodation we found in Sherpur, and bring in the required amount of supplies before the severe weather set in.

The combination against us was very considerable, and the number increased with extraordinary rapidity as the enemy approached Kabul – at the last there could not have been less than 100,000 men against us – too overpowering a number to meet in the open, so there was nothing for it but to wait patiently for the opportunity which the enemy gave us on the 23rd December. The principal men opposed to us are now at Ghazni, they are doing all in their power to keep up the excitement, partly to prevent those who, if left alone, might join us and partly to induce the disbanded soldiers and other enterprising spirits to join them, and by stopping up all the roads leading from the NW and S to Kabul to prevent our communicating with, or drawing supplies from, outlying districts. They cannot persuade the people to attack us again, and we are practically independent as regards supplies. Our position here is very different to what it was a month or six weeks ago as regards defences; I am quite confident that I can hold Sherpur and the Bala Hissar, and also prevent the city from being occupied by the enemy unless the townspeople were to join them en masse.

I think my views about the future of Afghanistan are much the same as yours; hold on to the west and leave the east as soon as the country has been settled, and satisfactory arrangements made for its future government. It would never do to go away before then; we have upset such a government as there was, and are bound to do all we can to set up another. It looks difficult now, but as soon as winter is over, and troops can move about a great many difficulties will disappear – one great difficulty is to find the right man to make Governor of Kabul. I don't really know who would be strong enough to hold his own here without our direct aid, and yet somebody must be found, for I certainly do not think we should remain another winter in this part of Afghanistan, if we can possibly help it.

I am glad to hear from you that the Ministry are likely to remain in office, it certainly would be a calamity if the Liberals got into power now. They tell me that Mr Gladstone has done for himself in Scotland, and has now no chance of being returned for Mid Lothian.[40]

I hope Lord Cranbrook and the other members of the Government will not allow me to be spoken of as a murderer! I thought I was tolerably callous to newspaper abuse, but I confess to having felt greatly put out [?by] a paragraph I read in the *Daily News* a few days ago. I am quite certain that Martial Law has never been carried out with less severity than during the last few months in Kabul, and that I have been so merciful and forebearing as the safety of my force, and the object for which it came to Kabul admitted. A Commander has only the Government he is serving to look to, and unless he is strongly supported by them, he has a poor chance of being done justice to.

The situation has been surrounded by difficulties, however, I need not trouble you about them. I feel satisfied that my case is in good hands, and that whatever Radical Papers may write, or Radical Members may say, I shall not be condemned by the Public when they know all that has been done here.

IOR MSS Eur D/951/3

112
Adjutant-General India to Roberts

[Manuscript copy]   Fort William, Calcutta
                                        9 February 1880

In my letter of this date No. 1626, I informed you that under the orders of His Excellency the Commander-in-Chief I should address you more in detail concerning the manner in which Brigadier General Massy exercised the Command of the troops in the action of the 11th December.

2. In now doing so I am commanded to state that His Excellency has after the most careful consideration viewed the circumstances in so serious a light as to necessitate the removal of Brigadier General Massy from the Command of the Cavalry Brigade in the Field.

The Commander-in-Chief has come to this conclusion with much regret for it is necessarily extremely painful to him to have to take such a step in the case of any Officer but naturally more so in that of one, who has from previous service established a reputation which has led to his being sent to this country from England specially to Command a Cavalry Brigade in the field.

3. But the requirements of the service must of course be superior to personal considerations in such matters and His Excellency is

satisfied that these requirements cannot be adequately met by any action short of Brigadier General Massy's removal.

4. The Commander-in-Chief was not satisfied with Brigadier General Massy's conduct on the night of the 8th October when he shut the Cavalry under his Command up in a walled enclosure and allowed the enemy to escape. Sir F. Haines accepted at the time your view of that matter as conveyed in your report of the 22nd November 1879 and trusted that Brigadier General Massy would by subsequent conduct remove the unfavourable impression thus created.

5. The following details of the affair of the 11th December however show Brigadier General Massy to have been as wanting in judgement as in military appreciation of the circumstances in which he was placed.

(1) His leaving the road by which he was ordered to proceed, and taking Cavalry and guns unnecessarily into a country intersected with water courses.

(2) It does not appear that he had a single scout out in any direction and this naturally resulted in his advance guard finding itself suddenly in the presence of the enemy.

(3) Having sent away a troop to look for Brigadier General Macpherson his small force was weakened to this extent and this troop never rejoined him.

(4) His orders were not to engage the enemy until he had joined with Brigadier General Macpherson. Instead of obeying this order he came into action in ground extremely unsuited for the arms under his command against a force of 10,000 men without in the least knowing where Brigadier General Macpherson was.

(5) Once in action he commits the grave military error of continually moving forward his guns thus losing their fire for the time. The enemy meanwhile advancing and enveloping his flanks.

(6) His having dismounted 30 Lancers with carbines to stop the advance of 10,000 men.

(7) Retiring the guns over a line of country by which it had not been previously ascertained they could be moved.

(8) These ill judged proceedings rendered it necessary to order the Cavalry to charge large masses of the enemy in order to give time to extricate the guns.

(9) These charges resulted in a serious loss of life, and finally the guns had to be spiked and left in the hands of the enemy.

6. Under all the circumstances, it is impossible for the Commander-in-Chief to permit Brigadier General Massy to continue in Command in the field, and I am therefore directed to request that immediately on receipt of this letter you will communicate His Excellency's decision to this Officer and order him to proceed to Peshawar there to await further orders.

He is to report his arrival at Peshawar to the General Officer Commanding for the information of the Commander-in-Chief.

7. I am further to request that you will be so good as to select an Officer for the temporary command of the Cavalry Brigade and report to me for His Excellency's orders whom you would recommend for the permanent Command.

RP 154–3

113
Roberts to Colley

[Printed copy]   Kabul
                                        11 February 1880

As statements appear repeatedly in the newspapers to the effect that there is a want of cordiality between myself and the Generals under my command, I write these few lines that the Viceroy may be assured such is not the case.

I am on the best possible terms with every General and every Commanding Officer serving with the Force. I know perfectly well the advantage it is to a General in command to keep men with him, and I am not likely to fall out with my officers.

Bright is the only one who could have a grievance from the fact of my having superseded him, but nothing can be nicer than he has been throughout – most loyal and cordial. He knew me as a boy, and we have been friends for years.

I cannot conceive what has given rise to the newspaper reports which are absolutely without foundation.

Weather is very cold now, but the troops continue healthy.

RP 101/CCVII

114
General Order by Roberts

[Manuscript copy]   Kabul
                                     15 February 1880

The Lieut General is pleased to direct that each Regiment of the 1st Division, and also the 24th N.I. and 45. N.I. shall at once take in hand the training of 60 men per Regt. (including N.C.Os) as mounted Infantry.

For this purpose the Regimental Transport is to be utilized and a sufficient number of Yaboos[41] in each regiment will be equipped by the Director of Transport with the Kandahar pad which has been found the most suitable for the purpose.

Each pad is to be fitted with a pair of rough stirrups, a strong strap or bala Tang to go round the animal, and with strings in front to tie on a pair of Saddle Bags, and behind to tie on a great Coat.

The pattern of saddle bags approved is now with the Brigd General Baker & the Director of Transport will be good enough to have enough of these made up from any suitable material available – In these Saddle Bags are to be carried 60 Rounds of Ammunition, each man's Canteen & Rations for one day & a day's grain for each Yaboo and the weight in these are to be equally divided –

Each Yaboo will be provided with a Snaffle Bridle a Picketing rope & peg & his blankets, and each man is to carry some sort of whip or stick. Each man's blankets are to be folded and placed over the pad and under the seat. His Great Coat when not worn is to be neatly rolled & tied on behind.

Each man will carry the usual amount of ammunition, on his person and when mounted will carry his rifle slung across his back – A Small Warren's cooking pot will be supplied to each detachment of British Soldiers.*

The Mounted Infantry will work in fours, generally one man holding four ponies while the other three act as Infantry, but it will be question for after decision whether one man can conveniently hold more than four ponies as is done at the Cape by "ringing" them.

Some notes on this subject by Major Cooke Brigade Major 1ˢᵗ Brigade 2ⁿᵈ Division[42] are circulated for general information.

To superintend the training of these Detachments and to consider all points which may add to their efficiency the following Committee is appointed

> Brigadier Genˡ Baker CB President
> Lᵗ Col. Hudson 28 P.N.I.
> Lᵗ Col. Brownlow 72ⁿᵈ High.
> Lᵗ Col. Low Director of Transport
> Major White 92ⁿᵈ Highlanders[43]

---

* The question of cooking pots for Native Troops will have to be decided. Each squad of four to be of the same caste.

NAM 7804–76/23

115
Government of India to Secretary of State

[Printed despatch]   Fort William, Calcutta
                                                                18 February 1880
No. 41 of 1880

The telegram from His Excellency the Viceroy to Your Lordship's address, No. 365E.P., dated 24th January 1880, repeated a telegram from Lieutenant-General Sir F.S. Roberts, K.C.B., V.C., Commanding at Kabul, furnishing a statement of the executions which have been carried out under his orders. General Roberts has now submitted a statement in which are shown, amongst other particulars, the crimes for which capital punishment was inflicted in each case. We now forward, for the information of Her Majesty's Government, a copy of this statement, together with a copy of the letter from Sir F.S. Roberts, No. 112, dated the 27th January 1880, which accompanied it.

2. The following abstract shows in an abbreviated form the information contained in General Roberts' report:-

Nature of charges	Number executed	Number released
Dishonoring the bodies of the officers of the Embassy	4	–
Possessing property belonging to the Embassy	4	4
Being armed within five miles of camp	6	15
Attacking escorts in view to releasing prisoners	4	–
Murdering camp followers; participation in the attack on the Residency; inciting people to rise; carrying arms, treacherously firing on and killing wounded soldiers	69	57
Total	87	76

3. General Roberts' telegram of the 23rd of January reported that ninety-seven persons had been executed. His later and fuller report of the 27th states that sentence of death has been carried out only in eighty-seven cases. In explanation of this discrepancy it is stated by General Roberts that, when the first return was prepared, some persons who had been convicted of more than one offence were, by oversight, entered twice on the record.[44]

PP (HoC), 1880, LIII (C2523)

116
Memorandum by Roberts

[Printed]   Kabul
                                       27 January 1880.

With reference to certain statements made in an article entitled
"Martial Law in Kabul", which appeared in "The Fortnightly
Review", dated the 1st of December 1879, and bore the signature
of Mr Frederick Harrison, I would make the following observa-
tions regarding the proclamation of Martial Law in and around
Kabul on the 12th of October last:-

1. The civil government had ceased to exist, order had to be
restored (for all was anarchy on my arrival here), and to suppose
that this result could have been brought about in a country like
Afghanistan without the adoption of measures which I maintain
the circumstances fully justified, and which the result has proved
to have operated beneficially for the Afghans themselves, is to
betray total ignorance of Afghan character.

Martial Law is not altogether one-sided in the advantages it
confers. Here it actually protected the Afghans from themselves,
by the knowledge that swift and sure but just punishment would
overtake outrage or treachery.

2. My troops were placed in the heart of a hostile country and
encamped within a mile of a densely populated city, whose inhabitants alone exceeded tenfold the strength of my force.

In addition to the natural hatred which every Afghan feels
towards a foreign invader, there is a strong underlying current of
fanaticism which, unless promptly checked, becomes at times, and
especially against a Christian enemy, uncontrollable.

Every man in Afghanistan is invariably armed, and only too
ready to convert a trifling dispute into a bloody quarrel.

3. In the proclamation I distinctly stated that, for certain past
offences, namely –

(a) Having been engaged in the attack upon the Mission;

(b) Having in possession, after a certain fixed date subsequent to the proclamation, property which had belonged to the late members of the Embassy; and

(c) Having borne arms against their lawful sovereign at Charasiah; the punishment was death, on conviction by the constituted tribunal.

I further notified that in future –

(d) Those proved to have mutilated our wounded; and

(e) Any person found bearing arms within a radius of five miles from the city of Kabul,

would be liable on conviction to suffer a similar penalty.

4. I do not suppose that any person will be found to impugn the justice of clauses *a* and *b*, or deny that the fact of finding property which had belonged to the murdered members of the Mission in any person's possession was strong presumptive evidence that the possessor had been more or less directly concerned in the attack upon the Residency. Yet every opportunity was given to those with whom such property was found to come forward and explain, and all who did so escaped. Concealment after the proclamation was issued naturally led to the inference that no satisfactory explanation was forthcoming.

The repeated statement of the ex-Amir, when a guest and ally in our camp, that "all who fought against us at Charasiah were traitors to him", confirmed the decision at which I had arrived regarding clause *c*. Rewards were offered for the apprehension of these men, as it was known that all the regiments concerned in the attack upon the Mission took part against us at Charasiah, but in no instance were the soldiers thus brought in executed, unless proved to have taken a part in the attack upon the Residency, or to have committed other of the crimes enumerated in the proclamation.

Four hundred rupees in all was paid in rewards, but of this sum two hundred rupees was given as compensation to the family of a man in the service of Sirdar Wali Muhammad, who was killed when arresting an armed band of troops.

Clause *d* requires no defence, and I would point out as the result of the disarming clause the entire immunity which this force has enjoyed from assassination or fanatical attacks by individuals, and, further, so widely was the rule circulated, and so thoroughly well was it understood, that but few have suffered for its non-observance; all who proved that they were ignorant of the terms of the proclamation were released.

5. I cannot allow that the terms of the proclamation were unduly severe when looked upon either as punishment for past treachery of the most infamous description, or as a possible preventive of the mutilation of the wounded and of quarrels probably ending in bloodshed.

6. A Military Commission, presided over by a general officer, and whose members were drawn from officers of standing and experience, tried every case; and without their deliberate verdict and sentence, and with (I trust) calm and dispassionate consideration by me, not one sentence of death was awarded, confirmed, or carried into effect.

All that the accused had to urge in their defence was considered, remands were invariably granted when rebutting evidence was stated to be forthcoming, and in all cases where reasonable doubt existed, those on their trial reaped the benefit of it.

To question the good faith of the decisions of the Military Commission amounts to nothing short of casting discredit upon the honesty of the verdicts of all military courts.

7. The exigencies of my force rendered it imperative that each day numerous foraging parties should be despatched in various directions, and often to considerable distances from camp; the operation of the disarming clause enabled this duty to be carried on with much smaller guards than would otherwise have been required, and so relieved my troops of a very necessary but irksome duty.

I would further point out that the result has been that not a single case of assassination, outrage, or quarrel has occurred since our troops arrived at Kabul.

8. The establishment of martial law, instead of "meaning terrorism, slaughter, and violence, within such limits as a soldier thinks convenient", as the writer of the article in question asserts, is, as I understand it, a means of maintaining order and of preventing collisions between the troops and camp followers and the natives of the country; to those who may have to decide between us I confidently leave this point. The people have been treated well, their grievances have been inquired into, and, if possible, adjusted; for every article brought in for sale they have been liberally paid, and labour has commanded a price unheard of under Afghan rule.

9. There are other assertions made by Mr Harrison, with a few of which I will deal. He states that "no quarter was given to anyone found firing upon us, or to prisoners taken in fight." This statement is incorrect. If reference is made to two or three straggling Goorkhas having during the engagement at Charasiah, on the 6th of October last, set fire to the clothes of four Afghan bodies in whom life was virtually extinct, this does not call for the wholesale condemnation of our troops; and if the offenders had been discovered they would undoubtedly have suffered the most severe punishment. On the other hand, it may be mentioned that on this very occasion several wounded Afghans were taken into hospital and treated side by side with our own soldiers.

"All who took up arms against us were treated as mutineers, rebels, and murderers." I trust I have shown that such was not the case.

"It is laid down on system that the troops are to enter the enemy's country . . . that they are to kill and burn, ravage and destroy, as far as may be requisite, to secure "submission". . . This assertion is untenable in the light of the facts already stated.

One fort, near Kabul, has been destroyed as a punishment to its owners for treacherously cutting up our wounded when lying helpless on the ground on the 11th of December.

One fort in Kohistan, the property of Mir Bacha,[45] who headed the recent rising against us – and

One fort in Maidan, whose proprietor refused to pay the customary revenue, declined to come in and tender his submission, and treacherously fired upon a small party of our troops.

None others have been interfered with, except certain villages near Sherpur cantonment, which, for purely military reasons, it was necessary to destroy. Ample compensation has invariably been paid, fresh ground granted in other localities, the families thus deprived of their homes have been provided for temporarily in the city, and every attention paid to their comfort.

10. I attach a copy of the instructions which were issued for the guidance of the Military Commission referred to.

MEMORANDUM

The following instructions are issued for the guidance of the Military Commission, of which Major-General T. Hills,[46] C.B., V.C., is President:-

1. All prisoners, not belonging to the force, will be brought before the Commission.
2. All natives of the country found with arms in the city of Kabul, or within a radius of five miles, and all persons suspected of being soldiers, will be made prisoners.
3. Every soldier or civilian who took part in the massacre of the British Embassy on the 3rd of September last will be executed.
4. The cases of all other prisoners will be inquired into and referred for the orders of the Major-General Commanding Kabul Field Force.

PP (HoC) 1880, LIII (C2523)

117
Roberts to Major-General Dillon, Assistant Military Secretary War Office

[Printed copy]   Kabul
                                  23 February 1880

I am sending you by this mail three sets of photographs which I think perhaps Her Majesty The Queen and Their Royal

Highnesses the Prince of Wales and the Duke of Cambridge might be graciously pleased to accept. They are not so good as I could wish, but give a fair idea of Kabul. They are taken by the Sappers and Miners. I will send you some more copies next week. One set you will perhaps kindly make over to Lord Napier with my best respects.

I have not much news to give you this mail; all military operations in the neighbourhood of Kabul are at a standstill in consequence of the severity of the weather; snow falls frequently, and renders the country quite unfit for the movement of troops. At Jellalabad and other places of lower elevation it is different, and General Bright has recently done good service in exploring the Laghman valley. Nearly all the leading men have paid their respects to the General, who has not had occasion to fire a shot. He will now direct his attention to Hisarak, the district which lies between Jagdallak and Tezin, and with I hope the same result. Affairs are of course still very unsettled, but I think I can see signs of some satisfactory conclusion being arrived at without great delay. Afghans are even more suspicious than other Asiatics, and require very careful handling, but so far as I can judge matters are progressing fairly well.

In my last letter I mentioned that the management of the Cavalry and Horse Artillery action on the 11th December was not conducted as I could have wished, and I now learn that it has been decided to remove General Massy from the command of the Cavalry Brigade. I am much distressed about this, but I was afraid it would go hard with him. His own report, I think, shews clearly that he did not appreciate the position he was placed in. It is a most unfortunate business altogether, and poor Massy is in terrible grief. I have always held the opinion that the leader of cavalry in the field requires to be possessed of peculiar qualifications. History proves this to be the case, and the wars of the last two centuries have not produced more than half a dozen real Cavalry Generals. Of course it will occur to you that such being the case I can hardly hope to be more fortunate than others have been before me. I do not expect to be so, but I have had now for some considerable time opportunities of judging Massy, and have arrived at the conclusion that he is wanting in the military instinct, prompt decision and quick action which go far towards making a good cavalry leader.

At the same time I would not wish it to be inferred from his failure in this particular capacity that I consider Massy unfitted for professional employment; on the contrary I believe, but this is of course better known to His Royal Highness and the authorities at the Horse Guards, that he was an excellent regimental officer, and I think that in another position, where those instincts in which he is deficient would not be so actively called into requisition, he would do good and valuable service.

In my despatch detailing the operations here in December last, I was particularly careful to sift thoroughly the various reports of the Brigadier-Generals concerned, as by a recent ruling of the Government of India it has been decided that these are not to be published (as was formerly the case) as appendices to the principal despatch. My report of Massy's operations was almost word for word a reproduction of the despatch which he himself sent in, and in order that there should be no possible misunderstanding, I sent for, and read over to him, what I had written. I then told him that I feared it would condemn him, and that I was prepared, if I had misunderstood him, to make any corrections that he deemed fair.

The decision which the Commander-in-Chief came to, namely, to replace Massy by another officer, seems to me to be the only one at which His Excellency could arrive in the interests of the service; and though Sir Frederick Haines may not be able to provide me with a Murat or a Kellerman, I feel certain His Excellency will give me the best officer he can, and one who, as far as he can judge, possesses the qualifications I believe to be wanting in Massy.

Massy is about to proceed to India, and will meet the Commander-in-Chief at Peshawar, whither Head Quarters are now moving. He will then be able to state his case fully, and I am in hopes that Sir Frederick Haines will feel himself justified to a certain extent in mitigating the terms under which Massy leaves this, and permit him to resign his appointment. This, in consideration of his services, and the fact that he was, from a very early date in his military career, crippled by a wound, will I trust so far tone down the circumstances of his departure that he may still hope for employment of some more suitable nature. The whole matter is one which under the most ordinary circumstances would be painful to any one in my position, but in the present case it is doubly so, as Massy is an old friend of mine, and one for whom I have a strong personal regard.

I trouble you with this detailed account of all that has occurred, as the removal of Massy is sure to cause a considerable commotion, and you will doubtless be desirous of knowing the facts of the case.

Sir Frederick Haines has of course made an official report for the information of His Royal Highness, but some of the points I have mentioned would scarcely perhaps find a place in such a report.

I am glad to see from Reuter's telegram that Mr Stanhope has read out in the House the letter I wrote to him on the 10th January, and I hope I shall now be acquitted of having treated Afghan prisoners with undue severity.

The troops continue very healthy and are in famous spirits. Nearly all the wounded men have recovered; the exception is Colonel Cleland.[47] I saw him this afternoon and fear he has not long to live.

I have got an Afghan tea urn for you and am having a second one made.

RP 101/CCXIV

118
Roberts to Major-General Greaves, Adjutant-General India

[Printed copy]   Kabul
                                            9 March, 1880

* * *

Massy left this on the 1st March, and, in accordance with the instructions conveyed in your telegram, placed in my hands the statement he proposed submitting to the Chief in his defence. I advised him to say nothing but to throw himself on the Chief's mercy; that it was impossible he could free himself from blame, and the less publicity that was given to the whole affair the better for his sake. I enclose you copies of the letter I wrote to Massy, and of the one I proposed sending to you, both dated 25th February. I did not send it to you at the time as Massy evidently did not think it would help him and asked me not to do so; you can tear it up. I send it now that you may see the line I took with Massy – for I think you somewhat misunderstood me when I telegraphed suggesting that the Chief should delay settling matters with the Government of India and the Horse Guards regarding Massy's removal from the Brigade Command in India until His Excellency had seen Massy. You are quite right no doubt that, if a man is not fit to command in the field, he should not hold a position which may require him to take the field at any moment. I have always advocated this, and it was perhaps a little inconsistent of me to suggest any other course in Massy's case, but sending him home straight with the whole business fresh in the memory of every one seemed to me a terrible punishment, particularly for a man like Massy who has been cracked up all his life, and has been living on a reputation for which there is apparently no foundation. I forwarded his letter of explanation yesterday together with my own remarks. I think you will agree with me that his defence is foolish to a degree; he tries to lay the whole blame on me, and shews clearly that he never understood his position as a Cavalry Commander. I am sorry to see that *The Pioneer* takes his part; this is, no doubt, owing to the fact that his father (so I am told) is the Paris correspondent of that paper. Cory's article in *The Civil and Military* about the Chief's letter acknowledging receipt of my despatch amused me much, and though Cory said I never could see a joke, I thought I had discovered one in that article. I never for a moment thought of the Chief's letter being anything but what I am sure it was intended to be, *viz.*, a cordial acknowledgement of the services of this force, and, as I told you in my telegram, I was extremely glad to get it . . .

RP 101/CCCXXIII

119
Roberts to Viceroy

[Printed telegram]   Kabul
                                                15 March 1880

Personal. Your Excellency will I am sure excuse my suggesting
that once the Government of India has approved generally of any
operations that may be determined upon in Afghanistan the
Commander-in-Chief should be required to leave the commanders
in the field practically unfettered.[48] Mr Griffin and I are quite
capable of undertaking any work that may be required once we
have received instructions of Government, and I am quite sure
that the less we are interfered with after that the better for ourselves and for Government: a certain latitude in our conduct of
operations, and in our dealings with the people is very desirable,
especially in a country like Afghanistan where the condition of
affairs is so constantly changing and where the movements of
troops must depend on the political situation, which can be best
understood by those on the spot. I trouble Your Excellency with
these views, as I am somewhat alarmed that once the Chief reaches
Peshawar, His Excellency will wish to take a more direct part in
Kabul affairs than may be desirable; and I am very anxious that
matters should, as far as possible, be left as they have been,
especially as I believe that for the future the military work will be
subordinate to the political.

RP 101/CCCXXVIII

120
Viceroy to Roberts

[Manuscript telegram]   Calcutta
                                                16 March 1880

Personal and Secret. On 13th Instant I sent following telegram to
Secretary State. Message begins. Personal and Secret. Necessary

to find without delay some native authority to which we can restore Northern Afghanistan without risk of immediate anarchy on our evacuation of Kabul not later than next autumn and if possible earlier. No prospect of finding Indian [sic] country any man strong enough for this purpose. All agree that country would rise in favour of Abdool Rahmnan if he appeared. I anticipate that Russia will not let him appear till we have been forced to recognize and subsidy some weak ruler (32530). Immediately after our withdrawal Abdul Rahman would enter Afghanistan country would rise our recognised and subsidized ruler would fall and our position become most embarrassing. I think it essential to prevent contingency thus foreseen. This can only be done by promptly securing Abdul Rahman if after exclusion of Ex-Amir he is generally felt to be the only man who has any chance of uniting or subduing all parties. His acquisition of power after we withdraw is inevitable better he should owe it to us than to Russia. If he obtains it without our aid our acquiescence in his requisition of it will be regarded throughout Central Asia as a political defeat. Time presses. I therefore advocate early public recognition of Abdul Rahman as legitimate heir of Dost Mahomed and open deputation of Sirdars with British concurrence to offer him throne of Northern Afghanistan as sole means of saving country from anarchy. This Russia could not openly oppose or resent. I attach no importance to any conditions she might make with Abdul Rahman he could not keep far off to the detriment of his own interests which would be sufficiently identical with ours if he depends on our subsidy and were controlled from our advanced Frontier. Abdul Rahmans family profess grateful devotion to us. They might accompany Stewart to Kabul and there assist Griffin in rallying adherents and preparing for reception of Abdul Rahman. I have reason to believe Abdul Rahman would willingly accept Northern Afghanistan without Kandahar and Herat as some time ago he proposed their partition to present Kandahar Ruler and Sher Ali would be less alarmed by Abdul Rahman at Kabul than by son or brother of Ex Amir.[49] Do you approve? Message ends. Yesterday I received following reply. Message begins. Personal and secret. Your telegram of yesterday. Assuming that Abdul Rahman is acceptable to the country and that he would be contented with Northern Afghanistan it is desirable to support him at Kabul. The more spontaneously any advances to him on the part Sirdars and the less appearance of British influence the better but where is he? and how do you propose to learn his wishes and intentions. If invited by chiefs every inducement to bring him to Kabul should be then held out. Public recognition should not precede but follow his (21429) by Sirdars and his acceptance of the position. Not desirable at this moment to raise new and great questions. Message ends. Communicate to Griffin and Lyall on arrival and use every effort to ascertain where Abdul Rahman is. Acknowledge receipt of this.

RP 37/79

121
Viceroy to Roberts

[Cypher Telegram]   Calcutta
                                                     17 March 1880

Personal. Your telegrams of 15th on the subject of alteration in the nature and extent of your command by Commander in Chief are receiving my most earnest attention.

RP 37/83

122
Roberts to Viceroy

[Printed telegram]   Kabul
                                                     19 March 1880

Personal and Secret. Many thanks for Your Excellency's kind telegram of yesterday. In support of my suggestions regarding desirability of leaving command here practically unchanged I have just learned by General Order of 10th instant, that each of the two divisions here is to have a separate commander of Artillery and Engineers. This seems to me quite unnecessary; one commander of each branch will be more economical and certainly more practical. It will be very difficult to divide the Engineers' work according to divisions, and I had proposed to keep the artillery in one body to be used as the requirements of the service might dictate. I am most reluctant to trouble Your Excellency with this matter, and I am still more reluctant to take any steps that could appear as if I were taking advantage of Your Excellency's confidence in me to protest against or criticise arrangements made by the Commander-in-Chief, nor do I wish that His Excellency should know of my action unless Your Lordship should consider it necessary to acquaint him, as it would doubtless cause considerable unpleasantness between me and all at Head Quarters, but it seems to me absolutely necessary in the interests of the public service that the commander at Kabul should be practically independent, that all details should be left in his hands, that all chance of friction and clashing should be reduced to a minimum, and that his work should be made as light and easy as possible. This would not be the case if one of the divisions were in any particular a separate command, such as having its own Commandant of Artillery and Engineers, more especially as both of the officers now ordered up happen to be senior to those holding similar positions in the division I am personally to command, and who have been with me throughout the campaign. I do not ask for a second divisional commander as I hope to be able to do all the work required, but I would strongly urge for Your Excellency's consideration that the troops here may be treated as one force in two divisions, and may have only one Commandant of Artillery and one of Engineers; that I may be held responsible for the efficiency of all the troops, for the safety of the military position at Kabul, and for the conduct of any operations that may be required. Unless this is accepted and disturbances arise the result will probably be a serious military complication, it being impossible in my opinion for matters to be conducted properly except by the commander on the spot, and it will probably end in the Commander-in-Chief urging the necessity of coming to Kabul himself. I have received a letter today from the Quarter Master General giving me directions as to what particular points I should hold round Kabul to ensure the safety of my position, and I am told that it is unnecessary to hold a certain point, to which I attach great importance. Such directions would remove all direct responsibility from me, and would place both the Commander-in-Chief and myself in false positions. The commander on the spot can alone be really responsible, and should, I respectfully urge, be allowed to act as he thinks best and as circumstances at the time may demand.

RP 101/CCCXXXII

123
Lytton to Roberts

[Holograph]   Calcutta and Barrackpore
                                           20/21 March 1880

Private & very confidential

I am ashamed of not having sooner thanked you for several very interesting letters of which the last received is dated 5th of March. But I have purposely postponed writing to you till I could write with adequate certainty on various important points connected with military as well as political matters, which have been engaging my constant attention during the last fortnight. Your telegram of the 15th only confirmed the increasing alarm with which I had for some time been contemplating the probable consequences of the assumption by Sir F. Haines of the command of the field forces from the base at Peshawar. I think you are aware of the circumstances in which I was induced to sanction that arrangement, as a "Compromise" suggested by Sir Edwin Johnson, for the purpose of "rehabilitating" the CinC who had demanded the personal command of the whole Spring Campaign with his Head Quarters at Kabul. I consented to it with great reluctance and misgiving and only on the assurances of the Military Dept. that it would not practically alter the CinC's relations towards the General Officers commanding in the field. What has been going on, however, during the last few weeks shows that this was a delusion. The CinC already in anticipation of his new powers has been interfering with everything and if this were not promptly stopped I feel sure that the consequences might be very serious. The receipt of your Telegram, therefore, determined me to lose no time in addressing to Sir Edwin the Confidential Note of which I enclose a copy (for your private & personal information only). [Not included] In accordance with this Note, the orders authorising the CinC to assume command from the base have been cancelled. And H.E., who has been informed that things are to revert to the status quo ante, – will not proceed to Peshawar. I trust that this will sufficiently relieve your mind, and that you will have no further cause for apprehension or complaint; – but, should that not be the case, pray write or telegraph to me freely. The new Adjutant General, Greaves, is an able energetic soldier, who is disappointed & dissatisfied with his present position in consequence of Sir F. Haines' decision, which I regret, not to appoint or accept a Chief of the Staff. Hence it is the incessant endeavour of Genl. Greaves, to get the entire virtual control of military operations, little by little, through the CinC, into his own hands, and he chafes at any authority which stands in the way of this result. From this cause alone there is a disposition at headquarters to restrict your authority & cripple your freedom of action – but this disposition is intensified by a circumstance which I know you are well aware of, that the Head Quarters staff has never been friendly to you. I fear you have also enemies in your own camp, and this too is I daresay not unknown to you. The fact is, men are envious of you; and Envy has no conscience. You have however the complete confidence of myself & the Home Govt; and you may reply upon me to prevent the bulls of Bashan from trampling you when they wax fat, and kick: but I cannot always prevent these animals from encompassing you round. Be on your guard about Brabazon.[50] I am sure he means no harm, and has no personal ill will to you (though he has to Baker) but he "is nothing if not critical" and his estimate of his own judgement is overweening. If he writes home (as I fear he does) in the same tone & spirit as those in which he writes to me, his letters must do mischief; though I think they are likely to do more harm to himself than to others. When I can find time to write to him, I shall give him a hint to moderate his critical ardour. But he is not likely to take it. Pray consider all I have said on this subject as <u>very</u> private & confidential.

* * *

RP 37/84

124
Viceroy to Roberts

[Manuscript telegram]   Calcutta
                                              25 March 1880

Personal.
I have today sent the following minute to Mily Dept. Minute begins It having been decided that His Excellency the Commander in Chief will not assume the direct and personal command of the troops in Afghanistan the present minute defining the relations of Lieut Gen Roberts and Lieut Genl Stewart to the Govt of India and to the Commander in Chief has been drawn up by me in consultation with His Excellency the Commander in Chief. Each of those officers is to be considered as a Genl Officer holding an independent command in the field and will be directly responsible to the Govt of India for the organisation of the forces under his Command, for the disposition of those forces and for the conduct of mily operations subject only to the genl scheme submitted by the Commander in Chief and approved by Govt or to any changes which may be made in that scheme under the authority of Govt. All reports referring to the organisation of these forces, their disposition and the conduct of military operations will as hitherto be rendered to the Commander in Chief for the information and orders of the Government of India. In the event of a concentration of the

forces now respectively under Lieut Gl Stewart and Lieut Gl Roberts Lieut Gl Stewart as senior officer will assume command.[51] Minute ends.

RP 37/85

125
Roberts to Edward Stanhope

[Holograph]   Kabul
                                                   31 March 1880

Your letter of 26th February reached me on the 28th Instant. I am very much obliged to you for it, and for sending me the copy of Mr Harrison's second article on Martial Law in Kabul.

Long ere this you will have received the statement of all the cases brought before the Military Commission for trial. I understand that it is considered to be satisfactory by the Government of India, and I hope that it will be viewed in the same light in England, and that it will enable you to answer any questions that may be asked on the subject in the House. I was careful to shew the exact charge upon which each prisoner was tried, and to give the instructions which I had drawn up for the guidance of the Commission. These instructions were issued three days before the proclamation of the 12th October, and it is unlikely in the face of such instructions that I should have ever contemplated executing men for merely fighting against us, though I now see that the wording of the proclamation is liable to cause people to believe that such a course was intended.

The Extracts from the Papers and telegrams quoted by Mr Harrison have misled that gentleman in many points.

I will mention three. Neither General Saifudin, nor the man of that name who was wounded at Charasia, were executed. The reasons for their being released are given in the official statement – under any circumstances the second Saifudin would have been released unless it could have been proved that he had taken a part in the attack on the Residency.

Sultan Aziz is called a Barakzai, and blood relation of the reigning family – the truth is that he was an illegitimate son of a Barakzai – the father is a man of no importance, and that the son by reason of his illegitimacy was practically distinct from his father's family.

We know of no General called "Kaispuk", possibly the name may have been misspelt although to the best of my belief no person having the rank of general was executed. Two Resaldars were executed named Atta Mahomed and Kabir, who are recorded as N^{OS}.24 and 25 in the statements which you possess. The latter may possibly be Kaispuk.

With regard to the cases mentioned at pages 444–445 of *The Fortnightly Review*, I have only to observe that any soldiers who were executed, suffered not because they resisted British arms but because there was evidence implicating them in the attack on the Residency. They all belonged to regiments concerned in the attack on the Residency.

The only matter to which Sir Donald Stewart could have referred was a communication from me to him regarding two persons who had escaped from Kabul into the Kandahar district, and whom I did not think it right to leave at large. I therefore asked Sir Donald to take measures regarding them, or to send them back to Kabul. Anything that Sir Donald Stewart may have written home was, I have reason to know, strictly private, and the use made of his letter seems to me to be indefensible.

I think I have now replied to all the points raised in your letter.

Stanhope MSS U 1590/0305/1; printed copy in RP 101/CCCXLII

126
Roberts to Viceroy

[Printed copy – private]   Kabul
                                            31 March 1880

I enclose for Your Excellency's information a copy of a letter I received by the last mail from Mr Stanhope; as also a copy of my reply to the same: I hope this will meet with Your Lordship's approval. Mr Lyall and Mr Griffin have both read it, and think it is all that is wanted. The article by Mr Harrison in *The Fortnightly Review* I have made over to Mr Griffin, who will probably reply to it.

On receipt of Mr Stanhope's letters I telegraphed in cypher to General Stewart as follows: "What did you write home about me and the Military Commission here? Mr Stanhope writes that your correspondents have made great capital out of your letters. As they were of course private, it seems an extraordinary use to have made of them."

Sir Donald replied as follows: "Never wrote to any one except Norman, to whom I expressed disapproval of your punishing persons who merely fought against you. I expressed my views on this subject to Government, and Viceroy in reply approved of them and directed me to act on them. The question was at the time generally discussed, and in writing to Norman I probably gave my opinion very freely in the confidence of private friendship, but he was not authorized to make public use of what I may have written. I do not think I ever wrote to any one else on this subject except my wife, and she has not spoken to any one regarding it. More by post." I felt sure that Sir Henry Norman was General Stewart's correspondent, but I certainly am astonished to find that he should have made use of private letters to assist those who were trying to get up a case against me.

* * *

Your Excellency may rest satisfied that there will be no friction in our work here. Mr Griffin is of the greatest assistance to me and we have but one object in view, *viz.*, to bring the difficult task before us to a satisfactory conclusion. I hope we may be able to do so, and in time to admit of our leaving Kabul in the early autumn.

I cannot express to Your Excellency how grateful I am for the support you have afforded me and for placing me in command of the troops at Kabul, and on the line of communications. I am quite sure it is right that the commander at Kabul should be supreme, and I am satisfied that had the Commander-in-Chief taken over charge at Peshawar, His Excellency would have found it necessary to have come on to Kabul where the military and political action must go hand in hand, and must be determined by events which, it is quite possible, may change very rapidly.

I shall be on the look out for Sir Donald Stewart and will assist him either in the direction of Ghazni or Kushi as he may require.

RP 101/CCCXLIII

127
Roberts to Lyall

[Manuscript telegram]   Kabul
                                               4 April 1880

Private. Think carefully over best permanent line of communication between Northern India and Kabul. I am almost inclined to recommend that we should retire altogether to Peshawar, giving up both Khyber and Kuram routes; but hesitate to place my views on paper until I hear from you that their advocacy will not compromise Gov^t. Conditions have changed so completely during last year that reasons which brought about Gandamak Treaty and question of scientific frontier no longer exist. Our strength has been felt. Afghanistan as Kingdom and formidable military power has passed away. We can return to Kabul at any moment. Kandahar must inevitably be the line by which operations against Russia will have to be carried on. Our energies should be concentrated in that direction and husbanded. If so, I am inclined under existing conditions to recommend non interference with tribes North West to reduce unhealthy Peshawar to small native garrison, to concentrate troops in healthy localities, Rawal Pindi and Attock, to bridge Indus and complete railway, and to reserve our strength for the supreme effort we must be prepared for. Please advise.

LyP 24/ff. 149–50

128
Lyall to Roberts

[Manuscript copy]   Camp Pinjor[52]
                                           16 April 1880

I joined the Viceroy here on the 14th, we go to Simla tomorrow. He is not in very good spirits, but having tendered his resignation with that of the Ministry, and being ready to stay for a time if so asked, he is composedly awaiting instructions. His Earldom is secure. Of course all larger questions, not immediate are more or less in suspense; but we have discussed the future plans and prospects of our dealing with Afghanistan, and I think HE would be quite prepared to issue definite orders for withdrawing the troops in the early autumn. It will not be a glorious conclusion; and in India the people will say, as they say already that we have found the Afghans too hard a nut to crack; but to me the argument that we shall get nought and lose much by staying, seems unanswerable. As I have written to Griffin, I don't believe in the possibility of discovering, and setting up a friendly Amir; and there seemed to be, in his speech of the 13th, a little too much about the Govt[t] selecting and approving the future Amir. I think we must rely on our position at Kandahar as affording us a reason for evacuating North Afghanistan, and leaving the people much to their own internal devices. I talked to HE about the passes to be kept in future; he still holds to the Kuram line, but I think him open to conviction, though I fear now that the final arrangements may not come in his time. I am persuaded, however, that the Liberals will do nothing hastily.

Abdurrahman appears to keep strictly in reserve. I suppose it is on the cards that he may be secretly organising, with the Maidan and Ghazni leaders, a general coalition against us; though his more probable game is to let us depart quietly, and not to compromise himself.

It is thought here that the special correspondents of the Indian newspapers are let rather deep into the political views and calculations of Kabul; I suppose it must be impossible to keep dark the drift of our policy there, but just now the situation is critical and their reports are rather full.

I am going to have a talk with General Massy. I suggested to his brother here that the General might call on me to talk about Kabul matters and I guess he will come, but he has probably said already anything he has to say about executions.

* * *

LyP 24/ff151–153

129
Foreign Secretary India to Roberts

[Printed copy]
Pinjore
16 April 1880

Precedence. Following message sent 8th April to Stewart, not clear whether repeated to you. Begins. Viceroy desires me to say that your political powers will be commensurate with your military authority and supreme over the whole area of your command but when you have assumed that command you should regard Mr Lepel Griffin as your political Chief of Staff. Ends. Letter follows.

LyP 129A/f102

130
Viceroy to Secretary of State (Cranbrook)

[Manuscript telegram]
Pinjore
16 April 1880

I respectfully submit that services rendered by Lieut. General Sir Frederick Roberts since the massacre of the Embassy deserve some special mark of favour from the Crown. Under ordinary circumstances the name of Genl Roberts would only be submitted together with names of others at close of present operations and

reward for military services would be granted by Ministers irrespective of party. But General Roberts services have been political
as well as military. You are aware he is specially obnoxious to
powerful section of Liberal party and I fear he will be made victim
of party feeling. As General Stewart is about to supersede Roberts
in chief command on juncture of his force with Kabul force fitting
occasion for rewarding Roberts is presented and I strongly urge
his claim to special reward.[53]

RP 37/96

131
Roberts to Griffin

[Printed copy]   Kabul
                             17 April 1880

I return your letter to Lord Lytton with very many thanks for letting me see it.

I need not say how gratified I am at your kind expressions about
me; in return let me tell you that no one could possibly appreciate
your services more than I do, and that my regret is that you were
not with me from the first. I feel now how invaluable your able
help would have been to me, and how much I should have bene-
fited by your advice, particularly during the first few weeks of our
arrival at Kabul.

I am personally much distressed at the idea of being superseded
by Sir Donald Stewart, having been here from the beginning I certainly hoped to see the ending of the business; but as Sir Donald is
so much my senior, I cannot of course object to serve under him in
a military capacity; moreover, I have a great personal admiration
and liking for him. With regard to political work I am prepared to
give it up altogether, if my doing so would enable you to remain
on. I have for long held the opinion that while war lasts, there
should be but one supreme authority, but the stake is so great and
your departure from Kabul would be now such a calamity that, if
you will allow me, I will write to Lord Lytton and beg of him to

place all political authority absolutely in your hands. Sir Donald Stewart would then, in virtue of his rank, command in Northern Afghanistan, but neither he nor I would have anything to say to the political duties. Pray think over this solution to the present difficulty.

RP 101/CCCLIII

132
Roberts to Viceroy

[Printed copy]   Kabul
Private   18 April 1880

Mr Griffin has shewn me a letter which he is sending by this post to Your Excellency on the subject of Sir Donald Stewart's exercising political authority over Northern and Eastern Afghanistan, as soon as he is in a position to undertake general control of all the troops now with him and at Kabul. On reading Mr Griffin's letter is struck me that the way out of the difficulty would be to propose to Your Lordship that the political and military duties should be divided, placing the former absolutely under Mr Griffin, and the latter under General Stewart; but Your Excellency will see from the enclosed letter, which I forward with Mr Griffin's permission, that he is not disposed to accept this solution of the difficulty.

Having commenced the work at Kabul, I am naturally most anxious to see it through, and it will, I am free to confess, be a very great disappointment to me to hand it over to any one else, specially now when matters are, I trust, progressing towards a satisfactory and speedy solution.

I cannot, however, urge any reason why I should not serve under Sir Donald Stewart; he is an officer for whom I have strong personal liking; and if it should be considered desirable to place the supreme authority at Kabul in his hands (keen as the disappointment would be to me) Your Lordship may be sure that I would afford him every possible assistance, and accept the situation as cheerfully as my nature would admit.

I was under the impression that the Kandahar Column would not come further in a north-easterly direction than Ghazni, and that while Sir Donald Stewart exercised, as well as the distance and difficulty of communication would allow, a general control over military affairs from that place until the time came for the two forces to retire – Sir Donald's by the Kuram route, and mine by the Khyber – matters at Kabul would be left much as they are, and that the political control and management would remain undisturbed.

I see so many arguments in favor of this procedure that I trust I shall be excused for recommending it strongly for Your Lordship's consideration. If, however, there are reasons which militate against such an arrangement, I can see no other way out of the difficulty than that which Mr Griffin is unwilling to accept.

I am, as Your Excellency is aware, strongly of opinion that, while war lasts, the supreme authority should be vested in the Military Commander, but the stake at Kabul is now so great, and the loss of Mr Griffin would, under existing circumstances, be such a calamity to the State, that I have no hesitation in recommending that, rather than lose his services, the military and political duties should be separated, Sir Donald Stewart being placed in charge of the one and Mr Griffin of the other. I am prepared to give up the political work altogether; at the same time I will most loyally afford Mr Griffin every assistance in my power.

It will, I know, be a great satisfaction to Your Lordship to learn that my relations with Mr Griffin are of the most cordial and friendly character: I thoroughly appreciate the able way in which he is carrying on the very difficult task before him, and my only regret is that I had not the benefit of his advice and counsel at an earlier period, especially during the first weeks of our arrival at Kabul.

I do not think I need say more, except to assure Your Lordship that whatever decision may now be arrived at regarding the conduct of affairs in Northern Afghanistan, my hearty co-operation may be unreservedly depended upon.

RP 101/CCCLV

133
Griffin to Roberts (Enclosure to 132)

[Printed copy] Kabul
Private Not dated

I have delayed the despatch of my letters to His Excellency and the Foreign Secretary till tomorrow. To the first I have added a postcript merely saying that I have shewn you the letter. The kind expression of your letter to me I thoroughly appreciate, and it is the greatest pleasure to find that you consider my services so valuable, but the solution of the difficulty which you suggest is not one which I could accept.

I came here with the intention of loyally placing my best work at your disposal, and I had no *arrière pensée* or any thought to evade the conditions under which I accepted the appointment.

I confess I had some misgivings as to possible friction, but from the first day your uniform kindness and full confidence in me have altogether removed the possibility of anything of the kind. I could not accept the position of taking full political authority, as it would be both contrary to the conditions on which I came here, and would suggest the doubt whether my objection to serve under General Stewart was not due to a wish, when my resignation would be inconvenient to Government, to induce them to make me supreme in political matters. Nor do I think that it would be advantageous to the public interest. The real objection to the severance of chief military and political functions is no doubt found in conflict of authority between high officials, each in his own sphere independent. Generally I think the advantage is greater than the loss, but our relations are and will remain such that I do not think any change that can be made would be beneficial, while I should lose the benefit of your intimate knowledge of affairs of the people and of the country.

I desire no change, and am perfectly content with my position. I cannot but think that His Excellency had not specially considered the difficulty and indeed danger in now making any change in the direction of political affairs, and that he will, when the matter is represented, favorably reconsider the orders which have been passed. General Stewart, whatever military exigencies may compel him to take military command, can have no title to political authority in matters of which he is ignorant, and where his interference will undoubtedly cause disaster. If you would also write to His Excellency, it would add great weight to my representations.

RP 101/CCCLV

134
Roberts to Baker

[Holograph]   Kabul
                                                 20 April 1880

Pray excuse my having kept your note to the Duke of Cambridge so long, but I am still seedy, and have been lying down the greater part of the day.

I like what you have said very much, but I would suggest your inserting somewhere, or adding at the end, words somewhat to the following effect – "There can be no possible doubt that Macpherson's and Massy's forces on the 11th Decr were together more than sufficient to dispose of any enemy that Mahomed Jan or his friends could bring against them; and that if Massy instead of engaging the enemy with his own column alone, had carried out Sir Frederick Roberts's orders (as I think everyone will admit he should have done, even if he had received no orders, seeing that his force consisted of Cavalry and Horse Artillery alone and that he was operating in a very enclosed & difficult country and over ground which in every way suited the tactics of an irregular enemy) and communicated with General Macpherson, keeping his own little column concealed until the infantry of General Macpherson appeared on the scene, the result could have been a total and complete dispersion of the Enemy who must then have fallen back on Argundeh where I was waiting for them".

NAM 7804–76/27

135
Roberts to Viceroy

[Printed telegram]   Kabul
                                                      21 April 1880

Clear the line. Personal and private. The clear-the-line telegram from the Commander-in-Chief dated yesterday has been forwarded by me to Sir Donald Stewart. I respectfully solicit that I may be empowered to tell Sir Donald Stewart not to act upon it until Mr Griffin's and my letters of the 18th instant reach Your Lordship. The minute recorded by Your Lordship dated 24th March, a copy of which reached me yesterday, defines the relations between General Stewart and myself, as I have always understood they would be when that officer reached Ghazni, and that I should be independent of him unless a concentration of our two forces took place. I can honestly say that nothing has occurred since the date of Your Lordship's minute, which would necessitate any change being made in those relations, and unless there are very urgent reasons for General Stewart's coming to Kabul, may I express an earnest hope that he will not be allowed to finish the operations which I commenced, and which I believe Your Lordship considers I have conducted loyally, and not without some credit to myself and benefit to the State? To be superseded now, when matters are, I hope, progressing towards a speedy and satisfactory conclusion, would be a mortification and a blow to my reputation that I could never recover, and which, unless I have failed in my duty, I trust Your Lordship will spare me.

RP 101/CCCLXI

136
Roberts to Viceroy

[Printed telegram]   Kabul
                                                      23 April 1880

Personal and private. I am most grateful for Your Excellency's gracious telegram of yesterday. I quite understand the position, and Your Excellency may depend on my serving cheerfully under General Stewart and helping him in every way to the best of my ability. I have not been very well lately, and may perhaps not have viewed matters in a proper healthy light.

RP 101/CCCLXII

137
Lyall to Roberts

[Holograph copy]   (?Simla)
                                                   29 April 1880

Private

I am exceedingly sorry that Stewart's going to Kabul should have caused you so much disappointment; and I can easily comprehend that it should be unpalatable to you; though I feel certain that it will not be viewed publicly, in the light in which it at first appeared to you. As you now know, the orders regarding Stewart's political powers were issued long before I saw the papers, indeed I only came upon the telegram by accident, and discovered that it had not been repeated to you. I spoke to HE about it; but he did not anticipate that the Commander in Chief would order Stewart to Kabul; nor did I see clearly how the distribution of political powers could be arranged so as not to follow the military command. But I have observed no symptoms of any general interpretation of these arrangements as derogatory to you. Most people seem to think that they naturally follow by inevitable rules of seniority. Griffin has written to me vehemently on the subject; and I must say to you privately that he seems to me on the brink of a seriously false step, when he writes about resigning etc. I mention this because he mentions that you entirely agree with him. I cannot understand in what way the change affects him so substantially or upon what public grounds he could possibly justify his resignation of a position which affords a most fortunate opening towards distinction for a man of his standing in the Service. And I think he should be cautious about writing to me in this strain, unless he really wishes me to act officially upon his declarations – but as I have a great personal esteem for him I am keeping all such letters private.

I myself have no very strong hopes of our bringing the correspondence with Abdurrahman to any very important or satisfactory conclusion. I guess that he will hold off and attempt to negotiate, and finally wait till we evacuate; and I doubt his coming to Kabul, as this might compromise his position, and look as if he had accepted the rulership of North Afghanistan only, whereas he will be very reluctant to give up his claim to the whole Kingdom of Dost Mahomed. However, we shall see – if he declines to come to Kabul, and proposes a meeting at some other place, it will be for you on the spot to decide whether this is practicable and reasonably safe for our officers; you had better settle all such details without reference, unless you desire it, to us for orders – as time presses, and Abdurrahman represents, I believe, our sole chance of making any arrangements whatever before we leave Kabul in the Autumn. The withdrawal early in Autumn is positively fixed, so far as the Gov^t in its present state of transition can fix anything. Lord Ripon leaves England very soon, I believe he will be in India towards the end of June, if not earlier; he is evidently coming out as fast as possible and all this indicates that there is to be a sharp change of policy. The Liberals are treating Lord Lytton ill; they have announced the new Viceroy without any formal intimation to Lord L that his resignation is accepted, and they are forcing him to leave India in the very hottest time of the year. I could not have credited such conduct towards a Viceroy; but this is the edge of keen party animosity. Personally, I am intensely sorry and I feel deeply for Lord Lytton, while publicly I foresee the damage that India will suffer by being thus involved in the party feuds of England. Lord Rippon [sic] is elderly, a gentleman in every sense, not supposed to be unduly vigorous, but he may be bringing out some vigorous instructions, though I don't see that he can do our Afghan proceedings much harm. Nevertheless, if we have aught to do, we should do it quickly. I hope you will write to me in all confidence regarding your own wishes and interests; and I will let you hear how politics go here. It would be a real pity if we, who had worked together all this sea of Afghan troubles, for the last 10 months, could not manage to hold on particularly now that, as I trust, we are in sight of port.

I can't get hold of General Massy but he talks – I guess he avoids me. Simla is desperately dull, as might be expected. By the way, I am very glad you telegraphed back to me, on the 27th, desiring to avoid mention to AR of Kandahar and the date of evacuation. I was overruled in Council on both points, I wanted to omit mention. As to Russia, it was sufficient to say enough to reassure him on his fear that we wished to insist on some conditions distinctly adverse to his Russian friends. But the point is, to bring him in.

LyP 24/ff160–63

138
Lytton to Roberts

[Holograph]   Simla
                                                   2 May 1880

Personal

In reply to my confidential telegram to him recommending a public recognition of your services by the late Gov^t before its surrender of office, Lord Cranbrook has informed me that the Horse Guards & War Office to which he was obliged to refer my recommendation were of opinion that an exception could not properly be made, more especially in the then circumstances of the Gov^t, to the decision previously taken by it, that all rewards for services connected with the present Afghan Campaign should be deferred till after the close of the Campaign, and the receipt of the customary official reports and recommendations from the Gov^t of India in regard thereto.

My little effort therefore, about which I was not very sanguine, has been ineffectual so far as regards the immediate attainment of

its object. But as I understand from Lord C. that my recommendation, and the fact of its having been made, will remain on record
at home, I am hopeful that it may have been not altogether fruitless. In any case, your military services throughout this second
Campaign have been so conspicuous and beyond question, that I
do not think it will be practically in the power of any Gov^t however
ungenerously disposed, to grudge or shirk the full recognition of
them. And I know that they are no less highly appreciated by the
Queen than they are by your ever cordially attached.

RP 37/99

139
Roberts to Lyall

[Holograph]   Kabul
                                               8 May 1880

Private

Thanks for your letter of the 29th April. Before this you will
know that all has been satisfactorily settled between Stewart
and Griffin. I told Griffin from the first that he would find
Stewart a most pleasant and easy man to work with, and I am
quite certain that he and Stewart will go on just as well as he
and I did.

Of course, I don't like making over the Command but it is fortunate that I have to do so to a man I like so much and know so
well as Stewart. We shall carry on together all right but I look forward to the end of the Campaign, and the more so as Lord Lytton
will not be in office much longer. The Liberals have treated his
Excellency extremely ill, I feel more than I can tell you for him,
both on public and private grounds; having to take a family home
at this season is really very serious.

I am glad it has been decided that the Army is to leave Kabul in
the Autumn, I am sure that it is the right course to pursue, and, if
in the meantime some satisfactory arrangements can be made with

Abdurrahman, our lengthened occupation of the country will not have been in vain.

Lord Ripon has made an admirable selection in Major White, 92nd Highlanders, as Military Secretary; he is quite one of the best men I know for such an appointment; clever, gentlemanly and a first rate soldier.

I see in the Papers that there is some chance of the Frontier Medal being given for this war. This will be a great disappointment to the Army. A large majority of the Force have already got the Frontier Medal, and as there is a Afghanistan Medal in existence, I have always imagined that should be given again this time. In the 1839–42 Campaigns, three, if not four, medals were given – Ghazni, Kabul, Jellalabad, and one (I think) to Pollock's force.[54] One would now be sufficient but it should be a medal that all engaged in the War should receive. I don't like troubling Lord Lytton about such matters now, but if ever the question comes up in Council, I hope you will do what you can in the matter.

* * *

The fact is that wheeled artillery is of little use in Afghanistan and now that the screw gun battery has arrived we can well spare a horsed battery.

Before our next campaign, we must organise more mountain batteries, they are cheaper and more efficient in a country like this.

LyP 24/ff164–66

140
Roberts to Dillon

[Printed copy – Private] Camp Saidabad, near Kabul
10 May 1880

I want you kindly to interest yourself about the medal to be given for this campaign. A local Indian paper states that the "Frontier Medal" will be bestowed with clasps for Ali Musjid, Peiwar Kotal and Kabul. I trust I may be excused for saying that it will be a great disappointment to the army if this is the case, especially to the Native portion, a large majority of whom are already in possession of that medal.[55]

Native soldiers value medals much, as you who have been so long in India probably know; they hand them down as heirlooms, and their descendants consider that the possession of a medal which belonged to their father or grandfather fairly entitles them to be looked upon as faithful servants of the Sirkar.

It is expressly desirable that the Native Army should at the present time, be made as popular as possible, so that men who have done good service may clearly understand that it is to their advantage to remain in the ranks, and that recruits may be induced to come forward and fill up the many gaps which now exist in almost every regiment. After every campaign a certain number of sepoys are inclined to take their discharge, but I believe that with judicious treatment and a liberal amount of leave, many of them could be kept with their regiments. All ranks are in good heart now, and very proud of their doings, and well they may be, for never before have Native troops done better or more loyal service.

I crossed the Shutar Gardan last September with sundry misgivings as to the way in which the Pathans with this Force would behave, but even they, with scarcely an exception, have been thoroughly loyal, and have fought for us as well as the Sikhs and the Goorkhas have. This is very remarkable when we consider the fanatical temperament of Pathans generally, and the manner in which their religious feelings are so easily worked upon by Moollas and others.

Many of the Native troops will have been absent from India for two years by the time this war is over, and those who have seen service on the frontier before and who may not be entitled to one of the clasps now to be given, will return to India without any recognition of their services in the shape of a medal. It is to my mind a matter of such considerable importance that I venture to trouble you with this letter, and would ask you, if an opportunity offers, to place it before the Duke of Cambridge. I am sure that His Royal Highness will never regret giving the subject very careful consideration.

I would have written to you before about this matter, but knowing that a medal for the first Afghan War is in existence, I never doubted but that it would be given for the present war, and this feeling was shared, I believe, by nearly every one under my command, all of whom are much concerned at the statement in the papers . . .

RP 101/CCCLXXX

141
Roberts to Lyall

[Printed copy]   Kabul
                                                 12 May 1880

No. 11–K–L

With reference to the wish expressed by you when at Kabul last March, I have prepared a memorandum regarding the best line of communications connecting India with Afghanistan.[56] I now beg to submit the same for the consideration of His Excellency the Viceroy and Governor-General in Council.

2. His Lordship will observe that while I advocate the exclusion of Afghan control over the whole of the country acquired by the provisions of the Treaty of Gandamak, I am in favor of the withdrawal of our troops to the limits of the frontier held by us previous to the present campaign excepting in the direction of Kandahar.

3. My reasons for this are explained in considerable length in the memorandum: they are briefly as follows:-
I. – the altered conditions of Northern Afghanistan since operations commenced, consequent on the overthrow of the Amir's power.
II. – the announced intention to maintain a British garrison permanently at Kandahar.

4. We are thus committed to the communication with Kandahar being secured, and are in my opinion relieved from the necessity of incurring military responsibility in the direction of the Khyber or Kuram.

RP 101/CCCLXXXIV

142
Roberts to Viceroy

[Printed copy]   Kabul
                                                     22 May 1880

Private

I am quite ashamed to trouble Your Excellency with my own personal matters at a time like this, but when Your Lordship has leisure I shall be very grateful if you would advise me as to whether it would be desirable for me to submit an application for the appointment of Secretary to the Government of India in the Military Department. I understand that Colonel Allen Johnson does not care to remain and would like to be relieved at the end of the present Simla season.

   My objections to applying are –
(1) I have never yet directly or indirectly asked for any appointment since I entered the service.

(2) My wish is to go home as soon as the campaign is over, and were I to be appointed Secretary to the Government, I could not accept it unless I were permitted to take leave as soon as a *locum tenens* could be found; certainly not later than February or March 1881. I have been more than 11 years away from England, and am sure that I could not undertake steady desk work for any length of time without having at least a year's rest.

   My reasons for wanting the appointment are –
(1) There are very few appointments in India open to an officer of

my rank, and I do not think I could exist in command of an ordinary division of the army in time of peace, even if His Excellency, the Commander-in-Chief would nominate me for one, which is doubtful.

(2) I am absolutely dependent on the service, and could not possibly manage, except for a short time, as an unemployed Major-General.

(3) I think I could be useful to the State in the position of Military Secretary, especially if the proposals of the Army Commission are likely to be taken up. Few officers know the army, or the officers of the army better than I do, and I fear that, unless some changes are in the first instance made in the personnel of the Military Department, considerable difficulty will be experienced in getting the recommendations of the Commission carried out. My ambition is to be Member of Council or to command one of the Army Corps, should they ever be formed, but I fear that for some time to come the Horse Guards and India Office authorities would think me too junior in rank, and perhaps *not old enough!* for such a command.

I am very anxious to hear whether my views about the permanent line of communication between the North-West Frontier of India and Kabul meet with Your Lordship's approval; if they do not, I need not say that the memorandum which I sent privately to Mr Lyall on the 12th instant will never see light in an official form.

RP 101/CCCLXXXVI

143
Roberts to Lyall

[Printed copy – Private]   Camp in Logar Valley, near Kabul
23 May 1880

I am, I daresay, unnecessarily anxious lest the Viceroy should make over office to his successor without placing on record the policy by which the Government of India has been guided in carrying on the Afghan War up to the present date, and the determination it had come to of withdrawing the army from Northern and Eastern Afghanistan during the next few months, or even sooner, should it be found possible to make satisfactory terms with Abdur Rahman.

Lord Lytton has no doubt thought of the value such a state paper would be to him and his party, and very possibly has already prepared it: but should His Excellency not have done so, and you see no objection, would you kindly let my idea be known to the Viceroy?

It is quite evident that the Liberals will work exactly on the same lines as the late Ministry have been doing, but unless this is clearly shown, any success that may be achieved with Abdur Rahman, or any credit that may be due on account of an early retirement from the country will be claimed by the Liberals.

If the views contained in the memorandum which I sent to you on the 12th instant meet with Lord Lytton's approval, and His Excellency feels himself able to advocate both the Kuram and Khyber routes being henceforth left without *military* control, this would take the wind out of the sails of the Liberals, and would conclusively prove the wisdom and success of Lord Lytton's Afghan policy.

RP 101/CCCLXXXVII

144
Viceroy to Roberts

[Manuscript telegram]   Simla
                                          3 June 1880

Personal. Your telegram of the second. I deeply sympathise but as your sincere friend most strongly urge you not to leave your post till close of war which will be I trust not later than October. I feel sure your premature retirement would be generally misinterpreted to your detriment.

RP 37/105

145
Roberts to Viceroy

[Printed copy]   Kabul
Private   4 June 1880

I am greatly obliged for Your Excellency's cypher telegram of yester-day in reply to mine soliciting your approval to my leaving Kabul.

I now trouble you with these few lines in further explanation of my desire to get away.

After promising Your Lordship that I would serve on, and assist Sir Donald Stewart to the best of my ability, I was determined to try and do so, but I find the position so irksome and the work so uninteresting that I long to be off. Moreover, I am not well, and the doctors urge me to go.

If I could be of the slightest use to Your Lordship I would stay at all hazards, but the time for that has now passed; I am not required here and can get no credit by remaining; the contrary may perhaps be the case.

I thought, at first, that as a soldier I was bound to see the war out, and to accept any position while service was going on, how-ever distasteful it might be; but I do not think this is expected of me; my departure would be accounted for by a medical certificate, which would, I trust, prevent the public being under any wrong impression as to the reason of my leaving the force.

The troops may, and probably will, be withdrawn in October, but I much fear that between this and then no satisfactory arrangement will have been made for the future government of the country. We shall have to go away, either without putting up any ruler, or being satisfied with one who would in all probability be displaced as soon as our backs are turned.

However, I will not trouble Your Excellency with my political forebodings. I have explained fully my reasons for wishing to leave Kabul. If Your Lordship will sanction my doing so I shall be very grateful; if you still think that I should remain I will do so, and will make up my mind to stay till the end of the war, unless my health should break down in the meantime . . .

RP 101/CCCXCIII

146
Roberts to Dillon

[Printed copy – Private] Kabul
9 June 1880

Many thanks for your few lines of the 13th May, received last evening – 26 days from London to Kabul!

I hoped to have sent you with this a memorandum giving all the information you wanted about the Massy case, but it cannot be copied in time for today's post, and I am afraid that tomorrow's will miss the mail at Bombay. However, I shall risk it, and it is possible that it may reach you with this. I have confined my remarks strictly to the manner in which General Massy exercised his command while with this force, and I trust that His Royal Highness will consider that I have not said anything more than the occasion requires.

The memorandum will be addressed to you, but I am writing to W.K. Elles[57] to have it printed for me, as I cannot expect people will take the trouble to read it in manuscript. When printed, Elles will consult you as to its distribution. Pray decide whether copies should be sent to the clubs and papers, or whether it should be treated as an official document.

My object is to satisfy His Royal Highness –
(1) that General Massy has been treated most leniently;
(2) that my forces were not disposed in a rash manner;
(3) that I had every reason to expect success; and
(4) that Sherpur was never in danger.

I really care little what the press says, and am a firm believer in the saying that "Truth is seldom insulted with impunity". So that if it is the wish of the Duke of Cambridge that the memorandum should be deposited in the archives of the Horse Guards, please do not think that I shall be disappointed.

I propose sending a copy of the memorandum, together with a copy of this letter, to the Adjutant-General in India for the infor-

mation of Sir Frederick Haines. The whole business is, as I have
said, most distasteful to me, and I hope I have now finished with
it. . .

RP 101/CCCXCV

147
Roberts to Lyall

[Printed copy]   Kabul
                                        7 July 1880

Stewart has written to the Viceroy recommending that we should
commence withdrawing from Kabul soon after Abdul Rahman
crosses the Hindu Kush and comes within easy distance of the
capital.

I hope this proposal will receive your support.

The people are beginning to get very restless and excited, not
on our account, or because the hostile feeling against us has
increased, but in consequence of the near approach of Abdul
Rahman. The Sher Ali faction is consolidating itself, and it is
quite evident that on, or soon after Abdul Rahman's arrival in
Kabul, there will be a struggle between him and the opposition
party.

Now it is most desirable we should be away before this struggle
takes place, and it seems to me also desirable that we should not be
committed to Abdul Rahman until he has shown that he is able to
maintain himself as Amir.

Having encouraged him to leave Badakshan, and cross the
Hindu Kush, we cannot, of course, throw him over, but I don't
think there is any occasion for us to do more, at the present time,
than let him take possession of Sherpur, and give him the guns we
intend leaving behind.

There is doubtless a strong feeling against Abdul Rahman.
Many think that his advent will be followed by a Russian occupation of Afghanistan. A Tajik, named Abdul Kadir, who was for
some months last winter acting as Governor of Ghazni, sent me a

SEPTEMBER 1879 TO OCTOBER 1880

message a day or two ago, saying that the Afghans would infinitely prefer being our riyots to subjects of Russia, and that, if there was the slightest chance of the Russians coming, they hoped we would not leave the country. That we were guided by a book as the Muhammadans were; that we owned the existence of a Prophet as they did; and that we respected their women and children. The Russians, he understood, had no book, owned to no Prophet, and if they came to Afghanistan, there would be no hope for their families. It was a curious communication, but interesting as a sign of the times, and, as I believe, fairly representing the feelings of the people.

* * *

LyP 24/f176

148
Roberts to Adjutant-General India

[Printed telegram]   Kabul
                                          30 July 1880[58]

Personal and secret. I strongly recommend that a force be sent from this to Kandahar. Stewart has organized a very complete one consisting of nine regiments of infantry, three of cavalry, and three mountain batteries. This will suffice to overcome all opposition *en route* it will have the best possible effect on the country, and will be ready to go anywhere on reaching Kandahar, being fully equipped in all respects. He proposes sending me in command.

I am sure that but few Bombay regiments are able to cope with Afghans, and once the Kabul Force leaves this country, the chance of sending a thoroughly reliable and well-equipped column will be lost. The movement of the remainder of the Kabul troops towards India should be simultaneous with the advance of my division towards Kandahar, it being most desirable to limit the area of our responsibilities as soon as possible. At the same time it is imperative that we should now show our strength throughout Afghanistan. The withdrawal, under existing circumstances, of the whole force from Kabul to India would certainly be misunderstood, both in Afghanistan and elsewhere. You need have no fears about my division. It can take care of itself, and will reach Kandahar under the month. I will answer for the loyalty and good feeling of the Native portion, and would propose to inform them that as soon as matters have been satisfactorily settled at Kandahar, they will be sent straight back to India. Show this to Lyall.

RP 101/CCCCXIX

149
Lyall to Roberts

[Printed copy]   Simla
                                          4 August 1880

Greaves showed me your telegram to him [148]; and I at once did all in my power to further your desire to command the division for Kandahar, as I have the fullest confidence that you are the man for this business; and a finer command, or a more important expedition, no General need ask for.

In regard to political matters, you will understand, from the official letter which I am sending, that the best line to take is to have nothing to do with matters not directly concerned with your military expedition. The word 'political' has, in my opinion, been very troublesome to us in Afghanistan, and a military commander exercises, as such, a very wide discretion in dealing with all matters which concern his troops. Whatever you do, do as a military commander in a hostile country, not out of any separate authority or jurisdiction whatsoever; and above all things avoid political engagements or declarations.

You may always rely on my doing my best to support you; and I greatly hope to hear from you by telegraph that you have received this note, and the letter which the Viceroy wrote to you yesterday.

We have nothing else to do in Afghanistan beyond settling accounts with Ayub, and I know that, if you get a chance, you will wipe off all his score for us.

Poor Burrows seems to have blundered; but it was all wrong to leave him out on the Helmand facing that army of Ayub's and all the ghazis, with a set of raw Bombay troops. I felt what was coming, and kept recurring to Windham's affair at Cawnpoor in 1857, when we got a thrashing from a strong body of regulars with good artillery, aided by a crowd of irregulars and badmashes.[59] I wanted the Bombay people at Kandahar to concentrate at all hazards, and to withdraw from Kelat-i-Ghilzai, but most people were in a hurry to disperse Ayub.

LyP 24/f180

150
Roberts to Adjutant-General, India

[Printed copy]   Kabul
                                                   6 August 1880

Will you kindly order two or three Madras and Bombay Army Lists, latest edition, also Bengal ones, to be sent to meet me at Kandahar.[60]

The force will be ready this evening; tomorrow we make a short march, and afterwards will push on as fast as possible. I have magnificent troops and first rate commanders, so we ought to do well.

You will, of course, have instructions waiting for me at Kandahar; it is absolutely necessary, in my opinion, that Ayub should be punished, if he has fallen back towards Herat. I hope I shall be authorized to go as far as Farrah after him. With my troops I am quite sure of not getting into trouble. As soon as the business is *really* over the Bengal Troops should be allowed to return to India, but they would be as much disappointed as I should be, were they to be ordered away from Kandahar until matters have been properly settled.

On reaching Kandahar I shall be senior officer; please have this

explained to General Primrose,[61] and see that I am placed in political as well as military charge. I know St John[62] well and like him
much. We are sure to get on, but I will never again accept a command in the field with any division of authority, as there practically has been here since the arrival of Mr Griffin. I am writing to
Mr Lyall on this subject.

RP 101/CCCCXXI

151
Roberts to Lyall

[Printed copy]   Kabul
                                                  6 August 1880

I have received from Sir Donald Stewart a copy of your telegram
of the 5th instant, conveying political instructions regarding the
march of the troops under my command to Kandahar.

The instructions will be strictly attended to.

I wish, however, to make the following remarks which I shall be
obliged by your submitting to His Excellency the Viceroy.

When I accepted the command of the Kabul Field Force last
September it was on the understanding that I was to be supreme
in political, as well as military matters. This position *outwardly* I
maintained until the arrival of Sir Donald Stewart, who relieved
me by virtue of his superior rank.

I use the expression "outwardly" for practically after the
arrival of Mr Griffin, I was not supreme in political affairs. His
advent caused a division of authority which to my mind is most
dangerous whilst an enemy's country is in military occupation.
I promised Lord Lytton that there should be no friction, and
that nothing should occur on my part which could possibly
cause an interruption of the public service. This promise I fulfilled most scrupulously; at the same time I determined that
nothing should ever induce me again to accept a military command on service unless I was politically supreme. It is unnecessary for me to give my reasons in this letter. I will only support

them by saying that Sir Donald Stewart, as you know, holds the same opinion.

Under existing circumstances it is not possible for me now to make any reference to the Government of India; my duty is clear, to take command of the troops placed at my disposal, and proceed to Kandahar with the least possible delay, and to carry out any instructions I may receive to that end. As soon as I have accomplished the task entrusted to me, I must beg that I may be allowed to resign my command unless the Government of India think proper to place me in supreme political, as well as military, charge. My actual experience of the situation since Mr Griffin has come to Kabul has satisfied me that without this I could not carry on my work with satisfaction to myself, or with benefit to the State.

Lieutenant-Colonel St John is a personal friend of mine, and his great local knowledge will be of the utmost value to me, but of course it would not do if he were permitted in any way to interfere with my perfect freedom of action as regards the object of the expedition. I quite understand that the Government do not wish me to take any part in the domestic affairs of the Kandahar State, but otherwise Colonel St John's relations towards me should be the same as they were towards General Stewart when that officer commanded at Kandahar.

It is too late now for me to receive an answer to this, even by telegram, before I leave Kabul, but I trust that you will have instructions sent to meet me *via* Kandahar.

RP 101/CCCCXXII

152
Lyall to Roberts

[Manuscript telegram marked 'Precedence']   Simla
                                              7 August 1880

Private. Your political instructions give you full latitude of action for the purpose of your military expedition, and the political officers in your camp are of course subordinate to you. I strongly recommend no further questioning on subject of instructions, and reliance on my support here, but do nothing, especially in South Afghanistan except upon military grounds and for military objects.

LyP 24/f182

153
Lyall to Roberts

[Printed copy]   Simla
                                                  20 August 1880

I inclose a letter for you from the Viceroy. I hope my demi-official replies to your letters of the 6th and 8th August from Kabul about your political authority will have reached you. It is not possible to draw fine distinctions in the matter, but whenever I have half an hour's talk with you, I hope to convince you that the present arrangement is by far the best and simplest way of giving you complete authority to do anything you think fit on military grounds. The Government does not want any one to hold any important political powers – i.e. powers to act in politics without reference to the Government – in South Afghanistan just now; the Viceroy would not hear of Primrose assuming such powers.

We all trust most fervently that you will get first to Kandahar or, better, within striking distance of Ayub. We have heard rumours that he has been accompanied from Herat by European officers, anyhow his troops were skilfully handled when he defeated Burrows.

I suppose I need not remind you that some extra vigilance in keeping your troops in order, and in forestalling by precautions any possibility of the recurrence of the stories about ill-treatment of wounded and prisoners by our soldiers,[63] would not be thrown away. I do not write more, as this may be long in reaching you – believe in our great anxiety for your success. I wish I felt as confident in the Kandahar defence as I do in your attack, but our troops sit cooped up ingloriously, and a bold and cunning enemy might do them a mischief.

LyP 24/f184

154
Ayub Khan to Roberts

[Printed translation]   Kandahar
                                         19th Ramazan 1297H

May this letter find you in perfect health and strength. After
which be it known to you I have at all times regarded the English
Government with friendship and still continue so to regard it. I
have not altered in this. Before this time you despatched to me
from Kabul several letters by the hand of Sardar Abdul Salam
Khan but these were seized in Kandahar and were not allowed to
be forwarded to me.[64] They kept your letters and sent on others
of their own. I too on several occasions made known my friendship but received no fitting reply until such time as the news
reached me that Sardar Sher Ali Khan was marching on Herat
and had arrived at Girishk. I marched and came to Farah. I there
received news that troops had been sent to Washir. I left Farah
and when I reached Washir the army of Sardar Sher Ali Khan[65]
retired and at Girishk they all dispersed. After that I was
informed that the English had halted at Kushk-i-Nakhud. On
the receipt of this news, I thought it well that my troops should
not take the road by Kushk-i-Kakhud but should proceed by that
of Maiwand, and I hoped that the English might show me
friendship. Early in the morning when my troops were marching
by Maiwand, in pursuance of my orders, in the neighbourhood
of Maiwand the English army came and began to fight. What
was pre-ordained came to pass. I have given you the particulars
and this is the real truth. On no account will I relinquish the
friendship of the English Government. If the Government have
been informed in any other sense the real truth is what I have
written. I now write to you in this friendly manner that you may
write and tell me in a friendly way what you think is the best
course for me to pursue, and these affairs may be settled in an
amicable manner.

PP (HoC), 1880, LIII, C–2736, 34, enc. 2.

155
Roberts to Ayub Khan

[Printed copy]   Robat
                                                    29 August 1880

In answer to your letter asking my advice, I can only recommend
you to send in the prisoners in your power to Kandahar, and submit yourself unconditionally to the British Government.

PP (HoC), 1880, LIII C–2736, 34, enc. 3

156
Roberts to Viceroy

[Printed telegram]   Kandahar
                                          1 September 1880 (6 p.m.)

Clear the line. Ayub Khan's army was today defeated and completely dispersed with, I hope, comparatively slight loss on our
side; his camp was captured, the two lost guns of E–B Royal Horse
Artillery were recovered, and several wheeled guns of various calibre fell to the splendid infantry of this force: the cavalry are still in
pursuit. Our casualties are Captain Straton, 22nd Regiment,
Killed; 72nd Highlanders, – Lieutenant-Colonel Brownlow,
Captain Frome killed, Captain Murray and Lieutenant Monro
wounded, 7 men killed, 18 wounded; 92nd Highlanders –
Lieutenants Menzies and Donald Stewart wounded, 11 men killed
and 39 wounded; Lieutenant-Colonel Battye, 2nd Goorkhas, and
Major Slater, 2nd Sikhs wounded.[66] It is at present impossible to
ascertain the casualties amongst the Native troops, but I have no
reason to believe they are excessive; full details will be telegraphed
tomorrow. The quite recently murdered remains of Lieutenant
MacLaine, Royal Horse Artillery, were found on the arrival of the
British troops in Ayub Khan's camp.[67] Ayub Khan is supposed to
have fled towards Herat.

RP 101/CCCCXLV

157
Viceroy (Lord Ripon) to Roberts

[Holograph]   Simla
                                              6 September 1880

* * *

And now before I conclude, I must say a few words upon a matter, about which your wishes have only just come to my knowledge after a decision had been taken which is, I understand, inconsistent with them.

I allude to your desire to retain for the present the command of the Punjab Frontier Force. It was represented to me sometime ago by the Military Department that that post could not be held in accordance with the Regulations by a General Officer and that consequently when you became a substantive Major General in Dec^r/78, the appointment ought to have been declared vacant and another officer appointed. This, it appears, was overlooked at the time, but when attention was drawn to it, it seemed to me that I had no alternative but to regard the Command as vacant and to appoint another officer to it which I accordingly did, selecting Colonel Kennedy[68] for that purpose. The matter has therefore gone too far for the steps taken to be recalled even if the regulations would permit that to be done – and I am consequently, I am sorry to say, only in a position to express my regret, and I do so most sincerely, that I am unable to forward what I now understand to be your wishes upon this subject.

I send you this explanation at once because it would be very painful to me that you should think for a moment that, after such services as you have just rendered to the Government, I was indifferent to your wishes or inclined lightly to disregard them.

RP 63/6

158
Viceroy to Roberts

[Holograph]   Simla
                                             6 September 1880

<u>Confidential</u>

I have just directed Mr Lyall to send you a telegram investing you
with the chief political authority in Southern Afghanistan, and I
therefore write now to give you a general outline of my views upon
the political situation in that part of the world, so far as my imper-
fect information as to the present state of affairs there enables me
to form any judgement upon it – But I must premise by saying
that you must not regard my private letters as a substitute for official correspondence; all orders issued to the officers of the
Government ought to be matter of record, and the true use of private communications is to elicit a free interchange of views
between the Viceroy and those who are acting confidentially under
him –

I need not point out to you that the invasion of Ayub Khan, the
mutiny of the Wali's army, the active support given to the enemy
in so many parts of the province of Kandahar, and the proof which
is thus afforded of the very small hold, which Sher Ali has upon
the country, renders necessary a reconsideration of our whole
position.

I have always held and I hold still that we are bound to observe
the most scrupulous good faith towards Sher Ali; but our engagements to support him on the throne were obviously made in the
belief that he had at all events some substantive position of his
own, and that there was a fair hope that he would be able within a
reasonable time to "consolidate his powers" to use the expression
employed in Lord Lytton's letter of recognition. After what has
happened lately it seems to me very difficult to suppose that he
has any powers of his own to consolidate or that he is really more
than a man of straw, whose political existence depends entirely
upon the presence of our troops.

Under these circumstances it is evident that it is of first importance that the most perfect freedom should be preserved to the Government with regard to the measures which they may ultimately think it right to adopt, and I trust therefore that you will carefully avoid anything calculated to commit us in any way. The proverbial three courses lie before us; we may either annex the country; or we may give our support to Sher Ali or to some other nominee of our own; or we may restore the Province to the Ameer of Kabul. For the present it should be your endeavour to leave it perfectly open to us, as far as depends upon you, to adopt whichever of these courses we may prefer. The subject has not yet been fully discussed in Council and I am not therefore in a position to say what our decision may be; but I have little doubt that Her Majesty's Government would be glad to be relieved, if it can be properly done, of the burden involved in the prolonged maintenance of a British Force at Kandahar.

I propose to send Mr Lyall very shortly upon a special mission to Kandahar in order that he may inform himself fully of the state of political affairs there and may be able on his return to furnish me with a detailed report upon them; until that report has been received and considered the position must be regarded as entirely provisional, and the liberty of action of the Government carefully preserved. The instructions contained in Mr Lyall's letter to Sir D. Stewart of the 3rd August, to which I request you strictly to conform, will put you in possession of the general principles by which the Government wish you to be guided. [not printed]

The avoidance of all entangling engagements, a considerate treatment of the population of the people of the country, an absence of all unnecessary severity, and the observance of the utmost possible neutrality in the internal affairs of the Province until the decision of the Government as to the arrangements to be made for the future has been pronounced, are the objects which you should keep steadily in view, and which you should regard as the basis of the policy, which it is our wish that you should follow. I have entire confidence that you will appreciate and will adhere to them.

I am aware that you are naturally anxious now that the military duty entrusted to you has been so admirably performed, to bring your troops back to India as soon as possible. You may rely upon it that your wishes in this respect will be consulted to the utmost but I am sure that I may count upon your being ready to remain at Kandahar as long as the exigencies of the public service require that you should do so.

I have only to add in conclusion that I beg you to write me fully and frankly, and to express your views to me without reserve.

RP 63/13

159
The Queen to Roberts

[Holograph]   Balmoral
                                                9 September 1880

The Queen Empress is anxious to express personally to Sir F. Roberts her high sense of the very great service he has rendered to his Sovereign & country by his grand march & brilliant victory which came at a very critical time.

The Queen would also wish to thank him and all the brave officers & men under his command & express her deep sympathy with & anxiety for the wounded as well as her sorrow for those of her gallant soldiers who fell "for Queen & Country'. The fate of Lieutenant Maclaine has given all a thrill of horror.

She trusts that the health of Sir F. Roberts & all her troops will continue good & that success may attend them till the blessings of peace are restored.

This is the sincere & daily prayer of the Queen Empress.

RP 65/2

160
Roberts to Adjutant-General India

[Printed telegram]   Chaman
                                                10 September 1880

Please inform the Commander-in-Chief that the state of my health necessitated my leaving Kandahar temporarily.[69] I have passed the Medical Board, and the Doctors urge my going home at once. Change to Pishin will no doubt be beneficial and enable me to remain until October, but I shall esteem it a favor if His Excellency will arrange for my being relieved then, as I feel that I could not carry on this high and responsible command with satisfaction to myself. I much regret having to make this application so soon after His Excellency has been pleased to appoint me to the command of the troops in Southern Afghanistan, but my health has been failing for some time past.

RP 101/CCCCLVIII

161
Viceroy to Roberts

[Telegram]   Simla
                                                10 September 1880

Clear the line. With great pleasure I inform you that the Queen has created you a GCB and that you are to succeed Chamberlain as Commander in Chief Madras. Accept my hearty congratulations on this well deserved recognition of your eminent services. Stewart succeeds Johnson as Military Member of Council.[70]

RP 63/16

162
Viceroy to Roberts

[Manuscript telegram]   Simla
                                          10 September 1880

Clear the line. Government wish for your opinion as to whether it
is necessary on military grounds for us to maintain permanently a
British Force at Kandahar or whether you might retire from that
advanced position at or in advance of Quetta holding pass Kojak
Amrand range or to within old Scinde Frontier. If you approve
retiring from Kandahar state which of the latter alternatives you
prefer. Reply by telegram.

RP 63/17

163
Roberts to Viceroy

[Printed telegram]   Camp Gatai
                                          13 September 1880

Your Excellency's clear-the-line message of 10th instant. On military grounds I am in favor of maintaining a British Force at
Kandahar, which is a position of the greatest strategic value; there
is no place short of Kandahar which possesses the same advantages.

It is of course essential that a post so far advanced should be
provided with a sufficient and properly constituted garrison
able to maintain itself and also to act on the offensive. With a
good commander and efficient troops, the force need not be
larger than the district could without difficulty support. The
long line of communication is at present no doubt a cause of
anxiety, but with proper management and time this would right
itself.

RP 101/CCCCLIX

164
Roberts to Lyall

[Printed copy – Private]　　　　　　　　　　Chaman
14 September 1880
(23rd Anniversary of the Assault of Delhi)

I do not know how my suggestion will be received that a special medal should be given to the troops who marched from Kabul to Kandahar; if favourably, perhaps the idea of my Second-in-Command, General Ross, may also find acceptance, that the medal should be in the form of a gun metal star. There is some reason in General Ross' proposal.[71]

Perhaps it was wrong of me to moot the subject, but I did so in the fulness of my heart, knowing that no other reward would be so acceptable to the gallant troops I am so proud to command. When we reached Kandahar, they were just at that pitch of enthusiasm and determination, that had Ayub's army been composed of three-fourths Russians, I should have attacked him with perfect confidence. Nothing could have stopped the gallant fellows. Had they wavered or hesitated, our loss would have been much heavier; everything, but pluck, was in favor of the enemy, but our success was a certainty; anything to the contrary never entered into my thoughts, though I was prepared for a more stubborn resistance, if necessary.

All is going on well, even in the matter of forage and supplies, on the line of communication. I am not in despair. Things do not look bright at present, but I am glad I came here to see and judge for myself. At Kandahar itself I have no immediate anxiety, but it will not do to leave too many troops there for long or we shall suffer later on – if we stay there.

Shall we?

RP 101/CCCCLXIII

165
Roberts to Adjutant-General India

[Printed copy] Camp Gulistan
18 September 1880

No. 41–Miscellaneous

In obedience to Adjutant General telegram of the 4th
September, which reached me at Kandahar on the 7th instant, I
have the honor to submit the following remarks regarding the military situation at Kandahar at the time of my arrival.

2. Previous to the force under my command reaching Khelat-i-
Ghilzai, the investment of the town and citadel in occupation by
the troops under the command of Lieutenant-General Primrose
C.S.I. was complete. At that time, however, Sirdar Mahomed
Ayub Khan gave up the ground to the west of the city, which his
army had held since the beginning of August, and massed his
troops behind the Baba Wali Pass, in the defensive position from
which he was dislodged on the 1st September; simultaneously, the
villages encircling Kandahar were relinquished, and the garrison
were free to move outside the walls.

3. On the 27th August heliographic communication was opened
with the garrison from Robat, twenty miles distant, and
Lieutenant-Colonel St John rode into the cavalry camp, escorted
by a squadron of the Poona Horse.

4. On the 31st August, I was met by Lieutenant-General Primrose
and a large number of the officers of the garrison, when I was riding into Kandahar. On that occasion, and subsequently, I could
not help being struck by the tone of depression that pervaded the
accounts of their situation, which the officers of the garrison
themselves gave; these indicated a want of confidence in their ability to resist an assault if such had been made, and represented that
the morale of the larger proportion of the troops, already seriously
affected by the defeat at Maiwand and the subsequent disastrous

retreat, had, after the sortie of the 16th August, fallen very low.[72] I allude more particularly to the native soldiers of the garrison; one and all, however, bore testimony to the unfailing good behaviour and creditable bearing of the men of the Royal Artillery and of the Bombay Sappers, not only during the investment, but in the very trying time of the retreat from Maiwand.

5. Although the extent of the city wall, which was, of necessity, included within the defences held by the garrison, demanded a large number of men for its protection, the height and thickness of the walls themselves made it almost impossible for an assault to be attempted. It is true that scaling ladders had been prepared by the enemy, and an idea gained ground that an assault would be made, but in my opinion such an attempt could only have been disastrous to the assailants if the defenders were at all determined in the resistance offered.

6. The system of defence adopted by Lieutenant-General Primrose was, I think, generally satisfactory, although the formation of a continuous wire entanglement along the base of the walls appeared unnecessary, and the elaborate precautions taken for securing the gates &c were calculated to reduce the confidence of the garrison in their ability to resist attack by offensive action, which should at all times have been possible for so large a body of troops as that which remained under Lieutenant-General Primrose's command. I believe I am absolutely correct in stating that, until within two days of the arrival of the relieving force, the British flag had not been hoisted, – a significant omission which is much to be regretted.

7. I attach notes regarding the actual condition of the garrison, their state of health, the amount of supplies available &c., which have been furnished at my request by Lieutenant-General Primrose.

8. The object of, and reasons for, the sortie of the 16th August, which was attended by such terrible loss of life on our side, are

best known to Lieutenant-General Primrose; and the effect, how-ever, of this reverse upon the garrison was very apparent. An examination of the village of Deh Hajji, and enquiry made unoffi-cially could only lead to the conclusion that the sortie had been made without sufficient reason.

9. It is impossible to conclude without recording my opinion that, in physique and fighting power, the Bombay sepoy generally is unfit for service in Afghanistan. The people in the neighbourhood of Kandahar speak of them with open contempt, and many, I understand, predicted that on the departure of the Bengal troops, in April last, troubles would arrive.[73]
[Attached three appendices (1) on supplies, labelled Statement A, (2) on sick and wounded, labelled Statement B, (3) a description of the Kandahar defences, all tending to show that the garrison had been in no real difficulty]

LP 126/ff161–63

166
Roberts to Adjutant-General India

[Printed telegram]   Segei
No. 43L   20 September 1880

In continuation of my confidential telegram of date, I have the honour to submit, for information and for the orders of His Excellency the Commander-in-Chief in India, the proceedings of a Court of Enquiry assembled at Kandahar to consider certain let-ters written by Brigadiers General Burrows and Nuttall, regarding the behaviour during the action at Maiwand and the subsequent retreat of Lieutenant Colonel Malcolmson, C.B., Commanding 3rd Scinde Horse, and Major Currie, Commanding the 3rd Bombay Light Cavalry.[74]

2. These leters were submitted to me by Lieutenant-General Primrose, C.B., on the 7th September, when he visited me by

appointment; they had, however, been in his possession since the beginning of August.

3. I pointed out to Lieutenant-General Primrose the serious difficulty created by his failure to take action in the matter at an earlier date, and feeling it impossible to arrive at any decision regarding the very grave imputations made against the character and reputation of the two officers previously named, I at once directed the assembly of a Court of Enquiry, naming Major General Phayre, C.B., as President.

4. It will be observed that Lieutenant Colonel Malcolmson and Major Currie have been allowed to remain in command of their respective regiments till now, and that Lieutenant Colonel Malcolmson was wounded in the sortie of the 16th August; this is very much to be regretted. The very decided opinion expressed by the Court of Enquiry has left me, however, no option in the matter; I have therefore solicited the approval of His Excellency to my ordering Lieutenant Colonel Malcolmson and Major Currie to be suspended from the command of their regiments and from military duty, until His Excellency's orders upon the proceedings now forwarded can be received.

5. These proceedings have been received direct from Major General Phayre, C.B., the President, and have not been remarked on by Lieutenant-General Primrose. Since they were despatched from Kandahar, Major-General Phayre has telegraphed that a further statement regarding this matter has been forwarded. As however the conclusion arrived at by the Court in the proceedings terminated on the 16th instant leaves no doubt upon the subject, I have at once represented the case. The further statement will be forwarded immediately it is received.

HP 38/pp 126–27

167
Haines to Roberts[75]

[Manuscript copy]   Simla
Private   22 September 1880

I have telegraphed my congratulations to you on the successful accomplishment of your most brilliant march and on the equally brilliant victory you gained as a finale to it, but I cannot refrain from telling you by letter how deeply indebted I feel to you for the masterly and energetic manner in which you have given effect to the views and intentions held by the Government of India and by myself when we despatched you on your adventurous march to Kandahar. Although this was effected without military incident of note, this march will ever stand out as a proof of the endurance of our soldiers, and of the skill enterprize and organising power of their Commanders, you being at their head. Regarding your fight of the 1st I shall have to speak hereafter, and you may be sure that I shall do so in no grudging terms, but I shall express all the admiration I feel as to the skill with which you designed it, and the valour with which your designs were carried out.

I cannot tell you how I regret the fact that failing health will take you away from your most important field of action, for I can have no doubt that, failing you, the command in Southern Afghanistan will have to be provided for apart from the ordinary course of things. This command is one which requires unbounded energy and activity, qualities which as far as I at a distance am able to judge have not hitherto been applied to it. I have had the greatest difficulty in getting the most ordinary reports from Kandahar. Almost every military item of intelligence has reached me through the Foreign Office, a most unsatisfactory state of things. Even now the list of killed and wounded at Maiwand has not been received. I am looking forward with great interest to the receipt of your reports on the military situation at Kandahar as you found it.

I am extremely glad you have taken the Maris and Atchakzais in hand.[76] I hope they will be well trounced; once done it will be done for ever. They thoroughly deserve it. Do you notice how much events have forced upon us the policy we initiated after my inspection of Jacobabad in 1877 when we proposed to so advance the Sind outposts as to [?extend the hand] to Dera Ghazi Khan, a proposal which wrung from Johnson the exclamation "Good God, this is annexation". The line taken up in consequence of the alignment of the rail is a good deal in advance of our views but it is a mere enlargement of them.

I must now be permitted to congratulate you on the more recent honours which have been so worthily bestowed upon you viz GCBship and the Commander-in-Chiefship of Madras. There is but one voice in this matter; they have been fairly won by long, continuous hard work and a staunch upstanding under much difficulty and under heavy responsibility. I wish you health long to enjoy both the honour & the place. The honour you will greatly prize I know, and believe me the place too is well worth having. I cannot say that the latter ever did me much good in a pecuniary point of view, except as enabling me to defend and keep up a good position, but I think you will find all the surroundings exceedingly pleasant, for the work will interest you much, and I am certain that contact will lead you to take a deep interest in the welfare of the old Coast Army, whilst socially you and Lady Roberts will delight both in Madras and Ootacamund. If my local knowledge should prove of any value to you, it is at your disposal. I would strongly recommend you to secure the house in which Sir Neville Chamberlain now lives at Madras, "Rutland Gate" and at Ootacamund you should take Woodcock Hall – at least that was the best house available in my day. Its situation is quite peaceful. I trust you and Lady Roberts may find a five year residence at Madras as pleasant as I found it in years gone by. But the first thing you have to do is to get home as soon as you can, so as to utilize every moment you have at your disposal for laying up a stock of good health in a good climate. If you make good the wear & tear you have undergone in the course of the last two years you will not find Madras at all a trying climate, taking it in connection with the trip to Ooty and with occasional excursions to Bangalore & etc.

I hope you have found accounts of Lady Roberts and the

Children. The news of 1st September must have greatly rejoiced their hearts. Please remember me to them. Shall we see you at Simlah before you go home?

HP 31/40

168
Roberts to Lieutenant-General Sir Donald Stewart, Military Member of Council

[Printed copy – Private]   Quetta
                                            24 September 1880

Your cypher telegram of the 23rd reached me this morning.

I do not see my way to doing as you propose, and putting the case about my successor here before the Commander-in-Chief. It would be like running a lance into a hornet's nest. I should never hear the end of it. You know Phayre better than I do. I have no hesitation, therefore in giving you privately my opinion of him, but that is very different from expressing an opinion officially to the Chief. Even if called upon by the Chief I should object to speaking openly to His Excellency as I would to you. I could not do otherwise without being prepared to bring proof for my reasons which would be scarcely possible.

Besides, remember that I am not in any way responsible for the selection of a commander for the troops in Southern Afghanistan; I tell you as an old friend that I do not think either Primrose or Phayre is the sort of man to be placed in such a position; and that, so far as I can judge, the Officers Commanding Brigades are inexperienced and not up to their work. I have of course not seen much of them, and could not officially condemn them. At the same time I feel tolerably certain that I have taken their measure fairly accurately.

The question as to who will command when I leave is one which should be settled without delay, for it is just possible I may have to go away sooner than I would wish. I have promised Lord Ripon that I will remain as long as His Excellency may desire, and

I hope I shall be able to do so, but I am feeling far from well again today, and have great difficulty in getting through my work. Yesterday I was much better, and may be all right again tomorrow; the climate is exquisite, and I am taken every care of by Sandeman[77] – but the fact is I require rest.

You can show this letter to the Viceroy if you think proper. It is but right that His Excellency should know the views and opinions of those holding responsible positions under the Government.

RP 101/CCCCLXXIV

169
Viceroy to Roberts

[Telegram]   30 September 1880

Minister at Teheran telegraphs as follows. Begins. Meshed Agent reports that Herat correspondent writes on 12th Instant saying that he has ascertained that two English officers were taken prisoners by Ayub Khan. Sent to Foreign Office. Ends. Do you think that Ayub has still a British officer in his hands.

RP 63/24

170
Major C.B. Euan Smith[78] to Roberts

[Holograph]   Camp Quetta
                                               30 September 1880

Pretyman has just been over here and has told me that you wish to know whether from the enquiries which I made while at Kandahar there is any reason to believe that Ayub had in his camp on the 1st Sept. or at any other previous period any other European prisoner than poor Maclaine. I have thought perhaps that you might like to have my opinion in writing and I therefore trouble you with this note.

I am as convinced as I can be that Ayub took no other European prisoner than poor Maclaine.

The universal testimony of all whom I examined – previous to the action – after the action was over – and on the spot at poor Maclaine's tent where I went under orders received from you – was unanimous that Maclaine had been the only European prisoner taken.

Had there been another the fact must have been known and would have certainly been stated!

In Maclaine's tent where I extricated all the small things lying about (and subsequently made them over to Slade) there was no sign of there having been any other occupant; and I went into several of the tents near his and found nothing indicative of the presence of a European.

If there had been another European prisoner he would almost certainly have been killed as poor Maclaine was – but his presence in camp and his subsequent escape (even if he had escaped) must have been known and would certainly have been divulged.

The Kizzilbash[79] prisoner who came in after the fight, must have known and would have stated the fact if any prisoner had escaped or been taken away.

Lastly I found in Maclaine's tent a pencil memorandum noting briefly the events of each day – very shortly and briefly. He would certainly have mentioned the fact had there been another European prisoner. There was however no mention or hint of this being the case – the memo. came to a sudden stop on the 15th August – no European could have [been] taken subsequent to that date.

It is most improbable that any European could have [been] taken near Maiwand and not brought into Ayub's camp. His captors would have been too anxious to reap the reward by delivering him up. But even in this case the fact of his detention must have leaked out. It is not at [?all] the sort of secret that could be kept in Afghanistan.

In my opinion there is every reason to discredit any rumours which would point to the existence of another European prisoner in Ayub's hands – I cross questioned very many people concerning this but the invariable answer was that Maclaine was the only prisoner.

RP 63/25

III
October 1881 to July 1885
Commander-in-Chief Madras

Roberts reached England on 16 November 1880, to find himself a public hero and, as a corollary, an emergent rival to Wolseley, hitherto 'our only general'.

In a crowded round of public engagements, a speech at the Mansion House on 14 February 1881 stood out, because for the first time in public he tackled the subject of Army reform, putting himself in direct opposition to Wolseley on this issue. He claimed that the short-service soldier was inferior in stamina and fighting power to the old long-service man and that the problem was compounded by the linked-battalion scheme which meant that the home battalions were constantly being weakened by the need to send out drafts of young, untrained men to keep the overseas battalions up to strength. He advocated a home army, which might approximate to a militia, and a foreign service army, based on a return to long-service engagements. In attacking thus the core of the Cardwell reforms, he found a warm supporter in the Duke of Cambridge.[1]

Within a fortnight of this speech, the Government received news of Colley's defeat at Majuba in the First Boer War. It selected Roberts to go out as Governor of Natal and High Commissioner of the Transvaal, and Commander of the British forces there. It was a clear rebuff to Wolseley who had filled the same job only a year before.[2]

Roberts left Dartmouth on 5 March 1881, reaching Cape Town on the 29th, only to find that, in the interim, the Government's initial resolve had given way, under Radical pressure, to a negotiated settlement; he left Cape Town twenty-four hours later. There is no reference to this episode in Roberts' papers, which may be an indication of his irritation, and it is significant only as marking a further stage in the rivalry with Wolseley.

He was in time to hear the debates in both Houses on the Votes of Thanks to the commanders in the recent Afghan war, in the course of which a motion by Tim Healy, the Irish MP[3] to delete Roberts' name, because of his alleged 'atrocities', was heavily defeated. When the rewards for the campaign were published in the summer of 1881, Roberts received a baronetcy and £12,500. He felt that these rewards contrasted meagrely with those given to Wolseley for the Ashanti campaign [189, 190].

Shortly before he was due to sail for India, he was asked to take the position of Quartermaster-General of the British Army, in succession to Wolseley, who was moving on to the more senior position of Adjutant-General. Roberts gave grudging acceptance but the offer was withdrawn almost immediately [171, 172, 173]. It was renewed in December 1881 [174, 175] but refused [178, 179]. In fact, Roberts had been a pawn in a game designed to defuse the Royal opposition to Wolseley's appointment.[4]

He reached Madras at the end of November 1881. Childers had described Madras as 'a good place of observation' [172] and so it proved since, without neglecting his primary task of making the Madras Army fit for war, Roberts had time to survey developments and events outside Madras and India.

The papers in this Section may be grouped loosely under five main themes:

(a) work to improve the efficiency of the Madras Army;
(b) the continuing Russian advance towards India and the defence of the North West frontier
(c) developments and events outside India;
(d) the reform of the British Army;
(e) the progress of Roberts' career.

A firm believer in the theory of the so-called 'martial races', he arrived in Madras convinced that the Madras native regiments were not capable of being matched against either the better regiments of the Bengal Army or serious foes such as the trans-Indus tribesmen, let alone the Russians [184].[5] He thought that something might be done to improve their fighting power by building on their better discipline and intelligence – the Madras Sappers and Miners, for example, were renowned for their efficiency. An early step was to convert the 1st and 4th Madras Native Infantry (both of which had served creditably in Afghanistan) into Pioneer regiments and to try to secure operational experience for them on the Frontier [207, 209]. Musketry was an activity in which the

Madras sepoy might be taught to excel and Roberts devoted much personal effort to this. The Madras Army was widely scattered, often in small, one-battalion stations, which made formation training difficult. In the middle of January 1884, Roberts held a Camp of Exercise at Bangalore which brought together some 9,000 men for a week of manoeuvres [196]; smaller-scale camps were held at other stations as opportunity offered [209]. Writing to Napier, he was able to show after three years a lengthy list of improvements during his tenure [209].

Two other issues may be considered here. On the Bengal pattern, the Madras Government (including Army Headquarters) spent the winter months in Madras and the summer months in the hills, at Ootacamund some three hundred miles away. Roberts found this inconvenient and inefficient, and moved the Headquarters permanently to Ootacamund, a decision much criticised in the Madras Press [205]. The Ilbert Bill, which provided for Europeans to be subject to the jurisdiction of native Indian magistrates and judges, caused a storm throughout the European community in India. Roberts' letter to the Viceroy on the subject is revealing on his own racial attitude, which did not change in his time in India [191].

Russia and the North West Frontier continued to occupy his thoughts. In the summer of 1883, he produced a major paper, *Is an invasion of India by Russia possible?*[6] The paper ran to 17 pages of print but a useful summary is given in a letter to Dr William Markby, the Professor of Indian Law at Oxford [199]. The purpose of the paper was frankly polemical:

'It is time for us to throw off the feeling of confident security in which we seem to be living, and to realise the fact that an ambitious Power, confident in the might of her two millions of armed men, is approaching nearer and nearer to our borders, gathering strength with every onward movement.'

Roberts circulated it widely to those in positions of power and influence [198]. He was able to follow it up in May 1885 when, with the Pendjeh crisis at its height, Stewart asked him for ideas on where Russia might most profitably be attacked. The resulting paper – '*What are Russia's vulnerable points, and how have recent events affected our frontier Policy?*'[7] – was familiar enough to those who had seen his paper of 1877 [4]. Perhaps the most significant part was the conclusion that the British garrison in India needed to be increased from 65,000 to 80,000, or even

90,000, and that massive expenditure was needed to develop trans-Indus communications [215]. Roberts used the paper to strike up a correspondence with Salisbury [216, 217].

He had been nominated to command one of the two army corps which were to be mobilised for war, and in January 1885 he travelled up to Rawal Pindi to attend the meeting between the Viceroy (Ripon) and Abdurrahaman, inspecting the troops of his Army Corps as he went. En route, he met Lord Randolph Churchill and together they inspected the 17th Bengal Native Infantry which was going to Suakin as part of Sir Gerald Graham's second expedition against Osman Digna. The 17th was a Hindu regiment, recruited from Lower Bengal, and Roberts expressed serious doubts about its fighting quality. When it broke and fled at Tofrek, six weeks later, he reminded Churchill of his prediction [213]. The incident was to have an unforeseen repercussion.

At Madras, Roberts watched with critical interest Wolseley's expedition to Egypt in 1882 [184, 185, 187],[8] and his attempt to rescue Gordon in 1884-5 [211]. His intellectual curiosity ranged over the project for a Channel Tunnel [182], the future use of machine-guns [210], the choice of new guns [193, 194] and the proper function and equipment of light cavalry [206]. He watched also the slow and obstructed passage of the major recommendations of the Eden Commission, particularly the proposal to abolish the separate Presidency armies, which was stubbornly resisted by the Duke of Cambridge [177, 179, 180, 183].[9]

His criticism of short-service engagements had been largely met in July 1881 by an extension of the initial engagement for the infantry to a minimum of 7 years with the colours, and by regulations which would prevent soldiers being sent overseas below the age of 20 or with less than one year's service.[10] The two-battalion regiments introduced in 1881 were a not unsuccessful attempt to overcome the problem of moving men between battalions without destroying unit loyalties. Roberts increasingly saw the real problem of recruiting as the unattractiveness of military service, and its low social status. He set out his views in a wide-ranging paper – 'Free Trade in the Army' – published in the review *Nineteenth Century* in June 1884.[11] Its message was put thus:

'The basis of any future reforms should be –

(1) That soldiers should be made to understand exactly the terms under which they enlist, and once they have accepted those terms, no change should be made in them without their consent.

(2) That army service generally should be made easier and freer; the

status of the soldier raised; and, so far as may be practicable, more consideration paid to his wants and feelings.

There must, in fact, be free trade and reciprocity in the army, by which I mean, the sweeping away of many hard and fast rules, which now unnecessarily hamper the soldier's life, from the hour of his enlistment until the day of his leaving the army.'

The initial engagements of either 3 or 12 years which he favoured and which were introduced at this time, in effect created the home army and the foreign service army he had advocated in 1881.

He was keenly aware that among the serving soldiers, it was boredom and petty restrictions which led to drink and crime. The solution, as he saw it, was, in part, temperance [203], and, in the longer term, the establishment of regimental institutions [238, 241].

As Macgregor had perceived earlier,[12] Roberts was ambitious and he was now in a position to aim at the highest posts in India and at home. His status is exemplified by the range of his correspondents and, perhaps particularly, by the volume of his correspondence with the Duke of Cambridge.[13] His serious ambition centred on succeeding Stewart, but there were two major obstacles – Wolseley [218, 221], and the antipathy for him in Liberal circles [189]. An unexpected window of opportunity opened in June 1885 when the Conservatives replaced the Liberals. Stewart hastened to announce his retirement in order to give Roberts his opportunity [219]. Wolseley remained the favourite [218] but finally rejected the post. Randolph Churchill, the new Secretary of State for India, was strongly in favour of Roberts as a result of their meeting in India; indeed, his son, Winston Churchill, claimed that his father was the prime mover in securing Roberts' appointment.[14] Equally importantly, Salisbury was in favour.[15] Roberts received the news of his appointment at the end of July 1885 [220]; the Government fell five months later.

171
Roberts to Hugh Childers, Secretary of State for War

[Printed]   Hampton Court
                                                 10 October 1881

I have thought very seriously over our conversation of yesterday. I had no anticipation of being offered an appointment in England, and all my preparations have been made, as you are aware, for going to India.

These arrangements have put me to considerable expense, which my very limited income is not well able to afford, and I have looked forward to the Madras command as a means of, at least, recouping myself for this outlay, and of meeting other heavy expenses, which I would not have incurred without such a prospect before me.

The present Government must, I think, be aware how ready I am to respond to any call of duty, and after what you were good enough to say to me yesterday, I can not but feel that I ought now to be guided by something higher than personal considerations; and, therefore, should it be the opinion of Her Majesty's Government that I can render better service to the country and the army by holding office at the Horse Guards, instead of going to Madras, I am willing to forego all private inclination, and to accept the appointment of Quarter Master-General, if the offer is made to me. I would, however, wish this acceptance to be subject to the condition that I may be allowed to proceed to Madras, and hold the command of the army there for, say, 6 months; this would help me pecuniarily, and would be of great advantage to me officially, as enabling me to become better acquainted with the Madras army, and to see something of the Madras Presidency, Burma, &c.

Nearly everything I possess is now on its way to India, and in equipping myself for the position I expected to hold in Madras, I have already spent more than double the allowance (£1,000) granted by the Indian Government for outfit, &c.

I will not close this without expressing to yourself, personally, the gratification I feel at the very handsome terms in which you have made known your wishes to me on this subject, and how much I value the high opinion you have formed of my capabilities, and the interest you have shewn in my future career.

RP 101/CCCCXCI

172
Childers to Roberts

[Holograph]   Dover
                                               18 October 1881
Confidential

I promised to let you know, by the 20th Oct., whether the offer of the Quartermaster Generalship would be made to you, which you confidentially told me you would accept if made by that day; and I now have to inform you, with much regret, that the arrangements under which the office would become vacant have not been made, so that your promise is at an end. It is a great disappointment to me that the plan, from which I hoped that so much public benefit would result, has fallen through; but, although I can only do so confidentially, I am anxious to assure you how very sensible I am of the public spirit and high motives which prompted your reply to my enquiry, and that I still hope that the day may come when I may have an opportunity of shewing how highly I value your services & character.

I fear that I shall not see you before you leave England, but I hope that you will write to me from time to time when you have leisure; and if I can serve you in any way you may rely on my desire to do so.

I hope you will like your command, & find Madras at any rate a good "place of observation". I do not myself look forward to quiet times in the world, at least in Europe.

RP 17/2

173
Roberts to Childers

[Printed copy] London
20 October 1881

I thank you very much for your letter of the 18th instant.

I will not disguise from you that I am not sorry matters have so turned out as to admit of my taking up the Madras command. At the same time, it would have been a great pleasure to me to have worked under you at the War Office, to have taken part in the organization of the army (a subject in which I am so deeply interested), and to have rendered any help in my power to make the army efficient.

I assure you I feel much the kind expressions you make use of in your letter, and I appreciate your wish to have me in a post of responsibility in England as thoroughly as I value the confidence you have placed in me.

It is, of course, a matter of some importance to hold an appointment, the pay of which is fairly good, but I need not tell you that I am at all times ready, most cheerfully and willingly, to serve anywhere, or in any capacity that the Queen or Her Majesty's Government may desire.

RP 101/CCCCXCII

174
Childers to Roberts

[Holograph] War Office
23rd Dec. 1881

Private

You will, I believe, by this mail receive a letter from the Duke of Cambridge offering to recommend you to me for the appointment of Quarter Master General at Head Quarters, on the understanding that you need not take up the office until towards the middle of 1882. The Duke is aware, in general terms, of what confidentially passed between us, in the month before you left England.

I have not seen the words of HRH's letter, & I therefore do not know precisely how he puts his proposal before you; but what I have asked him to express is that your acceptance of the office (nominally so much less in value than the one you now hold) should be a matter entirely for your own discretion, that is to say that you will not be prejudiced in our eyes if you find it more to your advantage to decline it. At the same time, speaking in <u>my</u> interest and that of the public, I may say that I hope you will be able to conclude that it will be for your advantage to come to Head Quarters, & Lord Hartington has told me, in confidence, that he is of the same mind.

However do not let this [?carry] too much weight with you. What I hope you will carefully consider is whether having regard to all the circumstances of your past career, your age, and the high estimation in which you are held, it would be of advantage to you to hold, for five years, the second highest office at Head Quarters under the immediate eye of the Commander in Chief and the Secretary of State, or to remain in a high Command in India.

RP 17/3

175
Duke of Cambridge to Roberts

[Holograph]   [?London]
                                                23 December 1881
<u>Private</u>

Though I have not yet heard from you since you left England, I think it right to send you a line to say that the Quarter Master Generalship at home will be vacant on April 1st, when Sir Garnet Wolseley is to succeed Sir Charles Ellice[1] as Adjutant General. Mr Childers is under the impression that you are anxious to succeed Sir Garnet in the appointment he vacates, whilst my impression is decidedly the other way, & that in every point of view the

Command in Chief at Madras is a better position for you than the one at Home. Having this opinion I suggested he make a selection at once of some other officer, but as Mr Childers is in doubt, I proposed to him that I should write to you to ask you frankly what your wishes are in this respect and I do so accordingly, and should be glad if you would telegraph to me your reply, in cypher if necessary, merely to state what you prefer. However much I should at all times rejoice to see you on my Head Quarters Staff I see no special reasons for setting aside what you would like best to do yourself, or what would be most conducive to your future interests. Hoping that you have had a good journey out & with the compliments of the season, I remain.

RP 15/6

176
Roberts to Lieutenant-Colonel G. de C. Morton, AAG India[2]

[Printed]

Camp near Tonghoo[3]
24 January 1882

When I was at the German manoeuvres, I was much struck with the way in which company officers instructed their men; recruits are, practically speaking, made over to the captains of squadrons and companies, who teach them everything. I remarked upon this in my report, and said that I thought we might usefully take a hint from the Germans in this respect. I have now (as I fancy other Commanders-in-Chief have) been called upon by the Horse Guards to give my opinion in detail on this subject, but before replying I would much like to know what you think about it. I am, of course, quite aware that there are many things in our army so different from the Germany army that we cannot copy them altogether. For instance, their recruits come in the same number and on the same day in each year; officers know, therefore, exactly what they have to do, and when it must be done. With us recruits are enlisted throughout the year, and there must be a constant succession of awkward squads, which no regimental officers, unassisted by an adjutant and sergeant major, could be expected to take in hand. Then, again, the German officer knows that the men he instructs will remain in his company or squadron during the years they have to serve in the ranks, and that they will return to the same regiment, if not battalion, in the event of the reserve ever being called out. This, again, is very different from our system. With us, recruits are no sooner fit for the ranks than they are sent from the battalion in which they have been drilled and may never be seen again. Even should the reserve be required, it is very unlikely, except in the case of the Guards, that men would join the battalion in which they had been drilled, or in which they had served their time with the colours.

Still, I think that our officers might do more with their men than they do at present, and that by some arrangement for recruits to be, in the first instance, sent to, and drilled at, some central depôt, regimental musketry instructors might be done away with altogether, and adjutants confined to what I imagine they were originally intended for, the commander's office and to be his staff officer on parade.

If you will give me your opinion I shall be much obliged. I hope to be in Calcutta shortly after you receive this, and you could by then, perhaps, have a short memorandum prepared for me.

RP 97–2/X

177
Roberts to Duke of Cambridge

[Printed]   Rangoon
                                                5 February 1882

Private

I cannot thank Your Royal Highness sufficiently for the very gracious letter of the 23rd December, which I received a few days ago. It would have been acknowledged sooner, but I have been on tour in an out-of-the-way part of Burma, and owing to the absence of roads and railways, communication in this Province is at present very slow. I much regret this, for I am afraid Your Royal Highness may have been surprised at not hearing sooner from me.

The offer of the Quarter Master Generalship is a most tempting one, and I should consider it a great honor to serve on the Head Quarters Staff. Had Your Royal Highness expressed any wish for me to return to England, or could I flatter myself that I could be of use to you, Sir, I should have had no hesitation whatever in accepting the appointment. But, as Your Royal Highness has been gracious enough to consider my interests, and kind enough to permit me to refuse the offer, I have come the conclusion, after thinking over the subject very carefully, that it will be better for me to remain in India for the present. I telegraphed in this sense to Your Royal Highness yesterday.

I shall write to you again, Sir, shortly, and give an account of my inspections in Burma. This letter is merely to explain the reason of my having been so long in replying about the Quarter Master Generalship, and to assure Your Royal Highness that I fully appreciate the great honour conferred on me by having such an important appointment offered to me.

RP 97/1/III

178
Duke of Cambridge to Roberts

[Holograph]   [?London]
                                          10 February 1882
Private

Your very interesting letter of January 1st from Ootacamund has reached me & since then your telegram in reply to my letter on the subject of the Quarter Master General Appointment about to become vacant at Hd Qtrs.

I think you have come to a very <u>wise</u> decision in <u>not</u> accepting it & for my part I never expected from what passed between us before you left that you would, but Mr Childers was so impressed with the idea that you were <u>anxious</u> to become Q.M.G. that I had no alternative but to make you the offer, & though I should gladly have seen you here by my side in the Office, I think you have done the right thing in retaining your position in Chief Command at Madras, a high & most important post which I feel assured you will fill with great credit to yourself & to the advantage of the public service. A selection has at once been made for the Q.M.G. appointment, which I think will now be filled by Lt General Arthur Herbert.[4] I am in great hopes moreover from all I hear <u>confidentially</u>, that the India Office at home will not <u>agree</u> to the Military Committee's Report as regards the abolition of the Chief Commands in the two Minor Presidencies, & that you will therefore, as also General Hardinge, see no organic change made in your responsible positions.

I am very glad you have at once undertaken a long & unhurried inspectional tour of your extended Command, commencing with Burmah, a most important & interesting country, seldom visited by superior authorities. As far as you have gone, you seem to be fairly satisfied with the condition of the troops, though local arrangements in many I believe require amendments to which you can now give your more powerful support by personal observation & experience.

I am glad you are able to give me yourself a good account of our European Troops & the General Officers in charge, & that you think highly of General Payn,[5] of whom I have a very good opinion, and who has of course had an anxious time of it lately, as <u>Acting</u> Cdr in Chief. I hope also that on further acquaintance with the Madras native troops you will be able to appreciate their merits. I know they have perculiarities, and physically they are certainly inferior to the troops of the Northern Presidencies but their dress, which I rejoice to hear is likely to be amended, is greatly against them, and I must say I have always understood that they have done any work to which they have been put in a very creditable manner, and their discipline has been more easily maintained at all times than may have been the case earlier in Bengal or Bombay. I am so glad you are going back to Madras via Calcutta where you will have an opportunity of conferring fully & freely with Sir Donald Stewart, which I think will be of great advantage to the public service, as the closer the intercourse is between the three Cdrs in Chief, the less friction there is likely to arise, and the better it must be for the general interest of the three Armies. I hope you will continue to write to me, whenever you have time or matters of interest to communicate and I remain . . .

RP 15/7

179
Note by Roberts on the Despatches from the Government of India to the Secretary of State for India, reviewing the report of the Indian Army Commission

[Printed]   Calcutta
                                               18 February 1882

I have read with great interest the several despatches submitted by the Government of India, during the past year, to the Secretary of State for India, reviewing the report of the Indian Army Commission.

   As a member of that commission I strongly urged–
   (a) the formation of four army corps in place of the three Presidential commands,
   (b) the reorganization of the staff, and
   (c) *a reduction in the number of regiments of Native cavalry and infantry.*

   I was also in favour of the changes proposed in the artillery, *viz,* the reduction of a certain number of garrison batteries, and the substitution of a few mountain batteries for batteries of Horse and Field artillery.
   The only recommendation I did not approve of was that to reduce the number of regiments of British cavalry and infantry. I

pointed out that these corps contained the only reserve of British officers we had in India; that, in the event of war, every officer taken from the Native army for the staff, transport and commissariat department, &c., would have to be replaced by one from a British regiment, and that if there were troubles in Europe, while we were at war in India, we could scarcely expect that trained officers would be sent out to us. We should then have to content ourselves with cadets from Sandhurst and Woolwich. I am glad to learn that this proposal has not been accepted, and that it has been finally decided to maintain the cadres of British cavalry and infantry at existing numbers. This is a wise measure, and well worth the money it will cost.

While I was in England many arguments were brought forward by officers who had held high postitions in India against the recommendations of the Army Commission; the proposal to do away with the Presidential commands, especially, was disapproved of. I was told that my opinions had been formed without sufficient experience of the minor presidencies, and that I would be sure to alter them when I had been a short time a Commander-in-Chief. It was urged that it was essential to the dignity of the office, and to His Excellency's position in the eyes of the Native officers, noncommissioned officers and sepoys, that the Commander-in-Chief should be a Member of the Council, and that I would find it very difficult, if not impossible, to carry on the command of the Madras army, with satisfaction to myself, unless I retained the title of Commander-in-Chief. I have not been very long in command of the Madras army, and it may perhaps be considered somewhat presumptuous of me to offer an opinion on the duties of such an important post, until I have become better acquainted with the work that has to be done; but I feel that I have seen enough to convince me that the views I originally held are correct, and I have no hesitation in recording my opinion in favor of the proposed changes.

One point which has struck me, has, I see, been remarked upon by the Government of India in their despatch of the 29th July last. I allude to the fact "that the greater part of the Madras army is serving in territories, of which the civil administration is directly under the Government of India." When my tour ends this cold season, I shall have inspected the four regiments of Native cavalry and three-fifths of the regiments of Native infantry in the Madras Presidency, but, with the exception of the small garrisons of Madras itself, St Thomas' Mount, Palaveram, Bellary and Vellore, these regiments are located at places over which the Madras Government has no control, *viz.*, Burma, the Central Provinces, Hyderabad and Mysore States.

It is the same with the British portion of the army. The greater part of the artillery, both the regiments of cavalry, and six out of the nine regiments of infantry, are quartered at stations independent of the Government of Madras. It is unnecessary to point out the inconvenience of such an arrangement, or "the needless trouble, embarrassment and delay to all concerned" owing to the interposition of the Government of Madras between the troops at those stations, and the authority which really administers the business connected with them.

The success of the proposed measures will mainly depend upon decentralization being strictly carried out; if any attempt is made to concentrate all executive work at Army Head-quarters, it will altogether neutralize the advantages that would otherwise be gained by the formation of the army corps. It is essential that the commanders of these corps should be left to manage their own affairs, subject only to a general control by the Commander-in-Chief in India. I am satisfied that if this desideratum is not lost sight of, the armies of Madras and Bombay will benefit considerably by becoming more closely associated with the Commander-in-Chief and Head-quarters in India. Hitherto these armies have scarcely had a chance; this could not, perhaps, be avoided under existing circumstances, but I am sanguine enough to believe that once the scheme has had a fair trial, no soldier, British or Native, in the armies of the minor presidencies, would wish to revert to the present system.

I am fully prepared to admit that the Army Commission made a mistake in recommending that the Commander-in-Chief in India should not be a Member of Council. After perusing the despatches and thinking over the very high position the Commander-in-Chief will hold, and the great responsibility that will be placed upon him as Commander of the four army corps, I am decidedly of opinion it is very necessary that he should be a Member of the Supreme Council.

But I can see no reason on military grounds why the commander of an army corps should be a Member of the Council of a Presidency. He will have to look to the Commander-in-Chief in India, and through him to the Government of India, for anything he may require for the troops under his command. At the same time, I can understand that, on political grounds, it might be desirable for the commander of the Madras and Bombay army corps to be Members of the Councils of those presidencies. They might be so ex-officio without altering their position relatively towards the commanders of the army corps of Bengal and the Punjab, in which provinces no councils exist.

RP 97–2/XVI

180
Roberts to Duke of Cambridge

[Printed]   Kampti
                                       28 February 1882

Private

My last letter to Your Royal Highness was from Rangoon on the 5th instant; since then I have spent a week at Calcutta with Sir Donald Stewart, with whom I had many talks. I had also a long interview with the Viceroy.

Amongst many matters the question of the Army Corps was discussed, and all the despatches from the Government of India to the Secretary of State for India on this subject were given to me to read. Nothing could be more complete and exhaustive than they are, and I am very hopeful that, if Your Royal Highness can afford the time to study them, in connection with the Army Commission report, the objections which you, Sir, now have to the proposed changes will be removed, or at least considerably modified.

I am aware that the recommendations of the Army Commission did not altogether commend themselves to Your Royal Highness, and that they have met with opposition from Sir Henry Norman and other officials of Indian experience. I have never heard definitely how Lord Napier of Magdala views the several proposals but I am under the impression that His Lordship is against doing away with the Commander-in-Chiefships of the minor Presidencies, and is also against any reduction being made in the number of regiments of Native Cavalry and Infantry.

I have such a great respect for Your Royal Highness's and His Lordship's opinions, and I am so anxious to carry out your wishes in every possible way, that I should almost have hesitated to abide by the opinions I held when a member of the Army Commission, after learning that those opinions did not meet with the approval of such high authorities as Your Royal Highness and Lord Napier of Magdala, had I not read the despatches above alluded to. These despatches endorse, in a remarkable manner, the recommendations made by the Army Commission. They are the result of serious thought and much consultation on the part of a Council who have great experience of the India of the present day; and who, from having taken no part in the proceedings of the Commission, or having had any connection whatever with its composition or recommendations, approached the subject with minds unbiassed, and with but one wish, *viz.*, to do the best in their power for India, and the Indian Army.

One great advantage which the Government of India of the present day possesses in considering a question so intimately connected with the Indian Army, lies in the fact that one of its members is an officer like Sir Donald Stewart. No one in authority, either in this country or at home, has such a vast and varied experience of India as he has; and no one is better acquainted with the Native Army of the past and present, or with the military requirements and resources of India. The despatches are the embodiment of Sir Donald Stewart's views, and were, I believe, agreed to by every member of the Council: the only dissent being disapproval on the part of Major-General Wilson[6] to that portion which deals with the subject of the Indian Staff Corps.

It seems impossible that there should be such a consensus of opinion in favour of the proposed changes, if those changes were not calculated to improve the condition, and add to the efficiency of the Army in this country.

Almost the only recommendation of the Army Commission I did not approve of was that in which it was proposed to reduce the number of regiments of British Cavalry and Infantry. I pointed out that these corps contained the only reserve of British officers we had in India; that, in the event of war, every officer taken from the Native Army for the Staff, Transport and Commissariat Departments &c, would have to be replaced by one from a British regiment, and that, if there were troubles in Europe while we were at war in India, we could scarcely expect that trained officers would be sent out to us. We should, then, have to content ourselves with cadets from Sandhurst and Woolwich.

I am glad to learn that this recommendation has not been acted upon, and that it has finally been decided to maintain the regiments of British Cavalry and battalions of Infantry at existing numbers. This is a wise measure, and well worth the money it will cost.

My conclusions were formed entirely in the interests of India. Mr Childers comes to a similar decision from an Imperial point of view, and, in my opinion, his arguments are unanswerable. They might, I think, have been applied with equal force against any reduction in the number of batteries of Artillery.

India does not, in my opinion, need a greater strength of Artillery than she has now, and it was because the instructions to the Commission were to consider the requirements of India only, that I agreed to a reduction in the number of batteries; but I quite see that India may, in all fairness, be called upon to bear her cost of any reserve England may have to keep up; and, if it had been known, that the batteries considered unnecessary for India would have been broken up on their return to England, I think that some of the members of the Commission would have hesitated to propose any reduction, and would have contented themselves by recommending that a certain number of batteries of Horse and Field Artillery should be converted into Mountain Batteries. Nearly every officer, who filled any position of importance or responsibility during the Afghan Campaign, holds, I believe, the same opinion as regards the value of Mountain Artillery in a country like Afghanistan. I should have been very glad to see the Mountain Batteries, recently raised, given as an addition to the Artillery strength of India; but the Commission was distinctly told that the expense of the Army must be reduced and the problem to solve was, how this could best be done without impairing its efficiency.

I much wish I could persuade Your Royal Highness that the proposed measures will be advantageous to the Army in this country, instead of, in any way, injuring it. No change will be made in the status of the native soldiers, nor will there be any decrease in their numbers. And, as regards their viewing the formation of Army Corps with suspicion, and the change in title of Commander-in-Chief to that of Lieutenant-General Commanding with dislike, my belief is that they will not give the matter a thought. The Army Corps Commander, even if he loses a little in social position, will, in reality, have much more power than the Commander-in-Chief of a minor Presidency has now. Sir Donald Stewart is quite aware of the importance of decentralization being strictly carried out, and of the danger of concentrating all executive work and patronage in the Head Quarters of the Army in India.

At present, a local Commander-in-Chief has no voice in the expenditure, and no control over the several departments, on which the troops he commands depend for supplies and stores. In fact, his responsibility is limited to the discipline and military efficiency of the regiments, &c., in the Presidency. With the Army Corps system it is intended to make the commander the real head of all military matters, and to leave him to manage his own affairs, subject only to a general control by the Commander-in-Chief in India.

RP 97–1/VI

181
Roberts to Adjutant-General, London

[Printed]

Kampti
28 February 1882

In reply to your letter* calling upon me to report confidentially for the information of His Royal Highness the Field Marshal Commanding-in-Chief, as to whether, in my opinion, the officers generally of corps and battalions can be made more available for the drill and instruction of the non-commissioned officers and men under their command, I have the honor to submit the follow remarks.

* No. 7693–3221, dated 1st December 1881.

2. I have long been of opinion that troop and company officers might be brought into closer relations with, and that they should be held more responsible for, the general efficiency of the men under their immediate command.

3. Under the present system these officers have, in reality, but little to say to the instruction of their men, who are handed over to them when they are considered by the adjutant and his staff fit to join the ranks, and are taken away from them again for their annual course of musketry, or whenever they seem to require any special training.

4. Not only would it be beneficial to the men to be more immediately under the eye of their troop and company commander, but the officers themselves would be gainers; for nothing conduces so much to the mastery of a subject as having to teach it to others.

The question to be determined is where the duties of the adjutant should end and those of the troop and company officers begin?

I do not allude to the instructor of musketry, as I propose to dispense with the services of this special officer.

5. If the conditions of our service were similar to those of the German army, it might be possible to restrict the adjutant to being the commanding officer's Secretary in the orderly room, and his staff officer on parade. Looking, however, to the fact that, in the English army, recruits are enlisted all the year round, and are continually joining the battalion by twos and threes, it does not seem advisable to make any change in the present method of their preliminary training *viz.*, under the adjutant, assisted by the sergeant major and non-commissioned offices as drill instructors.

6. In Germany the recruits join their battalion in one batch on a certain date every year. They are placed at once in the charge of the officer commanding their squadron or company, who is held responsible that the men are fit to join the ranks on a fixed date. The squadron or company commander takes an interest in the men from the first; he knows that they will remain in the regiment or battalion the whole time they have to serve in the ranks, and that they will return to the very corps in which they were drilled in the event of their being called out as reserve men.

7. With us the system is very different. The requirements of foreign service, and of the small wars in which England is so often engaged, render it difficult to say where a recruit may be a few months after his enlistment, and quite impossible to predict to what battalion he would be posted, should his services be required while in the reserve. Troop and company commanders could not, therefore, be expected to teach recruits the goose step or squad drill; indeed, it would under the circumstances be a waste of their time and intelligence to employ them upon such work.

8. My recommendation is that the recruit should be left with the adjutant until he has passed his preliminary drills, and then be made over to the commander of his troop or company, by whom the higher portion of his training should be completed.

9. This evidently was the method in force in the earlier days of the British army. Every endeavour was then made to develop the com-

pany system, under which captains and subalterns were brought into intimate relations with the non-commissioned officers and privates. A knowledge of each other was thus obtained, and a feeling of confidence engendered between the several ranks, which had the effect of creating an interest on the part of the officer in the soldier, and of calling forth a responsive and willing obedience from the latter.

10. To enable troop and company commanders to carry on their work satisfactorily, it is very desirable that *(a)* they should have greater autonomy with regard to the training of their troops and companies than they have now. In fact, they should be left to instruct their men pretty much as they like: their prospects of advancement being dependent, in a great measure, upon the general efficiency of the units which they command; *(b)* the drill season should be progressive; instead of the present system of regimental parades, which takes up all the time, parades for the first six weeks or so should be under troop and company commanders, and the men should be put through a complete series of setting up, squad, company, musketry, skirmishing, shelter trench and outpost drill by their troop and company officers; *(c)* at the end of the six weeks the troops and companies should be brought together under the commanding officer, and exercised as a regiment or battalion, passing on afterwards to brigade drill and field manoeuvres; during this period majors, and when practicable captains, should have frequent opportunities of commanding the regiment or battalion on parade; *(d)* some of the routine duties which obtain largely in garrison towns, and which consume a great deal of the time that might be more usefully employed, should be modified.

11. Under the new Army Act, courts martial will not henceforth require the attendance of so many officers as members, but more than this is required; and I hope it will be possible to come to some arrangement by which guards and fatigues will be materially reduced, and officers will not be perpetually called away from their troops and companies to serve on garrison and regimental

boards, or to give their opinions on such articles as tents, clothing, groceries, &c., things about which the large majority of officers cannot possibly know anything. Unless some modification is made in this custom, I am afraid it will be impossible that the proposed training of men by their own officers can be efficiently carried out.

12. For the annual course of musketry troops should be told off as they are now, but their instruction should be conducted entirely by their own officers, who ought all to be quite competent to perform this duty, without a specially appointed and paid instructor. Troop and company commanders should be encouraged to impart to the non-commissioned officers and men some instruction in subjects as surveying, reconnaissance and elementary field fortification. These subjects would interest the men, would raise the standard of intelligence generally, and would prevent the officers themselves from becoming rusty as regards their own knowledge.

13. These proposals will doubtless meet with a certain amount of opposition. Some commanding officers will object, for they would miss the daily parades, and would be apprehensive that their corps would "get out of hand", and some troop and company commanders might dislike, while some might be found incapable of performing, the additional duties required of them. My answer to the former is that their time can be more profitably employed in preparing themselves for higher commands than by continually drilling their regiments and battalions; and, as regards the latter, I am convinced that the large majority of British officers are not only quite capable of instructing their men, but that they would gladly welcome the introduction of any system under which they would be entrusted with more important and responsible work than they are now.

14. If these recommendations are adopted, the adjutant's duties, beyond those of the orderly room, should be confined to the preliminary drilling of recruits, and to serving as staff officer to the commander of the regiment or battalion on parade and in the field.

15. Whether the foregoing suggestions will demand a change, such as the introduction of the double company system in the infantry, and the squadron in the cavalry as administrative and tactical units, is a matter for consideration; there is much to be said on both sides; at all events such an organization would seem to correspond with the present proportion of regimental field officers. Moreover, with a field officer in command of squadrons and large companies, it might be made possible to settle matters of minor rewards and punishments, and promotion of rank and file and non-commissioned officers without centralizing all power in the hands of the Colonel commanding. This would give squadron and company officers a greater hold over, and interest in, their own men, adding to their importance and, therefore, to their feeling of responsibility. At the same time I venture to think such a measure would tend to diminish crime generally, and to lessen the number of more serious offences which have now to be dealt with by commanding officers and regimental courts martial.

RP 97–2/XIX

182
Duke of Cambridge to Roberts

[Holograph]   [?London]
                               24 March 1882

<u>Private</u>

I have received your interesting letter[7] in which you put forward your view of the arguments in favour of the changes proposed by the Military Committee, which are strongly supported by the Viceroy & his Council, whilst they do not I believe find much favour at the India Office, & are entirely objected to by myself, Lord Napier of Magdala, & <u>almost</u>, if not <u>all</u>, the Military men now able to judge of such matters, & a large body also of Indian Civilians of standing & position. I thought it will be as well for me to send you at once my views as drawn up just a year ago in May on this subject. To those views I adhere & I have not heard one single argument to modify or change my opinion in any respect, and I am afraid your letter has made no sort of impression upon me on the main features of the case though I doubt not that you are right about the improvements which may be effected & which by your General Order you are endeavouring to bring about by an immediate change in the mode of enlistment. I am rather surprised to find that Sir Donald Stewrt is so favourable to the new Scheme. I was rather under the impression that he had accepted it on assuming office but not that he very much liked it. I am so glad you are undertaking your tour of inspection which will be most useful to the Madras Army.

RP 15/9

183
The Channel Tunnel[8]

[Printed]   Ootacamund
                                         17 April 1882

For some time past, and especially during the recent controversy, I have thought much about the proposal to make a tunnel between Dover and Calais, and I have come to the conclusion that we are better without it.

Commercially, the scheme would probably be a success.

It is not to be supposed that the promoters of such a project, including capitalists, engineers, speculators, and scientific men generally, have omitted to consider thoroughly whether the construction of a Channel tunnel is feasible, and whether it will, eventually, pay a fair dividend on the capital expended.

Socially, I think there would be but little change.

No doubt there would be an increased passenger traffic between the two countries, if the journey from London to Paris could be made in the same carriage; but it would be of the same class of people that travel now, and would not appreciably, if at all, increase the flow of continental mischief-makers to London. A far larger number of people would, I believe, be induced to travel, if steamers were built, large enough to accommodate railway carriages; and, if sufficiently commodious harbours were constructed, for such steamers, on the coasts of France and England.

Politically, in my opinion a tunnel would be a source of great danger to England, and this point I do not think has been sufficiently considered by those who can see nothing to fear from the projected scheme. No one acquainted with the form of our Government, or with the English character, can suppose that we should ever be prevailed upon to make such arrangements as would render it practically impossible for an enemy to seize the Dover end of the tunnel, either by a *coup de main*, or by treachery. Even, if we admit that the tunnel could be made absolutely secure, would not its existence reduce us to a level with those nations on the Continent of Europe whose boundaries are conterminous? Would it not entail our keeping up a larger standing army than has hitherto been found necessary? And would it not, in a measure, justify the scares with which people in England are frequently disturbed, as to the possibility of an invasion?

From a military point of view, more has been adduced for, and against the construction of a Channel tunnel than from any other. And, although it would seem a comparatively easy thing to come to a conclusion, as to whether England could be rendered as safe from invasion with the tunnel, as she is without it, there is no phase of this much debated question which has given rise to more speculation, or to more diverse arguments.

Although defiles have frequently been taken advantage of from the passage of troops during war, notably in 1866 when the Russians[9] under the Crown Prince, entered Bohemia by Nachod, I confess I do not think a narrow road under the sea, 20 miles and upwards in length, leading into a hostile country, could ever be made use of for the advance of a large army. But I am ready to admit that the possession of the Dover end of the tunnel would be of the greatest possible assistance to an enemy, in the event of an invasion by sea being determined upon. I do not say that an invasion of England would be an easy matter, or that, even if an enemy got a footing upon our shores, we should not be able to deal with him. But I am confident that such an undertaking is not impossible. In fact, in war nothing is impossible. If then, an invasion is practicable without a tunnel, it surely would be easier with one.

The possession of it, even for a few hours, would be of such priceless value to an enemy, that he would spare no expense to secure it.

Under these circumstances would it not be wiser for us to discountenance the construction of the Channel tunnel? As a nation it cannot benefit us, and it might become a source of great danger.

Though I trust we shall always be able to maintain our supremacy at sea, we must remember that other nations are gradually becoming great maritime powers, and that one, at least, is doing its utmost to rival us in the number, size, and speed of its war vessels.

If ever an invasion of England is attempted, such an enterprise will not be undertaken without the most careful preparations, and without adopting every measure, recognised as fair in war, to ensure success. Why should we permit any step to be taken which could, by any possibility, assist such an enterprise? Or why should we do away with the inestimable advantage we now possess in an insular position?

RP 97–1/XI

184
Roberts to Stewart[10]

[Printed]   Ootacamund
Private   30 June, 1882

As it seems probable that troops may be despatched, ere long, from India to Egypt, I cannot resist writing to you to express my earnest hope that only those regiments, best qualified in every way for service abroad, will be selected, and that the Government of India will not be induced by any feeling of sentiment to form the force indiscriminately from the armies of the three presidencies, as was done in 1878.

I was away from head-quarters when the expedition started for

Malta, and had nothing to say to its constitution; but I confess to having been considerably alarmed when I heard that regiments of Madras and Bombay infantry had been sent from India with the possibility of meeting a European enemy; and to a feeling of intense relief when the force returned without having had occasion to fire a shot. A small portion of the force would, no doubt, have done credit to the Indian army in any part of the world in which it might be employed, but some of the regiments would, most assuredly, have disgraced it.

It is of no use our trying to persuade ourselves that the whole of the Native army is capable of meeting an enemy from Central Asia, or of taking their part in a campaign anywhere out of India. They are not capable of this, and nothing will ever make them so. It is not a question of efficiency, but of courage and physique; in these two essentials the sepoys of Lower India are wanting. No amount of instruction will make up for these shortcomings; and it would be extremely dangerous for us to flatter ourselves that we have an army in India of so many thousand men, ready to take their part in any war England may be engaged in. Such is not the case, we shall be only deceiving ourselves, and be calculating upon a force the greater part of which would most certainly fail us in the hour of danger. Regiments recruited in Madras, Bombay, and the lower parts of Bengal, could doubtless be better depended upon, if their complement of British officers were larger than it is at present, but even then I would strongly deprecate their being employed *out* of India, within the limits of which they will, I dare say, do well enough.

It was because I held these opinions that, as a member of the Simla Commission, I so strongly urged, and have since so persistently advocated, the reduction which has recently taken place in the Native army. We have a force still left which is sufficiently large for anything likely to occur *in* India, and for the defence of our frontiers, and if we are required to join in a war *out* of India, which is likely to last for any length of time, we must raise regiments to take the place of those on service. Fortunately the material in certain parts of the country is so good that such regiments would, in a very short time, be quite fit to do ordinary duty in a cantonment, and to provide drafts to keep up the strength of the corps in the field. It would not be politic, nor is it necessary, to maintain a larger number of regiments composed of the warlike spirits to be found in the north of India than are absolutely necessary for peace duties. But it is satisfactory to know that this good material is available, and that there would be but little difficulty in inducing the very best class of Native soldier to take service when the time of trouble comes.

To those who can discern no difference in men, and who think that every one who wears a uniform must necessarily be able to fight, the reduction of a certain number of regiments of the Indian Army must appear a suicidal policy, especially when there seems to be every prospect of troubles, not only in Europe, but also in Asia and Africa. To my mind, however, it is the best thing that could have been done for our future welfare in India, and I rejoice that the Government have had the firmness to carry out the measure in the face of such considerable opposition as they have met with. We have got rid of several regiments which could never have taken their part creditably in a campaign beyond our frontier; and if we have to replace them temporarily, we can do so with corps composed of men who are soldiers by nature, many of whom have already passed through our ranks, and who are quite capable of forming efficient regiments with a minimum number of British officers.

I have studied the native character carefully; I have been with our soldiers under various circumstances; and while I would pin my faith on, and go anywhere with those I believe in, I should be extremely sorry to find myself in command of an army in the field, composed of troops taken promiscuously from the three presidencies.

So long as the Native army had only to fight against men of much the same stamp and calibre as themselves, they were fairly dependable, and on some occasions distinguished themselves; but when they came into contact with the Sikhs, it was quite apparent that they were overmatched, and that they were unable to cope with the hardier races of the north. Now, we cannot disguise from ourselves the fact that, if our Native soldiers are ever again to be engaged in a war, the possibility, indeed the probability, is that they will have to meet very different foes from those which they have hitherto encountered.

I often thought when I was at Kabul how formidable the Afghans would have been had they been led by Russian officers; we should, under such circumstances, have required many more than the 25,000 picked troops we had to keep open our communication through the Khyber, and to hold our own in eastern Afghanistan.

If it be decided to despatch a force from India, the only troops I would recommend being sent from Madras are the sappers, whom I believe to be more efficient than either the Bengal or Bombay sappers, and from Bombay the two Baluch corps. The rest of the force should, in my opinion, consist mainly of Sikhs and Goorkhas. In each brigade of infantry I would have two British and two Native regiments. With a force composed of such troops, no commander with Indian experience need have any hesitation in meeting an Eyyptian, Turkish or even Russian army, but it would not be prudent to enter upon a campaign against such enemies with less efficient material.

You are most welcome to show this letter to the Viceroy; indeed, I would like His Lordship to see it. But it is not necessary, nor is it desirable, that I should make these opinions public while I am holding an important command in India.

In this, I am sure, you will agree with me.

RP 97–2/XXXV

185
Stewart to Roberts

[Holograph]   Simla
                                           6 July 1882

. . . We have been asked by the Home authorities to furnish a small force – a Brigade – for the protection of the Canal from Suez to Ismailia.

Seeing that the section to be protected is about 50 miles in length I recommend the following force for the purpose

1 Mm By jointed guns
2 Garrn Batteries with 12 guns
1 Reg^t native Cavalry

	1 Infy Divn	1 Pioneer Reg^t	2 Co^m Mad Sappers	Supports of 2 Reg^{ts} Mad N.I. to be sent to Aden.
63 Foot	72 Hig^1			
20 P.N.I.[11]	29 Beloochies			
45 Seiks[11]	(1 Bo N.I.)			

The Government wishes the Hindustani[12] element to be better represented in the force and with this view it was arranged that an additional Native Infy. Regiment should be attached to each Brigade. The Corps selected are the 7 B.NI. and Regiment from Madras. Besides this a Reg^t of Bengal N.I. takes the place of the Pioneer Regiment and 2 Cos. of Sappers from Bengal are added to the force which now stands thus

1 (British) Mountain Batty
2 (D^o) Garrison
1 Reg^t N Cavalry (13 B.C.)

	(63 Foot		(72 High^d
	(		(
	(20 P.N.I.		(29 Beloochees
1 B^{de}	(45 Seiks	2 B^{de}	(16 Bo N.I.
	(7 Ben N.I.		((?) Mad N.I.

1 Reg^t Ben N.I.
2 Cos Madras Sappers
2 Cos Bengal Sappers

Reserves

2 Regiments Mad N.I. to go to Aden

What you say about the quality of the troops of the different armies is to a certain extent true. Everybody knows that they are not all alike, and no one would dream of pitting an inferior Regiment against Europeans.

At the same time I am unable to agree with you that none but the northern races should be sent to Egypt.

Our men are not likely to meet anything but Egyptian foes there and if our Hindustani troops are unequal to coping with them I don't see how we can pretend to hold India very long.

Of late years our Hindustani troops have not had fair play and if they have lost some of their military spirit the fault lies at the door of the authorities, who never gave them a chance of showing what they are made of.

I think it would be a profound political blunder not to avail ourselves of the present opportunity of testing the quality of these classes.

For my own part I believe they will acquit themselves creditably in the hands of competent officers, and I consider that the Government is well advised in allowing representation from all three Presidencies to join the Expeditionary force. It is surely our duty to do all in our power to increase the efficiency of every section of our military Establishment, and if we do not avail ourselves of such opportunities as now present themselves we practically help to destroy those qualities upon the development of which we annually spend so many millions of money.

These are my chief reasons for concurring in the arrangements that have been made by the Government in detailing troops for Egypt, but they are not the only reasons that can be put forward in support of the course pursued. No one knows better than yourself that some of our best Regiments had enough of fighting in Afghanistan, and you can understand that such Regiments might not relish at the present moment another foreign campaign of 2 or 3 years beyond sea. I don't think it prudent to put too great a strain on our best soldiers, and it is certainly not wise to have all our eggs in one basket.

The question raised in your letter is of very great importance, but after looking at it from every point of view I think we have done the right thing.

[PS] We have just been ordered to send transport to take on the 72ⁿᵈ to Suez whenever the authorities at home think it necessary to seize Port Said. I have proposed to send with the Regᵗ a company of Madras Sappers as they will be very useful if works of any sort are to [be] required at Suez.

RP 78/1

186
Roberts to Stewart

[Printed]   Bangalore
                                                 21 July 1882

Yours of the 8th instant reached me a few days ago; you must not mind if I reply to it somewhat at length, for the subject we are discussing is one in which I am most deeply interested, and which, for the last six or seven months, has occupied a considerable share of my thoughts.

I quite agree with you that "it is our duty to do all in our power to increase the efficiency of every section of our military establishment"; and I also agree that, if it is certain none but Egyptian foes are to be encountered, it is politic to allow our Hindustani troops to form part of the force ordered to be held in readiness for service in Egypt. But my object in writing to you on the 30th ultimo was from a fear that the present troubles in Egypt might lead to further complications, and that our troops might possibly have to meet others than Egyptians, who, unless they are belied, are not likely to prove very formidable enemies.

You say "everybody knows that our troops are not alike, and no one would dream of pitting our inferior regiments against Europeans."

Can you be sure of this? What would have happened in 1878, if matters had resulted in a British force being sent to Turkey? The Indian contingent would certainly not have been left at Malta or Cyprus, and if it had landed on Turkish soil, the British commander would justly have concluded that troops would not have been sent all the way from India unless they were intended to fight; and that it would be quite prudent for him to make use of them against any enemy he might meet.

Even officers who may have seen hard fighting are not always competent judges of soldiers; it is not surprising then if military men who have never been on service, and civilians generally, should form an erroneous estimate of the fighting powers of soldiers, and think, as I said in my last letter, "that every one who wears a uniform must necessarily be able to fight."

Sir Frederick Haines was throughout the Sutlej and Punjab campaigns, and commanded a regiment at Inkerman, but even with such experience as this, he never seemed to me to be able to estimate soldiers at their proper value, and would, I am certain, have been extremely surprised if any one had expressed an opinion in favour of Sikhs and Goorkhas over Madras troops, whom he ought to have known well, having been connected with them for some 15 or 20 years during his career. Nearly every one I have met in Madras has much the same opinion on this subject as Sir Frederick Haines, an opinion which, I believe, is generally shared in by the authorities at the India Office, and by most people in England. You, of course, know how very erroneous such an opinion is, and thoroughly appreciate the difference between the several sections of the Indian army; but it is because 99 men out of 100, or I might say 999 out of 1,000, do not understand how great this difference is, or indeed that there is any difference at all, and because I feel so strongly how dangerous it would be to our future in India if the views of this great majority were acted upon, that I cannot resist letting those in power know the conclusions I have formed.

Unless our rulers are aware that certain regiments in India are inferior to others, the very fact, that a force prepared for service in Egypt in 1882 was drawn from the three presidencies, would be accepted as reason for selecting the same kind of troops in the event of an army having to be formed on the north-west frontier of India, or sent out of the country against an enemy more to be dreaded than the Egyptians.

I have been reading lately the history of the Madras army, and I cannot find any occasion on which its fighting qualities were ever severely tried. The men often suffered considerable hardships, and considering that their pay was often months in arrears, they behaved, on the whole, very loyally. But a study of the campaigns and battles which took place in the latter half of the eighteenth century, prove conclusively that the brunt of the fighting was always borne by the Europeans, and that the casualties amongst the native troops were never very serious.

The capture of Seringapatam in 1799 ended the wars in southern India, and none of the regiments of the Madras army have seen service since then, except the few which were employed in Burma in 1825–26, and again in 1852–53, in China in 1840, and during the mutiny of 1857–58.

The fact is that the Madras sepoy has never encountered a formidable enemy, and nearly 100 years of peace have almost quenched any martial spirit there may have been in him. In the wars with Hyder Ali and Tippoo, Madras soldiers were fighting against men of much the same kidney as themselves, and though they were usually greatly outnumbered, they had the advantage of having British officers and sergeants to drill and lead them, and British soldiers to take the posts of honor and danger.

It would never do to make these opinions public and so long as we are obliged to maintain troops composed of men who are not born soldiers, we must make the best we can of them, and do all in our power to render them as efficient as it is possible for them to become. No one recognizes the necessity for this more than I do, and it is from considering carefully, during the last six months, how this is to be done, that I have found the opinions formed some time ago about the Madras army are correct, and have satisfied myself that it would be extremely dangerous to employ soldiers of southern India, except on the most ordinary kind of service.

During the recent campaign I was most anxious to give Hindustanis a chance, and at my request the 11th Native infantry was sent to join me in Kuram. I would have included the regiment in the force detailed for Kabul in September 1879, but it had become very sickly, and the commanding officer had shewn so little aptitude for his position, that I thought it wiser to leave it behind; and I certainly did not regret having done so when, later in the year, I found that I was only able to maintain myself at Kabul from having troops with me on whom I could thoroughly depend.

I grant you that a Bengal sepoy is far superior to the ordinary soldier of the two minor presidencies, and that he has on some occasions behaved with great gallantry. But he came to an untimely end in 1857; those that remained to us after that time felt that they were insulted and lowered by being mixed up with men of inferior castes. Their spirit was broken, and I doubt very much if anything could be done now to revive it. Moreover, it must not be forgotten that Hindustani regiments have never been tried, during the present century, with the reduced complement of offi-cers. They do not possess the material out of which really able Native officers are formed, and I think we may be sure that, if the old sepoy army had proved itself capable of meeting such enemies as the English had to deal with in the southern parts of India, the organization which then existed would have been maintained, instead of the number of British officers with each battalion being trebled and quadrupled, as was done in 1796.

I quite agree with you that it would not be prudent to call too often upon our best regiments, especially as it is in them that the greatest number of casualties are sure to occur in a campaign. But, at the same time, I am very confident that those are the very regi-ments which would cheerfully respond when real work has to be done, provided they were assured that their interest in India would be cared for during their absence, and that they themselves would be liberally treated.

I did not hear that any of the corps which returned to India in 1879–80 experienced difficulty in getting recruits. The Punjab frontier regiments I know did not; the 5th Punjab Infantry had to stop recruiting before it left Kabul; and 5th Punjab Cavalry wrote to me, not long after their arrival at Kohat, that their number was complete, and that they had not enlisted such a promising lot of young men for a long time. All this shows, I think, that the service in Afghanistan was not unpopular. The men were clothed and fed well, and taken every care of; their family remittances were paid regularly, and they returned to their homes with their pockets full of money. So long as this is the case, and so long as the Government are wise enough to treat the Native soldiers liberally, we need have no anxiety as to their willingness to go on service; certainly not such men as Sikhs, Goorkhas and the majority of Pathans, who love fighting and the excitement of war.

On the whole, I am inclined to think that you and I have the same opinion on this question, which, as you say, is one "of very great importance". I only wish that all in, or likely to be in, authority, understood the Native army as well as you do. I should not then be as anxious, as I confess I am, about the future.

If the Viceroy has time I shall be very glad if His Lordship would read this letter.

RP 97–2/XXXVIII

187
Stewart to Roberts

[Holograph]   Simla
                                                   3 August 1882

I have been so busy of late that I have not hitherto had time to answer yours of the 21st. There is not a word of that letter in which in the main I do not concur. The only one indeed in which I do not quite go with you perhaps is in your estimate of the Bengal Hindustani. The non employment of this class since the Mutiny has no doubt impaired their military qualities or perhaps it would be more correct to say that officers in general do not estimate their military qualities as highly as they did before the Mutiny. I don't think there is anything surprising in this because I entertain a little of this feeling myself. At the same time I recollect that the old officers of my own Regt – Colonels Paul & Smith – told me of the performance of the Sepoys in Java and in the Nepaul war, and the little I saw of the fighting qualities of the old . . . at Peshawar led me to think that there is very good stuff in Hindustanis if it is placed in good hands.[13] Surely you are wrong in supposing that the people about the Gov^t here and at the India Office suppose that all native troops are equal.

Norman, R. Strachey & Eden[14] know perfectly well what the value of the different races is. Indeed I should say from telegrams now coming from the India Office that this matter is being fully considered there now.

Considering the suspicious attitude of Turkey I have advised the Viceroy to inform the authorities at home that the part of the Indian Contingent required to move into the Delta should be comprised of from $\frac{1}{3}$ or $\frac{1}{2}$ of the European element.

The native troops will do capitally for Canal work, but it is hardly fair to put too great a strain on them.

Between ourselves I will tell you why I have not recommended the employment of Seiks & Ghoorkas in Egypt. This [is] because there is no telling when we may need them at home.

There is an uneasy feeling in some parts of the country among the Mahomedans who are very much disposed to rouse the sympathies of their co-religionists in favour of Arabi.

The Sultan has <u>said</u> that he will proclaim Arabi a rebel but he for some reason not yet explained does not seem inclined to fulfil his promise.

The Egyptian peoples are doing their best too to create ill feeling all over the East against the English and this being so we think it desirable to keep our best Hindoo troops in India.

If Wolseley will strengthen Macpherson as I have suggested I am confident his force will be quite good enough for the Egyptians – but I am not so sure they will be quite equal to the Turk.

I shall write to [?Crozier][15] in this sense and I have also told Macpherson what my views are.

I dare say you heard that we had nothing to say to the peculiar composition of Macphersons force – that was done at home. The War Office will give us no information about their plans and we are working entirely in the dark.

The S of S has asked if we can give more troops and our reply is that we can give another Brigade of Infy and two or three Batteries of art. if necessary. Fancy them sending the Lifeguards to Egypt! Is it not ridiculous.

I don't like the political outlook in Europe at all. The Gov^t seems to have alienated every power more or less. The departure of the French from Egypt is a good thing in itself but in these days one hardly likes being without friends.

RP 78/2

188
Roberts to Adjutant-General India

[Printed]   Camp Mysore
                                             22 October 1882

In reply to your letter No. 2610–D., dated 1st July 1882, forwarding copies of a Circular* on the subject of the increase of crime in

the British Army in India, and request-
* No. 2547–D., dated 28th   ing me to submit my views on the same
June 1882.   for the information of His Royal
                             Highness the Field Marshal

Commanding-in-Chief, I have the honor to offer the following remarks.

The causes which have produced the increase of crime, in my opinion, are –

(1) The non-deterrent nature of the punishments which courts martial have now only the power to award under the new Army Act, and the prohibition of cumulative sentences.

(2) The system of sending out bad characters, and releasing offenders from prison before the expiration of their sentences, for the purpose of accompanying regiments and drafts to India.

(3) The fact that men who find the restraint of a soldier's life irksome, and who, if at home, would desert, have no other means in this country of getting out of the service than by repeatedly committing acts of insubordination.

(4) The absence of military prisons generally in India, and especially in the Madras Presidency.

There is a remarkable consensus of opinion amongst the officers whom I have consulted, that these four are the main causes of increase of crime in India. But they think, as I do, that the more general introduction of the short service system into this country has also had a great deal to do with it, in consequence of the great deterioration this system was rapidly bringing about in the non-commissioned grades.

It seems desirable to consider each cause separately.

With regard to the first. To show how necessary it is that punishments for severe crime should be more deterrent than is possible under the existing law, I cannot do better than invite attention to what occurred in 1870, when the army in this country was in such a state of indiscipline that the Commander-in-Chief, Lord Napier of Magdala, was compelled to recommend the enforcement in India of all sentences of penal servitude up to a limit of five years, and of the full term of imprisonment in all cases, as the only means of effectually checking crime. The proposal was sanctioned, and in the very first year the crime of insubordination fell from 160 to 66, and in successive years it continued to fall until the low rate of 35 was reached in 1874.

Enforcing sentences of penal servitude in India was in accordance with the Mutiny Act, but with the expiration of that Act, this check upon insubordination ceased, and now a prisoner sentenced to a term of penal servitude, or of imprisonment exceeding 12 months, must be sent home, unless, in the case of imprisonment, the court shall, on special reasons, otherwise order.

As the partial increase of violent crime in 1880, and the great increase in 1881, have been co-incident with the change in the law, there can be but one conclusion, and I trust that it will be found possible to modify section 131 *(2)* of the Act of 1881.

It also seems very desirable that the Act should be altered so far as it prohibits cumulative punishments.

In my opinion grave crimes of insubordination will not be effectively repressed until the ill-disposed soldier is made to know that every crime will involve its own punishment without limit as to terms of imprisonment.

For contempt of court, for instance, a crime which has, I believe, become more frequent since the introduction of the Army Act, a soldier can now only be imprisoned, with or without hard labor, for a period not exceeding 21 days: under the old law, a District court martial was competent to award the offender a further term of imprisonment up to two years. Nothing would offer a greater check to the commission of this offence, and to the repetition of offences, than a return to the old system of cumulative punishments; particularly if the law be altered as I have recommended above, so as to allow of imprisonment and penal servitude up to the limit of five years being carried out in India instead of the United Kingdom.

(2) This cause requires no explanation. It is evident that men of notoriously bad character, recently released from prison before the expiration of their sentences, can be no acquisition to a regiment.

With regard to the 3rd cause, it seems to me that no comparison can fairly be made between the crime rate of India and that of the United Kingdom.

In India men are seldom able to desert, and their only chance of escaping military duties is by committing such offences as will ensure penal servitude, or long terms of imprisonment. At home these very men desert when they are tired of soldiering, and remain in civil life until necessity forces them to re-enlist. This fraudulent re-enlistment, and the consequent steady flow of hardened bad characters through the ranks, is, perhaps, the greatest stumbling-block to any real reform in the morals of the army.

It has often been proposed that instead of the old plan of marking offenders with D or BC (which was abolished out of deference to humanitarian feelings) every soldier, officer, as well as private, should be tattooed with a distinctive mark on entering Her Majesty's service. This mark ought and would by all men of good character, be considered as an honourable badge, and not as in any way degrading. It might be optional with those now in the service to be tattooed, but, unless I am much mistaken, few who wear Her Majesty's uniform would be found without the mark, once it had been decided that all soldiers were in future to wear it. By such a measure desertion and fraudulent enlistment would be greatly, if not altogether checked.

The want of a sufficient number of military prisons in India has been represented, from time to time, by successive Commanders-in-Chief. In the Madras Presidency there are only two, *viz.*, at Bangalore and Secunderabad. The result is that a number of military prisoners have to be confined in ordinary civil jails, where they do not meet with the same strict discipline, and in fact where they are too comfortably off. It is well known that a certain class of men prefer an easy jail to regular duty with their corps.

The 5th cause, *viz.*, the deterioration of the non-commissioned grades owing to the more general introduction of the short service system is now met by the improvement which has been made during the last few months in the position and prospect of non-commissioned officers. This is already beginning to have its effects, and, as time goes on, I believe this class will regain its old influence, and with the happiest results.

Under the original conditions of the short service many good men would not accept promotion; they knew they were only to remain for a limited time in the army, and it was not worth their while to undertake the responsibility attached to the grades of corporal and sergeant, and to separate themselves from their friends amongst the privates. The consequence was that we were getting a class of non-commissioned officers into the army who were without power or influence, and who, from not knowing how to deal with men, were often the cause of soldiers committing serious crime. As, however, I remarked before, the difficulty connected with non-commissioned officers has been met. Indeed, this class is now infinitely better off than it was under the old organization. But, as regards private soldiers, we must accept the fact that amongst these a certain number will always be found whose vicious and depraved habits can only be restrained by the severest punishments.

In former days the better specimens of old soldiers used undoubtedly to exercise a considerable moral and restraining influence over their younger comrades, whose feelings were also worked upon, in no small degree, by a desire to maintain the good name of the regiment in which they had elected to serve. Now, there are but few old privates, and the period a man has to serve in the ranks is so short, that it tends to make him regardless of consequences, and prevents the development of that *esprit de corps* which has done so much for our army. The loss of these valuable adjuncts to the maintenance of discipline and good order, made it all the more necessary that the punishments for military offences should not, at all events, be of a less deterrent nature than formerly; and yet, almost coincident with the more general application of the short service system to the ranks of our battalions, the Army Discipline Act was introduced, under the provisions of which punishments for serious crime (at least so far as India is concerned) are not so severe as they were under the old law.

In conclusion, I beg to state that I do not think service in India is unpopular with soldiers generally, though doubtless in many parts the climate is very trying, and the lengthened confinement to barracks extremely irksome. Much has been done of late years to improve the condition of soldiers in this country, but we must not, on this account, cease in our endeavours to counteract the bad effects of the long, tedious, hot weather days.

Every encouragement ought to be given to rifle shooting. Camps of exercise, if only on a small scale and for a short period, should be the rule, and not the exception, and it would be well to have gymnasia constructed and institutes established at all the large stations. Everything of this sort tends to relieve the monotony of a soldier's life in India, and consequently to reduce crime. Many a man who chafes at constant barrack square drill, is happy enough in camp or at field manoeuvres, and enjoys the relaxation which gymnasia, institutes, &c., offer.

RP 97–2/XLV

189
Roberts to Mountstuart Grant Duff, Governor of Madras

[Copy in Roberts' hand]

Ootacamund
25 December 1882

Private

I enclose a copy of the letter I have written to Mr Childers on the subject about which I spoke to Your Excellency the other day.

I don't suppose it will have any effect but I could not allow such a marked difference in the bestowal of rewards for two campaigns to pass without a challenge.

The fact is, as I have hinted in conversation to you, I feel very keenly the manner in which I was treated by the present Ministry on my return from Afghanistan.

It would almost seem as if I had been made the scape goat of party strife, for without doubt my services received but scant acknowledgement (according to the standard of the present day) from the Government; partly, I imagine, from their antagonism to the policy which brought about the war in Afghanistan, and partly also from an unjust and quite unfounded suspicion of theirs, that I had allied myself to their opponents as a political partisan.

So far from this being the case I had always studiously avoided mixing myself up in any way with politics, having a strong opinion that, so long as a soldier is actively employed, he belongs to the country, and should be the loyal servant of the government of the day.

Curiously enough it fell to my lot during the war in Afghanistan to serve, in turns, both a Conservative and a Liberal Government, and I never anticipated that, after an arduous campaign which lasted 2 years, and which was brought to a successful conclusion by the decisive action at Kandahar, my services would be weighed in the somewhat fickle scale of politics.

I felt this considerably at the time but I feel it infinitely more now that I have seen how generously the services of soldiers can be rewarded by a Liberal government.

Your Excellency has, I think, had opportunities of judging how

273

untrammelled I am by political prejudice, and can, therefore, understand how surprised and disappointed I was to find myself received with unmistakable coldness by the government of the day; as if, forsooth, I had been a political opponent, instead of a soldier who had tried to do his duty to the State.

Pray excuse this spontaneous outburst of feeling. I had not the slightest intention of troubling you with it, but my letter to Mr Childers has brought forth what has been for a long time working in my mind, and my pen has run on apace.

Copy enclosed in RP 97–1

190
Roberts to Childers

[Printed]   Ootacamund
                                                   26 December 1882

Although you are no longer at the War Office, I am sure you will not object to my writing to you on a personal matter, especially as the circumstances connected with it occurred while you were Secretary of State for War. You will no doubt remember my writing soon after my arrival in England, to say how gratified I should be if the temporary rank of Lieutenant-General, which I held while in command in Afghanistan, could be made permanent. In reply you informed me that you regretted my wish could not be complied with as the regulation, under which such promotions had previously been made, was obsolete; that General Wolseley had been refused his promotion for South Africa; and that it had been decided not to reward General Officers by making permanent any local rank they may have held on service. Although at the time much disappointed, I naturally accepted the decision, and felt that, under the new ruling, nothing could be done for me. I now see that for the Egyptian Campaign Lord Wolseley has had his local rank of General made permanent, and that Sir Archibald Alison, who was only a Major-General in command of a Brigade, has been promoted to the rank of Lieutenant-General.[16]

I need not assure you that I do not grudge these two distin-guished officers their well earned reward, but I can't help thinking myself very unfortunate for having come under a ruling, which after all was not obsolete, but apparently only in temporary abeyance, and which it has now evidently been determined to rein-troduce. Many officers who were junior to me while I was in Afghanistan have been promoted over me during the last two years; more than one of them actually served under me, and other similar instances will doubtless occur if I am to wait for promotion in the regular course of seniority. From this you will see how much my future career may be affected by the refusal to confirm my local rank.

I commanded 25,000 men while at Kabul, and rather more than that number while at Kandahar. I held the local rank of Lieutenant-General for nearly a year, and only relinquished it owing to my health failing after two somewhat trying years of field service. This step I was most loath to take, and only did so at the earnest advice of the medical authorities, as the Viceroy of India had begged me, on public grounds, to retain the supreme political and military command in Afghanistan.

RP 97–1/XXVII

191
Roberts to Viceroy

[Printed]   Fort William, Calcutta
                                             8 March 1883

As Your Lordship was pleased to speak to me last Sunday on the subject of Mr Ilbert's Bill,[17] I trust I may be excused for venturing to express myself a little more fully than I did on that occasion.

Your Excellency will doubtless remember that when Mr Grant Duff recorded his opinion some months ago on the question of revising the Code of Criminal Procedure, he stated that, though sorry that this subject had been mooted, he could not but admit that in equity there should be no difference between British and

Native gentlemen holding similar positions in the covenanted Civil Service. In this view I concurred, looking on the proposed measure as a logical sequence to the acts of former Governments. It would, I thought, be as unreasonable to deny the Native gentlemen of the Civil Service the full privileges enjoyed by their British colleagues, as it would be to bestow on a Native of India a Lieutenant's or Captain's commission in Her Majesty's Indian Forces, and then to refuse him the right of commanding a mixed detachment of British and Native troops. But although thinking thus I endorsed Mr Grant Duff's views, I feel that I ought to have said how much opposed I had always been to the admission of Natives either to the covenanted Civil Service, or to an equality with the commissioned officers of Her Majesty's army.

The universal dissatisfaction which has now been shown by the European population of India, seems to me to prove that my feelings as to the proper relative positions of British and Native gentlemen in the service are shared by most of our countrymen here; and it is a matter of regret to me that I did not express my views more fully as a member of the Madras Government.

The question has now assumed paramount importance, and as it is one which must give Your Lordship considerable anxiety, I hope I am justified in informing Your Lordship what I think myself, and what has come under my own observation as to the present state of public opinion.

During the 32 years I have been in India, I remember no measure of Government which has called forth such a bitter feeling of opposition as this Bill. This feeling has made way among all classes, the non-official, the civil service, and worst of all, the military; and I cannot but believe that if the Bill is carried, the consequences may be more serious than Your Lordship has hitherto contemplated.

Having gone so far, it may be difficult to abandon our position, but I for one am ready to admit that I was not at all prepared for the fierce agitation that is now going on, and that had I foreseen it, I would have strongly urged that the question should be allowed to rest for the present.

RP 97–2/LVIII

192
Roberts to Stanhope

[Printed]   Ootacamund
Private   8 May 1883

I had no intention of troubling you so soon again with a letter, but I cannot resist writing in order to draw your attention to the present state of the Army.

From all accounts the recruiting market is most unsatisfactory, and I am informed that an attempt will be made to remedy the serious deficiencies existing in the ranks of our Army, by the short sighted method of once more lowering the standard of measurement required of recruits, and of again reducing the age at which they may be enlisted. I earnestly trust that such ill advised expedients may be strongly opposed. Mere numbers of ill grown lads do not create a fighting army, and though no doubt cheaper and easier to get hold of than well grown ones, they are in the long run more expensive to the State. The price saved by an "economical Government" in accepting recruits of inferior physique instead of competing in the labor market of the day is more than counter balanced by the cost of nursing, and too often of invaliding such striplings, from India and the Colonies. In short, obtaining recruits by lowering the standard is in reality a cheap but ineffectual way of showing more numbers on paper.

It is further an act of deception on the part of the Government practised towards an ignorant and long suffering public, who are told that they possess an army of so many thousand fighting "men". Now, one of the chief arguments used by the advocates of the short service system in England, and certainly, if true, a powerful one, was that recruits would not enlist for long service in sufficient numbers, although they would do so freely for short service.

The fallacy of this argument has at length been clearly proved. After a twelve years' trial of the new system we are now confronted by the serious fact that recruits will not come in, that the strength of the British Army in India is about 5,000 men short, that the

Artillery at home is some 1,500 and the Guards about 1,000 below their normal strength; and further that there seems no probability of these deficiencies being made up except by again lowering the standard, and accepting as recruits the worst classes of the population, both morally and physically.

I think you will give me the credit of not being an obstructionist, although I have felt it my duty on more than one occasion to draw attention to the weak points of a system, borrowed from the Germans, ill adapted though it is in every way to English needs, and to the small and ubiquitous English Army. The advocates of the system appear to have entirely omitted from their calculations the essential differences between the armies of the two Nations. The German Army is in fact a highly trained militia; ours is employed all over the world and is in numbers too small ever to produce an efficient reserve. That a really strong reserve is necessary for England to back up her small fighting line I am well aware, as must be every practical soldier; that such reserve is now or ever can be formed out of our very limited regular army, I entirely and absolutely deny. Why, instead of the 60,000 men promised us in 1882, we had the other day according to Mr Childers about 28,000 reserve men on paper? What I am now afraid of is that every effort will be made by the Government to patch up the short service system on its present lines, notwithstanding its too palpable failures, instead of frankly acknowledging that it has failed to meet the varying conditions of the British Army.

Why should we have copied the German system which we did in shadow without getting the substance of it, when we had all the material ready to hand wherewith to build up an English system – a system based upon our national traditions, and one capable of being adapted to all our wants? This was quite feasible, and would have been a real instead of a sham reform. I allude to what I have long considered to be the only solution of England's difficulties with regard to the conditions of service of her army, and her voluntary enlistment system, *viz.*, the necessity of her possessing two armies, one a home army or militia on a short service basis, the other a foreign service army on a longer service basis; both armies to be intimately connected on the territorial lines, the one feeding the other, and receiving back a certain number of its old and trained soldiers. This was the idea which I had in view when I spoke about the Army at the Mansion House, and later on when I wrote on the same subject in the *Nineteenth Century*.[18]

I will not attempt to go into details here, as I feel I have sufficiently wearied you already. Moreover, I hope, ere long, to put my views on this very important subject before the public. Meanwhile let me recommend you (if you have not already done so), to read a most able and convincing article on the present state of our Army by General Sir L. Simmons which appeared in the March number of the *Nineteenth Century*.[19]

RP 97–1/XLII

193
Colonel Macfarlan's proposal to have a light field gun for India

[Printed]   Ootacamund
                                             23 May 1883

The proceedings of the Madras Government (No. 1261, dated 26th February 1883) forwarded for my information copy of a Military despatch,* relative to the steps to be taken for providing a new breech-loading equipment for horse and field artillery, for home service.

* No. 3, dated India Office, London, 18th January 1883.

This despatch enclosed a letter† from Colonel D. Macfarlan,[20] ordnance consulting officer for India, in which that officer recommends, that, if the Indian Government determine to introduce a new breech-loading equipment, it should be lighter than that adopted at home, and should not exceed 30 cwt. for each carriage, exclusive of limber, gunners, and their personal equipment. In support of these views, Colonel Macfarlan urges that, as regards India, "mobility is

† Dated Charlton, 9th December 1882, to the Military Secretary, India Office, London.

of relatively greater importance than gun power, taking into consideration climate, bad roads, long marches, inferiority of horses, and mountainous countries." And he says that "keeping our artillery in India light will enable us, when the emergency arises, to use the horses of the country, and perhaps eventually to get rid of the necessity for the costly and possibly precarious Australian supply."

After careful consideration of the subject, and the recent experience of a 2 year command in Afghanistan, I am unable to agree with Colonel Macfarlan's views.

I consider it essential that India should possess the most powerful gun manufactured, and that the question of gun power is more important than that of mobility. The best kind of artillery for service in a mountainous country, such as that on, and beyond the north-west frontier, is –

(1) a gun that can be carried on strong, active pack animals; and
(2) the most powerful gun that can be taken into the field.

Mobility is, of course, of immense consequence when a sudden and rapid movement is required; but, for operations on the rocky, hilly country beyond the frontier nothing is so mobile and suitable as mountain artillery. This should consist of the present 7-pr. in one piece, which is just the thing for short ranges, and for rapid operations over difficult ground. To be supplemented by a more powerful gun; if possible a better gun even than the new jointed gun. It should be in two pieces, each piece weighing not more than 220 lbs. In each battery I would have four such guns, say 9-prs. or 10-prs., and two howitzers capable of carrying an eighteen pound shell.

In the countries I am alluding to, there are, practically speaking, no roads. It is seldom that artillery can move faster than infantry can march, and no horse or field battery can make any impression upon the thick mud walls of which all forts and houses in these countries are built. For these reasons I am in favour of using the most powerful gun which can accompany troops into the field.

I do not mean to say that no horse or field batteries should form part of an army operating beyond our north-west frontier, but I am decidedly of opinion that the greater part of the artillery, on such an occasion, should consist of mountain and heavy batteries.

For India itself, I see no necessity for a lighter field gun than that proposed to be introduced at home. Good roads and a network of railways are being rapidly constructed, and the greater part of the country consists of vast tracts of level expanses; conditions which are all in favour of a heavy field gun.

Again, it is desirable, for many reasons, that the equipment of the various batteries in England and India should be similar. For instance, quite recently batteries were sent from this country to operate, side by side, with some batteries in South Africa and Egypt. A different equipment would have been manifestly inconvenient.

The advantage of a lighter gun claimed by Colonel Macfarlan, *viz.*, "to use the horses of the country," and thus get rid of the Australians,[21] does not commend itself to me. We have never really depended upon India to horse our artillery. At first, when but few horses were procurable from other places, bullock draught was chiefly resorted to; then came the expensive stud system in Bengal, with Arab and Persian horses in Madras and Bombay. Efforts are now being made to improve the blood and bone of the country horses, but I should doubt their ever becoming powerful enough for artillery purposes, however light the gun may be. We must either start studs again, or import horses. Australians answer admirably, and are fairly cheap; the breed is steadily improving, and the supply is unlimited. The horses we now get would compare favourably with those purchased for the artillery at home.

I would strongly dissuade Government from taking any steps to discourage the Australian market. If we keep our batteries properly horsed, and have a reserve of horses in India, sufficient to meet the demand of one year, I don't think we need fear any such grave emergency arising as would jeopardise our supply of remounts for artillery purposes.

RP 97–2/LXII

194
On the Desirability of having a more powerful Armament than the 7-PR Jointed Gun for British Mountain Batteries in India[22]

[Printed] Bangalore
22 July 1883

In a Minute, dated 23rd May 1883, on Colonel MacFarlan's proposal for a light field gun for use in India, I adverted to the great value of mountain artillery in all operations on and beyond the frontier of India, and advocated the introduction of a more powerful armament for British mountain batteries than the 7-pr jointed gun.

I understand that the authorities at the Royal Arsenal, Woolwich, are prepared to construct a jointed 9-pr. M.L.R. mountain gun, weighing about 450 lbs., with a steel carriage in two parts, weighing 210 lbs. and 215 lbs., respectively, and having a hydraulic buffer attached to it. These weights, though they may be considered as the maximum, are not beyond the carrying power of the best mules in our batteries.

Such a gun would be most valuable in hill warfare, and I strongly recommend that the Home Government be requested to construct one or two of this weight and calibre, and have them carefully tested.

With reference to the carriage, I would observe that as regards the particular service for which it would be required, there would seem to be no objection to a hydraulic buffer like that made for 12-pr. B.L. field gun being fitted to it, but it is desirable that conclusive experiments should be made in England, with the carriage as well as the gun.

Should the experiments prove satisfactory, each battery might have 4 9-pr. guns, and to render the armament really effective, I would give in addition two jointed B.L.R. howitzers capable of throwing a large shell; possibly a shell similar to that constructed for the proposed new heavy field gun would be the most convenient, with a view to simplicity of ammunition.

For mountain warfare, no doubt a M.L. howitzer would be preferable, especially in a battery of M.L. guns, but the well known want of accuracy in the fire of a M.L. howitzer, makes it almost imperative that a B.L. howitzer should be introduced, provided that the Royal Gun Factory can construct one sufficiently simple and strong to stand rough usage.

Personally, I see no serious objection to the existence of M.L. guns and B.L. howitzers side by side in the same battery. The ammunition (except perhaps the fuzes) would in any case be dissimilar, while the uniformity of velocity and consequent accuracy of range are so much greater in a B.L. than in a M.L. howitzer, as to more than compensate for any trifling disadvantages which might arise from this new system.

Believing, as I do, that the subject is one of grave importance, I earnestly invite the early attention of Government to the consideration of further development in the power of our mountain artillery in India, and would strongly urge that the War Office may be communicated with in the matter.

The above proposals are not intended to interfere with the armament of Native mountain batteries, which, for the present at any rate, should consist of the 7-pr. gun, in *one* piece; a very useful weapon for short ranges, and for rapid operations over difficult ground.

RP 97–2/LXIV

195
Roberts to Colonel Hughes, Deputy Adjutant-General India

[Printed]   Ootacamund
                                        18 October 1883

I am delighted to hear that you are to suceed Napier Campbell; at the same time I am very sorry that you are leaving head quarters. Sir Donald has not told me who is to be the next Deputy Adjutant General; I am anxious to know this, for we may have to work together. I have quite made up my mind to go home when Sir Donald does, if I am not to succeed him; nothing would induce me to serve in India under Wolseley; he told Elles[23] he hoped to come to India! We are both very sorry you will not be at Bangalore; I hope, however, to see you in Calcutta next February; I propose going there for a few days, but Lady Roberts has not quite made up her mind whether she will accompany me or stay here with the children. In July she goes home again for 3 or 4 months, so as to be with our boy during the summer holidays.

I am glad you approve of my last letter to L'Estrange.[24] He has not written since. Now, old fellow, I want your opinion as to what I am to do with the enclosed paper.[25] I commenced writing it about a year ago, and then left it until August last, when I felt impelled to finish it. At first I thought of sending it to the *Nineteenth Century*, as that magazine has the widest circulation, and my object in writing the paper, is to stir up the British public, who have been educated into a disbelief of any hostile intentions on the part of Russia, and to a horror of interfering in Afghan affairs. But I do not feel quite sure whether I ought, holding a high position under Government, to publish such a paper, and whether I should not, in the first instance send it to the members of the Government. My fear is that they will simply pigeon-hole it, and that, not having public opinion to force them to action, they will let matters slide until it will be too late for us to interfere, with any hope of success, to save Afghanistan from Russia. All my trouble would then be thrown away.

There is a third course (as Mr Gladstone would say), *viz.*, to publish the paper in the *Quarterly* if the Editor would accept it, but I do not think that an unsigned article on such a subject would carry much weight, and I have a dislike to writing anonymously, especially as I have, in this case, been rather down on Sir Henry Norman, and as I disagree with the conclusions of a strategist like Hamley. On the other hand, the fact of my name being attached might confirm Russia on many points about which she must be more or less doubtful. My belief, however, is that Russia has a pretty accurate knowledge of the situation, and it seems to me more important that the British public should be told clearly and plainly how matters stand, than that anything should be concealed for fear of enlightening Russia. You will observe that I do not mention the actual strength of the force we could put into the field; such information would doubtless be valuable to Russia, and I have carefully avoided all political controversy, confining myself to a simple statement of facts as regards the past. In this way I hope to attract Conservatives, Liberals, and possibly even some Radicals.

I know that some men advocated the abandonment of Kandahar, because they feared that our next move would be to Herat. Upon such men the views I have expressed will have great effect. Dr Markby, Professor of Indian Law at Oxford, and an ex-Judge of the Calcutta High Court, pressed me to make my opinions known on this point when I was at home. He is a very advanced Liberal, and he told me that the knowledge that Kandahar would be the limit we ought to go to, would lessen considerably the opposition which men, holding his own views, had offered to a forward policy.

It does not seem advisable to detail the many ways in which we could trouble Russia in the event of her crossing the frontier of an Afghanistan friendly to us. She would, under such circumstances, be much in the same position that we should be were we to become entangled in the passes of a hostile Afghanistan. A few British and well disposed Mahomedan Native officers would enable Afghan troops, and the tribes on the line of Russia's advance, to worry the invaders pretty considerably. With this short explanation, you will be able, I hope, to advise me which of the following three courses to adopt –

1st. – Publish in the *Nineteenth Century*.
2nd. – Distribute copies among the members of the present Government, reserving to myself the right to publish afterwards, if they take no action.
3rd. – Publish in the *Quarterly Review*.

After coming to a conclusion, please send me a telegram saying which of the three courses you would recommend. I should like to receive your answer before the 29th, as we leave Ootacamund on that day.

When you write, I shall be glad to have your opinion on the paper, and please tell me whether Hamley is the kind of man to dislike having his views criticised. I hardly know him, but I propose writing to him (if I publish) to explain more fully my reasons for disagreeing with him.

Of course you will treat this letter and the enclosed paper as strictly confidential.

RP 97–2/LXXV

196
Roberts to Duke of Cambridge

[Printed]   Bangalore
Private   28 January 1884

I was unable to write to Your Royal Highness last week, as the manoeuvres were going[26] on and I was at some distance from the Head Quarters Camp. Since then the camp has been broken up and the troops are now *en route* to their respective stations.

On the whole, the manoeuvres were well executed. I enclose an account of each days proceedings together with my remarks as Umpire in Chief, it may interest Your Royal Highness to read them. The troops had some long marches, but there were no signs of fatigue, and everything was carried on with spirit. To a casual observer the country looks easy, but in reality it is difficult, being much cut up by ravines and irrigated land; cavalry and artillery require specially good ground-scouting, and even then find difficulty in moving rapidly.

In all peace manoeuvres the attack has the advantage, as the troops composing it advance much more quickly than would be possible on actual service, unless the umpires are constantly on the alert. This was certainly the case with us, but irrespective of that, the attacking force had the best of it. General Prendergast[27] displayed considerable skill in concealing his movements, and in bringing a far superior force to that of his adversary to bear on the decisive point. He had the advantage of his Staff and Commanders; Lt Colonels Morton of the 14th Hussars and Gatacre, 77th Regiment,[28] as AAG and AQM General respectively were very useful; the Infantry Brigadiers (Elles and Dixon)[29] are both intelligent, particularly the former, who handled his Brigade well, as soon as he got confidence; Lt Colonel Rawlins managed the Artillery satisfactorily; and Colonel Hooper (2nd Madras Cavalry), though far from being a brilliant cavalry officer, conducted his reconnaissances and scouting duties better than Colonel Russell (12th Lancers).[30] Neither of these last named officers, however, seemed to recognize the importance of obtaining intelligence of the enemy's movements, and did not afford their Generals as much assistance as they might have. Sir Charles Keyes[31] was nearly out-manoeuvred the second day, and was fairly beaten the third. Neither of his Infantry Commanders (Gib and Brett)[32] shewed much talent or enterprise, and his Artillery was but feebly handled. In the absence of any RA Lt Colonel, Major Sandham commanded the two batteries, I was not favourably impressed by him, or by the battery commanders, Major Lavie and Captain Nugent.[33] The three battery commanders on the other side (Lt Colonel Swinley, Majors Anderson and Broadfoot)[34] are quite above the average, and contributed much to the success of General Prendergast. Lt Colonel Russell disappointed me; his regiment is in an admirable order, and on the parade ground he is all that could be desired, but I doubt his ever making a good cavalry leader. Your Royal Highness would have been pleased to see the British Infantry working, the 7th Fusiliers and 43rd especially did well; the latter get over ground in quite a remarkable manner, the reason, I believe, being that the Company Officers are allowed to command their own men and have them well in hand. The 7th are of unusual physique and have some good officers, though the Colonel (Beauchamp)[35] does not seem particularly bright. The 2nd Battalion South Wales Borderers (24th) are a fine body of men, they are however weak in numbers and it struck me that they are not in quite the same form as when I saw them at Secunderabad in December 1882. Lt Colonel Caldwell[36] is not, I understand, a very wise commanding officer; nothing has come up officially, but from what Sir Charles Keyes told me privately, I thought it necessary to have Colonel Caldwell warned that I expected him to be more conciliatory both to his officers and men. The 2nd Battalion Middlesex Regiment (77th) have improved much in looks during the last two years; they are also far below their strength and are evidently commanded throughout by the Colonel (Colquhoun),[37] this prevents their being as useful in the field as a battalion in which the company leaders are allowed to look after themselves. The native corps held their own fairly well, and one or two which had come from out-of-the-way stations, notably the 10th and 12th, improved even in the short time they were at the camp. The night march under Sir Charles Keyes, across a really difficult country, was quite a success. Indeed, the field firing was the only failure, and this miscarried most unaccountably. General Prendergast, who had the management of it, is very keen and unusually intelligent, but for some reason or another he failed to give any reality to the operation. The march past was well done, and I think that the Madras troops, in their new uniform made a favorable impression upon the "foreign officers".[38]

* * *

RA Add MSS E/1/10611; printed
RP 97–1/LXXIII

197
Childers to Roberts

[Holograph]   [No location]
                                               29 January 1884

Thank you very much for your letter, and for sending me your paper on Free Trade in the Army. There is much in it with which I cordially agree, and the whole deserves careful weighing by those in authority. But I will venture to make a few remarks on one or two points of detail.

1. I was not aware that the minimum height in the Line in 1870 was 5ft 8, and that the better Short Service recruiting here was due to its reduction. In 1870 a very large addition was made to the Army, I think 10,000 men, & this necessitated nearly doubling the no. of recruits. But when I took office the height was fluctuating between 5ft 4 & 5ft 5. I fixed it at 5ft 4, and raised the age, & the result was a far more rapid recruiting than the no. fixed by Parliament. I had to check this, too much so as it turns out, and Ld Hartington restored the state of things to something better than it was (as to recruits) in 1880. Now we are getting them at the rate of 37,000 a year, & Wolseley's figures on health are conclusive as to their character.

2. You speak of our using in war the system of bounty to attract volunteers, from other Battalions. This is what I stopped. No one can be transferred except within the same Rgt., and I sent out Wolseley's army to Egypt without a single transfer. We had prepared another Army Corps also without a single transfer. I speak of the Guards & Line, not the Cavalry which is on the old system.

I wish you could read on this subject the paper to which I have had access as to the state of matters in the old Peninsula War, in the Duke of York's time, and again in the Crimean war.

I pass from these points of difference to those on which I cordially go with you. Especially do I think that the Service should be made more popular, by kindness & by concessions to the reasonable wishes of the men. This is not wanted for recruiting, as recent figures shew, but it would I think be useful in itself, & raise the men in each others' esteem & that of the Public.

As a matter of fact the Army at home has been (I think rightly) sacrificed to the Army in India; you have no recruits, no very young men, & full leave & power to keep for longer service the magnificent force entrusted to you. The money part is practically in your hands, & so is the treatment of the men. Reading your paper again I should say that the one object, quod organisation, to be cultivated is to impress on your men that they belong to a Regiment not a Battalion; that they are supplied on this system with Regts., and this is their family. We are able at home to find plenty of recruits, your part is to <u>keep</u> what every foreigner regards as the splendid force which is wholly in your charge.

RP 17/5

198
Roberts to O.T. Burne

[Holograph]   Calcutta
                                                   26 February 1884

The accompanying Paper[39] will, I think, interest you – and in most of the views put forth you will probably agree. I learn that the authorities have been roused to the necessity of taking some action with regard to defining the Northern boundary of Afghanistan, and that a proposal to communicate with Russia on the measure will shortly be submitted to the Home Government.[40] Unless you have any one else to run, I hope you will remember how pleased I should be to act as the British representative. The Russians, if they agree to a commission, will certainly name some high official and it is desirable that we should have at least as big a man. I think I should carry more weight with the Russians, and certainly with the Afghans. I can talk Persian enough to get along, and it would be an immense advantage to me, if ever I am to have a frontier command again, to see the country over which a Russian army would have to pass, and to ascertain the resources in supplies, transport etc. I should like to take men like St John and Ridgeway with me, and leave one or both at places where it might be decided to locate British officers.

I have given a copy of the Paper to the Viceroy who, I'm afraid, hardly appreciates it. H.E. is very averse to admitting the necessity of an active policy. Please show it to any one you wish to so <u>in confidence</u>. I do not at all object to my views about Afghanistan and Russia being known, but for obvious reasons it is undesirable that my opinions about the Native Army should become public property.

IOR MSS Eur D 951/3

199
Roberts to Professor William Markby, Oxford

[Printed]
                                    Calcutta
                                    26 February 1884

Do you remember our conversation at Oxford in February 1881, on the subject of Kandahar and writing to me a few days later suggesting that I should put the views I had expressed to you on paper? I hesitated for a long time to do so, but affairs seem to me to be progressing so rapidly on the North-West Frontier of Afghanistan, that a few months ago I followed your advice. I quite intended sending you a copy of the paper,[41] but I found I had entered upon such very confidential matter, such as, for instance, the insecurity of our position in India, the possible danger the Native Army might be to us, &c., &c., that I decided on printing a very few copies, just enough for the Viceroy, Sir Donald Stewart, and the Members of the Government out here and at home. I wish I were near enough to show you what I have written; my object is –

I.   – To point out the importance of Aghanistan to India, and the necessity of our keeping it free from Russian influence.

II. – The desirability of settling the Afghan frontier, and letting Russia clearly understand that if she comes beyond the line laid down, she must be prepared to go to war with England.

III. – That we must not expect much from the people of India, and that if we vacillate and adopt a shrinking policy, we shall not be able to depend upon the Native army.

I show what Russia's progress has been during the last twenty years, and that England and Russia must meet ere long in Asia. I review our past policy and show how completely we failed to make friends with the Afghans, and I point out that our relations with Abdul Rahman now are much what they were with Sher Ali ten years ago, but that in the mean time the positions of Afghanistan, Russia and England have materially altered. That "in fact the situation presents infinitely greater difficulties than in Sher Ali's time, and may necessitate the acceptance on our part of heavier responsibilities than would formerly have been necessary". I then say that "England's only chance of preventing Russian influence from becoming sooner or later supreme in Afghanistan lies in her speedily substituting a bold and firm policy for the half-hearted proceedings of the past, and by endeavouring in every possible way, to place ourselves in some satisfactory relationship with the people of Afghanistan. They must be assured that we have no designs upon their country and that even should circumstances require a British occupation of Kandahar, the direction of all internal affairs would be left in their hands; we must guarantee them the integrity of their kingdom; we must be prepared to hold out advantages as great as they might accept from Russia; and they must be made to see that their interest and ours are identical and that our policy would under no circumstances be liable to change, as it has hitherto changed." I point out the difficulties of our dealing with an Amir, who has no power over his own country, and ask "whether it would not be better for us to accept the fact that the country is in a state of disintegration, and to endeavour to deal with it as so many distinct Provinces," and I add that "the most effectual way of gaining a hold over the country, without offending the susceptibilities, or incurring the dislike of the Afghans would be to convince them of the benefits they would derive from their commercial system becoming closely connected with that of Hindustan." I then point out the advantage of completing the railway to Quetta, and the civilizing effect it would have all over Afghanistan.

So much for (I)

With regard to (II), I urge that "no time should be lost in defining the northern boundary of Afghanistan. It should run from the Tejend river near Sarakhs to Panjdeh, and thence to Khoja Saleh, or any other point that will include all the cultivable portion of the Afghanistan Khanates." I then go on to point out the necessity "of Russia being made clearly to understand, that she will not be permitted to interfere with Afghanistan, and that any encroachment on the northern boundary of that country, would be a *casus belli* with England" and the desirability of England having early and accurate information of Russia's movements.

I then proceed to discuss the line by which Russia would probably advance, supposing we are unfortunate enough to lose our hold over Afghanistan, and the course that would be best for us to adopt under such circumstances. I think it nearly certain that, while a small force would move on Kabul *via* Balkh, the main army would take the Herat-Kandahar-Kabul line. "Hence the reason for Kandahar being to us a point of the very greatest strategical importance" Sir Edward Hamley has given it as his opinion that from Kandahar an enemy would proceed by Quetta and the Bolan pass. I think not because –

(a) Strategically and politically, it is the line which would be "the easiest for us to defend."
(b) "It enters upon a poor and unimportant country, and would bring the invader near the sea – the last place at which the commander of such a force would like to find himself."
(c) "It is the furthest point from the Punjab, which province it would be the object of the invader to seize first."

The strength of the invading army is somewhat difficult to calculate, but I have said that it would depend more upon the resources of the country, as regards supplies and transport, than upon the number of men that would be available. The probable strength of our own force, I can estimate more definitely; one thing is certain, that only a limited number of our native troops could be depended upon to fight against a European enemy, and unless we show a bold front, and let it be clearly seen that we intend to win, even these few would most assuredly question the policy of remaining faithful. This is a point apparently lost sight of by those who advocate waiting to be attacked, but it is one that requires to be carefully considered, as indeed must the question of the Native army generally. Our several armies are useful in their different ways, and will prove valuable instruments in our hands, or the reverse, according to the way we make use of them. The army is the great danger; if properly managed it will do well; if misunderstood and misapplied, it will prove a broken reed. Under the most favorable circumstances our force would be a small one compared to what we might have to meet. Its operations should, therefore be combined to a single line, in order that its strength might not be frittered away in detached columns.

"That line should be the one which presents the least difficulties in a political and physical sense; it should require the minimum number of men to hold it, and should admit of the maximum number of men being concentrated at its extreme point, whence we could take the offensive, and strike a blow with our fullest strength, as soon as the opportunity for action arrives."

I then discuss the four routes we have to choose between, *viz.*, the Khyber, the Kurum, the Gwuleyree[42] (near Dera Ismail Khan) and the Bolan, and give my opinion in favor of the Bolan.

"Kandahar is evidently then the goal, which we should make for, and though it would doubtless be necessary to hold certain points at or near Kandahar, *under no circumstances should we be persuaded to send an army beyond Kandahar*, except for the purpose of fighting a battle, and dealing the enemy a crushing blow on ground which we could previously select. *An advance to Herat is now altogether out of the question.* With Afghanistan friendly to us, such a measure should be unnecessary; with Afghanistan against us, it would be unadvisable. Under the last named condition, we could not reach Herat before the Russian, and its distance from India, would necessitate the employment of a force infinitely larger than we could hope to mobilise."

This will give you some idea of the scope of the paper. You will, I am sure, give me credit for not being an alarmist, and throughout the paper, I have shewn that I have no desire to annex Afghanistan, or any part of it. I advocated retaining Kandahar because it seemed to me certain that we should have to return there ere long, but I do not now wish to see any advance beyond our present frontier. All I would urge is that we should make ourselves as secure as possible up to that frontier; that we should endeavour by all means in our power to improve our relations with the Afghans, and that we should, at any rate, delay the inevitable meeting of Russia and England in Asia, by entering into a treaty which could not be broken without risk of war. I have not the slightest objection to my opinions on the subject generally being known, but I would of course wish that my opinion of the Native Army should be treated *most confidentially*.

I am sending you by this mail a paper on a different subject; it is not much in your line, but every one must be to a certain extent interested in the army. In the face of recent speeches you may have some difficulty to accept what I have written. Recruits are coming in because the standard has been reduced lower than it has ever been, and medical inspections are somewhat leniently carried on, but the difficulty of keeping men in the army after they have been caught has not been faced. It is to a certain extent a question of money, but unless the service is made popular the money will be thrown away. We are some 4,000 men short in India, notwithstanding the offer of Rs. 120 bounty, and the jubilee over the success of recruiting.

RP 97–1/LXXXIII

200
Roberts to Stanhope

[Holograph]   ?Calcutta
Private   3 March, 1884

I sent you, a few days ago from Calcutta, a copy of a Paper[43] I was induced to write on reading Lord Hartington's speech at the Mansion House last August. My first idea was to publish the Paper, but I thought that my suggestions would be more likely to receive consideration if I offered them to the responsible authorities; this I did some little time ago. I have not heard yet from Lord Hartington, but unless I am much mistaken, Lord Wolseley's speech at the dinner given by the Artists' Corps of Volunteers for Sir Fred Leighton was intended as a hint to me that he, at any rate, does not share my opinions. Recruits are coming in because the standard has been reduced lower than it has ever been before, and medical officers are told not to be too particular with their inspections; but you may have observed that the Artillery, which require a better class of men, cannot complete their numbers. We are still about 4000 men short in India, not withstanding that nearly 7000 men were attracted by the Rs 120 bounty to extend their service. I feel sure that the terms of enlistment recently sanctioned for the Guards will have to be made applicable to the Line, but it will be a very dangerous and a very expensive measure, unless some attempt is made at the same time to make the Army popular. I took some trouble to find out the reasons why soldiers object to prolonging their service, and regimental officers will, I think, tell you that I have given the correct ones, and that I have not overstated them.

We are anxiously watching General Gordon's movements in the Soudan. Graham's success at Tokar should help him considerably, but he has a difficult task, and one which nobody else could hope to bring to a successful issue.

I am glad to see that the Government have decided to complete the railway to Quetta, or rather Pishin; I am sending you a Paper which will show you how important I consider this railway and how much I hope it will improve our relations with the Afghans. If we can keep on friendly terms with them, and prevent the Russians from gaining influence in their country, we are not likely to have any serious trouble in India. Kindly consider my Paper confidential; I have given copies to Lord Ripon and some members of the Government and though I have no objection to my views being known (except as regards the Native Army) but so long as I am holding an appointment conferred on me by the present Ministry, I would rather not be held up as the advocate of a policy which cannot but be distasteful to them after all that has occurred, and which there are already signs they will be forced to adopt, if they remain long enough in office.

It seems to me very necessary that no time should be lost in coming to some agreement with Russia regarding the Northern boundary of Afghanistan, for until this has been decided upon, it is difficult for us to say to Russia "You must not come any further". The boundary has never been defined, and neither Persia, Russia, Bokkhara, or Afghanistan could tell you how it should run.

You will readily understand how desirable it is that my opinions about the Native Army should not be made public. As I have said "Our several armies are useful in their different ways, and while it would be dangerous to employ the greater number of them against a Western army, it would be scarcely less dangerous for them to know that they would not be so employed."

Stanhope MSS U1590/0305/1

201
Major-General Sir Charles Brownlow, Assistant Military Secretary, War Office, to Roberts

[Holograph]   London
                                                   20 June 1884

Private

Thanks for yours of 23rd inst.

I am glad to have such an honest expression of your opinions on the relative value of the several classes that the uninformed public lumps together under the head of "Indian troops".

Hardinge & Haines are both prepared to go anywhere and do anything with Madras or Bombay sepoys provided they wear the special pattern of knickerbocker or pugree that each has invented, or that they have been instructed in a particular mode of attack!

Nothing sickens me more than the nonsense that is talked on this subject, and the use or abuse of the idea that we have 500,000 Indian soldiers panting for death in the Soudan or anywhere else. This contemptible delusion has I believe a great deal to say to the apathy of our rulers as to the hopeless condition of the British Army at home, if not in India.

We swagger and dictate to the world and yet we are quite unable, not only to put 10000 men in the field, but to send that number to India to complete our Establishment.

If any considerable body of Indian troops go to Egypt I hope you may go with them, but I hope still more that no such troops may be sent. There is no idea of it at present, & I am watchful to prevent it if I can. No good can come of a connecting link between India and the mess we have made of Egypt.

As to Russia I am in no immediate alarm if we keep cool and do not take troops <u>away</u> from India – black or white.

I never doubted her evil intentions, but I must admit that I did not, until Skobeleff took Geok Teppe,[44] believe in her power to advance as rapidly as she has done. From first to last the idea has dominated me that the goodwill of the Afghans was worth more to us than any factor in the question and I still hold obstinately to the belief that we did well to surrender Candahar.

Remember that I have always been for holding Peshin in force sufficient to enable us to recover our lost ground in a week, and for completing not only the railway from Scinde upwards, but the Thal Chotiali road[45] from Dera Ghazi. I do not believe in the zone of love wherewith we should have begirt ourselves by the occupation of Candahar – I know too well how much we are loved outside the cantonment pillars of Peshawar.

As to fortifications a good supply of entrenching tools will enable us to do all that we shall want to do, not at Candahar but on the Helmund.

I am glad you have reopened the question of your leave. Let me know when it comes home. You are very right to get a respite from work & from India while you can.

I need not say that I am too much of an Indian not to pray and work for you as regards the succession to Stewart. I like Wolseley very much but I do not like to see everything I have venerated turned upside down.

RP 12/1

202
Officiating Military Secretary (Captain Ian Hamilton) to Commanding Officers of 14th Hussars and 67th Foot

[Printed]   Poona
Confidential   3 July 1884

Sir Frederick Roberts has been much struck by the good behaviour of your men, as evinced by the small percentage of court-martial cases. He is anxious to do something which will mark his appreciation of good conduct, and which may still further encourage good behaviour in the future. His Excellency's own idea is that some of those restraints which are essential to discipline in an average or indifferently behaved regiment might safely and advantageously be relaxed in a corps which was well behaved. What is your opinion on this point? For instance, all well conducted men might be excused tattoo, or their tattoo might be postponed, say, half an hour, if that would be considered a boon.

Kindly let me have your ideas on this subject for His Excellency's information; also, any suggestions which may occur to you on the matter of giving good characters more tether.

RP 97–2/XCVI

203
Roberts to Reverend J.G. Gregson[46]

[Printed]   Ootacamund
                                   6 July 1884

I have the pleasure to send you my annual subscription to "the Soldiers' Total Abstinence Association"; you will receive at the same time from my Military Secretary a further sum of Rs. 260, contributed by the officers on the head-quarters staff of the Madras army.

I am making enquiries as to the possibility of meeting your wish to have a recognized room set apart in each set of barracks for the branch society of the association. I quite understand how desirable it is that your temperance work should be placed on a permanent basis, and it would be a pleasure to me to help you in this, or indeed in any other way.

I naturally hear a good deal about barrack life, and I am quite convinced that all who have the welfare of the soldier at heart, cannot do better than to subscribe to your association, and thus assist to promote discipline, contentment and health in the ranks.

It is difficult to give statistics in support of the assertion, but I have little doubt it could be proved that serious crime in the army is almost entirely due to the effects of drink. I am not an abstainer myself, and if I thought that soldiers could trust themselves to drink in moderation, I would not advocate their taking the pledge; but unfortunately, experience shows that few can resist the temptation to exceed, and for this reason I am always glad when I hear that a soldier, especially a young soldier, has joined your society. If the large majority of our men took, and kept the pledge, I am convinced that there would be a great improvement in the matter of health, and a corresponding diminution in the number of courts-martial.

RP 97–1/XCVII

204
Roberts to Grant Duff

[Printed]   Arkonum Railway Station
                                                 8 July 1884

I hear privately from Sir Donald Stewart that the Viceroy has submitted my name, amongst others, to the home authorities, to accompany the commission destined to determine the northern boundary of Afghanistan.

Stewart says:- "If you would like the employment, I would advise you to make interest at home *at once*." I should like to go of all things, and I have both written and telegraphed to Lord Northbrook and Sir Henry Rawlinson, but I hesitate to do so to

Lords Kimberley and Granville,[47] as I know so little of them. The selection, no doubt, rests with these two latter, and if you think you could write, or, better still, telegraph, to either or both of them, I shall be very grateful. Should you telegraph, I will gladly pay all expenses.

It seems to me very desirable that an officer of rank and some reputation in the east should be sent with the commission, and that every advantage should be taken of this opportunity to get accurate military information of the country. I have many friends amongst the Afghans who would help me if necessary; I can talk Persian, and though I have unfortunately allowed my French to get somewhat rusty, I am brushing it up, and in a couple of months I hope to be able to converse fairly well.

RP 97–2/XCVIII

205
Roberts to Stanhope

[Printed]   Bangalore
Private   12 July 1884

As it is possible that the question of the Government of this country proceeding to the hills for a certain number of months every year may be brought before Parliament owing to the agitation now going on in Madras, I venture to trouble you with these few lines in order that you may be in possession of the true facts of the case, so far as I myself am concerned.

Soon after my arrival here I found that considerable difficulty was experienced in carrying on the work at Army Head Quarters, owing to the offices being divided, and that if I wish to carry out my desire to spend the greater part of each year inspecting the troops under my command, it would be necessary to find some one place where the offices could be permanently located. The choice lay between Madras and Ootacamund; I selected the latter for the following reasons: it is healthier, it is a more economical arrangement to the State, and it is the place at which the

Government usually resides during the time when I was not likely to be so much on tour.

The Government of Madras and the Government of India approved of my proposal, and in due course the Secretary of State for India sanctioned the transfer of Army Head Quarter offices to Ootacamund. The local press took but little notice of this at the time; the measure was in accordance with the decision which had been arrived at in Bengal some 20 years previously, after the question as to whether Army Head Quarters in India should be permanently located at Simla or in Calcutta had been very fully discussed; and it was very similar to the arrangement existing in Bombay, where for years past Poona has been the seat of Army Head Quarters. Probably nothing more would have been heard of the matter but for a proposal recently made by the Controller of Military Accounts to remove his office from Madras to Bangalore. This office has hitherto been in Fort St George, occupying barracks belonging to the troops, some of whom were obliged in consequence to live in places quite unfit for British soldiers. Government agreed with me that such quarters as were required by the troops should be vacated, and that accommodation should be provided for the offices elsewhere. As no convenient place could be found in Madras, the Controller proposed that his office should be moved to Bangalore, where several Government buildings have recently been vacated owing to the removal of the ordnance depôt from the old fort. Mr Grant Duff is to meet me here in a day or two when the matter will be finally settled. Should the buildings prove in every way convenient, the Controller's office will no doubt be transferred here, as it is absurd to suppose that the Government would incur the expense of hiring or constructing offices in Madras while suitable accommodation exists elsewhere, unless, of course, it was necessary that the offices should be located in Madras itself. In this case there is no necessity, as the Controller's work does not in any way require him to be near the local Government. His is an Imperial, not a Presidential office; this is exemplified in the Bombay Presidency where the office of the Controller of Military Accounts is located at Poona, and not in Bombay itself. The possibility of the removal of the

Controller's office from Madras has produced the present excitement, and on the 3rd instant a meeting was held in that city, at which a resolution was passed to memorialise Parliament, protesting against the annual move of the Government to the Hills, and urging that Army Head Quarters should be brought back to Madras.

It is, of course, very desirable that the Commander-in-Chief should attend meetings of Council whenever any important measure has to be discussed, or when he is unable, owing to the season of the year, to carry on inspections. At other times, his duty requires him, in my opinion, to be with some portion of the army he commands. I know from experience how much an army benefits by being frequently visited by a Commander-in-Chief, and after talking the matter over with Mr Grant Duff, on my first reaching the Presidency, I decided, with His Excellency's full concurrence, to see as much as possible of the troops; they are widely scattered, and some of them are in such very out-of-the-way places, that although I have travelled about for several months in a year, I have not yet been able to visit every station. In Bengal, the Commander-in-Chief finds that he can only spend a limited time in Calcutta every year, and General Hardinge is very seldom in Bombay. It is not, I understand, looked upon as a grievance by the residents of those cities, who very properly consider it better for the head of an army to be looking after the troops he is responsible for than sharing in the pleasures of a gay capital. Unfortunately for me, the good people of Madras have hitherto seen more of former Commanders-in-Chief than they have of me, and they resent my being so seldom amongst them. Owing to the want of communication it was not possible for my predecessors in the old days to travel about as I do, and for the same reason the Government could not go to the hills as it does now. But with a daily increasing railway system it would be strange if I left any military station unvisited, and equally strange if the Members of the Government did not avail themselves of the facilities to spend the hot weather months in a climate where the work of the State can be performed far more efficiently than in the plains.

The memorialists base one of their arguments against this

annual move to the hills on the grounds that the present scale of pay in India was originally fixed upon as a compensation for having to live in a bad climate. This was, no doubt, one reason, but a still stronger one I suspect was the necessity of attracting a superior class of Englishmen to the country. Anyhow, nothing can be reasonably urged on the score of pay, for the expense of living has increased so considerably of late years that what may have been a high salary 50, or even 20 years ago, cannot be considered so now; besides, I believe I am right in saying that the allowances of nearly every high official have been to a certain extent reduced during the same period. My two immediate predecessors were quite right when they told me I should find that my pay was only just sufficient to enable me to fill creditably the position of Commander-in-Chief; were it less, or had I to incur additional expenses by keeping up a house in Madras, I should be forced to resign the command.

As a matter of fact, the agitation is not the effect of any widespread feeling of the Europeans or natives of this Presidency. It is an effort made by the trades-people and press of Madras to try and revive the declining importance of their capital. Bombay is rapidly becoming the chief representative of the mercantile strength of the British in India, and in this Presidency, even less than in Calcutta and Bombay, the theory will not bear stating that only at the capital can the Government keep itself "in touch" with Indian public opinion.

The way to keep touch is to travel about amongst the people; this Mr Grant Duff has done most thoroughly. His Excellency never spares himself, and has never been for any length of time consecutively in the hills. He has visited every district in the Presidency, and is now, at this unfavourable season, on a lengthened tour.

Trusting you will excuse me for taking up so much of your time.

RP 97–1/CX

206
Roberts to Colonel Keith Fraser[48]

[Printed]   Ootacamund
                                                  8 August 1884

. . . You ask me about the scouting, &c., of the 9th Lancers in
Afghanistan. I need scarcely tell you how thoroughly I appreciated
the good qualities of this fine regiment – whether in quarters or in the
field, their conduct, turn out, dash and gallantry left nothing to be
desired, and could not have been exceeded by any cavalry in the
world. But I must confess to you that after many opportunities of seeing their fitness for the work, I came to the conclusion that scouting
was not their strong point. The men are not to blame for this. The
fault is in our system of training; in the absence of real work on an
enemy's frontier; and in the few opportunities cavalry have of taking
part in extended manoeuvres, and in practising reconnaissances at a
distance from the parade ground. The constant outpost and detached
duties which our Native cavalry have to perform, give the men a confidence in themselves, and an individuality you seldom find in the
British trooper. I do not wish for a moment to compare British and
Native cavalry, and I am only alluding to some of our best native regiments in northern India. These are a rough and ready lot, without
any pretensions to the smartness, efficiency in drill and general turn
out, which are the distinguishing characteristics of their British comrades, but you will find on service that from their practical training
native soldiers are able to shift at once for themselves, and seem to
know instinctively what is required of them. Please do not think from
this that I would advocate the employment of Native cavalry in
Europe; they would be out of place there, but I would like to see some
system of training devised by which our British cavalry would gain
some of the experience and self-confidence which our Native cavalry
on the Frontier now learn in the ordinary course of their duties.

In India, we have many more opportunities of doing this than
you have at home. There, I see great difficulties, and the only way
is to have, as you propose, combined Horse Artillery and Cavalry
manoeuvres annually on Salisbury plain, or any other suitable

place. Such exercises would have the best result if carried out in a broad and liberal spirit.

Among the British Cavalry regiments which have been in India of late years, I have heard the 11th Hussars spoken of for their intelligence when reconnoitring. I have often admired them on parade, but I never saw them in the field or at a camp of exercise. The regiment with which I have been most impressed is the 14th Hussars; there scouting is far above the average, and I attribute this in a great measure to the experience they gained in South Africa, which no doubt gave the men that self-reliance it is so difficult to acquire on the parade ground. At some small manoeuvres near Secunderabad in 1882, it was a pleasure to see the way the 14th Hussars worked; wherever you moved you found a Hussar scout watching you, and utterly declining to fight so long as his orders were to keep touch with the enemy. This is usually the great difficulty with our cavalry; you saw the 12th Lancers at Bangalore; the 9th Lancers in Afghanistan worked much in the same way. There is that tendency on the part of officers and men to court collision with the enemy to the detriment of their primary duties as scouts which led to the curious spectacle of Russell's brigade being chased out of the village of Tellahunka by the skirmishers of the 43rd, who had been permitted to advance unwatched over a fairly open country for at least 3 or 4 miles.[49] I am issuing instructions to the cavalry regiments in this command to go through a course of instruction in reconnaissance; it seems to me most necessary that this subject should be most carefully studied by all cavalry corps before taking part in manoeuvres, and I think that all officers and non-commissioned officers should prove that they thoroughly understand how to conduct a reconnaissance before they are promoted.

Cavalry should be armed with the best rifle that can be conveniently carried, and either steel scabbards should be abolished and wooden ones substituted, or some combination scabbard should be provided by which the men's swords could be kept sharp, instead of being blunted every time they are drawn.

In considering the question of cavalry equipment, I would strongly urge arrangements being made by which the sword could be carried on the saddle over the shoe pouch when the men dismount to use their carbines, and the carbine slung over the man's back whenever the enemy is reported near. I am aware that most cavalry men will object to this latter proposal, but please remember that I only advocate it in the immediate presence of the enemy; on all other occasions the carbine should be carried in the bucket. I feel very strongly on this point, for on one occasion in Afghanistan, we lost upwards of 40 carbines which remained in the buckets when the riders had been dismounted; either through being wounded themselves, or owing to their horses falling or being shot. And I myself personally witnessed the distressing sight of several men of the 9th Lancers trying in vain to defend themselves with their lances, with their swords dangling between their legs; had they had their carbines, they might have saved their lives. I would rather see our men have only one weapon for mounted work, either a sword or a lance, on one of these he should depend entirely so long as he is on his horse, and when dismounted he should trust to his firearm. If a mounted man has a pistol (as I believe was proposed after Graham's battles in the Soudan), [50] he would be apt to use it on horseback, when he is much more likely to injure friend than foe (I saw a 9th Lancer man in 1857 shoot his Captain's charger dead!), and if the firearm is only to be used on foot, it should be the best kind of rifle or carbine that can be carried conveniently by a cavalry soldier. I am strongly in favour of increasing the number of men in each cavalry corps; the foot soldier can, as you say, be turned out fit for service in a short time, but it takes much longer to train a cavalry soldier, and I agree with Sir Frederick Fitzwygram[51] that after spending three or four years in the reserve, a man would not be of much use as a cavalry soldier. I am also a warm advocate of any step which would tend to make the army popular, such as permitting men, or certainly non-commissioned officers serving abroad, to visit England at stated periods. You will see that my views on the advisability of doing everything to make a soldier's career attractive, are strongly expressed in "Free trade in the Army", published in the June number of the *XIXth Century*.

RP 97–1/CXII

207
Roberts to Lieutenant-General Wilson, Military Member

Ootacamund
9 August 1884

Your letter of the 2nd reached me this morning, and I at once sent you a telegram expressing a hope that it would be found possible to keep the 1st Madras Pioneers on the frontier until the end of the cold weather, when I propose to locate them at Bangalore. The regiment is sick no doubt, but I am under the impression that advantage has been taken of a certain number of men being in hospital to exaggerate the sickness. I have not heard of many deaths, while I have heard that the commanding officer and 2nd-in-command have been doing all they can to get the regiment brought back to Madras at once. Lieutenant-Colonel Tyndal, the 2nd-in-command,[52] sent in his papers as soon as he heard that I had recommended the regiment should be kept away for 6 months more; very bad form, I thought, seeing that a wing of the corps was under orders to join the Zhob expedition. I understand, however, that he is no loss.

It will have a bad effect if corps can get their own way in such matters, and I am induced to think that if the regiment were told that they would remain until the end of the cold season, sick or not, we should hear no more of the men being ill. Then, as regards the 4th Pioneers, it is really most important they should spend 18 months on the frontier; they are prepared to go, and they pride themselves on having been with the 15th Madras Infantry, the healthiest corps, in the Khyber in 1879–80. I do hope you will agree with me and give orders accordingly. I really feel it very necessary for the future efficiency of the Madras army that my views should be given effect to.

RP 97–2/CIV

208
Stanhope to Roberts

[Holograph]
Boston, Lincs.
26 August 1884

I was very glad to receive your explanation of what has recently taken place about the Head Quarters of the Madras Army. It is very probable that the whole matter may now be forgotten here, especially as Parliament is not sitting, but on the other hand it is not unlikely that the whole question of going to the Hills – and especially the move to Simla – may be raised next Session by Mr Gorst,[53] who is taking some interest in it since his visit to India. In that event it will be well for me to know the reasons which have governed your action in Madras in this matter. And it certainly seems to me that you make out a strong case.

I feel the greatest possible interest just now in the Frontier question. But we shall have an uncomfortable & disturbed autumn.

Our news from India strikes me as uncomfortable. The recent outbreak of seditious writing is a disagreeable symptom. Even if [it] be thought wise to take no effective notice of it. The best cure for it would, I think, be to bring back Lord Ripon.

RP 82/3

209
Roberts to Lord Napier

[Printed]
Bangalore
10 October 1884

I was very glad to receive your letter of the 18th August; my only regret is that it did not enclose the paper about the Madras army which Your Lordship mentions having commenced. I hope that you may yet find time to finish it, and that you will send it to me. What you say about the necessity of our employing young men in various parts of the country, even though they may not be the best material for soldiers, is very true, and having enlisted such men, we must do our best to improve them. Madras sepoys have many things to commend them, and I am satisfied that much can be done with them. Their misfortune is having no frontier, and in having taken but a small share in the wars of the last 60 or 70 years.

As you ask me to let you know what I have been able to do for the Madras army, I will enumerate some of the ways in which I have endeavoured to effect improvement:

(1) The men are now dressed in a really nice uniform, and I have reason to believe that they are well satisfied with the change, which was made without expense to them. The question had been under discussion for a long time before I took command, and I found that nearly all the senior officers, both British and native, were much opposed to any alteration. . . I took the opportunity of being at Secunderabad to collect representatives of all corps within a reasonable distance; I then explained to commanding officers that it was desirable to adopt one pattern uniform for the whole army, and that I should like to hear which one of the many was most generally approved of. At the same time I had a smart-looking sepoy of the cavalry and another of the infantry dressed in the uniform I thought most suitable. I left the party for a couple of hours to talk the matter over amongst themselves, and on my return I found that the verdict in favour of the uniform I had proposed was almost unanimous!

(2) Two regiments are now equipped as Pioneers; every man who did not wish to become a Pioneer was allowed to select some other corps to serve in, and his place was taken by a volunteer from another regiment. One of the Pioneer regiments has been employed on the Baluchistan frontier for the last year, and a part of it is now with the Zhob expedition. The second corps is on its way to relieve the first, and will, I hope, spend at least a year on the frontier.

(3) An improved plan of lines has been sanctioned, and one set has just been built at Trichinopoly. The sepoys did the work almost

entirely; this they had not been in the habit of doing, and I was assured there would be great difficulty. I went to Trichinopoly when the lines were marked out, and have visited it several times since; the men were slow at first, but they soon improved, and are now quite satisfied with the work they have done. Each Native officer has a house to himself, instead of living with the other men of the company, and the bachelors have a separate quarter to themselves away from the families.

(4) No sepoy is allowed to be married, or if he is married to have his family living with him, for the first three years of his service. Government hesitated to sanction this, but I was able to prove that some such custom existed in many regiments, and that the majority of the men were in favour of it. The order does not have retrospective effect.

(5) Messes for recruits have been established in every regiment, and are gradually becoming popular, so much so that in some corps bachelor sepoys have asked to be allowed to join them.

(6) Every regiment now has a small gymnasium. Government refused assistance, either in starting, or transporting the gymnasium when regiments moved in relief, so an inexpensive apparatus has been provided out of regimental funds, the same pattern has been adopted, and there should be no difficulty in exchanging gymnasia. Four men of each regiment are being instructed by the nearest British corps, and they, when competent, will teach the recruits and line boys of their own regiments, and such other men as may be willing to go through the course.

(7) Farriers belonging to the native cavalry now attend the Poona course, and commanding officers report favorably of the result.

(8) Whenever it is possible, regiments march in relief instead of travelling by rail, which I found had been the custom in this presidency.

(9) A camp of exercise was held at Bangalore this year, and smaller

camps have been held each year at several stations. Government has now agreed to give an annual grant of Rs. 5,000 which will admit of manoeuvres on a limited scale being carried out at most of the larger stations.

(10) Places of refuge have been arranged for at every station where they are likely to be required. At most places in the presidency a fort of some sort already exists; these have been, or are being, put in order; all reserve ammunition is being stored in them, the ranges of all prominent objects have been ascertained and noted, and orders have been drawn up detailing the measures to be adopted in time of trouble.

(11) At Bangalore an entrenchment has been constructed in a suitable position to serve as a place of refuge, and in which the ordnance depôt will be placed. Hitherto this has been located in the old Bangalore fort, some 3 miles from cantonments and beyond the native city.

(12) Orders have been drawn up for the protection of the Hyderabad Residency, and arrangements made, by which the General Officer Commanding at Secunderabad can be quickly informed, night or day, of any sudden disturbance in the city.

(13) The unsatisfactory position of the entrenchment at Secunderabad has been pointed out to Government, and also the danger of permitting the treasure, amounting usually to 70 or 80 lakhs of rupees, being placed under a small native guard in the Hyderabad Residency. Government, however, decided not to move the treasure, and to make the best of the present entrenchment. This is now being done, but the position is most unsatisfactory, and instead of the Hyderabad Subsidiary Force being able to take the field during any disturbance, the greater portion of the troops would be required for the defence of the entrenchment and Residency.

(14) Sanction has been obtained for a soldier's exhibition to be

held at Bangalore next year. This will be the first exhibition of the kind in the Madras Presidency.

(15) Some of the Madras and Bangalore volunteers took part in the Bangalore camp of exercise, and the Volunteer movement is being encouraged in every way. A new corps has just been raised at Trichinopoly and Negapatam, called the South of India Railway Volunteers.

(16) A scheme has been started for the employment of discharged native soldiers as Commissionaires, very similar to that proposed for the Bombay army by General Hardinge.

(17) There is a considerable improvement in the shooting of the Madras Army, and the interest, in rifle practice, is year by year increasing.

I trust that you will not think that I am writing in any boastful spirit. I have had unusual opportunities of knowing what an army requires, and I should not be doing justice to the training I received, when serving under Your Lordship as Quarter Master General in India, did I not try to do all in my power to benefit the army I have the honor to command. I feel that the Madras troops are capable of being improved, and that in some ways they have the advantage over other native soldiers. They are certainly more intelligent, mainly because they are better educated. I have purposely avoided anything like pressure, and have endeavoured to lead rather than to drive. Soldiers are naturally conservative, and I should have defeated my own ends if I had not endeavoured, in the first instance, to gain the confidence of both officers and men. Some of the measures introduced have, I know, been distasteful to a certain class, but on the whole they have been accepted most loyally, and I have every reason to speak well of the assistance I have received from all ranks.

It is very kind of Your Lordship to express a hope that I may have health enough to succeed to the Commander-in-Chiefship in India. My eyes trouble me occasionally, and I want to take a run home to get advice about them, otherwise, I am very well. My ambition is to be at the head of the army in India, but I think it probable that I shall not succeed Sir Donald Stewart, in which case my intention is to resign my present appointment and go home with Sir Donald. I should not be content to serve under any other Chief in this country, and having this feeling, it would be unwise of me to remain.

RP 97–1/CXIX

210
Remarks on Machine Guns

[Printed]   Madras
                                              25 January 1885

One 10-barrelled and one 5-barrelled rifle calibre Nordenfeldt guns[54] were sent to Bangalore in July last, and, after some practice, a series of interesting experiments were carried out with them.

2. The guns were fired at ranges varying from 300 to 800 yards in competition with marksmen of the 1st Oxfordshire Light Infantry, firing with Martini-Henri rifles: they were also tried at a range of 2,450 yards against 9-pr. guns firing shrapnel shell.

3. The accuracy and power of a weapon which, when worked by men unskilled in its use, can fire 777 shots in 2 minutes at a range of 1,200 yards, and obtain about the same number of hits as fifty first class shots, firing for the same time with Martini-Henri rifles, must be acknowledged by all.

4. It seems clear, therefore, that machine guns must play an important part in future warfare, and the consideration of their organisation and use in the field is of the greatest interest and importance.

5. Great diversity of opinion exists as to the tactical position which should be assigned to machine guns, and this because there has been no practical experience of any value to decide the question.

6. Personally I am not in favor of machine guns forming part of the equipment of artillery. They appear to me to be essentially an infantry weapon: there is nothing in their manipulation that requires any knowledge of artillery matters, and their fire is but a multiplication of infantry fire.

7. In what way machine guns can best be utilized in war can never be satisfactorily settled until some opportunity offers to try them, but I am inclined to think they are better suited for defence than for offence. I can understand their being used with advantage as an offensive weapon under certain conditions, as, for instance, during street firing; the passage of a river; to cover a landing or an infantry attack; but their rôle I conceive to be a defensive one.

8. In gateways, ditches, or other weak points of fortresses, in bridgeheads, stockades, places of refuge, &c., they would be simply invaluable, and I consider it most desirable that a certain number of the best description of machine guns should be available in this country.

9. It has been suggested that machine guns could be appropriately utilized as escorts to artillery, as an adjunct to cavalry, or with mounted infantry. I think it quite possible that any such guns which could be carried on mules or ponies might be of great assistance to mounted infantry, but I am not at all in favor of using them with cavalry or as an escort to artillery.

10. As I have said before, these guns should not form part of the equipment of artillery, and it is now generally admitted that no special escort should be provided for batteries, the real safety of the guns being confided to the other arms. The movements of cavalry would certainly be hampered by having machine guns attached to them; any assistance they might require could be better afforded by horse or field artillery.

RP 97–2/CXXVIII

211
Roberts to Grant Duff

[Printed]   Kampti
                                             8 February 1885

I am very anxious about Wolseley's force; it is greatly scattered, and we must now expect that the tribes will be hostile.[55]

Dongola is the important point: so long as the Mudir keeps with us all may go well, but should he joint the Mahdi (and he has been suspected by many all along), communication with Egypt would be at once cut off, and then it would go very hard with our troops. Reinforcements could only reach them *via* Suakim, and under the most favorable circumstances, several weeks must elapse before a properly equipped force could march to Berber. I could never understand why Wolseley insisted upon the Nile route. After toiling all the way up the river, he was no nearer Khartoum at Dongola than he would have been at Suakim, which is a perfectly secure base.

The Mahdi either by accident or design has played a good game. Khartoum fell into his hands just as Wolseley had committed himself by dividing his force. It is a most serious business, and I hope that it will not be made worse by attempting to assist Wolseley with too small a force. For such an operation the best commander and the best troops England and India can produce are required.

RP 97–2/CXXX

212
Viceroy (Lord Dufferin and Ava) to Roberts

[Holograph]   Calcutta
                                             4 March 1885

You will have heard of my intended interview with the Amir. It will take place at the end of this month or the beginning of April. I daresay it would interest you to be present, and if so, I need not say how much pleasure it would give me to accommodate you and Lady Roberts and your Staff in my camp.

Perhaps your Military Secretary will let Lord William Beresford know of how many persons your staff will consist.

RP 27/f2

213
Roberts to Lord Randolph Churchill, MP

[Printed copy]   Poona
Private   15 April 1885

You may remember my expressing doubts as to the fighting qualities of the 17th Bengal Infantry, one of the regiments you saw at Allahabad. According to the *Pall Mall Gazette* correspondent it was the only regiment which broke during McNeill's fight,[56] and I hear that the men quite lost their heads and fired wildly, being more dangerous to their friends than their foes. I deeply regret this, but it is what I expected, and confirms the fears I have always had of employing Hindoostani sepoys against a determined enemy.

RP 97–1/CXXVII

214
Roberts to Sir Henry Rawlinson, Member of Council of India

[Printed]   Ootacamund
Private   3 May 1885

* * *

You of course will know all that passed at Rawal Pindi between the Viceroy and the Amir. Throughout the negotiations Lord Dufferin wisely kept his own counsel, and we in the camp heard nothing that went on, but I much doubt whether His Excellency was able to arrive at any satisfactory conclusions as to our future dealings with Afghanistan. He was unfortunately obliged to work with the Amir alone, but in a country like Afghanistan it does not necessarily follow that arrangements made with the Ruler should be concurred in by the people.

Abdul Rahman Khan has no councillors or any one about him whom he trusts, and although by means of great severity he has made himself feared, and has got a certain hold over the country, he is thoroughly hated, and his subjects would gladly take advantage of any chance to get rid of him. Then his health is very bad; his Doctor, who was in our service, and with me in Kabul, told me that he suffers from kidney disease, and is not likely to be long lived.[57]

It is impossible to say whether Abdul Rahman was in earnest and meant all he promised, but I confess I cannot help having grave suspicions of every Afghan. The Afghans want, of course, to keep their country independent, but it is impossible to say which side they would eventually join when they find that they must throw in their lot with one or the other. It is a quaint country to be associated with; if we please the Amir we may disgust the people, while if we secure Herat for the Afghans we may be doing just what the northern tribes do not want. Of one thing I am quite sure, that while it is advisable we should not prematurely force ourselves upon the Afghans, we must avoid anything like timidity or vacillation in our dealings with them; any such action would effectually alienate them from us. It is also very necessary that we should not place ourselves in a false position towards them; they cannot, for instance, understand our holding aloof when Panjdeh[58] was attacked, more especially as we had gone there to check the Russian advance, and it was in accordance with our advice that the Afghans had abstained from attacking the Russians when they might have done so advantageously. The Boundary Commission is now, I fear, somewhat discredited in consequence of having left the Afghans in the lurch at Panjdeh. Lumsden and his party could not perhaps have acted otherwise, but it will be difficult to explain this satisfactorily to the Afghans, and another accident of the sort would, in all probability, turn the whole of northern Afghanistan against us.

You say that you would like to know my views of the plan of the campaign, if there is to be one. It seems to me that war is inevitable, and unless Russia agrees to withdraw her troops to where they were when Lumsden started from England, I would send an army corps at once to Kandahar, taking care to explain to the Afghans beforehand our object in going there. As soon as arrangements could be made, I would move the army corps on to Herat, its place at Kandahar being taken by a second corps, in order to ensure our line of communication being secured without being dependent upon the Afghans. As you are aware, I have hitherto considered that Herat was beyond our sphere of action, and that our operations should be confined to the neighbourhood of Kandahar. When I formed this opinion I never expected that Russia would attempt so forward a movement until she was better prepared than we believe her now to be. I thought that she would wait until she had consolidated her power in the Khanates, had brought Merv into easy communication with the Caspian Sea, and had completed her railways as far as Sarakhs. Russia would then have been so powerful, and would have gained such influence in northern Afghanistan, that it seemed to me we could scarcely hope to save Herat. Now, I think that if we act with boldness and decision, the chances are in our favor, and that even if we cannot reach Herat before the Russians, we ought to be able to turn them out of it, and inflict such punishment upon them as would prevent a recurrence of the Afghan frontier question for many years to come.

However successful we may be, I confess to being fairly puzzled as to where the future frontier of Afghanistan should be fixed. This to my mind is the most difficult part of the present problem. If we agree that it is to be along the north portion of Afghanistan, what guarantee shall we have that its integrity will be observed, and that we shall not be called upon to incur the same vast expenditure of lives and money that now appears imminent? Then, on the other hand, if it be decided to draw the frontier much nearer to India, how should that frontier run? We must, under all circumstances, retain possession of Kandahar, but I really do not see what frontier we could propose which should give us that security it is of vital importance to the Empire we should obtain. The physical difficulties of the country between Peshawar and Herat, the fanatical nature of the tribesmen who occupy the greater portion of it, and the absolute uncertainty of knowing how far at any time the Afghans can be depended upon, all combine to render the solution of this question a difficult one. It may be that the results of the impending campaign will enlighten us on this subject, but I feel far more hazy about it than I care to confess when I consider all the experience I gained in 1878–80 of Afghanistan and the Afghans.

RP 97–1/CXXX

215
Roberts to Stewart

[Printed]   Ootacamund
                                                   26 May 1885

In your letter of the 1st instant you ask me if I could think of anything that would lead us to a vital point in Russia's armour? I have been considering the matter over, and send you the result. It seems to me impossible that we can seriously injure Russia without having allies to assist us. At the same time we cannot afford to remain inactive, while Russia is massing her troops on the Caspian-Askhabad-Sarakhs line, and probably also in the neighbourhood of Tashkend and Samarkand. The question is surrounded by difficulties, and I am afraid we shall never be sure of peace in India if we allow Russia to remain our near neighbour.

We shall have to maintain a far larger army than has hitherto been found necessary, and we shall be put to great expense in constructing fortifications, railways, roads, &c.

But how we can now keep Russia off is indeed a puzzle. I confess I mistrust the Amir. He must know that his troops would have no chance against the Russians, and yet he demurs to our assisting him with men. I can understand his not wishing to have an English army at Kabul, but with, or without his leave, one will, I think, ere long, have to go to Kandahar.

I have made no mention in my paper of Russia's possessions in the Pacific, for although we might trouble her in that part of the world, I cannot believe that anything we could do there would stop her movements in Central Asia.

I have sent two copies of the paper to Mackenzie Wallace.[59]

The telegram ordering the troops detailed for the second army corps no longer to hold themselves in readiness has puzzled me. The Guards are detained at Alexandria, and the Australian contingent at Aden,[60] and it is rumoured that the Russians are making demands which cannot be acceded to. I suppose that the Government has received some information, of which the public are still ignorant? Many thanks for writing to me. I am, of course, very interested in hearing all that is going on.

RP 97–2/CXXIVA

216
Roberts to Lord Salisbury

[Printed]   Ootacamund
                                                 8 June 1885

Central Asian affairs have progressed rapidly since I wrote to Your Lordship on the 19th April 1884. The Russians are now, as Mr Marvin[61] says, "at the gates of Herat," and it is quite time that we should decide how much further they are to be allowed to come, and what is to be our future frontier on the North-West. My views on both these points are contained in the enclosed paper, which I was induced to write, on being asked by Sir Donald Stewart whether I could think of anything that would lead to a vital point in Russia's armour. Without some ally it seems to me that we can only reach the Russians through Afghanistan, and that if we intend to drive them away from the confines of that country, we shall require a larger army than Lord Dufferin and Sir Donald

Stewart have been preparing. Even supposing we can operate through the Black Sea, Russia will, in my opinion, endeavour to act, as much as possible, on the defensive in that direction, while she pushes every man she can find transport for into Afghanistan. She well knows that that is our weak point, and it is there that she will try and bring pressure to bear upon us.

For this reason, I trust that if war is staved off now, there will be no cessation of warlike preparations in this country, and that the Peshin railway will be pushed on without delay to Kandahar. How differently situated we should be now, both as regards Russia and Afghanistan, if we were settled in force at Kandahar with railway communication to India! We ought to return there at the earliest date, even if we have to pay the Amir heavily for letting us have what we once possessed. I thoroughly agree with all that has been urged by Sir Charles Macgregor, Mr Marvin and others as to the strategical value of Herat, and the serious menace a Russian occupation of that province would be to India; at the same time, I believe that Afghan-Turkistan in the possession of Russia would be attended with still greater danger to us. In the one case, a British army at Kandahar would check any onward Russian movement; we should know exactly what was going on in our front; and should we find it necessary to take the field, the country is open and well suited to military operations. In the other case, we should be in complete ignorance of Russia's designs; we should have to watch a long tract of country, the features of which on the side of the mountains nearest Russia are but imperfectly known; and unless we have a loyal ally in the Ruler of Kabul, Russia's influence would soon be felt there, and would gradually extend through Chitral, Yasin, Gilgit and Kashmir to India itself. It would be very satisfactory if we could counteract this danger by fixing upon a frontier further advanced than the Hindu-Kush range, but this seems to me now out of the question; were there no other reason against it, the uncertain attitude of the Afghans would prevent our undertaking the task of defending a line extending from Herat to the most eastern part of the Oxus. However, even if the Hindu-Kush be decided upon, I hope that England would go to war with Russia rather than permit her to occupy any portion of Afghanistan after all our declarations to the contrary. A successful campaign would seriously injure Russia's prestige in Central Asia; it would give us time to put our frontier in a proper state of defence; and it would enable us to dictate such terms to Russia as would prevent a recurrence of the Afghan frontier question for many years to come. Trusting that Your Lordship will excuse me for taking up so much of your valuable time.

RP 97–1/CXXXVIII

217
Lord Salisbury, Prime Minister, to Roberts

[Holograph]   [No place]
                                               6 July 1885
Private

Your kind letter of the 8th June has just reached me. I am very much obliged to you for it. I am very glad to have the weight of your authority in favour of making a stand at Candahar. The extreme military theorists who would have us defend Herat are doing a great deal of harm. The evident impossibility of maintaining such a position without a crushing expenditure frightens the ordinary Englishman & he turns aside as impracticable all military warnings. The people who pine for a campaign beyond Herat are making the Pishin railway, & the fortification of Candahar, if not impossible, at least very difficult. I think the scientific frontier doctrine which was so much derided some years ago is master of the field now. The "friendly Afghan" doctrine which was opposed to it has pretty well broken down. This is at all events a symptom of returning sanity. But we are still the victims of an incurable attack of "brag". We cannot reconcile ourselves to the truth that if we will not provide cloth enough for the coat we want, we must cut down our coat to the cloth we have got. So many of our amateur, semi-military programmes go on the assumption that we had as large an army in proportion to the population of the Empire as other nations have. So we think we can do all that other nations do. Our people requires to have it driven into their heads that if they will not submit to a conscription, they must submit to a corresponding limitation of their exploits.

I am afraid the present Amir has a foot in both camps: & has agreed to refuse us all real access to his dominions.

RP 80/4

218
Brownlow to Roberts

[Holograph]   London
Confidential   9 July 1885

. . . And now about Donald Stewart's successor. I believe he has been offered within the last week Council[62] & I have no doubt he will accept it.

The object I hope & think is to appoint you, while the Conservatives are in office.

You have tout le monde in your favour, but Wolseley is a power in the land and if he insists on it he may get it – indeed I feel sure he will – for bear in mind that he is in a position to make himself very disagreeable here, and your best friend[63] may be glad to get him out of the way even at your expense, verb. sap.

Let us hope that he may not want to leave England. Next to yourself I think he is the best man for the place. In very exalted quarters perhaps Hardinge[64] would be the first favourite but God forbid he should ever be let loose upon India with his egotistical fads & follies. He has done very well in Bombay, but he would improve everything in Bengal out of all recognition.

When the matter begins to look settled I shall not forget to call attention to your wishes as to coming home for a few months. Wolseley arrives on Monday[65] & we ought to know something during the week. I should like

D. Stewart, Council London; F. Roberts, India; Chelmsford,[66]

Madras; C. Arbuthnot, Bombay; Macpherson, Council India;[67] Wolseley, Ireland – but Whitmore[68] laughs at my programme. Nous verrons. . .

RP 12/2

219
Stewart to Roberts

[Holograph]   17 July 1885

<u>Very Confidential</u>

Though I am very busy with my home letters I must write one line to urge you to put all your irons into the fire <u>without delay</u> if you want to succeed me. I may have to go home sooner than I expected and I am all the more willing to do so as you may have a better chance of succeeding me under the present Gov[t] than if Gladstone comes in again as he is likely to do in November. Don't ask any questions but write home at once as I may resign before the Election comes off.

Keep this entirely to yourself and lose no time in looking after your own interests in this matter.

I thank Lady Bobs for her advice which I am following with great benefit & success.[69]

RP 78/4

220
Viceroy to Roberts

[Manuscript telegram in Roberts' hand]   Simla
                                                30 July 1885

The Secretary of State requests me to inform you that the Queen will approve your nomination as Commander in Chief, and that military authorities agree to your coming home immediately. The question of Madras command standing over for the present. In transmitting this information I offer you my cordial congratulations.

RP 27/3

221
Napier to Roberts

[Holograph]   Harrogate
                                               31 July 1885

It would be difficult to express the satisfaction I felt on reading the announcement of your appointment to the Chief Command in India.

There was a strong impression here that Wolseley would get it but fortunately the Government had changed hands and his "Nile" extravagances were a warning! He would have done more mischief in India than Lord Ripon himself.

It would only be necessary to read his minute which is probably on record in the Foreign Office, shewing how he would turn the Russians out of Central Asia to learn what a dangerous man he would be for India, and I think his chance is over.

I rejoice for India and the Army which require changes for the better, to be made with caution and with a full knowledge of antecedents; and this no one could possess more than yourself. I sincerely trust that your health may carry you through your command and that if you have to draw the sword against Russia you may do so with a stronger army and more ample weapons and supplies for war.

* * *

RP 23–49/f22

IV
December 1885 to April 1893
Commander-in-Chief India

Roberts' facility with the pen, his unflagging energy, the very wide range of his responsibilities, both as administrator and operational commander, and his unusually long tenure as C-in-C India[1] combined to produce a daunting output of paper. In eight years as C-in-C, he produced over three hundred and seventy formal printed notes, memoranda and papers, many running to more than ten closely printed pages, and the whole amounting to more than thirteen hundred printed pages; in addition, his papers include several thousands of official, demi-official and private letters, both to and from him. A printed summary of his administrative decisions, produced at the end of his tenure – the 'Short Report' – runs to more than two pages.[2] In selecting papers for this period, the aim has been to indicate the most important areas of interest and at the same time to provide an indication of the total range.

He arrived back in India in December 1885 after three months leave in the United Kingdom to find the Army involved in a third Burmese war. The excesses of the ruler of the kingdom of Ava (Thibaw), the growing penetration of the French and a long history of Anglo-Burmese friction had led in October 1885 to a British ultimatum, and then to the bloodless occupation of the Burmese capital, Mandalay, by an expedition under Major-General Prendergast. Prendergast had had the misfortune to clash with the local correspondent of *The Times* and had been superseded in command by Macpherson, C-in-C of the Madras Army, in whose operational area Burma fell [228]. Macpherson died of fever within a month of reaching Burma and Roberts himself took over the command of operations, moving his headquarters to Rangoon in November 1886 [235, 237, 239]. The initial success had by then degenerated into what Kipling was to call 'a subalterns' war'[3] – a grinding guerilla war against small bands of rebels and dacoits which was to last another five and a half years [236, 237]. Roberts returned to India in February 1887, leaving the chief operational command in the hands of George White.[4]

As Commander-in-Chief, his primary strategic preoccupation remained the North-West Frontier, Afghanistan and the threat of a war with Russia, which the extension of the Central Asian railway eastwards from the Caspian appeared to render even more probable and dangerous [222, 229, 231, 242, 253]. The advent of a Conservative administration in August 1886 which was to remain in power for six years provided the necessary support and stability for a programme designed to secure an effective strategic frontier. Roberts' long-held view that the true strategic frontier of India lay along the Kandahar-Ghazni-Kabul axis, and that Kandahar, rather than Kabul, was the vital *point d'appui* [265], was now generally accepted in India and by men like Salisbury in England. The main elements of the programme were therefore

(a) improvements to the roads and railways infrastructure;
(b) the strengthening and re-equipment of the forces in India;
(c) the extension of control over the trans-Indus tribes;
(d) the organisation on paper of a striking force of two army corps and a reserve divsion to provide an immediate striking force in event of war with Russia [234].

The railway to Kandahar was completed as far as the border at Chaman although it was considered inexpedient to press for its extension to Kandahar [225, 229]. At the other end of the line the Indus was permanently bridged at Attock and the railway extended to Peshawar. In the middle, the Gomal Pass was opened up to provide a direct route to Ghazni. A mass of lesser improvements to roads and railways provided for quick and easy movement laterally.[5] At the end of the 1880s a new threat took shape as the Russians pushed south across the Pamirs [272].

These developments led inevitably to increased friction with the trans-Indus tribes, unsettled by the Afghan war. A succession of minor campaigns followed.[6] Improved mountain warfare tactics [250, 251] and improved armament meant that the balance of military advantage swung at this period against the tribesmen. When failure occurred, it was more likely to be due to political miscalculation, as in the Black Mountain expedition of 1888 [252, 266].[7]

Large reductions had been made in the native armies following the Second Afghan War. The Pendjeh war scare of 1885 began a reversal of these economies when approval was given to raising three new cavalry and nine infantry regiments [227, 232, 233, 240]. Roberts took the opportunity to increase the proportion of the 'martial races' [233, 254,

264]; by 1893, the proportion had risen from just over a quarter in 1881 to almost a half. Coupled with increases in unit establishments and an increase of nearly 11,000 in the number of British troops [240], the cuts of 1882 had by then virtually been made up.[8] With Mortimer Durand's collaboration, troops from the native states were equipped and trained to regular standards [244, 246] and Kashmir State troops took part in the Hunza-Nagar expedition in 1891.

Roberts' papers at this time reveal few signs of radical tactical thought. As has been seen, he saw machine guns as primarily weapons for static defense [210]; their incorporation into infantry battalions in a mobile role had scarcely begun when he left India. Even though a gunner himself, he does not seem at this period to have grasped the tactical opportunities presented by the new quick-firing, breech-loading field gun. He was ahead of his contemporaries in seeing that the primary role of the cavalry henceforth was as mounted infantry rather than as a shock weapon [223], although it was only with his accession to the post of Commander-in-Chief of the British Army, and with the experience of the South African War behind him, that he was able to impose this doctrine on the cavalry as a whole.[9]

The issue of short service still divided him publicly from Wolseley [268, 271] but he had moved on to regard the real problem for recruitment in the British army as the improvement of the actual conditions in the Army to match the improved social conditions outside. His 1891 paper 'National prosperity and its effect on the army'[10] continued a line of thought set out earlier in 'Free Trade in the Army'. This, together with his interest in temperance [243], found a practical expression in his scheme of regimental institutes introduced in 1887 [238, 241, 260].

The curious case of Captain Barry [247] reveals something of Roberts' concern for social and moral standards in the officer corps [226, 247].[11] He was often accused of favouritism and even of snobbery in his appointments [245] but his treatment of McQueen reveals his determination to weed out those whom he considered unsuitable for war [266].

The 'Short Report' claimed that Roberts' main organisational object was to carry out a system of decentralisation in India.[12] That is not very obviously the effect of the changes introduced but the paradox is explained in a later paragraph:

> an essential element . . . in such a policy must always be that the broad principles for each subordinate authority should be clearly laid down by one guiding spirit, independence in such matters being incompatible with that unity of purpose which is the soul of good administration.[13]

(One is reminded of Talleyrand's dictum that 'non-intervention' was a technical term which meant much the same as 'intervention'). While a good deal of unification and centralisation went on between 1885 and 1893, nothing was more important administratively than the improvement in the working relationship between the Commander-in-Chief and the Military Member, deriving from Roberts' proposal that in future business of mutual interest should be conducted on common files. In this way, a mass of time-consuming interdepartmental correspondence was avoided and decisions by higher authority reached more easily.[14]

A penalty of high command was close involvement with the Duke of Cambridge. The precise boundaries of the Duke's authority in Indian matters were not absolutely clear-cut, particularly in the case of senior appointments and promotions.[15] Given the Duke's natural vein of autocracy, fortified by nearly forty years at the helm, and his innate conservatism, he was bound to constitute a massive bulwark of obstruction, and Roberts found him a sore trial as time went on. He managed to keep their major differences to two – the proposal to abolish the Presidency Armies [249] and the promotion of George White. He eventually won both but the case of White is instructive in showing yet again his readiness to use the Press to assist his ends [248].

As the normal end of his tour approached in 1889, Roberts was still only 57 and could reasonably look forward to a further active post. The choice was limited in view of his seniority but Wolseley was coming to the end of his tour as Adjutant-General, the most senior post in the British Army after that of Commander-in-Chief, and it was a post which Roberts was keen to have. For reasons which are set out in the main Introduction, the post was offered and then withdrawn [255, 256, 259], and Roberts was invited instead to stay on for a further two years in India [261, 262]. As he was well aware, that meant the permanent loss of the Adjutant-Generalship but he assumed that the sacrifice would not go unrewarded. But when, in 1892, he rejected the offer of a further extension, he was offered only the somewhat derisory posts of Governor of Malta or Gibraltar. To add insult to injury, the Duke of Cambridge, who had actually been the root cause of all the trouble, professed ignorance of the offer of the Adjutant-Generalship, which drew an unusually tart reply [273].

When Roberts left India in April 1893, he was without any immediate prospect of employment in an active command. It was a somewhat ungracious end to an unparalleled career in India.

222
Roberts to G.E. Buckle,[1]
Editor of *The Times*

[Printed]   Calcutta
Private   6 December 1885

Although our acquaintance with each other is very slight, I venture to send you two papers[2] which I think will interest you. The first was written before the Russians reached Merv; even then you will see that I looked upon Herat as lost to us. The second I was induced to write last May in order to prepare the Government for the difficulties which would have to be encountered should it be determined to send a force against the Russians so far from our base as Herat.

My own opinion is that, however desirable it might be to despatch a British Army against Russia in the direction of Asia Minor,[3] the great struggle for supremacy in Central Asia must be decided in the valley of the Helmund. Russia knows full well that India is our most vulnerable point, and she will strain every nerve to injure us in this part of the world, while she acts on the defensive as much as possible in Asia Minor.

It seems to me very necessary –

(1) to disabuse the British people of the idea that Russia would find it difficult to subjugate Afghanistan. As I have endeavoured to explain in my second paper, her task, coming as she would from the north, would be very different to ours if we wished to conquer Afghanistan from the south;

(2) to bring it home to the people of England that a British advance upon Kandahar must be made simultaneous with any movement of Russia across the boundary now being laid down by the joint commisson,[4] and that British occupation of Kandahar would not, under such circumstances, be distasteful to the Afghans.

You are welcome to make any use you think fit of the two papers, but you will understand that I do not wish them published. In my present position it is obviously undesirable that I should appear before the public as the advocate of a policy to which the Government of the day may be averse.

RP 100–1/11

223
Roberts to Major-General Harman[5]

[Printed]   Near Delhi
                                                    18 December 1885

Would you kindly refer to letter No. 54 Cavalry General No. 71 dated 4th December 1884, signed by you as Deputy Adjutant General, and to No. 54 Cavalry General No. 94, dated 4th June 1885, signed by Colonel Blundell,[6] on the subject of "Cavalry Pioneer Equipment", and let me know whether a decision is likely to be arrived at soon

I am glad to see from the first letter I have quoted that "it is proposed to make the Pioneer equipment for each squadron complete, and to carry it on a pack animal in much the same manner as Colonel Russell[7] proposed." The subject is a very important one, and I am anxious that all Cavalry regiments (British and Native) in India, should have their entrenching tools so arranged as to be always with the squadrons and yet without adding to the weight which the horses have got to carry.

I feel very sure that in future wars Cavalry will be employed more and more upon dismounted work, and if I am right, it is essential that they should have the means of rapidly entrenching themselves. In this country a good supply of tools is provided; but as these are carried on mules, they can only be kept with the regiment so long as it moves at a walk. I have heard it urged that by taking a horse for the purpose the squadron is weakened, but surely one man and a couple of horses would not be missed from a squadron, and even if its *mounted* fighting strength is reduced to this extent, its *dismounted* fighting power would be materially increased by having the means at hand of throwing up an entrench-ment, destroying a bridge, or lines of railway and telegraph?

RP 100–1/VI

224
Roberts to Duke of Cambridge

[Printed]   Near Delhi
Private   19 December 1885

The Camp of Exercise has fairly begun, and I am present with the 2nd Division of the Southern Force at Goorgaon, some 20 miles from Delhi. This force, as I mentioned in my last letter, is com-manded by Sir Charles Gough. The division I am now with is under Brig-General East; the two Infantry Brigades are com-manded respectively by Colonels Wolseley and Dalrymple, the Cavalry Brigade by Colonel Bushman, and the Artillery by Lt-Colonel Alexander.[8] Nothing but preliminary Brigade drills have been attempted as yet; divisional work begins on the 23rd, and after Xmas day the Army Corps Commanders will exercise one division against the other. The two Army Corps are now 150 miles apart, but it is proposed to arrange the inter-divisional manoeu-vres so as to bring them within 100 miles of each other, at which distance operations will commence on the 4th January. Sir George Greaves will advance from the neighbourhood of Umballa to endeavour to raise the Siege of Delhi, while Sir Charles Gough, who is supposed to be covering the Siege, will move towards him with the object of giving battle as far from Delhi as possible. The two forces should come into contact near Paniput, famous for two great battles fought in its immediate neighbourhood, one in April 1526 by the Emperor Baber against Sultan Ibrahim, the other in January 1761 by Ahmed Shah against the Mahrattas. As it is desir-able that the manoeuvres should terminate at Delhi itself, the Northern will be reinforced (on paper) so as to oblige the Southern Force to retreat. To carry this out in order, and to enable the Southern Force to cross the Western Jumna Canal, an operation which will take several hours, I shall cause the Northern Force to halt for one day. In this way the whole of the troops should be collected in front of Delhi by about the 12th or 13th January, and the deciding battle should be fought on the 14th. The Viceroy proposes to reach Delhi on the 12th, so that His Excellency will be present on the last 2 days of the manoeuvres. The march past will come off on the 18th or 19th January, as may be most convenient to Lord Dufferin.

I am sending Your Royal Highness a set of the maps and orders which have been prepared for the manoeuvres. I hope that everything will go off well, and that the Foreign officers will be impressed with the workmanlike appearance and mobility of the Army in India. We ought to be thoroughly mobile, but I am not happy about our transport, and if one result of this Camp is to get that department placed on a satisfactory footing the money will have been well spent. All our shortcomings are being carefully enquired into, and Your Royal Highness may rest assured that no time or trouble will be spared to render the Army efficient.

As the 17th Lancers were not told off for the Camp, I have ordered a Squadron to come as it would be a pity if the Foreign officers did not see some representatives of one of our most picturesque and best turned-out Lancer regiments.

* * *

RA Add MSS E/1/11357; printed RP 100–1/VII

225
Roberts to Macgregor

[Holograph]   Camp Panipat
                                         10 January 1886
Private

I should like to have your views regarding the line the railway should take towards the Helmund – do you favour the Kojack route direct to Kandahar, or via Nushki.[9] Sir Donald, Wilson and Hope favour the former, Browne and the Engineers generally I believe the latter.[10]

The question must come on for discussion soon, and I want to have your opinion.

NMS I.A.886.1 1955–675/1/1

226
Roberts to Duke of Cambridge

[Printed]   Delhi
                                             22 January 1886
Private

I am much obliged for Your Royal Highness's letter of the 1st inst. received yesterday. I hope, Sir, that my letters from this Camp have given all the information about the manoeuvres that you wished for. The final operations took place on the 14th and 15th, and the two papers which I enclose, containing my remarks as the Umpire in Chief will, I trust, enable Your Royal Highness to gain a general idea of what took place. Curiously enough, on the same dates and on nearly the same ground, somewhat similar manoeuvres were carried out before the Prince of Wales.[11] General Hardinge then commanded the attack with Sir Donald Stewart as his 2nd in command; the defence was under Sir Charles Reid.[12]

On that occasion the brunt of the attack fell upon General Reid's left, and had General Hardinge concentrated his whole strength in that direction he would, in all probability, have succeeded. In the present instance, I believe that Sir George Greaves would have had a better chance of success had he followed, and improved upon, General Hardinge's tactics instead of advancing over the open country against Sir Charles Gough's centre. Be that as it may, I was much pleased with the spirited way in which the two days' manoeuvres were carried out, and I only regret that Your Royal Highness was not here in person to witness them.

The Southern Cavalry was handled in an intelligent and soldierlike manner by Brigadier General R.C. Stewart, whose hands were doubtless strengthened by Luck as one of his Brigadiers, while Brigadier-General Marter[13] did well with the Northern Cavalry when he had got the command of the whole into his own hands. He seemed to me, however, to be somewhat wanting in enterprise.

Your Royal Highness will have heard by telegram the ill fate which befell our march past. The day seemed fair enough when the troops started for the parade, indeed I was congratulated on having "Queen's Weather" but as the Viceroy reached the ground the rain commenced, and becoming heavier every moment, culminated in a heavy storm of thunder and lightning as we rode down the line. Everyone was drenched to the skin, but the march past was continued, the Viceroy refusing to take shelter while the troops were exposed. It was a bitter disappointment to us all that so splendid a spectacle should have been spoiled by the weather, but if anything could possibly have compensated for our regrets, it was the grand way in which all ranks, both British and Native, acquitted themselves during this most trying ordeal. After the passage of the guns and the cavalry, the ground was ankle-deep in mud, and it did one good to see the way in which the infantry pulled themselves together as they passed the Viceroy. The two corps which gained the most general approbation were the 74th (Highland Light Infantry) and the 45th Sikhs; the Rifle Brigade, the King's Own Borderers, the Manchester Regiment, and the East Surrey acquitted themselves most creditably. I was obliged to cut the Review short, and after the artillery and cavalry had trotted past (which they did most admirably), the troops reformed on the original alignment and advanced towards the flagstaff. This, I am told, was a most imposing sight, and was thought much of by the Foreign officers. Lord Dufferin was good enough to express his entire satisfaction with the parade and the appearance of the troops. I enclose a copy of His Lordship's speech, together with a present state, from which Your Royal Highness will see that there were nearly 36,000 men on parade.

Lord Reay accompanied the Viceroy to the parade, as did Sir Alfred Lyall and Sir Charles Aitcheson.[14] The first named seems very delicate, and I was glad to hear he was prudent enough to leave the ground soon after the march past commenced. I am told that in Bombay it is generally believed he will not be able to remain in India his full time. Admiral Sir Frederick Richards[15] also witnessed the march past, and I arranged for the Maharajas Scindia, Bhurtpore, and Ulwar to have suitable places assigned to them near the saluting point.

Yesterday morning, I presented new colors to the 2nd Battalion, Manchester Regiment, and made them a short speech, a copy of which I send Your Royal Highness. The regiment looked extremely well, and the ceremony went off without a hitch. It was a beautiful day, and I was glad that our Foreign friends should have had an opportunity of seeing how a British Regiment can march past in fine weather!

The Native Cavalry sports came off successfully before the Viceroy and the Foreign officers on the 18th Inst. The latter were much interested with what they saw, and to most of them the sight must have been a novel one.

I am very glad to hear that Colonel Knowles[16] is to succeed Brigadier-General Lyttleton Annesley as Adjutant General of the Bombay Army. He is, I believe, well fitted for the position. Whenever I think of him I recall to mind the gallantry and steadiness with which he behaved at the head of his regiment (the 67th) on the 14th December 1879, when covering the retirement of Macpherson's brigade into Sherpore.

I see that the Secretary of State for India has sanctioned the continuance of the Inspector General of Royal Artillery. This, I believe, to be a wise measure considering the many important changes that are about to be made in artillery equipment &c. Brigadier General Johnson has been nominated for this post, and in his place General Rowlands proposes to recommend Colonel Farrington of the West Yorkshire Regiment.[17] He is considered a good officer, and I hope his selection will meet with Your Royal Highness's approval.

I heard from the Duke of Connaught by yesterday's mail asking that he might put off his arrival in India until the beginning of July. This seems to me most advisable both for him and the

Duchess, and I telegraphed in this sense to Your Royal Highness today.

An unpleasant affair has occurred at a ball given in Delhi the evening before last. I was there for a short time and observed nothing wrong, but after I left there was some disturbance and more than one officer was the worse for liquor. I have only been able to bring it home to one, Lieut. Macdonald of the Border Regiment (34th).[18] He does not bear a very good character, and as he committed himself before the Foreign officers, I have put him under arrest, and have given him the option of retiring or being tried by a Court Martial. I hope he will send in his papers, if not, he must be tried, as it is necessary to make an example.

I leave here tomorrow for Allahabad where I remain one day with Sir Alfred Lyall and then proceed to Calcuttas. I shall only be there a few days as on the 31st I embark with Lord Dufferin for Burma.

RA Add Mss E/1/11 886; printed RP 100–1/XX

227
Roberts to Lord Randolph Churchill

[Printed]
Calcutta
1 February 1886

Private

Many thanks for your letter of the 6th January which reached me the day after I arrived here. I am very glad to hear that you succeeded in getting General Hardinge a K.C.B. He wished for a G.C.B. I know, but without some special war service it would be a difficult matter to receive a double promotion in the Order of the Bath at one time.

You warned me that the Conservative reign would be a short one, but I hardly expected that it would terminate as quickly as it has. I was hoping that the resignation would have been brought about by the Irish question in regard to which the majority of the

English people would assuredly have been on the Conservative side, now I am afraid that the Radicals will turn the agricultural question to their own advantage.

We start for Burma on the 3rd. We were to have gone today, but Lord Dufferin remained to entertain the Foreign officers at a ball. I wonder if you will see any of them? The two Germans leave for Europe tomorrow. One of the Americans has gone already and the other starts in a day or two. The French and Russians are desirous of making a somewhat extended tour. They go to Peshawur and I am arranging for them to see the entrance to the Khyber pass and to ride through the pass to Kohat. They were desirous of visiting Quetta and Pishin, but looking to the backward state of our railways and the importance of that line of communication, I thought it better to confine them to the Peshawur-Kohat direction. The Russians were evidently prepared for a refusal to their request to visit Quetta, and Commandant de Torcy, the only French Officer who applied to go there, understands that an exception could not be made in his favor.

The Italians are quiet going men who are quite satisfied to see what is shown them without asking questions. I enclose a copy of a speech made by General Saletta, the senior officer of the party, the last evening I spent in camp at Delhi when, as I think, I mentioned to you, I dined at the Foreign officers' Mess.

I had not overlooked the important matter of watching over the Viceroy's safety in Burma. Before the receipt of your letter I had telegraphed to General Prendergast to take every possible precaution, and I will see that every one is on the alert. I send you a paper by Lieutenant-Colonel Macneill[19] on the present situation in Burma. He is an enterprising officer, who spent some weeks in Mandalay about three years ago in the disguise of a photographer. I should like you to see him as he can tell you all about the behaviour of the Madras troops at Minhla,[20] where he was wounded. He is some relation of Sir Henry Rawlinson,[21] who should know his address in England where he goes on a year's leave.

Please note what Macneill says about dacoity in Burma. I do not think that Prendergast has been to blame. Burma has always been famous for dacoity, and in a difficult jungly country like Burma it is not easy to catch them. Besides it is not work for which troops are adapted, and I hope we shall be able to arrange, while the Viceroy and I are in Burma, for efficient Police being raised to undertake such duties.

I got an interesting letter from Ridgeway[22] a few days ago. He describes the new frontier as "utterly indefensible; tactically, strategically, politically, it could scarcely be worse." He seems to be much hampered by the arrogant behaviour of the Ameer's Agent who claims that every decision of the Commission should be referred to Cabul for the Ameer's sanction. The relations between the Russians and Afghans are, he says, not at all satisfactory (he alludes evidently to the Afghan soldiers, not to the people of the country), they (the Afghans) do not love the Russians, while the Russians are desirous of picking a quarrel with the Afghans. Ridgeway is much struck with the mobility of the Cossacks, who carry everything they possess on their own horses, and are the officers' servants as well. We must take a leaf out of their book in this respect.

Since I came to Calcutta I have been urging the Viceroy to sanction the nine new regiments being raised without delay. Once a Liberal Secretary of State gets hold of the India Office, all such measures may be stopped, unless a commencement has been made. Up to the present time only two out of the five Goorkha corps have been ordered, none of the Sikh corps are yet sanctioned, nor the formation of a reserve to the Native Army. General Hughes[23] is prepared to back me up, but I can see that the change of Government is already having an effect on the Viceroy and some of the Members of Council.

I have proposed that in all the new regiments, there should be an officer from Madras, and one from Bombay. Those Presidencies suffered by the reductions of 1882 even more than Bengal did, and as their Armies are never likely to be increased, it seems only fair that they should benefit, in a certain degree, by the additions now being made to the Bengal Army.

It is a matter of the deepest regret to me that this letter must be addressed to 2, Connaught Place, instead of the India Office. I can only hope that the Conservatives may soon be in power again, and that you may not be tempted to accept any other position than that of Secretary of State for India.

P.S. Would it not be possible to coin some name to designate the Tory party which would attract the public. "Conservative" does not represent the principles of the party at the present time, any more than "Liberal" does the principles of the opposition. Insist on the Radicals being called Radicals and get some suitable name for the Tory party.

RP 100–1/XXII

228
Roberts to Lord Randolph Churchill

[Printed]   Steamer "Clive"
                                              near Madras,
Private   28 February 1886

You will like to hear about our visit to Burma. We reached Rangoon on the 5th instant, and remained there until the 8th, when we left by rail for Prome, and thence to Mandalay in one of the Irrawaddy Flotilla's steamers. Mr Bernard met us at Rangoon, and General Prendergast joined the party a day's journey from Mandalay. Lord Dufferin must have been gratified with the reception he met with on landing at Rangoon. The streets were crowded, each nationality had erected a triumphal arch in their own particular part of the town, and the people generally showed their appreciation of the Viceroy under whose auspices the annexation of Upper Burma had been carried out. There is no doubt of the popularity of the measure so far as Rangoon is concerned. From Prome to Mandalay took a little more than three days. We landed in the afternoon of the 12th February, and drove in state to the palace, a distance of about 3 miles; the roads were lined by troops, three or four arches were erected, and at one or two places some of the inhabitants were collected, but there was no crowd, and I heard afterwards that the Burmese refused to believe that the Viceroy had come; they insisted that some much less important person had been deputed to represent him. The city is well laid out with broad streets and has the making of a fine place; some of the monasteries are quite beautiful, and the palace is a collection of singularly graceful buildings. Nearly all the houses are made of teak wood. Round the palace grounds, which are of considerable extent, is a strong palisading, backed by a high wall. A good body of troops can be accommodated inside, and for the present this will be the headquarters of the garrison.

Although there are nearly 12,000 troops in Upper Burma, the extent of country (about 90,000 square miles) to be occupied, and the absence of any police, have necessitated so much scattering, that Mandalay has been left without, in my opinion, sufficient troops.

Two more Native regiments are now on their way from Bengal: one of these is to relieve a Madras corps which has already been three years in Burma; the other (an Assam corps) will be stationed for the present at Mandalay. A police force is about to be raised, partly of local and partly of Hindustanis, and there are to be two police levies – one composed of Sikhs, the other of Hindustanis – for service on the frontiers. It will take some time before these will be fit for work, and in the meanwhile the soldiers must perform police duties. Mr Bernard is to be the head of the civil administration, and as it is very advisable that the military control should be centred in one officer, I proposed to the Viceroy that the commands in Upper and Lower Burma should be united under General Prendergast, and that, as a temporary measure, the military administration in Burma should be brought directly under the Commander-in-Chief in India and the Government of India. As the force in Burma is now composed of troops belonging to all three Presidencies, it was most inconvenient having to refer everything to the Madras Government, which has nothing to say to Burma. From the enclosed memoranda which I prepared for the Viceroy you will see how matters stand. All my proposals have been accepted and orders issued, – a procedure which would have been impossible without great delay, had it been indispensable to consult the Government of Madras. Instead, however, of Prendergast remaining in command, he is, under orders from

Lord Kimberley, to vacate on the 1st April, as I gather from your
telegrams to the Viceroy you would have ordered had you continued at the India Office. In his conduct of the military operations
Prendergast has, I think, done well. At Ava and in his dealings
with Theebaw he showed not only forebearance but firmness and
decision. A more excitable commander might have precipitated
matters and brought on a collision, the result of which would have
been great bloodshed and quite possibly the flight of the King. He
is wanting in knowledge of the world, and has not got sufficient
backbone, and it was this that caused him to run foul of Mr
Moylan and to deal too leniently with the Provost Marshal's case.[24]

Up till our arrival at Mandalay I had nothing to do with the
expedition. Under orders issued by the Government of India,
issued before I took over command, all reports were made direct to
the Military Department in Calcutta, while questions of discipline, &c., were dealt with by the Madras authorities. I protested
against this procedure, and pointed out that under such an
arrangement the Commander-in-Chief could not be held responsible for anything connected with the expedition, but owing to
Lord Dufferin's illness and my absence at the Camp of Exercise
no change was made until a few days ago. Now the commander is
directly under me and will communicate to me by telegraph all
that goes on. As Prendergast's successor I have named White;
though only a Brigadier-General, he is the best man in India for
the position; a thorough man of the world, and a most able soldier.
It will be necessary to give him local rank as Major-General, for he
is junior as a Colonel to Norman, the commander of Prendergast's
other brigade. Lord Kimberley ordered Colonel Hooper, the
Provost Marshal, to be tried by a Court Martial, but before
charges could be framed it was necessary to have a court of
enquiry. This I directed Prendergast to convene. I am afraid that
the reports telegraphed home by the *Times* correspondent are substantially correct, but Mr Moylan, no doubt, made the most of the
business.

You must be prepared for dacoity and internal troubles for some
time to come. Burma has never been free from them, and until the
people learn to respect our authority, and are satisfied that we

intend to annex the country permanently, they will not settle down.

It was only an hour or two before we left Mandalay that the Viceroy even knew that the present Ministry were prepared to adopt your policy with regard to Upper Burma, and until then it was scarcely possible to take any steps towards restoring confidence amongst the people. I hope all with go well now, and that it will not be very long before you will be able to justify the annexation of Burma by the increase its revenues will bring to the finances of India. We did not see a great deal of the country, but as far as I could judge, the people are quite prepared to accept our rule; dacoity is not the work of "patriots" but of restless spirits who have lived by the trade all their life.

RP 100–1/XXVII

229
Roberts to Viceroy

[Printed]   Karachi
                                              16 April 1886.

You will, I think, like to hear something of my experiences of Quetta and the Bolan Railway. Sir Donald Stewart had warned me that Quetta was not in an altogether satisfactory condition, but I confess that I was not prepared to find things so bad as they really are. This is, I dare say, partly because Quetta has hitherto been looked upon as nobody's child, and also because until quite recently our stay there seemed somewhat uncertain; but allowing this I cannot absolve the Brigadier General in command from blame, and I shall be glad when an opportunity offers of replacing Sir Oriel Tanner[25] by a more active and efficient officer.

Barracks for one battalion of British Infantry and a Mountain Battery have just been completed, but there are no subsidiary buildings, such as recreation rooms, canteens, Sergeants' messes, schools, &c. The few families at Quetta are in miserable quarters, and I have never seen soldiers so badly accommodated as the

Battery of Garrison Artillery in the Fort. The hospitals, both British and Native, are quite unfit for the purpose for which they are used, and it is not surprising that mortality and invaliding in the Quetta district have reached a high percentage. Sir Donald Stewart ordered a new hospital for the British troops when he was at Quetta last November, but for some reason or another no commencement was made until within a few days of my arrival. The building is now being pushed on, and the Engineers have promised that it shall be completed in every particular before December next.

I telegraphed to Colonel Sanford to meet me here, and have arranged with him (by a redistribution of sanctioned money) for providing funds for the immediate construction of barracks for the garrison battery and for a soldiers' institute. Much more is required to render the troops comfortable, but even if funds are forthcoming I doubt if more money than we have allotted to Quetta could be spent during the current year.

The temporary Bolan Railway is now within 23 miles of Quetta, and will probably be completed the whole way by the 1st July next. The total length of the line from Sibi to Quetta is 97 miles; the first 17 of these, as far as Rindli, are almost level. From Rindli to Hirok, 49 miles, the gradient is steep, being in some places as much as 1 in 25½. For the first 29 miles of this section, one engine can haul 8 vehicles, but for the remaining 20 miles only 5 vehicles can be taken at a trip. At Hirok there is a break in the gauge, and for the next 10 miles, as far as Darwaza, the metre gauge is used. Some of the curves on this part are very sharp, and the gradient in places is as much as 1 in 23½: over this portion, an engine can only take 3 vehicles. At Darwaza the broad gauge recommences, and from thence to Quetta the line runs through a fairly level country. A great deal of permanent-way for the Harnai line, and for any extension which may be decided upon hereafter in the Kandahar direction has already been brought to Hirok, and as soon as the line is finished to Quetta this material will gradually be conveyed there. The break of gauge is, of course, extremely inconvenient, and it will be a long time before the narrow gauge section between Hirok and Darwaza will be able to clear off the large amount of permanent-way which is now lying at the former place. There can be no doubt that this Bolan Railway will be of great assistance to the Harnai Railway, by enabling it to be completed much more quickly than if it had to depend entirely on its own carrying resources. The break of gauge, however, is a most serious drawback from a military point of view; moreover it seems to me that this line could never be relied upon owing to its liability to injury, if not destruction, by heavy floods.

The question then arises, what is to be done? The Harnai route alone could not stand any continued transport strain unless the line were doubled, and the temporary Bolan line would not afford any sensible relief to the Harnai railway so long as it has a break of gauge, and is carried over such very severe inclines. General Browne holds out no hopes of being able to double the Harnai line, and the break of gauge and steep gradients on the Bolan line can only be got rid of by constructing an almost entirely new railway.

It is of the first importance that we should have regular and rapid railway communication between our base on the Indus and Pishin, and onwards to the north and west of the Khwaja Amran range, but before any more money is spent on strategical lines it is very desirable that we should come to some definite conclusion as to the best means of securing the defence of India, and that all the country through which we may have to operate should be carefully surveyed.

RP 98–1/pp. 7–8.

230
Roberts to Major-General George White

[Printed telegram]   Simla
                                               6 May 1886

Urgent

I am quite sure that you will not sanction any expeditions to be undertaken without having thoroughly satisfied yourself as to their necessity, and that when they have to be undertaken the force employed shall be properly equipped and of sufficient strength to overcome all opposition; but I would suggest that the commanders of the several forces should be instructed to do all in their power to turn stockades and positions in jungly country, instead of attacking them in front, for we know from experience that Asiatics never have the heart to stand when their line of retreat is threatened. When, however, this cannot be done and a direct attack is inevitable, free use should be made of artillery before the attack is delivered.

RP 100–5/XIV

231
Roberts to O.T. Burne

[Holograph]   Simla
                                               21 August 1886

Private

I enclose three papers which will, I think, interest you.

(1) on the defence of the NW Frontier

(2) on a proposal to appoint Native gentlemen to the Army in the same grades as British officers.

(3) on the desirability of having a good road through the Kohat Pass.[26]

The last is, perhaps, the only one which will go direct to your office as a political question, and I hope you will be able to support my view as to the necessity of the road, and as to the desirability of placing the political control of the whole frontier directly under the Government of India. You know how nearly the administration of the Frontier was taken from the Punjab Government 8 years ago. I would now propose to leave the civil duties to be carried on as at present but to take away all political work. Practically this has been done, the substance has gone and only the

347

shadow remains. Formerly all correspondence with the Amir of Kabul was in the hands of the Lieut. Governor but it had to be taken over by the Gov^t of India the moment our relations with Afghanistan became serious. So on the Baluch frontier. The Punjab and Sind governments managed this between them. Now it is governed by an Agent to the Govr General. There only remains the strip from Dera Ghazi Khan to the Indus above Peshawar, and Hazara, and it seems to me most important that this should be in the hands of officers who would devote their whole time and attention to the Tribes, and do all they can to get an influence over them. This will never be done under the Punjab Gov^t, for they do not believe in getting hold of the tribes, and their District Officers have other work to do.

What do you think Russia's game will be this winter. Will she take advantage of our being occupied in Burma to advance into Afghan Turkistan?

IOR MSS Eur D 951/3

232
Note on the necessity of carrying out the proposed increase to the Native Army, and of forming a sufficient reserve.

[Printed]   Simla,
                                                    12 September 1886

I cannot too strongly urge upon Government the acceptance of the proposals made by the Military Member of Council in his Minute of the 21st August last, on the "measures for improving the efficiency of the Native Army". A year ago, when these measures were first discussed, it was decided that a reserve to the Native Army was necessary, and that three regiments of cavalry and nine of infantry should be added to its strength. The cavalry regiments have been added, but no commencement has been made with the reserve, and only three out of the nine regiments of infantry have been raised.[27] At the time this increase was decided upon, the annexation of Upper Burma was not, I believe, even thought of, and the sole reason for the increase was the demands that it seemed likely would be made upon our army in the direction of the North-West Frontier.

The probability that these demands will be made has certainly not diminished during the past twelve months, and in the meantime we have incurred responsibilities in Burma, which will for some time, at any rate, absorb a greater number of regiments than was thought necessary to be added to the Indian Army before the trouble in that part of the world commenced; so that we are in an infinitely worse position to undertake a war against Russia than we were a year ago. I hope that by next spring the force now in Burma may be somewhat reduced; but, under the most favourable circumstances, it will be necessary to keep a considerable number of troops in that province for some years to come, certainly as many as the addition it was recently proposed to make to the Native Army. Surely, then, instead of delaying longer to carry out the measures which were deemed necessary in September 1885, and which were sanctioned by the Secretary of State the following month, it would be wise and prudent to make even a larger increase than was approved of then, and to do all we can to form a sufficient reserve, the more especially as it appears to be generally admitted that the Russian danger is daily becoming more imminent. It must be borne in mind that it takes nearly two years to render a newly raised regiment fit to take the field. We have no reserve of soldiers of the old Khalsa Army[28] to fall back upon, as was the case in 1857; the training of soldiers is much more complicated than it was thirty years ago; and if our troops are to encounter a European enemy, it is absolutely essential that they should be as efficient as they can be made. Then, in regard to the necessity for forming a reserve, the statistics of the German Army show that at the end of the first year of a campaign 45 per cent of cavalry, artillery, and engineers are lost to the Army, and these numbers would have to be replaced. Hitherto, our casualties have not been quite so serious because we have only been fighting against Asiatics, but in a war with Russia we must be prepared for heavy losses; and unless there is some system of reserve, it will be impossible to fill up the gaps with efficient soldiers. A reserve cannot be organised in a hurry, and we have to find out by experience whether the proposed scheme will work properly and provide a sufficient number of trained soldiers to replace casualties in the field. My predecessor gave it as his opinion that without a reserve system the Indian Army would be unable to go through a protracted campaign. I most fully endorse that opinion, and I also cordially agree with all that Sir Donald Stewart urged as to the necessity of increasing the Army. I trust that the Government will hesitate no longer in giving full effect to the decision arrived at in 1885, and that orders will at once be issued to raise the six regiments of infantry to form the reserve on the terms proposed by General Chesney, and to authorise the introduction of "the new pension rules," "the good-conduct pay," "the half-mounting allowances," and "the increased pay to recruits." To meet these additional expenses I am prepared to agree with the Honourable Member's recommendations as regards deferring the supply of the new rifles to the Native Army and reducing the number of torpedo boats for our coast defences from 11 to 6 – not that I do not consider both these necessary, but the increase to the Army and the formation of a reserve are, in my opinion, of the first importance.

RP 96–1/XIX

233
Note on the necessity for increasing the efficiency of the Native Army

[Printed]
Simla
25 September 1886

I must apologise for having kept these papers so long, but the fact is that although I most cordially agree with everything urged by the Viceroy as to "The necessity for increasing the efficiency of our Native Army, without increasing our military expenditure beyond a certain definite amount," I have not, under the existing state of affairs in Burma, seen my way to make any distinct proposals on the lines suggested by His Excellency.

Until our troubles in Burma are in a fair way towards settlement, it is impossible to say how many troops will be ultimately required to maintain peace and order there; nor, until we know more of the country and its surroundings, can we determine whether any of the races with whom we have now, for the first time, come into contact, would be likely to enter our Army, and make efficient and trustworthy troops for service on the South-East Frontier.

One thing is most clear, that the annexation of Upper Burma will require us to keep up a larger army in India than has hitherto been found necessary, and another, that the efficiency of the army has become of greater comparative value than its numbers, now that, as the Viceroy remarks, "the cycle of our collision with inferior forces is probably closed."

If the first necessity be admitted, on its account alone it would seem imperative to make without further delay the additions to our Army which were sanctioned a year ago, before there was any thought of occupying Burma. These additions cannot now, as they were then, be looked upon as a reserve; they will, indeed, scarcely suffice to meet the demands of Upper Burma. As regards the second point, I go heart and soul with the Viceroy. We cannot, unfortunately, do away altogether with the soldiers of Southern India, or with the Hindustani regiments in Bengal, but I would limit their numbers to meet the actual requirements of the several localities within which they are enlisted. As Burma is to be a part of the Madras Command, and as the expense of sending other than Madras troops to hold that province would be almost prohibitory, we must include the garrison of Burma in the local requirements of the Southern Presidency, unless (as I trust may prove to be the case) soldiers of a superior fighting quality can be found amongst the tribes dwelling on or near the borders of Burma. We cannot, as the Viceroy justly remarks, afford to keep up a single surplus man of whose martial spirit there can be any doubt, nor can we depend upon receiving such reinforcements from England in the time of trouble as would enable us to equalize the fighting qualities of the Native troops of the three Presidencies in the manner suggested by the Secretary in the Military Department. From recent trustworthy information we know that England would have the greatest difficulty in placing even one Army Corps in the field; and the sooner we realize the fact that we in India would have, for some time at any rate, to depend upon our own resources in the event of England being engaged in a European war, the better for us.[29] It seems to me quite hopeless to expect, under such circumstances, the help of 20,000 men from home; and though "more Native troops of good quality, to say nothing of Native contingents and Frontier levies," might possibly be raised, if a sufficient number of British officers were forthcoming, we could not venture to place such troops in line against a Russian force. For such a service we must have the most efficient Native troops that can be formed, and by "efficient" I mean men drawn from the best fighting races who have been embodied long enought to be thoroughly trained.

As soon then as we know definitely the strength of the force which will be required for Burma, and have determined what share of this force it would get prudent to allow the Madras Army as at present constituted to contribute, I would get rid of every sepoy, not required for local purposes, from that Army, also from that of Bombay and from the Hindustani regiments of Bengal, replacing them by soldiers of the most warlike races, and locating the regiments thus newly formed near the places from which they would be recruited. No sentimental feeling should be allowed to interfere with the carrying out of this measure. After providing for the garrison of Burma, few, if any, of the newly-constituted Madras regiments would, I fear, be left for transfer to the North-West Frontier, but a considerable portion of the Bombay Army would be available. At present 3 regiments of Cavalry and 7 of Infantry belonging to that Presidency are quartered in Sind and Biluchistan, and it seems to me essential that these should be recruited from the Frontier tribes. The sepoy of the Deccan is quite unsuited to Biluchistan: – he thoroughly dislikes service there, and the casualties caused by the inclement climate amongst the Bombay regiments which have been quartered at Quetta, Pishin, and Thall-Chotiali during the last six or seven years makes him dread it still more. I would form a separate force for Sind and Biluchistan, much after the model of the Punjab Frontier Force –

such a force, indeed, as I hope to see eventually established in Burma. It should be part of the Bombay Army, as the Burma Frontier Force would be part of the Madras Army, but should never be required, during peace, to go further south and east than Karachi and Hyderabad.

Should it be urged that these measures would have the effect of increasing to a dangerous extent the more warlike races in our armies, and that there would no longer exist the same counter-poise to this element which is now afforded by having in our ranks a certain proportion of the races of Hindustan and Southern India, I would reply that whatever weight this argument may have, it sinks into insignificance when compared with the peril of con-fronting a European enemy on our frontier, without an army fit in all respects to cope with him.

RP 96–1/XX

234
Roberts to Viceroy

[Printed]   Simla
                                                     12 October 1886

A part of the proposed mobilization scheme programme is to arrange on paper for two Army Corps and a Reserve Division. It is very desirable that this should be done while there is leisure to think the matter over quietly, for there are many points which require the most careful consideration. We must make the most of the materials at our disposal by brigading the British and Native troops in such a manner so as to balance equally their different good and bad qualities; by selecting the officers best fitted for commands, and by associating with them Staff Officers whose special experience or qualities may supplement what they them-selves may be deficient in.

Any statements prepared beforehand would, of course, have to be periodically revised, but once the general principles have been accepted, the changes that would be necessitated by casualties, officers leaving India, &c., could be made without difficulty.

In preparing the enclosed statements, I have presupposed that your Excellency would wish me to command any large army that might be required to cross the frontier, and under this impression I have suggested that the Duke of Connaught should be given the 2nd Army Corps. He ranks next to Sir H. Macpherson, whom I have purposely omitted from the list of officers to be employed, as it seems to me probable that your Excellency might desire to have him with the Government of India during my temporary absence. It would, I presume, be necessary to find a place for the Duke of Connaught, and unless Sir C. Arbuthnot and Sir H. Macpherson are to command the two Army Corps, it would be difficult to provide for his Royal Highness in any other way. I have proposed that Brigadier-General McQueen should be Chief of the Staff to the Duke of Connaught: he has a thorough knowledge of the native army and considerable experience of war; he has a strong, independent character, and would never hesitate to give free expression to opinions he thought right, however much they might differ from those of his immediate superiors.

You will see from the enclosures the officers whom I consider best fitted for commands. Sir C. Macgregor I have made no mention of, but should his health be sufficiently restored to admit of his going on active service, I would certainly recommend him for a Division instead probably of General Gillespie.[30] I have entered Sir T. Baker for a Division, as I know him to be an excellent Commander in the field. His appointment would necessitate my looking for another Chief of the Staff. General Brackenbury is, I believe, the officer best fitted for such an important position; he is the only officer, as matters now stand, whose service would be required from England. I should be very much obliged if you will kindly let me know whether these proposals meet generally with your Excellency's approval, before I fill in the minor details of staff appointment, and pass the papers on to General Chesney. According to your present programme I find that I reach Bombay on the day you leave it; if you would wish to see me on any matter, I could easily arrange to be there one day sooner.

The senior officers who are omitted from my programme for employment in the field are –

Generals Dillon, Rowlands, Flood, of the British service. Generals Gib and Gordon, Madras Army, and Sir Charles Gough or General Macfarlan, Bengal Army; Major-General Murray, now Commanding at Meean Meer, I take no note of, as his time will be up on the 1st April next.

ENCLOSURES TO PRECEDING LETTER
First Army Corps.

Commanding	Lieutenant-General Sir CHARLES ARBUTHNOT.
Chief of the Staff	(To be named by Sir CHARLES ARBUTHNOT)
Commanding Cavalry Division	Brigadier-General LUCK (with the rank of Major-General).
Commanding 1st Infantry Division	Major-General Sir THOMAS BAKER.
Commanding 2nd Infantry Division	Brigadier-General WHITE (with the rank of Major-General).
Brigadiers of Cavalry	Sir HUGH GOUGH (Bengal) R.C. STEWART (Madras). R. MARTER (Royal).
Brigadiers of Infantry	1st Division – W.K. ELLES, Adjutant General, Madras Army; Sir JOHN HUDSON; a Bombay Officer, if Sir C. ARBUTHNOT can name one, otherwise Colonel LOCKHART. 2nd Division – Brigadier-General F. NORMAN, Colonel GALBRAITH, Colonel KEEN.[31]

Second Army Corps

Commanding	Major-General his Royal Highness the Duke of CONNAUGHT.
Chief of the Staff	Brigadier-General MCQUEEN.
Commanding 1st Infantry Division	Sir GEORGE GREAVES (Royal).
Commanding 2nd Infantry Division	Major-General GILLESPIE (Bombay).
Brigadiers of Cavalry	R. LOW. C.S. MACLEAN.[32]
Brigadiers of Infantry	1st Division – EAST (British), COLLETT (Bengal), HENNESSY (Bengal).[33] 2nd Division – KNOWLES (British), Adjutant General, Bombay Army; ANDERSON (Bombay); CHANNER (Bengal).

Reserve Division

Commanding	Major-General Sir CHARLES GOUGH, or Major-General MACFARLAN.[34]
Assistant Adjutant General	?
Brigadier of Cavalry	Colonel MACKENZIE, 3rd Bengal Cavalry.
Brigadiers of Infantry	Colonel FARRINGTON (British). Colonel H.M. PRATT (Bengal),[35] a Madras or Bombay Officer

RP 78–1/pp. 15–17

235
Roberts to Viceroy

[Printed copy]   Dharamsala
                                                  21 October 1886

This is terrible news about poor Macpherson. I was afraid from
what I heard that he would not be able to stand the climate, but I
never anticipated his dying. We had seen a great deal of service
together, and I feel very sad at his death. I am delighted that you
wish me to go to Burma. I hope I shall be successful, and that by
April next year the country will be quieted. Would you like
Clandeboye[36] to go with me. I would gladly appoint him Extra
A.D.C., but objection would certainly be raised at the Horse
Guards, on account of his having so recently entered the service,
but there is no reason why he should not accompany me as
galloper or orderly officer. Please tell Lady Dufferin that I will
take every care of him. I wish I could have sailed in the Mail
Steamer of the 28th from Calcutta, but it would be impossible to
get my horses and traps there in time. Unless I hear that your
Excellency wishes to see me at Simla, I shall make Umballa my
head quarters until the 1st November, and then proceed to
Calcutta.

RP 98/1/p. 19

236
Instructions for the guidance of General and other officers
commanding columns in Burma

[Printed]   Mandalay
                                                  20 November 1886

The following general instructions for the guidance of
Brigadier-Generals and Officers in Command of columns are
published by order of His Excellency the Commander-in-Chief
in India:-

1st. – Columns sent out for the pacification of a district, or in pursuit of a particular gang of dacoits, must be amply provided and able to keep the field for ten days at least. To enable this to be done without employing an undue number of transport animals, it is necessary that every endeavour be made to obtain grain for cavalry horses and transport ponies from the villages passed through; careful enquiry must be made as to where supplies can be obtained locally, and the line of advance determined accordingly. Arrangements must be made for replenishing the supply when necessary from depôts which must be formed at convenient centres when the nature of the operations may necessitate it. These depôts should be pushed forward from time to time as the troops advance. The work of a column obliged to return to its base of supply before it has had an opportunity of completing the object of the expedition must be more harmful than beneficial, as its failure emboldens the enemy and weakens the confidence of the people in our power to reach the offenders and to protect them.

2nd. – Where two or more columns are acting in concert, the details of time and place of movement should be settled beforehand with the greatest nicety, and the Commanding Officers of all such columns should be provided with the same maps, or tracings from them, so that subsequent changes of plan, rendered necessary by later information, may be understood and conformed to by all. Officers Commanding columns must do their utmost to get into, and keep up, communication with one another. This can be effected by –

> Visual signalling
> Spies and scouts,
> Patrolling.

3rd. – Movements to be executed in concert with the troops in other brigades or commands, or likely to tell directly or indirectly on the districts commanded by other officers, will be fully communicated to those officers, both beforehand and when in progress.

4th. – Brigadier-Generals are empowered to give very liberal remuneration for the effective service of guides and for information involving danger to those who give it. They may delegate this power to selected officers in detached commands, but a close watch must be kept on expenditure under this head. Opportunities should be afforded to timid informers who are afraid to compromise themselves by entering camp to interview officers at some distance out and in secrecy.

5th. – Cavalry horses and mounted infantry ponies must be saved as much as is compatible with occasional forced and rapid marches. On ordinary occasions the riders should dismount, from time to time and march alongside of their horses or ponies.

6th. – The special attention of all officers is called to the careful treatment of pack-animals, and officers in command of columns and parties will be held strictly responsible that the animals are properly loaded for the march, saved as much as possible during it and carefully attended to, and fed after it. Officers in command will ascertain by daily personal supervision and inspection that these orders are carried out.

7th. – It must be remembered that the chief object of traversing the country with columns is to cultivate friendly relations with the inhabitants, and at the same time to put before them evidences of our power, thus gaining their good-will and their confidence. It is therefore the bounden duty of Commanding Officers to ascertain that the troops under their command are not permitted to injure the property of the people or to wound their susceptibilities.

8th. – The most injurious accounts of our intentions have been circulated amongst, and believed by, the people, and too much pains cannot be taken to eradicate this impression, and to assure the people both by act and word of our good-will towards the law-abiding. Chief men of districts should be treated with consideration and distinction. The success of the present operations will much depend on the tact with which the inhabitants are treated.

9th. – When there is an enemy in arms against British rule, all arrangements must be made not only to drive him from his position, but also to surround the position so as to inflict the heaviest loss possible. Resistance overcome without inflicting punishment on the enemy only emboldens him to repeat the game, and thus, by protracting operations, costs more lives than a severe lesson promptly administered, even though that lesson may cause some casualties on our side. Arrangements should be made to surround villages and jungle retreats with cavalry and afterwards to hunt them closely with infantry. In the pursuit the broadest margin possible will be drawn between leaders of rebellion and the professional dacoit on the one part, and the villagers who have been forced into combinations against us. Bohs and leaders will generally be found heading the column of fugitives, and a portion of the cavalry should be directed to pursue them without wasting time over the rank-and-file of the enemy.

10th. – Unless otherwise ordered, columns of occupation should move in short marches, halting at the principal towns and villages. This will give Civil officers opportunities of becoming thoroughly acquainted with their districts, and give Military Officers time to reconnoitre and sketch the country.

11th. – Where troops are likely to be quartered for some time, bamboo platforms should be erected to keep the men off the ground. Tents, if afterwards provided, can be pitched on the platforms.

12th. – The greatest latitude will be allowed to Brigadier-Generals and Officers in local command in ordering and carrying out movements for the pacification of their districts. They will, however, report as fully as possible all movements intended and in progress, through the regular channel, for the information of His Excellency the Commander-in-Chief.

13th. – Civil Officers will be detailed under the orders of the Chief Commissioner to accompany columns. As they are in a position to reward loyalty and good service they will be able to obtain more reliable guides and intelligence than the Military Officers can hope to get. The Chief Commissioner has authorised selected Burmans, men of position who may look for official appointments, being employed as scouts by the Civil Officers of districts and being attached to columns. These scouts should wear some distinguishing and conspicuous mark or badge to prevent them being fired on by the troops. They should not be called upon to take the front when approaching an unbroken enemy, or where ambuscades may be expected, but their services will be most valuable in gaining information and later in hunting down the individuals of a broken-up gang.

14th. – Absolute secrecy must be maintained regarding movements against the enemy and every device resorted to to mislead him.

15th. – When Civil officers accompany columns all prisoners will be handed over to them for disposal. When no Civil Officer is present the Officer Commanding the column will, *ex officio*, have magisterial powers to inflict punishment up to two years' imprisonment, or 30 lashes. Offenders deserving heavier punishment must be reserved for disposal by the Civil Officers.

16th. – Officers commanding columns will be held responsible that the troops are not kept in unhealthy districts, and that when a locality has proved itself unhealthy, the troops are removed at the earliest possible opportunity. Military officers are responsible for the location of the troops. The requisitions of Civil Officers will be complied with, whenever practicable, but Military Officers are to judge in all matters involving the military or sanitary suitability of a position.

17th. – In the class of warfare in which we are now engaged, where night surprises and ambuscades are the only formidable tactics of the enemy, the greatest care must be taken to ensure the safety of the camp at night. To meet ambuscades, which usually take the form of a volley followed by flight, and which, in very dense jungle, it may be impossible to discover or guard against by means of flankers, His Excellency the Commander-in-Chief would wish the following plan to be tried:-

Supposing, for instance, the fire of the enemy to be delivered from the right, a portion of the force in front should be ready to dash along the road for 100 yards, or so, or until some opening in the jungle offers itself. The party should then turn to the right and sweep round with a view to intercepting the enemy in his flight. A party in rear should similarly enter the jungle to their right with the same object. The centre of the column would hold the ground and protect the baggage or any wounded men. The different parties must be previously told off, put under the command of selected leaders, and must act with promptitude and dash. Each party must be kept in compact order and individual firing must be prohibited except when there is a clear prospect. Past experience suggests the adoption of some such plan as the above, but in guerrilla warfare, officers must suit their tactics to the peculiar and ever varying circumstances in which they may find themselves engaged.

18th. – The Government have ordered a general disarmament of the country, as soon as the large bands of rebels and dacoits are dispersed. The orders for this disarmament direct that all firearms are to be taken from the people; but that a moderate number may be returned to responsible villagers who are loyal and are able to defend themselves. No firearms will be returned save under registered licenses; and licenses will be given only for villages which can produce a certain number (5 to 10) guns, and are either stockaded or fenced against sudden attack. The duty of disarming lies on Civil Officers and the police; but as it is desirable that the disarmament should be effected as quickly as possible, Officers Commanding posts and columns will give such assistance as may be in their power in carrying it out.

RP 96 1/XXIV

237
Roberts to Lytton

[Printed]   Mandalay
Private   20 November 1886

I have been sent by the Viceroy to try my hand at the pacification of Burma, which is, as you doubtless know, nearly as large as France, and just at present in a very disturbed condition. Here at Mandalay I am reminded by a multitude of details of the days when I was in Afghanistan, and in constant communication with Your Lordship, and I think it may interest you to hear some of my first impressions in this strange land. Not that there is the slightest resemblance between the two theatres of operations; indeed, nothing could well be more dissimilar than the inhabitants, climate, communications or productions of the two countries. But the greater issues are much the same, with this important difference that we intend staying in Burma – a determination which must, sooner or later, make itself felt amongst the people, with the best possible effect.

I am inclined to think that it is fortunate the Viceroy determined to send me here; not from any overweening self-confidence, but from the undesirability of the work falling into the hands of any officer unacquainted with what has been going on in Burma during the past twelve months. This is not altogether the kind of duty I would choose, but service in any shape or form has great attractions for me.

Partly owing to the rains which rendered certain tracts of the country impassable, and more recently by the inevitable delay from a change of commanders, a lengthened inaction has been forced upon our troops. During this period the dacoits have, without doubt, made head against us. The military being inactive the civilians saw with regret and dismay the loss of their prestige and authority; recriminations were beginning to be indulged in, and at poor Sir Herbert Macpherson's death things were certainly moving in a retrograde direction.

Bernard and White have done wonderfully well and made the

most of the means at their disposal, but, however sound their policy or able their plans, no commander strange to the position would be likely to accept them off-hand. A further delay must have occurred in the arrival of a new man, and much of the limited time during which active operations can be carried on in Burma would have been wasted.

Fortunately I am differently placed; I have the most thorough confidence in General White; all along I have been fully informed of his plans, and as his responsible chief I have quite approved of them. Having the somewhat complicated military situation at my fingers' ends, I need not, and shall not, lose one hour in carrying on a series of combined movements all over the country. With an equal good fortune I have the honor to reckon Sir Charles Bernard amongst my intimate friends, which will enable me, I trust, to carry the civilian element with me in any measures I may adopt. Finally, my long and frequent conversations with the Viceroy have given me an intimate knowledge of his ideas and wishes – an invaluable guide to me in this difficult undertaking.

I think there is but little doubt that we were at first inclined to underrate the difficulties which lay before us in Burma, and until quite lately there has been a fatal inclination to pare and scrape, especially in the matter of providing an efficient civil administration to replace the military as soon as the latter should have crushed anything like organized resistance.

For some time to come troops must be everywhere *en evidence*, to support civil authority and to terrify evil doers, but it is very desirable that all scattered posts should be taken by the police at an early date, especially in the unhealthy tracts of country. To enable this to be done more civil officers are required and an efficient police must be organized without delay. Police in Burma has always been a difficulty, but I see no reason why it should be an insurmountable one. We cannot hope to govern and country without employing a certain number of the inhabitants, and it behoves us to discover some means by which those enlisted for police duties can be made efficient and trustworthy. It was found necessary in the Punjab and Oudh, when we first annexed those provinces, to give the police a semi-military organisation, and this,

I think, must be done here. Young officers who enrol and train men are pretty certain to get some hold over them, and then it would be their business to watch them and see that they did not become discontented with our service. Hereafter the police may, perhaps, be made over to the civil authorities to be enlisted and trained, but to do so now would prevent our having anything like an efficient police force for many years to come.

I have already made preparations for a series of combined movements, some of which have indeed commenced, but I am averse to incurring responsibilities in the outskirts of the province until we have got the heart of the country well in hand. Although I see no prospect whatsoever of a speedy pacification, I hope that by working with system and energy during the next few months, it may be possible to get the main portion of the country sufficiently settled to admit of several regiments and batteries returning to India in the early spring, but I think it not unlikely that I may have to ask for further reinforcements in the meantime to enable the operations decided upon being undertaken with vigour.

With regard to our enemies, some fault has been found with the term "dacoit" and yet I think that there is a great deal more of the robber than the patriot about these gentlemen. I cannot ascertain that their actions are inspired by any higher motive than love of loot, and they slaughter a sepoy or brother Burman with perfect impartiality. They are most difficult to deal with after the larger bands have been dispersed. Whilst the pursuit is hot in their neighbourhood they hide their arms in the jungle, return to their villages and pose as peaceful labourers. When malaria or transport difficulties cause the troops to retire, they reappear again in their true colors, and as no Burman has been persuaded as yet to turn informer, it is not easy to get hold of a dacoit . . .

P.S. – If you think that Lord Salisbury would care to read my views on the situation in Burma, perhaps you would kindly send him this letter.

RP 100–1/LXXV

238
Roberts to Chesney

[Printed]   near Khyanyat
                                         12 December 1886
Private

For some time past I have been anxious to see clubs established for soldiers, either as a regimental or station institution, but difficulties have been raised, and experienced old soldiers, like Robertson, have not been able to clear them away. However, I cannot believe they are insurmountable, and it seems to me that, so far as British soldiers in India are concerned, the 50th Anniversary of Her Majesty's reign could not be commemorated in a more appropriate manner. My idea is that the club should take the place of the canteen, coffee-shop, and recreation-room.

The canteen is a relic of barbarism. I never visit one without thinking how impossible it must be for a soldier to have any self-respect who is required to take his glass of beer under the rules by which regimental canteens are governed.

Some corps have well-managed coffee-shops, and, so far as the space will admit, recreation-rooms are made fairly attractive; but it is impossible to say anything in favour of canteens. I am not prepared to assert that soldiers would drink less than they do now if their liquor were served out in a less repulsive manner: possibly they might at first drink a little more, but my belief is that after a short time, the mere fact of being able to get liquor when they want it, would, like the boy in the pastry-cook's shop, do away with the craving for it. Many men go to the canteen chiefly because they have nothing else to do, but if they had an attractive club where they could amuse themselves pretty much as they like, drink would in time become a secondary consideration, and not the first, as I fear it is now with most soldiers.

Recreation-rooms are far too small, and coffee-shops have no recognized place at all. What is wanted is a building sufficiently large to include the canteen, recreation-room, and coffee-shop, and to admit of the greater number of the men being able to spend their evenings in a respectable and rational manner.

There is a financial side to this question, and it is on this account that I would like to know whether you think the Government would be prepared to consider favourably such a proposal as a fitting way of celebrating Her Majesty's Jubilee. Of course I do not expect that money would be forthcoming for building clubs in every station, but if the principle I advocate were accepted, provision would be made for them at all new stations, and in the meanwhile existing buildings could be altered at a moderate cost, as has been done in the case of station hospitals.

Carefully considered rules would have to be framed for the management of soldiers' clubs, but this is a matter of detail about which I do not anticipate any difficulty.

RP 100–5/LXV

239
Lytton to Roberts

[Holograph]   8 January 1887
                                                Knebworth

<u>Private</u>

Your letter was so exceedingly interesting to me that I felt sure it must be interesting to Lord Salisbury; and I therefore sent it on to him at once. It was unlucky that the very next day brought with it the public outburst of the political crisis which had long been fermenting in the Cabinet and which came to a head with Randolph Churchill's resignation: so that I fear Salisbury must have read your letter with a mind much preoccupied. But in returning it to me a few days later he wrote "It is very interesting indeed. To judge by the Papers his forecast of success has been more than justified."

What you say of Bernard is a high testimonial to the merit of his administrative work in Burmah, and I was glad that the Prime Minister should have an opportunity of seeing – as, with the pub-

lic at least, there has been a pretty general impression at home that
Bernard had underrated the difficulties and requirements of the situation in Burmah, and that the slow progress made in the pacification of the new Province was largely due to weak Administration. I
have not only a real personal regard for Bernard, but of his abilities I
also formed, when I was in India, a very good opinion wh I sh^d be
slow to change: and it is therefore pleasant as well as interesting to
me to be assured by you that these imputations were undeserved. I
have no doubt however that by all the Civil Authorities concerned
the character of the work to be done in Burmah was more or less
underestimated immediately after the dramatic rapidity of
Thebaw's collapse, and that the mistake common to impecunious
Gov^ts was made of trying to do things too much on the cheap. White
I know is a good man. I sh^d be sorry to see Sir Griffin[37] appointed to
Burmah, which appears to be probable, but would rather see him
disposed of there than in the Punjab where he might be most mis-
chievous and a great thorn in the side of any Gov^t of India in the
event of renewed troubles in Afghanistan.

I was not myself in favour of your present Mission to Burmah –
not because I doubted for a moment that it would be productive of
great good in Burmah, but because it seemed to me like sending
for Sir William Gull[38] to attend a patient in the country – an
advertisement that the patient is in <u>extremis</u>. As a general rule I
think the proper place for the Commander-in-Chief is at Head
Quarters, unless he is required for field command in a really big
war beyond the British frontier. But in your own interest (which I
care most about) I think you were quite right to accept this mission without a moment's hesitation. You were sure to succeed in it
so far as success was humanly possible. It has kept you before the
public eye at home. It has enabled you to exhibit your administrative as well as your military ability – it has in many ways given you
new personal experience which you may hereafter find most useful, and it has not rendered you unavailable at a moment's notice
for any greater occasion sh^d it arise. Within the last few days the
news from abroad looks a little more peaceful, mainly because the
alleged military weakness of Austria appears to have alarmed
Bismark and renewed his anxiety to prevent for the present every

risk of actual conflict between her & Russia. And indeed I believe it may be said with truth that not one of the Great Powers at this moment really wishes for war, and that all of them have strong motives for avoiding war, <u>if possible</u>. But notwithstanding the force of this consideration my own impression is that a European war in the Spring is still highly probable. The whole European situation is undermined by a highly inflamed & inflammable condition of vital problems which cannot be solved by diplomacy alone. Mutual mistrust is universal & intense – nor do I see how these enormous armaments (the German especially) can much longer be maintained in a state of efficiency without being employed. It is fortunate for our interests abroad as well as at home (and in India also, I believe) that the secession of Randolph has, so far as one can judge, strengthened instead of weakening Lord Salisbury's Ministry. Randolph himself is now I believe sorry for what he has done and perceives that he made a great mistake.[39] His position when Parl^t meets will be an awkward one – but I don't think he has any intention of joining the Radicals. I hope that some progress has lately been made in the Organisation of our Army. But we are working on a rotten system; and I doubt if a sound system is possible compatible with Parliamentary Gov^t. . .

RP 37/119

240
Note on the urgent necessity of carrying out the sanctioned increase to the British and Native Forces in India

[Printed]   Calcutta
                                                  8 February 1887

I have had an opportunity of perusing Major-General Chesney's Note of 25th January, in which the effect on our Military strength of the recent annexation of Upper Burma is very clearly set forth, and I think it right briefly to record for the information of Government my entire concurrence with my honourable colleague's arguments and conclusions.

The increase to the Native Infantry of –
    5 Goorkha battalions,
    3 Sikh battalions,
    1 Pioneer battalion,
was fixed upon by the Government of India, and sanctioned by the Secretary of State in the autumn of 1885, as the least addition that could be made to that branch of the service, consequent on the threatening position which Russia had taken up in Central Asia.

It was then intended to proceed at once with the raising of these nine battalions, and I may, perhaps, usefully recall to the recollection of Government that the subsequent resolve to postpone their embodiment was taken when there was no opportunity of consulting the Military Member of Council or myself, and avowedly, as a temporary measure, to meet an urgent financial pressure.

In April 1886, after a discussion in Council, the Government agreed to raise the 5 Goorkha battalions, and 4 of these are now in course of formation; but it was then understood that the raising of the 4 remaining battalions, *viz.*, 3 Sikh and 1 Pioneer, would certainly not be deferred beyond 1st April 1887, and it was on this understanding that I acceded to the postponment of their embodiment.

I am not aware that there is any intention to propose a further postponement of the raising of these regiments, but I desire to endorse, in the most forcible manner possible, Major-General Chesney's opinion that our available strength of Native Infantry is at present below the point which the necessities of the case demand, and that it would be in the highest degree imprudent for us again to defer raising regiments which were considered an essential addition to our military strength in the circumstances of September 1885, and which the annexion of Upper Burma has now rendered doubly necessary.

I am quite willing, and indeed anxious, to enforce every possible military economy consistent with the efficiency of the army, but I can never agree that a proper field for economy can be found in any further postponement of the completion of the Native Infantry to its sanctioned strength.

I wish also to remind the Government that the sanctioned increase of the establishment of a Native Infantry regiment, from 832 to 912 of all ranks, is still held in abeyance, and that the army is therefore short of about 4,000 men on this account. I strongly urge that this increase be not again delayed; it is in my opinion a measure essential to the efficiency of the army, as regiments at their present strength, and with the new reserve system still undeveloped, are certainly, as our experience in Afghanistan fully proved, far too weak to withstand the strain of a campaign.

Again, as regards our strength in British Infantry, the increase considered necessary in 1885 was three additional battalions of 984 men each, and an increase of 100 men to each of the battalions on the Indian establishment; but, as General Chesney points out, the garrison of India, instead of being increased as was intended by three battalions, has actually, in consequence of the requirements of Burma, been reduced by one battalion.

Moreover, the promised increase of 100 men to the strength of the British battalions serving in India has been only partially carried into effect. We have, in fact, only got 50 men as yet per battalion, and our establishment of this arm, the backbone of our power, is on this account alone 2,500 men short of the sanctioned strength.

Major-General Chesney, at page 7 of his Note, while provisionally accepting the argument that financial difficulties preclude the immediate completion of the British Infantry to the authorised strength, expressly states that he does so in view "of the reasonable probability that in case of war we should be able to get more British troops from home"; but I am bound to say that the fulfilment of this expectation appears to me to be very doubtful, as I have recently been informed in a demi-official letter from the Horse Guards, that in the event of a European war, in which England might be engaged, we could not calculate on getting even the reserve men belonging to the battalions serving in this country.

It seems to me, therefore, that we should not rest until we have made it quite certain that "the 2,500 men still wanting to make good the rank and file of battalions should be supplied without fail next season," and I strongly urge that the necessary steps to secure this should be at once taken.

The same remarks apply with equal force to the six batteries of garrison artillery which are due next cold season, and which are indispensably necessary for the efficient manning of our sea-ports and frontier defences.

RP 96–1/XXVI

241
Note on the desirability of establishing Regimental Clubs for British soldiers in India

[Printed]   Simla,
                                                            4 May 1887

I cannot too strongly recommend to my colleagues the proposal to establish a kind of Club for the soldiers of every British regiment and battery in India.

Since the date (1860) when Sir James Outram[40] pleaded for the "cleanliness and decencies" of the Officers' mess being extended to the soldiers' canteen and refreshment-room, a remarkable change has come over the army. Nearly every soldier can now read and write, and in most corps the men, with very few exceptions, subscribe to the regimental library. In the barrack-rooms endeavours are often made to give the small space allotted to each man a home-like appearance by hanging pictures and photographs on the walls; while in the married quarters there are abundant evidences that a spirit of refinement is gradually spreading through all ranks. Of the many family quarters I visited during the past cold season, scarcely one was without an air of comfort and cleanliness; even the poorest private soldier's wife had made some humble attempt at decoration.

Notwithstanding this great improvement in the habits of the army, the "comparative squalor" of the canteen remains as it was at the beginning of Her Majesty's reign, while the coffee-shop is still officially an unrecognised institution, dependent on the energies and *esprit de corps* of the officers of the regiment for its very existence. No one can visit a canteen without a feeling of distress – not to say disgust – that British soldiers should in this enlightened age be condemned to such a degrading system. I never enter a canteen without thinking how impossible it must be for a soldier to have any self-respect, who is required to take his glass of beer under the rules by which regimental canteens are governed. The British Army in India could have no better or more lasting memorial of Her Majesty's Jubilee or one which would be so generally beneficial to soldiers as the abolishment of this relic of barbarism.

It is difficult to understand why no accommodation has been provided for the regimental coffee-shop, as more than twenty years ago (1864) the expediency of providing – "A reading-room, a recreation-room, and a regimental refreshment-room, all under the same roof, was recognised by the Government of India, and received the unqualified approval of Her Majesty's Government." Some corps have well-arranged coffee-shops, but they are generally worked under great difficulties, in a spare room or corner of a verandah, anywhere indeed where the stores can be collected and one or two tables placed at which a very limited number of men can take their evening meal.

So far as their size will admit, recreation and reading rooms are made fairly attractive, but in a majority of cases the space is far too small, and does not accommodate one tenth of the men of the regiment or battery. Reading and writing in the ordinary barrack-room is out of the question, for even if there were the usual conveniences, such as tables and chairs, the light in the evenings is quite insufficient.

Outside their barracks, there are no places of amusement in this country to which soldiers can go; they do not know what to do with themselves after dark, consequently they get into trouble either by wandering about the bazaars, or from spending too much of their time at the canteen.

What is required is a sufficient number of good-sized, well-lighted rooms, where soldiers can amuse themselves in a rational manner, and where they can have their supper and glass of beer with comfort and decency. It is not to be expected that buildings thoroughly suitable for these purposes could be specially erected at every station. We must make the best of what we have with such additional accommodation as may be absolutely necessary. What I would ask now is –

(1) that the establishment of Soldiers' Clubs may receive the approval of Government.

(2) that refreshment-rooms, as sanctioned by the Secretary of State for India in 1864, may be constructed without unnecessary delay, wherever it may be found impossible to provide for the same with the existing barrack accommodation;

(3) that a suitable supply of barrack furniture, lamps, &c., should be provided sufficient to render the "Clubs" as comfortable as may be considered advisable for soldiers.

I cannot bind myself to meet the cost of these Clubs by some specific corresponding reduction, as proposed by the Financial Member; but I can point to the many savings which have been made in military expenditure during the last 18 months, and I can promise to continue to use my best endeavours to economise in every way possible.

The Clubs themselves will, I feel sure, prove an economy in the end; and I cannot better express my ideas on the subject than by quoting what Sir James Outram wrote 27 years ago. That distinguished officer and soldiers' friend said:- "I maintain that were my recommendations adopted, the total aggregate expense of carrying them out would be covered in less than five years by the saving that would result in medicines, in medical comforts, in invaliding charges, and in the cost of replacing casualties; and I hesitate not to say that, were it otherwise, the expenses attendant on giving effect to my views are expenses which it is our bounden moral duty to incur, though we should thereby be driven to curtail our expenditure in other items."

RP 96–1/XXVII

242
Roberts to Charles Marvin

[Printed]   Simla
                                             14 May 1887

I have to thank you for another interesting letter, dated the 5th March last, in which, and in your reply to Colonel Malleson[41] in the *Fortnightly Review* of March, you clearly expose the fallacy of our ever hoping to grapple with the Russians in the neighbourhood of the Caucasus. Some few years ago I went into this question very thoroughly, and the result of my enquiries was to convince me that any action on our part between the Black Sea and the Caspian, or even from the Persian Gulf, against the Russians, would not only be most unprofitable but hazardous to a degree.

I know that a certain section amongst military men at home, and one which carries considerable weight with it,[42] is in favour of such a campaign, but for my part I believe that any one who would effectually "prick the bubble," as you so graphically put it, would be doing a great national service, and I am looking forward with considerable interest to your article in the illustrated *Naval and Military Magazine*. Before any responsibility is incurred in Europe, it behoves England to consider what demands will be made upon her, in the event of a war with Russia, from India, and from some of her important ports. It would be impossible to act solely on the defensive in India. We live by prestige, and we cannot afford to let our Native troops or the people of India doubt the maintenance of our supremacy, which they certainly would if we were to allow Russia to overrun Afghanistan. We must let it be clearly seen that we do not fear Russia, and that we are determined she shall not approach near enough to India to cause us serious trouble in our rear. Possibly before you receive this, important events may have occurred in Afghanistan. If the Amir can keep his Ghilzai troops loyal, he may weather the storm, but if they go against him, he would have no chance.

I am much obliged for your kind congratulations on the recent successes our troops have achieved in Burma. It is a most interesting country, and has, I believe, a great future before it. The backbone of dacoity is broken, and now that the police are gradually getting hold of the districts, I do not anticipate any further trouble, though for some time to come it will be necessary to keep a somewhat large garrison in the country.

RP 100–1/CXIX

243
Roberts to Bishop of Calcutta[43]

[Printed]
Simla
23 May 1887

The recent departure of the Revd. J.G. Gregson, the well-known Secretary to the Total Abstinence Association in India, necessitates some new arrangements being made to carry on the work, which that gentleman so successfully performed amongst British soldiers in this country.

Acknowledging, as I readily do, the necessity for total abstinence in many cases I am much impressed by the conviction that much more good would result, so far as the army in India is concerned, if the various societies, which now exist for the prevention of drunkenness, could be amalgamated. There would be more united action; funds would go further; the Government and the public would be more ready to assist the movement, and above all, officers would be more generally able than at present to become members of the association. It appears to me essential that the amalgamated society should be worked on a regimental basis, and that it should be absolutely undenominational in title as well as in spirit.

I earnestly hope that you will see fit to support my views in this matter, and that you will commend them to your Chaplains at all military stations, and invite them to assist in every way.

It may be that many soldiers have hitherto been unable to trust themselves to keep sober under a simple pledge of temperance, but soldiers are not altogether to blame for their habits of drunkenness. The canteen system has much to answer for. No one can visit a canteen without a feeling of distress – not to say disgust – that British soldiers should in this enlightened age, be condemned to resort to such a place of temptation, where they can only pass their time in drinking. But I am glad to say that the Government of India have determined that this shall no longer be the case, and have agreed to the establishment of regimental clubs or institutes. These will consist of a series of well-lighted rooms, in which the men will be able to amuse themselves in a rational and improving manner. The present canteen system will be done away with, and in lieu of it, a bar will be attached to the coffee shop and refreshment room, at which the men will be able to obtain beer (no spirits, I hope, certainly not undiluted) in moderation.

A remarkable change has come over the army of late years; nearly every soldier can now read and write, and in most corps the men, with few exceptions, subscribe to the regimental library. I am very sanguine that, as the status of the rank and file is still further raised, there will be comparatively almost as little drunkenness amongst the rank and file as there is now-a-days amongst the officers.

The admission of officers into the society will, I am convinced, be beneficial not only from their example, but from the direct interest they could take in the cause of Temperance.

I would propose that the new society should be called the "Army Temperance Association;" that it should include all existing Temperance Societies; that it should admit amongst its members not only total abstainers, but also those who do not think it necessary to bind themselves by a stronger pledge than that of Temperance; that it should be managed by a council and executive committee; and that the Revd. E.T. Beatty, whose services have been temporarily placed at the disposal of the Government of India by the Bishop of Madras, should be the secretary.

Should this project meet with Your Lordship's approval, may I hope that you will consent to join the council of the association?

RP 100–5/CII

244
H.M. Durand, Foreign Department, to Roberts

[Holograph]   Simla
                                         27 May 1887

I was speaking to Mackworth Young a few days ago about doing something to utilise the armies of native States, and he said he thought the Punjab States w^d gladly offer us troops, to be associated with ours, & drilled, if we would give them good weapons.

I am in favour of giving breech loaders to picked bodies of Native State troops – the numbers being of course limited, and the conditions being first, efficiency of drill & Equipment up to a given standard, secondly readiness to be called out whenever required for service.

The Viceroy, to whom I spoke yesterday, has no objection to my authorising the Punjab Gov^t to send up any proposal submitted by the States – but he wishes me to ask your opinion first as to the expediency of trying to bring about any measure of the kind I have described.

Would you mind telling me whether you think the general line right and the opportunity a good one?

If so it w^d be necessary to give the Punjab Gov^t some instructions for its guidance in shaping the offers of the States. They must not send up any requests which we could not grant, or the result will only be embarrassment. Could you give me any hints as to what should be aimed at and what avoided from a military point of view? Probably the less detailed their offers are the better?

While Dulip Sing[44] is in Russia, and undoubtedly doing harm among the Punjabis, a deliberate volunteering on the part of the Sikh States w^d be very opportune.

We must be careful not to bring upon ourselves a flood of troublesome proposals from elsewhere, but we might find the Punjab example bearing really good fruit.

I have lately read some notes by Barr,[45] one of our smartest political officers, which show that a couple of years ago he was in favour of a comprehensive scheme for utilising the State armies. He seemed to think much could be done in Central India and Rajputana.

I w^d not accept mercenary troops – only the troops of the States themselves – really local battalions or bodies of Cavy.

I will come over and speak to you whenever you like, but perhaps it w^d be better to let me know your opinion in writing if you do not mind.

Yours very sincerely,
H.M. Durand

245
Roberts to Dillon

[Printed]

Simla
2 August, 1887

Private

* * *

I am very much obliged to you for telling me the reports at the Horse Guards and War Office about the way in which I exercise patronage. I am not ashamed of helping my friends so long as they deserve it, but I would not put my own brother into any place for which he was not, in my opinion, fitted. I knew that men passed over would abuse me, but I am prepared to bear the burden, rather than promote men whom I believe to be inefficient. I may, of course, make mistakes, but I do my best, both by personal acquaintance and by carefully weighing opinions, to form a just view of all officers' characters, and I am gratified to find that, as a rule, my selections seem to be approved. The Viceroy has more than once expressed his admiration at the happy appointments I have made, and I feel pretty sure that the army trust me. It would save me an immense amount of trouble, and probably prevent my being occasionally misunderstood, were I to take men according to their rank in the Army List, but I know from experience the danger of putting officers in responsible positions, who have no other claim than age or seniority, and I determined that if ever I became a Commander-in-Chief, I would never appoint any one I did not believe to be in all respects fitted for the position he had to fill.

RP 100–2/LII

246
Note on the desirability of utilising the Armies of Native States

[Printed]   Simla
                                                  8 September 1887

I do not propose to discuss in detail the policy which is suggested
in Mr Durand's note; I will content myself by remarking that it is
a policy with which I agree most cordially, and one to which I
could give my fullest support. As I pointed out in a recent note on
our military preparations, it does not seem unreasonable that
Native States should be called upon to contribute in men, or
money, to the support of the power which ensures them peace and
prosperity, and the proposals now put forward by Mr Durand
would have the desirable effect of our getting a serviceable reserve
to the Native army at an unappreciable cost.

In the spring of 1885, when attending the Durbar at Rawal
Pindi, I was brought into contact with a good many natives of all
ranks, and I confess I was much struck with the feeling which
seemed to pervade all classes of a desire to come forward in support of our rule. There appeared to be a general wish to take a
part in the defence of the Empire, a wish that would, I feel sure,
be strengthened if the people were convinced of our determination to act with vigour, and of our ability to deal effectively with
any troubles that might arise beyond our North-West Frontier.
No better method of fostering this spontaneous wish to assist us
could, I believe, be devised than by our calling on the Native
States to bear their full share in the defence of India. In a State
paper written by Lord Lawrence's Government at the close of
his time as Viceroy, alluding to the possibility of "a Foreign
Power such as Russia ever seriously thinking of invading India
from without, or what is more probable, of stirring up the element of dissatisfaction or anarchy within it, our true policy, our
strongest security would, then, we conceive, be found to be . . .
in the contentment, if not attachment of the masses; in the sense
of security of title and possession, with which our whole policy is

gradually imbuing the minds of the principal chiefs and the Native Aristocracy, &c., &c.,"

This is a theory with which I believe, most men conversant with the present condition of our rule in this country would cordially agree. To ensure, however, such an ideal state of things, we need to have an efficient army, and to have an efficient army, there must be an increased expenditure. In the present state of our finances we cannot afford to add to our Military Estimates, another reason why the proposed scheme commends itself to one as a wise and statesmanlike policy. If Mr Durand's proposals are accepted, such portions of the Native States Armies as it may be decided to train should be made as efficient as possible. Whatever dangers there may be in such a course are fully outweighed by the many advantages which it offers. We cannot afford to take inefficient troops on service.

I see no objection to a beginning being made by inviting the Native States Chiefs of the Punjab to place a certain number of their troops at our disposal. Their active assistance to us in 1857 marks them out as being well fitted to lead such a movement, and when once the scheme is fairly launched, I am confident that other Native States will be eager to follow their example and prove their loyalty to the Government. Such a service would prove congenial employment not only for young men of good family in the Native States, but also for many restless and adventurous spirits for whom we have no place in our present organization. With a proper supervision by a certain number of picked British officers, selected partly for their professional qualifications, but principally on account of their tact in dealing with orientals, we should ere long receive a most valuable and material addition to our fighting strength. Before deciding upon the strength of the contingents to be provided by each State, it is, as Mr Durand points out, most necessary that we should be in possession of an estimate shewing the resources of the several States, and for such an investigation I would recommend that Major Melliss[46] should be employed on the footing as regards pay and position as suggested by Mr Durand.

Major Melliss has had experience of this sort of work at Baroda, and when he submits his report the Military Department will be able to inform the Government as to the amount of assistance which it may seem desirable that we should call on each Native State to provide.

RP 96–1/XXXVI

247

Roberts to Duke of Cambridge

[Printed]

Private

Simla
9 September 1887

* * *

I am sorry to say that another disagreeable racing case has occurred, and as these social matters often gain great publicity, and are as often misrepresented, I think it better to let Your Royal Highness know what has happened. At a sky [sic] race meeting at Meerut last month Captain Barry, R.A.,[47] had arranged to ride a horse called "Sultan" belonging to Lieut. Mahon[48] of the 8th Hussars, in a race called the "Sahara stakes". Captain Barry afterwards entered his own horse "Trumpeter" for the same race and got Lieut Templer, 19th Bengal Lancers, to ride for him. At the lottery the evening before the race Major Fell, 8th Hussars, saw Lieut Shortt, R.A., bidding for "Trumpeter", and as he understood that the bidding was really for Captain Barry, he bid for the horse himself and bought it in for R76. The horse "Sultan" was sold at the same time to Vet. Surgeon Clayton for R130. When the race was run the next day "Trumpeter" won by about a neck. This caused enquiry to be made, and the Stewards of the races decided that Captain Barry had intentionally prevented "Sultan" from winning the race. The Stewards were unanimous in their opinion and I understand that the following points told against Captain Barry.
(1) That he had had a trial, and considered his own horse the best of the two.
(2) That he entered his own horse after he had arranged to ride "Sultan".

382

(3) That he got another officer to bid for him at the lottery.

(4) That whether intentionally or unintentionally he rode "Sultan" so as not to win.

The Stewards at Meerut have prohibited Captain Barry from riding in races for six months, a decision which I hear has been upheld by the Calcutta Turf Club, to the committee of which Captain Barry appealed.

The Judge Advocate General, to whom I referred the case, points out that though Captain Barry might be tried under Section 16, Army Act, he thinks that from the evidence available a conviction would be far from a reasonable certainty. I agreed with this opinion, and except, perhaps, in the interest of Captain Barry, a Court Martial does not seem to me desirable. Under these circumstances I have caused Captain Barry to be informed that he must clear himself from the aspersions cast upon him by the Stewards' order; that he has placed himself under the stigma of a decision declaring him to have been guilty of conduct unbecoming an officer and a gentleman; that this decision has been passed by a competent tribunal (a social not a legal one certainly), but one that every gentleman engaging himself on the turf voluntarily subjects himself to; that the decision is equivalent to expulsion or suspension from a Club by decision of the Committee; that into the merits of the decision it is beyond the province of the Com^{dr}-in-Chief to enquire, and it rests with Captain Barry to show that the decision is wrong. Captain Barry, who was placed under arrest, has been released and given leave of absence until 1st November, with an intimation that if he fails to clear his character, or take satisfactory steps to do so within the time, I shall recommend to Your Royal Highness that he be removed from the service.

I trust, Sir, that you will approve of my action in this case, and that if Captain Barry fails to upset the decision of the Stewards, he will not be allowed to remain in the Army. An example is necessary, for I am sorry to say that some of the officers in India fail to remember that it is necessary for them to behave as gentlemen in racing matters. . .

RA Add MSS E/1/11901; printed RP 100–1/CL1

248
Roberts to Edmund Yates, editor of *The World*

[Printed]   Simla
                                             17 October 1887
Private and confidential

In *The World* of 21st September last there is a paragraph about Sir
George White, in which it is stated that, owing to his being a comparatively junior Colonel, the military authorities find it difficult
to make him a Major-General. I am sure you will allow me to give
you the following facts about General White, when I think you
will agree with me that the authorities ought to know exactly what
to do with him.

For the last eighteen months the General has filled a most
responsible position, and the present satisfactory condition of
Upper Burma is mainly owing to his intelligence, tact, soldierly
qualities, and great faculty for administering an arduous and
widely-extended command. At the close of the Afghan campaign I
strongly urged that Lieutenant-Colonel White (as he was then)
might be given the rank of Colonel. I had observed his unusual
ability for field service on more than one occasion in Afghanistan,
and I felt that his want of rank might be a serious loss to the
country. There are, it is true, 222 Colonels senior in that rank to
General White, but 73 of these belong to the Royal Artillery and
Royal Engineers, and get their promotion on separate lists. Of the
remaining 149, 97 entered the army after White, some of them
several years after, and all of these must, therefore, have superseded him at some period in their respective careers. Besides these
97 Colonels there are a good many Major-Generals who entered
the service subsequently to Sir George White.

If Colonels never had been, or never were to be, promoted for
service in the field, nothing could be urged in General White's
favor, but promotion to the rank of Major-General is yearly
becoming more and more a matter of selection, and during the last
few years several promotions have been made for distinguished
service in the field. However distinguished these officers may have

been, I cannot call to mind one who had a better claim to promotion than General White has. He has been thirty-four years in the army, or fourteen years longer than Lord Wolseley had been when he was made a Major-General; eight years longer than Sir Redvers Buller and Sir Evelyn Wood, five years longer than Generals Dormer and Brackenbury, and thirteen years longer than the late Sir Herbert Stewart.[49] I fail to see, especially in these days of selection, why the 222 Colonels senior to White should be protected from supersession by him, when he has proved himself eminently successful in the command of a very difficult operation.

I have pointed all this out to the Horse Guards in as forcible language as official correspondence will permit; and you are welcome to make use of the information, but I must ask you not to mention my name in any way.

RP 100–1/CLXVII

249
Roberts to Lieutenant-General Sir Charles Arbuthnot, Commander-in-Chief Madras

[Printed]   Simla
                                             1 June 1888
Private

I intended some little time ago to write, and ask whether you had formed any opinion as to the advantage or otherwise of the Army Corps system. It was merely out of curiosity, for at the time I had no idea that the question would be brought up again; in fact, I looked upon it as practically shelved. I had promised the Duke of Cambridge that I would not raise it while I was Commander-in-Chief in India, and no one in Council seemed to me anxious about it. I was somewhat surprised, therefore, a week or two ago to have a draft despatch sent to me conveying the opinion of the Government of India that the time had arrived when the introduction of the Army Corps system could no longer be delayed. This despatch has since been considered in Council and is now on its

way to the Secretary of State. At the time I thought of writing to
you, I did write to the Duke of Connaught, and I was glad to hear
from His Royal Highness that he was in favor of the measure
under certain safeguards to secure the interests and efficiency of
the Bombay Army. These safeguards are most reasonable, and are
almost identical with what we have recommended to the
Government at home. We have proposed that the Duke of
Connaught and you should retain the title of Commander-in-
Chief, and that you both, as well as your successors, should
continue to be members of the Local Councils. We have pointed
out the importance of maintaining the separate constitution and
segregation of the different local armies, and we have urged that
while the Commanders-in-Chief will have the command of the
whole of their own Army Corps, they should also have the services
of departmental officers with concurrent jurisdiction. In this way
decentralisation will be secured, and the Army Corps
Commanders will be placed in a proper position. If the Local
Governments had any power to deal with military matters there
might, perhaps, be no necessity for the proposed change, but the
force of circumstances has by degrees taken the several departments from local control, and amalgamated them under the
Government of India. In the same way the political authority of
the frontiers has been taken over by the Supreme Government,
and as a result very little of the Presidential system remains. In
fact, the Governments of Madras and Bombay have now little
more to say to their armies than have the Governments of Bengal,
the North-West Provinces, and the Punjab to the portion of the
Bengal Army which may happen to be located within their respective territories. The two armies, particularly that of Madras, are
scattered over districts with which the Governments of Madras
and Bombay have no concern, and during the four years I commanded in Madras, I cannot call to mind a single instance in
which the Local Government were able to afford me any assistance
or decide any question. Local Governments have no military
power now-a-days, and as it would be impossible to revert to a
system under which they practically managed their own affairs, it
would seem best to bring the armies they are supposed to govern

more directly under the authority by which these armies are really governed. The objections to the change which were urged a few years ago do not now really exist, and while the Government of Madras and Bombay will not be called upon to surrender any sensible degree of authority or patronage, the Commanders-in-Chief of those Presidencies will be distinct gainers by the change.

I do not think that the Duke of Cambridge will offer any further opposition when he finds that the Duke of Connaught approves of the measure under conditions which the Government are quite prepared to accept. My hope is that the change, if sanctioned, will not be distasteful to you. I have marked this "Private" as the Government of India would not like the matter to be made public until a reply has been received from the Secretary of State.

RP 100–5/CCXXVII

250
Roberts to Brigadier-General Galbraith[50]

[Printed]   Simla
                                               21 September 1888
Private

As some of the officers in your brigade are inexperienced in hill fighting, I would suggest your warning them all –

(1) Never to place troops in a picquet without its being protected by a "Sanga". Pathans are adepts at attacking under cover of stones and rocks, and at Umbeyla, one of our picquets held by British soldiers was *three* times rushed. No matter how secure the position may appear, it should be made strong enough to resist a rush of determined men.
(2) Before committing troops to a gorge or defile, or to working on lower ground, always secure the crest of the hill which commands the ground over which you have to advance. You will notice that the Pathans invariably hold the crest of a hill, and until they have been turned out of this, it is dangerous to advance.

(3) In hill fighting the advance must be slow; it does not matter how slow so long as you keep on moving. The enemy take heart the moment they see you halt. Young troops are apt to move too quickly at first, they soon get blown and are obliged to halt; this gives the enemy confidence; at the last a rush must be made, and in order that the men may be fit for this rush, they must advance at a very slow pace. Before moving from one position to another higher up the hill, time should be given to the supports and reserves to close up.

RP 100–6/CCLXXIII

251
Circular Memorandum for the information and guidance of Officers Commanding Batteries and Regiments, Hazara Field Force

[Printed]   Simla
                                              30 September 1888

I. – In moving up a hillside or spur in face of the enemy, the advance of our troops should be gradual – not too quick – but unceasing. The skirmishers in taking cover must never actually stop the general and steady advance of the line.

II. – Should the enemy be formed behind a "Sungurh" (stone breastwork) or an "Abattis",[51] the skirmishers will get as near as they can, keeping cover. If the position appears easily assailable, it should be taken at once by a simultaneous rush, and with a cheer; should however, the defences appear at all formidable, time should be given for the Artillery to come up.

III. – Should however, it be seen that the enemy are leaving their defences and descending the hillside to drive off our troops, an attack under any circumstances must be immediately made.

The initiative of attack must always be with our troops.

IV. – In hill fighting one great object to be kept in view is, to shake (if possible) the enemy's position with Artillery, before the Infantry assault.

The artillery can be employed for this purpose in two ways:–

1st. – During the slow but continuous advance of the skirmishers prior to an immediate assault.

2ndly. – When the infantry have taken up cover near to a "Sungurh", or "Abattis", and they are awaiting the final orders for an assault or charge.

V. – In making the final assault or charge on the enemy's position, care should be taken that the rush be not made from too great a distance, or the men will arrive out of breath. And as the troops advance to the charge, the louder the cheer, and the more the bugles sound the charge and the band plays, the better. The skirmishers, supports, and reserves should all advance and cheer together.

VI. – Uniformity of movement in the hills is neither expected nor is it desirable. It should be impressed on the men that all the requirements of hill campaigning are fulfilled when they adhere to the *one great rule,* viz., – *That each company is to hold together and follow its Captain or leader, and that the men should never separate from their companies* (companies of course keeping with their regiments). As the Captain leads, the men should follow in loose order, as the nature of hilly ground does not admit of precise movements.

VII. – Corps or companies, when halted, should at once sit or lie down to rest. The men gathered in groups round their Captain, in line or dispersed according to the nature of the ground.

VIII. – All bugling is to be strictly avoided except under the following circumstances. First when the final assault or charge is made on the enemy's position (as contemplated in paragraph II).

NOTE. – It must, however, be always remembered that no more time than is actually necessary should be lost in making these dispositions; any delay is always, by Asiatics, attributed to fear, and this false idea gives them courage.

Secondly, the sound from head-quarters of Brigades, on all which occasions the sound should be preceded by the regimental calls.

The above remarks apply equally to reserves and supports as to skirmishers.

IX. – When ascending a hill in face of an enemy, each corps should be prepared to support, if actually in action, the one in its front, without any orders from head-quarters of Brigades, should it be apparent that assistance is required. *The enemy, if attacking, must be met by a counter charge.* In like manner supports must, if necessary, assist skirmishers without waiting for orders.

X. – Skirmishers must not advance too quickly. The supports and reserves should be well up to the front.

XI. – When an advance of skirmishers has been ordered up any particular hill or spur in the face of the enemy, no one can do wrong in aiding such advance. The success of hill fighting is mainly dependent on the judgment, skill, and energy of regimental officers.

XII. – In withdrawing a piquet or covering party from a height in presence of the enemy, a few smart men should be selected to remain on the crest, with orders to make as great a show as possible to keep the enemy in check, while the main body retires to a position lower down the hillside; on a signal from the main body, these men should rapidly rejoin it so as to avoid observation by the enemy.

RP 96–1/LXI

252
Roberts to McQueen

[Printed]   Camp Theog
                                            10 October 1888
Private

I cannot tell you what a relief it was to me to get your telegram of the 9th instant, and to hear that you had reconsidered your decision about withdrawing from the Black Mountain.[52] I fully appreciate your difficulties, but the only way to get over them is to bring the tribes to submission, and teach them such a lesson as will prevent their troubling us again for many years. Withdrawal would, as you say yourself, "have a bad political effect and will be considered by the tribesmen as an immediate success." I am afraid they would consider it a permanent success, which would not be neutralised by any subsequent operations, however admirably they might be carried out in other parts of the Black Mountain. I say again I am delighted that you changed your mind, and I hope to hear in a day or two that you have ascended the Machai Peak and have got the tribes at your feet. You will then be able to work down the slopes of the mountain to the Indus and join hands with Galbraith. This is what was decided upon when the expedition was first talked about, and though the Lieutenant-Governor afterwards threw cold water on the proposal to advance as far as the Machai Peak, I have all along looked upon this as a necessity, and trusted to you and Ommaney[53] finding this out in the "wide discretion" given to you. The punishment of the Parari Sayuds is, I understand, a *sine quâ non*, and I do not see how you could hope to carry this out in a satisfactory manner with the two peaks, Chittabat and Machai, which overhang their territory, in the hands of the enemy. I think it possible you may not receive direct instructions from the Lieutenant-Governor for an advance to the Machai Peak, though I have written to him very strongly on this subject, but you should clearly understand that you are not restrained by political considerations from going to Machai if you think it advisable to do so from a military point of view. You may depend on receiving my full support; indeed, I consider it absolutely necessary that the military programme should be carried out to the fullest extent, and I hope to hear that every man of Nos. 1, 2, and 3 columns has bathed in the Indus. We shall never have such a chance again of dominating the Black Mountain tribes, and we should do it in thorough good style and completely. Look out for me on the 24th or 25th. I must try and get to Galbraith's column also.

RP 100–6/CCXCI

253
Salisbury to Roberts

[Holograph]   Hatfield
                                               11 October 1888

I am very much obliged to you for sending me a copy of your paper.[54]

I read it with great interest – the more interest, that in my humble civilian way I have been preaching the same doctrine for the last twenty years. When first I was connected with Indian affairs in 1866, Sir John Lawrence, & all under him, were never tired of maintaining the doctrine that India was to stay at home in event of war; & England was to fight Russia "in every part of the world". No one seemed to take the trouble to ask themselves at what point "in every part of the world" Russia was accessible to England. My impression is that Russia's next advance will be on Persia. She has no boundary engagement with us <u>there</u>, & can encroach without giving us here so plausible a cause of war. Therefore, though the next move <u>may</u> be on Affghan Turkestan, I think Khorassan more probable. Among many coils wh will result from this, there will be one advantage – that she will have time to show herself in her true colours, as a ruler, to the Affghans – before the time for their decision comes. After our Bulgarian experience, I look for great assistance from Russian brutality.

RP 80/5

254
Roberts to Arbuthnot

[Printed]   Murree
                                               6 April 1889

On receipt of your letter about the Madras Army, I wrote to Sir John Hudson[55] asking him his opinion of the Madras Sapper. You will see from his reply (which please return) that he estimates the Sapper's fighting qualities much as I do.

I feel for you and any one connected with Madras that it should be thought necessary to change the composition of the Madras Army, but if there are good reasons to doubt the fighting qualities of the present material, it is better to put all sentiment aside and do our best to improve it. Were there no European enemy near our frontiers, I would advocate leaving the armies of India much as they are at present, but our position has so completely changed during the last few years that we are forced to turn our attention outwards instead of inwards, as we have been in the habit of doing ever since we occupied the country. The dangers we feared such as "Native States armies", "Disaffection amongst our native troops", "troubles from Moplahs, Kookas, and Wahabis",[56] &c., &c., are all overshadowed by the fact of our suddenly finding ourselves a continental nation, liable at any moment to be forced into a war with a European power, possessed of an almost unlimited number of troops and of such vast resources as to be able to drive us out of India unless we have our army ready and fit to cope with it. Twelve or thirteen years ago I was against increasing the efficiency of any portion of the Native States Armies, and I thought it more prudent to arm our own native soldiers with an inferior rifle. Now, I would give our troops the best weapons that can be made, and I am sure that we would be depriving ourselves of what may be valuable aid if we neglect to make the best of the Native States Armies. My notion is that we must make every one in India feel that their interests are identical with ours, and that the Rulers of Native States especially must realise that they are trusted by us. You must not think that in drawing attention to the weak points of the Madras army, I have overlooked similar failings in the armies of Bengal and Bombay. On the contrary, I fully recognise the fact that many regiments in both these armies are composed of distinctly unwarlike material, and I have strongly urged that measures should be taken to remedy this unsatisfactory state of affairs with the least possible delay. Owing to the absence of a frontier to Madras (except in the direction of Burma) it may not be so easy as it is in Bengal and Bombay to enlist men with military instincts, but if we admit the want of such material in the ranks of the Madras army, I should not despair of the remedy being found, and if we do find it, so far from the change I advocate being the death-knell of the Madras army, it would I believe, go far towards restoring it to that estimation in public opinion which it formerly held, and which it has certainly done nothing to regain during the past three and a half years of its service in Upper Burma.

RP 100–6/CCCLXXXIV

255
Stanhope, Secretary of State for War, to Roberts

[Holograph]   London
                                        6 December 1889

Private

As I hear through Lord Cross that there is great question of endeavouring to retain you as C. in Chief of India for some time after the expiration of your term of service, I think it may be well to write a few words to you. If that proposal comes forward I need not say it would have my hearty approval, knowing what you are doing in India, but it seems to me that you should consider the matter from another point of view also.

As you are probably aware, the post of Adjutant General here also becomes vacant next year. What may be the exact position of his successor it is impossible yet to say. It may be that after the Report of the Commission known as Lord Huntingdon's[57] some considerable changes will be made. But, however that may be, there must still exist some post – whatever it may be called – for the highest military adviser. And whoever fills it would probably have to take on the work next autumn, when the term of the present Adjutant General expires.[58]

To myself – and I feel sure to H.R.H. the Commander in Chief also – it would be exceedingly agreeable if I am (in office next year, and) able to secure you for such a post. Of course the appointment is one upon which my colleagues in the Cabinet should be consulted, nor is it possible to foresee all that may happen by the time in question. But I should like to know very confidentially from you whether we might in such a case look to you as at all likely to be willing to accept such an appointment – and I certainly think that, before you pledge yourself to remain in India for a longer period, you should be frankly informed of my views upon the subject. I have mentioned to no one that I am writing to you upon it, & I know that you on your part will be good enough to maintain the confidential character of our communications.

RP 82/5

256
Roberts to Stanhope

[Printed]

Private

Calcutta
3 January 1890

I am greatly indebted to you for your letter of the 6th December, asking me whether I would be willing to accept the Adjutant Generalship, or the position which Lord Wolseley's successor would fill, should the report of Lord Hartington's Commission cause a change to be made in the staff of the Horse Guards.

I am deeply sensible of the honor you do me, and I gladly accept the offer you have made me. I would have written in this sense by last week's mail, but, as I telegraphed to you, I wished to talk the matter over with the Viceroy before giving a definite answer.

Lord Lansdowne had been good enough to ask me to remain in India after the term of my present command expires, and as I have received so much kindness and consideration from him, I did not like to do anything in the matter without consulting his wishes. Mr Rivers Wilson's[59] telegram reached me while travelling to Calcutta, and on my arrival here yesterday I showed your letter to the Viceroy, who was kind enough to say that, while he much regretted my leaving India, he could not but advise me to accept the important post you have offered me. At the same time Lord Lansdowne expressed a hope that some arrangement might be made to admit of my remaining in India for some little time, if possible over next cold weather. This would quite fall in with my own views, both on private and public grounds. I have always thought that it would be better for my successor to enter upon his duties in the spring than the autumn, as he would be somewhat at a loss how to spend the cold weather months profitably, unless he had gained some previous experience of the Council and the working of the several army offices. While however mentioning Lord Lansdowne's desire and my own inclinations, I hope you will understand that I wish to make no conditions, and that I shall be delighted to take up the appointment on any date you may name.

Thanking you very much for your kind thought of me, which has gratified me beyond measure.

RP 100–3/1

257
Viceroy (Marquess of Lansdowne) to Roberts

[Holograph]   Simla
                                          9 January 1890

Secret

I have no news this morning as to the Portugese dispute.[60] I shall probably receive a telegram this afternoon or evening.

I think you should be quite ready to act at short notice. If we are desired to occupy Goa, it will be necessary to decide beforehand what troops are to be employed & who is to command them. The force used should be strong enough to make it clear that resistance would be futile. The officer in command should be one whom we could trust to shew the utmost tact and consideration. We should, I take it, begin by intimating to the Portugese Governor that it had become necessary for us to occupy certain points on Portugese territory, & that we should do so in such strength that he would have no choice but to submit to superior force. He might be asked to depute an officer to arrange the terms of such an occupation which would be carried out with the utmost regard for Portugese susceptibilities. I have told the senior naval officer at Bombay to hold himself ready to send up a vessel or vessels of war.

In such a case would it be desirable to send up a political officer with the military force? A good deal would, I should say, depend upon the O.C. selected.

I will let you know as soon as I hear more.

RP 34/65

258
Roberts to Viceroy

[Printed]   Calcutta
                                             9 January 1890

If it should be necessary to occupy Goa, I would propose that a battalion of British infantry and a battalion of native infantry should be sent by sea from Bombay; these troops, with the war vessel or vessels which your Excellency has ordered to be in readiness at Bombay, should be sufficient to bring the Portugese to terms. At the same time I would move a battalion of British infantry, a battalion of native infantry, and a battery of field artillery from Belgaum to the Portuguese frontier, and, if necessary, to Goa itself, which is less than 70 miles by road from Belgaum. As the main part of the force would be taken from the Bombay army, I would like to consult the Duke of Connaught as to the selection of the commanding officer. I think, under any circumstances, it would be desirable to send a Political officer, one acquainted with that part of the country. The steps necessary are –

  (a) to tell the Duke of Connaught to detail the troops to go by
      sea;
  (b) to take up transport to convey the troops from Bombay to
      Goa;
  (c) to consult the Duke of Connaught about the officer to com-
      mand;

(d) to warn the Madras Commander-in-Chief that a certain portion of the Belgaum garrison may have to march towards Goa. There is an alternative measure, *viz.*, to send troops by rail from Belgaum to Londa junction,[61] or as much nearer to Goa itself as they can be taken by rail. In this case Madras troops would be employed.

I will do nothing until I hear further from your Excellency.

RP 99–1/LXV

259
Roberts to Stanhope

[Printed]   Simla
                                             12 May 1890

Please accept my best thanks for the telegram you have kindly sent, informing me that the cabinet accept your appointment of me as Adjutant General, and desire my presence in London next autumn.

I notice that "the Queen has not yet approved of the time – pending other arrangements", and I am in hopes this may mean that my successor will not reach India in time for me to relieve Lord Wolseley on the 1st October, the date on which, according to the official Army List, his tenure of office expires. To enable me to arrive in London by 1st October, I should have to leave this early in September, almost the hottest season of the year. For myself, this would not matter, and if you consider it necessary for me to take over the Adjutant Generalship on that date, I will, of course, do so, but it would entail my family being left behind, as it would be too great a risk for them to travel at that time. Unless, therefore, I am urgently required sooner, I shall esteem it a great favour if I can be allowed to remain in India until November, in which month my present appointment ends.

Should you not have informed me of the date on which I am to be relieved before you receive this, would you very kindly send me a telegram?

RP 100–3/XXVIII

260
Roberts to Viceroy

[Printed]   Mashobra (Simla)
                                             18 May 1890

My main object in the establishment of regimental Institutes was to
improve the tone of the British soldier by teaching him to appreciate a more respectable mode of life, in the hope that he would gradually become a better behaved man, and also because it seemed to
me that the educated men who now enlist ought to be treated with
more consideration than their predecessors in the army, most of
whom probably did not come from such decent homes.

In 1888 Institutes were only partially established, and it was
some time before I could get all commanding officers to believe
that the habits of their men could be improved, or that a well managed coffee shop would make up for the profits derived from a
canteen. I did not, therefore, expect any great change that year;
there was, however, a slight improvement in the conduct of the
soldiers, as evidenced by a decrease in the number of courts-
martial.

Last year, I am glad to say, the improvement was most marked
as your Excellency will see from the following statement:-

Bengal Army

	1888,	1889,	Increase	Decrease
per cent				
Total number of men punished	234	201	. . .	33
Number of cases of insubordi-nation with violence	307	257	. . .	50
Number of cases of drunkenness tried by court-martial	149	98	. . .	51
Number of men sentenced to imprisonment with hard labour	957	781	. . .	176
Number of men discharged with ignominy	110	79	. . .	21

In the Madras and Bombay armies the results are equally satisfactory. Put in the most appreciable form, the following figures
give the convictions by court-martial, as compared with the
preceding year:-

In Bengal the number of courts-martial decreased by 14.11 per cent.
" Madras   "   "   increased " 1.22 per cent.
" Bombay   "   "   decreased " 17.29 per cent.

but Madras has still the lowest record per cent. of strength and
Bombay the highest.

I trust that crime will continue to diminish as the men are
gradually induced to frequent the coffee shop and its comfortable
surroundings in preference to the liquor bar.

RP 99–1/LXXXIX

261
Stanhope to Roberts

[Holograph]   London
                                               21 May 1890

<u>Very confidential</u>

Please do me the favour to <u>destroy</u> this letter. It is really only to
add a word of further explanation why, to my great regret, we have
been compelled to forego the pleasure & advantage of having you
here as Adjutant General. The urgent wish of certain august persons to advance the claims of the Duke of Connaught, & the great
difficulties which have arisen in consequence of this & of the
recommendations of Lord Hartington's Commission, have led at
last to this result as the only means which presents itself of extricating ourselves from them.[62]

Her Majesty has all along been desirous that you should be
asked to remain on in India for a time.

I think that this word of explanation is due to you . . .

RP 82/21

262
Roberts to Lord Randolph Churchill

[Printed]   Simla
                                                             1 July 1890
Private and confidential.

Remembering your kindness to me on a former occasion when the highest post open to a soldier abroad was in question, and feeling hopeful that events have not caused you to regret the assistance you then rendered me, I venture now to trouble you with a short account of the reasons why I have been induced to accept an extension of the Commander-in-Chiefship in India.

In September last the Viceroy asked me whether he had my permission to recommend to the Secretary of State that I should be asked to remain in India for a time. I replied that I was prepared to do whatever the authorities desired; that I was deeply interested in my work, and would like to see the important measures which had been initiated during the last few years brought to a satisfactory conclusion. But that, on the other hand, there were reasons (chiefly family ones) why I should like to go home. I added that it had been hinted to me that Lord Wolseley would not be re-appointed, and that I might succeed him as Adjutant General; and that if I were not available owing to the tenure of my present command having been extended, some one else would get the post, and I could scarcely ever hope to hold it. I really care for only two appointments, the Adjutant Generalship at home and my present one, and I told Lord Lansdowne that I would rather leave the question as to whether I should be re-appointed out here or transferred home, to be settled by those who are best able to decide in which position I could be most useful to the State. Lord Lansdowne on this wrote to the Secretary of State representing his desire to keep me in India, and expressing his hope that my appointment would be extended for another year. A month or two later he told me the matter was practically settled, and that I would be asked to remain in India until the end of 1891. I heard nothing more till about Xmas, when I received a letter from Mr Stanhope, saying he heard through Lord Cross that there was a question of endeavouring to retain me as Commander-in-Chief in India for some time after the expiration of my term of service, and that while the proposal would have his hearty approval it seemed to him that I should consider the matter from another point of view. He said that the Adjutant General's term of service would come to an end in October 1890, and, although it was not possible to say what the exact position of his successor would be, there must still exist some post, whatever it might be called, for the highest military adviser, and that whoever fills it would probably have to take over the work next autumn when the post of Adjutant General would be vacant. Mr Stanhope added that it would be extremely agreeable to himself, and he felt sure to the Duke of Cambridge also, if he could secure me for such a position; that the appointment was one upon which his colleagues in the Cabinet would of course have to be consulted, but he would like to know whether I would be willing to accept such an appointment; and he certainly thought that before I pledged myself to remain in India for a longer period, I ought to be informed of his views on the subject. I showed Mr Stanhope's letter to the Viceroy, and then informed Mr Stanhope that I gladly accepted the appointment. There the matter ended until the 11th May last, when I received a telegram from Mr Stanhope informing me that my appointment as Adjutant General was accepted by the Cabinet, who strongly desired my presence in London this autumn. I acknowledged the receipt of the telegram, thanked Mr Stanhope for the appointment, and asked for orders as to the exact date on which I was required to be in London. Before my letter could have reached Mr Stanhope I received a second telegram from him, dated 29th May, in which he said that the decision had been arrived at to press me to continue my service in India, as it had been found impossible at present to choose a suitable successor.

I replied that, in order to meet the wishes of the Cabinet, I would be willing to remain in India for a limited time, but I wished to abide by my acceptance of the Adjutant Generalship, and I hoped that if I consented to remain I should not be deprived of the appointment. In acknowledging the receipt of this reply, Mr

Stanhope telegraphed that the Cabinet "have decided to ask you to extend your service for two years", and that his letters would explain that this compelled the withdrawal of their proposals as to the office of the Adjutant General. He added, "The exigencies of the public service urgently require you in India, and the Home Government will, of course, desire to take full advantage of your services here on your return, but cannot pledge themselves or their successors to any particular appointment."

I awaited the receipt of Mr Stanhope's letters, which confirmed the information he had telegraphed as to the difficulty the Cabinet had experienced in finding a suitable successor to me. I felt that I had not been well treated, but I agreed to the two years' extension, on certain conditions, as this seemed to me to be my duty. I cannot, however, help being extremely disappointed, for, after so many years in India, I greatly looked forward to the home appointment. My fear now is that, being so far away I may be overlooked when the time comes for filling up the Adjutant Generalship, or carrying out such alterations in connection with the same as may be decided upon in consequence of the recommendations of Lord Hartington's Commission.

I am anxious that you should know all that has occurred, and that my remaining in India is not in any way my own choice . . .

RP 100–3/XLIV

263
Roberts to Stanhope

[Holograph]   Simla
                                               20 July 1890
Private

If you can spare a few minutes I should esteem it a great favour if you would permit Lt Colonel Ian Hamilton to call upon you. He has gone to England on 3 months leave, and I should much like him to explain to you the course of musketry instruction which has been introduced for the Native Army since April 1889.

After it had been in force for one year, I submitted a report to the Horse Guards shewing how admirably it had answered, and recommending that it should be made applicable to the British Army in India. The Duke of Cambridge expressed his approval of the course but for some unnaccountable reason the Adjutant General[63] refused his consent. [Note in pencil 'Buller may be less prejudiced'] The new course is so practical and has so many advantages over the old one that I was most anxious the British troops in India should benefit by it; indeed, if I had had any idea that it would not have been accepted at home, I think I should have delayed adopting it for the Native Army. The improvement in the shooting and more particularly, in the "control of fire" of the native troops is quite remarkable, and it is greatly to be regretted that British soldiers cannot benefit equally with their native comrades. Colonel Hamilton served for several years on my staff before he was appointed to the Head of the Musketry Department in India. He is a particularly able, intelligent officer and I am sure you would be interested in hearing all that he can tell you about the Army in India.

Stanhope MSS U 1590/0305/2

264
Roberts to Chesney

[Printed]   Camp Khairabad
                                                     4 December 1890

What do you think of making enquiries as to whether we could get Zulus or some other good fighting men in Africa to enlist as soldiers for service in India at a reasonable cost? We shall probably have to improve the fighting qualities of some more regiments of the Madras and Bombay armies, and it would be wise not to have too many Punjab and frontier men in our ranks if good soldiers are procurable elsewhere. It seems worth while to enquire, and, if possible, to arrange for one of the two Bombay regiments about to be formed to be composed of Africans.

RP 100–7/CXXXVIII

265
Roberts to Viceroy

[Printed]   Simla
                                                         13 June 1891

I am much obliged for your Excellency's letter of the 11th instant,
and for the friendly criticism you offer on my note, dated 8th June
1891.

The note certainly does not give a direct answer to Lord Cross'
proposal that I should draw up a memorandum showing how we
could meet an attack by Russia on Afghanistan with the troops
now at our disposal. I consider that *in fact* it would be impossible
to meet such an attack with our present available force, and so it
would be impossible for me to show *on paper* how it could be done.
Practically, the defence of India and the opposing an attack on
Afghanistan by Russia are one and the same. In either case the
only course to pursue is to occupy the Kabul–Kandahar line, and I
have shown that we could not do this with the smallest chance of
success without the increase to the army in India which I have
named. I can, of course, alter the heading of my note, and call it
"an answer to the Secretary of State's proposal that a scheme
should be prepared to meet an attack on Afghanistan by the
Russians," or in other words, "for the defence of India, based on
the number of troops at present in the country". Or, a more appropriate title, perhaps, would be the words in paragraph 3 of the
note, *viz.*, "Is it possible for us to meet our actual and prospective
military requirements with an army that consists of 70,000 British
and 150,000 native troops?"

Your Excellency says that Lord Cross took exception to the
proposals contained in my memoranda of the 4th August 1890[64]
and 27th January, 1891,[65] "upon the ground that they were based
not only upon the occupation of the Kabul–Kandahar line, but
upon the assumption that we should make use of that line as a
basis for offensive operations beyond it."

In my present note I have not considered the possibility of any
movement beyond the Hindu Kush range. That must depend on

the consolidation of our power in Afghanistan, and on the course Her Majesty's Government may think fit to adopt in dealing with the Central Asian question. Personally, I think, it would be the height of folly to allow any influence but our own to be paramount throughout Afghanistan, and though a military occupation by us of the southern parts of that country seems to be inevitable, I am strongly in favor of maintaining its northern portion as a buffer between the Russians and ourselves. Once Russia and England become coterminous in the east, I can see no end to our troubles, or to the increase in the extent and cost of the military preparations which would be forced upon us by an aggressive and unscrupulous neighbor.

RP 99–1/CLXXXI

266
Roberts to McQueen

[Printed]   Simla
                                               25 July 1891
Private

Your letter of the 1st instant confronts me with the unpleasant dilemma of having either to disoblige a friend of seven and thirty years' standing, or else to recommend an appointment which I consider undesirable in the public interests. You are quite right in thinking that I approved of your work in the Afghan war, and my disappointment was all the greater that the promise of that campaign was not fulfilled in 1888.[66] I do not allude to your failure to meet my views with reference to the political part of your duties; about that there may be a difference of opinion, but your conduct of military operations was not such as would justify me in recommending you for a position which might any day entail your being again required to exercise command on service. The communications which passed at the time between you, the Adjutant General and myself, must have made you fully aware of my adverse opinion, and of the grounds on which it was most reluctantly formed. I shall, therefore, only say that it was with the deepest regret that I came to the conclusion that you were not fitted for an independent command in the field.

I was in hopes that, after what occurred in 1888, you would not have applied to me for further employment; but as you have done so, I am obliged to write plainly. I shall be glad, however, if your letter and my reply can be forgotten as completely as if they had never been written.

RP 100–3/CXLV

267
Roberts to Brackenbury[67]

[Printed]   Simla
                                            28 September 1891

I am delighted to find from your letter of the 26th instant that we are so much in accord as to what the British army should be, and I only hope that the difficulties of re-organising it will not prove so great as you anticipate.

I do not object to the enlistment of boys so long as they are not considered men, or included in the established strength of our regiments, and provided that sufficient inducements are held out to ensure a certain number of them continuing in the ranks when they reach maturity.

I have always felt that the navy should be England's main defence, and that our army should be just large enough to give some backbone to the auxiliary forces at home, and to defend our colonial possessions and India. In these days of huge continental armies I look upon expeditions to any part of Europe or Asia (except India, and possibly China under certain circumstances) as absolutely visionary.[68] At the same time I think that even with a far stronger navy than we have at present we should, in the event of a war with France, have to increase our army considerably, – probably double it. And of this I feel sure that whatever Cabinet may be in power, the Army in India will have to be strongly re-inforced should war break out with France and Russia, or even with Russia alone.

I am not sure that the spread of education and the increased love of individual liberty would deter men from enlisting under acceptable conditions of service. No difficulty, for example, is experienced in procuring a sufficient number of recruits for the Marines, a corps about 10,000 strong, and composed of long service soldiers, of exceptionally good character and physique.

I doubt also whether Parliament would raise any strong objection to increased expenditure on the army, provided the necessity for the increase was clearly established. At present politicians of both parties have reason to believe that a good deal of the money voted for the military services is spent unprofitably and wastefully; but if the inadequacy of the pay and other inducements held out to the recruit were fully explained to Parliament, I feel confident that the additional funds needed to render the army efficient would be forthcoming. We have an instance of the liberality with which demands are met in the grant of four millions for improved barrack accommodation which passed both Houses with scarcely a dissentient voice.

In matters of military administration I am inclined to think that there is not much to choose between Radical and Conservative Cabinets; and although my own tendencies are Conservative, I acknowledge that, in dealing with military questions, the Radicals possess the courage of their opinions, and generally carry out with less hesitation than their political opponents the measures which they consider as likely to increase the efficiency of the army.

RP 100–7/CCCVI

268
Roberts to Harman

[Printed]   Murree
                                               27 October 1891

In your letter of the 2nd October you say you are sorry that, in my paper reviewing the evidence given before Lord Wantage's committee,[69] I did not confine myself strictly to putting forward my own views and convictions, instead of criticising evidence which should be considered confidential until published with the report of the Committee. I am on tour now and have not got Gordon's[70] letter by me, but, unless my memory fails me, he told me that Lord Wantage wished for my opinion on the evidence given by the Duke of Cambridge, Lord Wolseley, Sir Redvers Buller, and Sir Evelyn Wood.[71]

I do not see how I could have given an opinion that would have been of any value without taking up the several points detailed in the evidence. My review is of course a confidential paper intended for the use of the committee, and the evidence with which it deals ought to be kept as confidential as if I had never seen it.

As you mention the subject, I may say I have been aware for some time there is a feeling amongst the general public that Lord Wolseley and I are greatly opposed to each other. The late Mr Smith mentioned this to me when I was at home in 1885. I told him then, as I tell you now, that, as far as I am concerned, there is no foundation for this feeling. There are some matters of extreme importance about which Lord Wolseley and I disagree, such as, for instance, the present system of service, and how England could best check a Russian advance towards India. With regard to the former, it was impossible that our differences of opinion could be concealed and as to the latter, I should think that the British public know nothing of our particular views.

Very soon after the introduction of the short-service system I saw that it was unsuited to our army, and after my experience in Afghanistan I determined to let the people of England know how unfitted boy soldiers are for war. As you are aware, I took the opportunity of the dinner given to me by the Lord Mayor, on the occasion of my being presented with the freedom of the city of London, to tell my story. I heard at the time that Lord Wolseley resented my speaking publicly on such a subject as army enlistment; indeed, Mr Childers, the then Secretary of State for War, begged of me as I was entering the Banqueting Hall not to broach it, as my doing so would offend Lord Wolseley and Sir John Adye, who were both present. I felt that I should be little short of a traitor to my country if I did not speak the truth, and the whole truth, on such an occasion, and I told Mr Childers so as well as I could during the short time (a very few seconds) we were able to talk together. This was in February 1881, and in the very next number of the *XIXth Century* Lord Wolseley wrote an article in defence of the short-service system. This, no doubt, gave rise to the idea that he and I were opposed to each other. We certainly are as regards that particular matter; he still favors the system; I believe it is killing the British army, but I should be very much ashamed of myself if on this account it would be sufficient for Lord Wolseley to propose anything for me to oppose it.

It is not to be supposed with my strong feelings against the present terms of enlistment that I should not take advantage of every legitimate opportunity to do all I can to get them changed.

My belief is that the army at home has come to its present state of inefficiency from officers in high positions not giving their opinions freely and honestly, and I deeply regret that absence from England prevented my being able to give evidence before Lord Wantage's committee. It was therefore with considerable satisfaction that I received Gordon's letter forwarding, at Lord Wantage's request, the evidence which you object to my having reviewed.

I treated all the evidences in the same way, and I don't think I can be accused of any feeling against Sir Redvers Buller or Sir Evelyn Wood. The former I have never seen, and the only communications I have had with him since he became Adjutant General to the Forces have been of a most friendly character. The latter I know very slightly, and I should gather from the evidence he gave, and from the work he has done at Colchester and Aldershot, that I am more likely to agree than disagree with him on most military matters.

Please excuse me for troubling you with this long letter, but I think it is right that you should be fully informed of my reasons for writing the memorandum which I sent you on the 8th September last.

RP 100–3/CLXXXII

269
Roberts to Viceroy

[Printed]   Bareilly
                                   11 January 1892

I feel the greatest possible dislike to writing to your Excellency on
the subject of this letter, and I regret that I did not bring it to your
notice when acknowledging the telegram in which you informed
me of Her Majesty's intention to confer a peerage on me.

When Lord Dufferin was leaving India he asked me if I would
accept a peerage; whether the question was put from himself or by
authority I cannot say, but in reply I told him that I was too poor a
man to make it right for me to put myself in such a position unless
a grant of money were given with it. I heard nothing more of the
matter until the receipt of your telegram on the 29th December. I
ought then, perhaps, to have told you what I said to Lord
Dufferin, but it seemed from the wording of your Excellency's
telegram that it was hardly open to me to make any conditions,
and it was extremely distasteful to me to suggest that the honor
should be accompanied by a grant. Since I entered the service I
have never asked for anything in the shape of an appointment,
reward or promotion, but on thinking it over it seems to me that I
have not been quite wise in accepting a peerage without the
where-withal to keep it up, not only on my own, but my son's,
account.

It may be urged that as the peerage has been bestowed upon me
for general, rather than for special war service, and as I have held a
well-paid appointment for more than the usual time, there is no
reason why I should be given a grant. The Commander-in-
Chiefship is no doubt well paid, but it is an expensive position,
and one in which but little can be saved. My private means are
almost *nil*, and with the baronetcy conferred upon me after the
Afghan war in 1881, I only received £12,500. This sum was
thought at the time to be quite inadequate, and I was often pressed
to allow the question to be brought before the public. This I would
not agree to, and more than once I had to tell Members of

Parliament that I would rather be without any grant at all than have the matter discussed in the House. I felt also that their wish to bring the matter forward was more for party purposes than for any real desire to do me justice.

I have not the slightest wish to compare my services with those of other soldiers who have been specially rewarded, but I think your Excellency will find that, with two or three exceptions, titles given to military men (who are generally poor) have been accompanied by a pension for two or more lives or a grant. During late years Lord Napier of Magdala received a pension of £2,000 a year for two lives, and Lord Wolseley has been given grants, amounting to upwards of £50,000. As a peerage to a poor man, unaccompanied by a grant, is such a doubtful benefit, your Excellency may perhaps feel inclined to place the matter before the Secretary of State for India.

RP 99–1/CCXXV

270
Sir John Strachey to Roberts

[Holograph]
London
5 March 1892

. . . Not improbably I shall have some day to ask your help. Lady Lytton has imposed on me a most difficult duty which I feel that I cannot refuse, that of writing a history of Lord Lytton's Indian administration. It will be a most difficult work, and it is not made more easy by the fact of the great friendship – I ought rather to say affection – which existed between us from the first day on which we met until the end, and by my having taken so active a part in the proceedings of his government. I hardly know yet how I am to begin, but obviously the most important and difficult part of the whole story will be the history of the Afghan business. There is a great deal about which the world has never heard the truth. All Lord Lytton's private papers have been placed at my disposal, and I shall get, where necessary, advice from Lord

Salisbury. But it seems very likely that I may come to matters – though I cannot yet tell what they will be – on which I shall be most thankful for your help, and in that case I shall not scruple to ask it. Lord Lytton had not very many real friends but you were always one of them and to the last he always spoke of you with the strongest regard. I need not say that there are a multitude of things regarding which the time has not come at which it will be possible to tell everything. I cannot pretend to be at all hopeful about the manner in which I shall be able to perform this task, but I could not refuse to do my best, and it became the more imposs-ible to shirk the work because Lord Salisbury agreed with Lady Lytton in wishing me to undertake it. Fifteen years ago I should have been less afraid of this sort of responsibility, but my powers of work have degenerated and I feel strongly that the older I get the stupider I become.[72]

RP 84/7

271
Roberts to Stanhope

[Printed]   Simla
                                             4 May 1892

In reading the parliamentary debate which took place on the 7th March last, I noticed that you are reported to have referred to me as being in favor of a long-service army for India, and to have remarked that few people at home concur in my opinion, which in fact is unsupported by any reliable evidence.

As this statement, coupled with your condemnation of long periods of obligatory army service exceeding twelve years in dura-tion, is liable to cause my views on the subject to be misunder-stood, I would beg leave briefly to point out what my recorded opinions really are.

I regard the present short-service system as being incapable of meeting our national requirements at home and abroad, and unsuited to the special conditions under which a voluntary army has to be raised and maintained. On the other hand, no one is more alive than myself to the impossibility and impropriety of reverting to the old long-service system. For ten years and more I have persistently urged that the soldier should be treated as a rational being, that his pay should be fairly commensurate with the wages obtainable by unskilled but adult civil labor, that the terms of his service should be as elastic as possible, and that life in the army should be rendered sufficiently attractive to induce a superior class of recruit to enter the ranks.

As regards the infantry, I think it is a mistake to bind the recruit to seven or eight years' color service before he has had any experience of a military life, and I would therefore enlist him in the first instance for three years' color service and nine years' reserve service. Towards the end of his three years' engagement the soldier should be given an opportunity of deciding whether he would prefer to extend his regimental service or to pass into the reserve. In the former case, his reserve service would be converted into service with the colors. On completing twelve years' color service the soldier, if he does not wish to take his discharge, and is physically and otherwise eligible, should be allowed to re-engage for nine years' color service, or to join the reserve for the same period. Subsequent to his re-engagement he should be permitted under reasonable restrictions to commute the remainder of his color service into an equal period of reserve service, unless military exigencies render his transfer undesirable. Similar conditions of enlistment would apply, *mutatis mutandis*, to the other branches of the army.

With reference to the reserve, I have always recognised the value of an adequate and efficient force of this nature; and, as pointed out in paragraph 10 of my 'Review of the evidence given before Lord Wantage's committee,' I believe that, if my recommendations were adopted, more reservists would be forthcoming than are available under the present system. In creating an infantry reserve for an army circumstanced like ours, there are two points which appear to me to be of the utmost importance. First, the line battalions at home and abroad should not be unduly weakened by passing into the reserve men who would prefer to prolong their service in the ranks; and secondly, arrangements should be made for the periodical training of the reservists, who without such training must rapidly deteriorate.

I originally put forward the proposals summarized above in an article in the *Nineteenth Century* entitled 'Free Trade in the Army', and I have since discussed them in greater detail in certain papers which have been submitted for your information. If the article and papers are referred to, it will be seen that I have not only deprecated a return to the old long-service system, but expressed myself strongly in favor of reducing the period of obligatory color service on first engagement from seven or eight to three years. You will understand, therefore, the awkward position in which I am placed by being represented to the House of Commons as advocating rigid and prolonged terms of color service, which, as a matter of fact, I was the first to condemn.

There is one other point on which I should like to say a few words. You alluded in your speech to the British army in India, which you believe to be much more efficient now than it has ever been before; and you compared the statistics of mortality and invaliding during a long-service period from 1868 to 1872 with those during a short-service period from 1886 to 1890 as tending to show that the improvement in the health of the troops is attributable to the present system of enlistment. I am inclined to doubt the correctness of this view, for while I admit that the British army in India has not sensibly deteriorated of late years, my impression is that the average drafts now sent out from home are as a rule inferior in *physique* and development to those supplied some years ago. It is true that a large proportion of the men who come out to India are converted in the course of a few years into mature and able-bodied soldiers; but this is mainly due to the great care that is taken of their health and general well-being from the date of their arrival in this country. In fact, the statistics quoted by you may be taken as a proof, not that youth is synonymous with a low rate of mortality and invaliding in a tropical climate, but that the sanitary conditions which affect the British army in India have been vastly ameliorated during the past twenty years. Barracks have been remodelled, pure water has been, or is being, brought into most of the principal cantonments, conservancy has been carefully attended to, numerous hill stations have been provided, and the extension of railways has enabled troops to be concentrated in the most favourable localities and invalids to be rapidly conveyed to convalescent depôts . . .

RP 100–3/CCXXXII

272
Note on a suggestion from the Secretary of State whether, in the event of Russia not agreeing to appoint a joint committee to define the boundary on the Pamirs, it would not be advisable for Her Majesty's Government to send a commission of exploration themselves

[Printed]   Simla
                                            31 August 1892

This is indeed a difficult question. It seems to me that we may discard all idea of being able to send, *via* Kashmir and Gilgit, a force large enough to cope with the one which Colonel Yanoff[73] apparently has with him. The difficulty and expense of transporting supplies of all sorts and munitions of war for even a small party would be very considerable, and, as Sir Mortimer Durand points out, the troops would have to go at once and wait at Gilgit until the spring.

There are two other routes by which the Pamirs could be reached, one *via* Bajaur to Chitral, the other *via* Kabul. The second of these could not be adopted without the Amir's concurrence, and the first would entail arrangements being made with the several independent tribes who occupy the country between Peshawar and Chitral, and now that Afghan troops are at Asmar it would probably be necessary to come to terms with the Amir. Were either of these routes then to be adopted, the Amir is a factor which could not be overlooked, and even were His Highness on the best of terms with us, I should doubt, in the existing condition of Afghanistan, whether he could secure the safety of a small party travelling *via* Kabul.

It seems to me then that all we can do from India now is to send officers to the Hindu Kush to watch the passes from the Baroghil to the Mintaka or Kirisht, for the purpose of re-assuring the people in that part of the frontier and of endeavouring to ascertain the exact strength of Yanoff's party. Above all I consider it essential that we should have an officer permanently stationed at Chitral, and in the first instance it seems desirable that Dr. Robertson should go there, as he is known to have influence over the Mehter.[74]

It would be necessary to request the Amir to warn his officers in the north-east frontier of Afghanistan that they must receive in a friendly manner any British officer who may be travelling in their neighbourhood, and assist them in every way instead of treating them as the commander of the post at Sirhind treated Lieutenant Malony last year.

This seems to me all we can do from India in the direction of the Pamirs. The question is one which must be dealt with from home, and we should, I think, strongly urge upon Her Majesty's Ministers the necessity for taking a firm stand and telling the Russians that their sending troops across the Pamirs, and seeking a collision with the Afghans, are indefensible acts, and distinctly contrary to the promises repeatedly made during the last few months by M. de Giers[75] to our ambassador at St Petersburg. I would say we cannot admit that there has been any change in the Pamirs, as asserted by M. de Giers, to warrant such action, and that any further advance of the Russian troops must end in a quarrel with us. We might add that after what has happened we cannot place any faith in the promise that Yanoff will "not pursue his reconnaissance beyond the Yashikul", especially as our information leads us to believe that he has himself reached Langar Kisht, close to Kila Panja, the head-quarters of the Deputy Governor of Badakshan, while part of his force is at Bozai Gumbaz threatening the Ishkaman valley leading to Gilgit.

My own belief is that the Hazara insurrection[76] and Yanoff's advance across the Pamirs are both part of the same plot, and that unless we act with decision we shall shortly hear that the rebellion is spreading in Afghanistan. It is certainly difficult to ascertain whether, and to what extent, the Russians are implicated in the Hazara business. They can afford the tribe valuable assistance without appearing on the scene at all, and if they are helping it, we may be sure that they will not permit the Amir's troops to get the better of the Hazaras.

Such a state of affairs cannot last long – either the Amir must coerce the Hazaras or he will find his whole country in rebellion against him.

I have said it is extremely difficult to know what part the Russians are taking on the north-west frontier of Afghanistan, but we have tolerably good information as to their action on the north-east frontier, and I would tell them plainly that unless Yanoff and the whole of his party clear off the Pamirs, until the boundary in that direction has been delimitated, we shall advance into Southern Afghanistan.

We can do but little on the Pamirs, nothing in fact to check Russia; but moving troops to the neighbourhood of Kandahar, or even letting the Russians know that we were preparing for such a move would, in all probability, make them hesitate to interfere further at present with Afghan affairs.

I would explain to the Amir exactly how we stand in reply to his letters of the 12th and 16th August on the subject of the collision between his men and Colonel Yanoff's troops, so that he may clearly understand that we can do nothing by force in the direction of the Pamirs, and that, if negotiations fail, it will be necessary, both for his sake and our own, that we should advance troops to the neighbourhood of Kandahar.

RP 96–2/CCCXLI

273
Roberts to Duke of Cambridge

[Printed]   Simla
                                                     12 October 1892

Private

I have to acknowledge with thanks the receipt of our Royal Highness's letter of the 16th September last, in which you inform me that the offer of the Governorship of Malta was made owing to your Royal

Highness's wish that I "ought at once to be considered for a high post on 'my' return from India". I am very much obliged, Sir, for your kind thought of me, but, as I have already explained, I have no desire to serve abroad after I leave this country.

With regard to Your Royal Highness's remark that you were unaware that the Adjutant Generalship had been offered to me, and that you, Sir, have always felt, as have the Government leaders, that India was my special sphere, I would like to remind Your Royal Highness that the Adjutant Generalship was definitely given to me in May 1890 by Mr Stanhope, and to assure you, Sir, that I should never have thought of accepting it, had I not understood that the appointment was made with Your Royal Highness's full concurrence.

I know too well, from my own experience here, how impossible it would be to carry on work with an Adjutant General who was not one's own choice, to have entertained for a moment the idea of occupying so high a post unless I was sure that I enjoyed the confidence of the Commander-in-Chief.

In December 1889, when first communicating with me about the Adjutant Generalship Mr Stanhope said:- "To myself – and I feel sure to His Royal Highness the Commander-in-Chief also – it would be exceedingly agreeable if I am able to secure you for such a post." It was this information, and the recollection that your Royal Highness had 8 or 9 years previously offered me the Quarter Master Generalship at the Horse Guards, which made me reply to Mr Stanhope in such a manner as resulted in my being given the Adjutant Generalship a few months later. Mr Stanhope then telegraphed to me as follows:-

"Your appointment as Adjutant General is accepted by the Cabinet, who strongly desire your presence here this autumn. The Queen has not yet approved of the time pending other arrangements so treat this as confidential."

It was, I think, natural for me to suppose that Her Majesty and the Cabinet would not have approved of my being made Adjutant-General without consulting Your Royal Highness and obtaining your consent. I certainly thought that Your Royal Highness knew all that passed between Mr Stanhope and myself, and in my letter to you, Sir, of the 21 June 1890, I alluded to the circumstances in the following words:-

"I am aware from Mr Stanhope's letters and telegrams that your Royal Highness approved of my being offered the Adjutant-Generalship in succession to Lord Wolseley, and that you subsequently agreed to my being asked to remain in India for a time. It is, of course, a great disappointment to me not to get home after the many years of service I have had in this country, and a still greater one when I am told that, as I am required in India, I could not be made Adjutant General, but I consider it my duty to adopt the course which the Queen, Her Majesty's Government, and your Royal Highness decided upon as most advisable in the interests of the public service. I must trust now to my being given health and strength to carry on my work as Commander-in-Chief for the additional time I have consented to remain in India, and that something suitable will be found for me when I return to England."

Whilst I am deeply sensible of Your Royal Highness's appreciation of my work in India, I trust that this very work, which has included the command of 70,000 British soldiers, may not be held to prejudice in any way my claim for a home appointment. I must own that, until the receipt of Your Royal Highness's letter under reply, such an idea never occurred to me, and even now I do not really believe that it was Your Royal Highness's intention to convey this impression when you say that you always considered India as my proper sphere of action.

As Your Royal Highness remarks, Sir Patrick Grant and Lord Napier of Magdala were given the Governorship of Malta and Gibraltar respectively at the close of their Indian careers; but, on the other hand, Sir Hugh Rose and Sir William Mansfield became Commanders-in-Chief in Ireland,[77] and, unless I am mistaken, Sir Hope Grant held the command at Aldershot.

RA. Add MSS E/1/128 57; printed RP 100–3/CCLXXXV

Notes

Unless otherwise expressed, the place of publication of books and articles mentioned is London.

Introduction

1   The Major-General's song from Act 1 of *The Pirates of Penzance*, first produced, at Paignton, in December 1879.

2   The importance of the VC in career terms in the late Victorian army is sometimes overlooked. In imperial or colonial warfare, leadership and courage counted for more than strategy or tactics, and possession of the VC tended to demonstrate that a man had both courage and leadership. The proportion of Indian Army generals with the VC was very high because of the large numbers of crosses (182) awarded for the Mutiny. Despite his extraordinary record of active service, Wolseley never received the award.

3   Roberts never served with the Royal Artillery. When he was appointed to a battery at Aldershot in 1859, he quickly secured a posting back to India.

4   Strictly speaking, the Bombay Presidency was responsible for the province of Sind, under a Chief Commissioner; Madras was similarly responsible for British Burma.

5   Residents and Agents were members of the Political Service – in effect, the Indian Diplomatic Service – recruited from the Indian Army and Civil Service, and controlled by the Viceroy as part of the Foreign Department. See T.C. Coen, *The Indian Political Service* (1971).

6   The Duke of Cambridge had pressed unsuccessfully after the Mutiny for control of the Army in India. Partly for that reason, he paid close attention to the senior posts in India and British Army officers occupied a disproportionate number of those posts. Between 1813 and 1900, for example, only six out of twenty-three Commanders-in-Chief India came from the Indian armies.

7   See, for example, Colonel de Lacey Evans' *On the Practicability of a Russian Invasion of India* (1829), and John MacNeill's *The Progress and Present Position of Russia in the East* (1836).

8   There is a voluminous literature on the Anglo-Russian rivalry in Central Asia and Afghanistan – see the useful bibliography in Peter Hopkirk, *The Great Game* (1989). The term 'Great Game' has lost much of its usefulness as a result of attempts to extend its scope in ways which add little to historical understanding or analysis – see, for example, Edward Ingram's article 'Great Britain's Great Game' in *The International History Review*, II (1980).

9 Lytton was Minister at Lisbon when offered the Viceroyalty. There is a great need of a full-scale, modern biography.

10 Roberts' strategical thinking at this time is most easily seen in three papers, *The advantages from a military point of view, of a good understanding between the Government of India and the ruler and people of Afghanistan* (4 August 1890, copy in RP 95/XXXIX), *The dangers which a reverse would expose us to in the event of war with Russia, and the best means of guarding against such an occurrence* (27 January 1891, copy in RP 95/XLV), and *On the sufficiency of the existing garrison in India to meet our actual and prospective military requirements in the event of Russia invading Afghanistan, even though the advance may be only intended to divert our attention from her real object of attack* (8 June 1891, copy in RP 95/LIV).

11 See Ian Beckett, 'The Stanhope Memorandum of 1888: a Reinterpretation', in *Bulletin of the Institute of Historical Research*, LVII (November 1984).

12 The Eden Commission proposal, for which Roberts claimed credit, was for four geographically organised Army Corps, including one covering the Punjab and Frontier, under the direct command of the C-in-C India.

13 The clash between Curzon and Kitchener in 1902–05, which the latter won, was over Kitchener's plan to amalgamate the Military Department and Army Headquarters, under the C-in-C. It proved workable only under a man of demonic energy and force; under a lesser man, it collapsed under the strain of the Mesopotamian campaign in 1915.

14 For a detailed account of railway development on the Frontier, see P.S. Berridge, *Couplings to the Khyber* (Newton Abbott, 1969).

15 See, for example, Adrian Preston, 'Wolseley, the Khartoum Relief Expedition and the defence of India 1885–1900', in *Journal of Imperial and Commonwealth History*, VI (1977–78).

16 See Joseph Lehman, *All Sir Garnet* (1964), pp. 286–8, 291–2.

17 'I think that Roberts has been quite the equal of Wolseley in the brilliancy of his successes, as well as in the importance of the field upon which they have been won. There is a general impression in the army that Wolseley has had much more than his share of opportunities of distinction: & he has certainly been fully rewarded. If Roberts were to be passed over for him, a painful impression would be produced.' Salisbury to Sir Henry Ponsonby (Private Secretary to the Queen) 25 July 1885 (RA E 30/179).

18 For macabre descriptions of executions at Kandahar under Hume, see Tim Jeal, *Baden-Powell* (1989) p. 63.

19 For the text of this proclamation, see Roberts' despatch of 15 October 1879 (RP 154–1).

20 Lytton to Roberts 5 January 1880 (LP 218/22, p. 16).

21 See Macgregor's diary for 14 November 1879 and 11 February 1880, in W. Trousdale, *War in Afghanistan 1879–1880* (Detroit, 1985).

22 'I consider that the Military Commission took the place of the old Drumhead Court Martial, and that it was not necessary to keep or prepare lengthy docu-

ments; in fact, we could not have done it . . .' Roberts to Lyall 29 January 1880 (RP101–1/CCXCIV).

23 Foreign Secretary (Lyall) to Roberts 4 January 1889 (LP 127B, p. 334).

24 Howard Hensman, *The Afghan War of 1879–80* (1881), pp. 228–9.

25 Macgregor did not believe that Roberts kept a record – see his diary for 13 February 1880 (Trousdale, op cit, p. 156).

26 *Report of the Royal Commission on the Organisation of the War Office and Admiralty (1890).*

27 'This cannot be allowed for one moment, and Sir Henry should take steps to prevent this even being discussed' – note by Queen on a letter from Ponsonby dated 4 March 1890. G.E. Buckle, *The Letters of Queen Victoria*, Third Series, Vol. I. In a letter to Ponsonby of 20 March 1890, she referred to 'this really abominable report' – *Letters*, op cit, p. 582.

28 Wolseley to Ponsonby 2 August 1890 – *Letters*, op cit, p. 625.

29 Buller became Adjutant-General and held the post until 1897. The Duke of Connaught went to Southern Command and Wolseley was rusticated to the Irish Command.

30 The Commander-in-Chief was statutorily barred from leaving India during his tenure of command. An enabling Bill (No. 226) was tabled in the House of Commons in April 1888 but not proceeded with. The Secretary of State for India (Cross) was unable to find time for it in 1890, or in 1892 when Roberts was again asked to extend but refused. There is a copy of the Bill in RP 12/48.

I. January 1876 to August 1879 – Introduction

1 No copy of this paper has been found among Roberts' papers at the NAM or in Lytton's or Napier's papers at the IORL.

2 Extract from '*Some of the "Turning Points" in my Career* (undated holograph manuscript in RP 225).

3 The Government of India had maintained a native vakil (agent) in Kabul for many years but he was essentially a news gatherer although occasionally used as a channel of diplomatic communication. What Salisbury wanted was a British officer resident in Afghanistan.

4 Colonel H.B. Hanna, *The Second Afghan War 1878–1879–1880* (3 vols., 1899–1910), I, p. 279. Hanna was prejudiced against Roberts for career reasons but his views here undoubtedly represented those of many officials in India at the time. For Colley and Cavagnari, see Biographical Notes.

5 Lytton's proposals are set out in a long memorandum to his Council, dated 22 April 1877 (RP 161/1), and later in a despatch to the Secretary of State, No. 86 of 1877, dated 17 May 1877 (RP 161/2). The Secretary of State proposed an amended plan but the subject died a natural death with the outbreak of the war. A North West Frontier Province, excluding Sind, was ultimately set up by Curzon in 1901.

6 Wolseley's acceptance and withdrawal are in LP 8/10, 11.

7 For these Russian initiatives, see Beryl Williams 'Approach to the Second Afghan War: Central Asia during the Great Eastern Crisis 1875–1878', *International Historical Review II, No. 2* (April 1980).

8 For a detailed account of the British progress to war see Maurice Cowling, 'Lytton, the Cabinet and the Russians August to November 1878 , *English Historical Review*, LXXVI (1961), pp. 59–79.

9 For details of Haines' war plans see RP 154/1.

10 There is no adequate analysis of the organisation, administration and equipment of the Indian Army in the last quarter of the nineteenth century, but see T.A. Heathcote, *The Indian Army* (1974) and Robson, *The Road to Kabul: The Second Afghan War 1878–1881* (1986), chapter 4.

11 For detailed accounts of the military operations see Hanna (op. cit), Robson, *The Road to Kabul*, and *The Second Afghan War: Abridged Official History* (1908). The official history, in six volumes, compiled by Macgregor, when Quartermaster-General India, was issued under a 'Strictly Confidential' classification and quietly suppressed. The only copies known to the present editor are in the IORL, one of which is Roberts' copy, transferred from the library of the National Defence College, formerly at Latymer (see IOR L/MIL/17/14/29).

12 For the text of the Treaty of Gandamak, see RP 161/10.

13 Field Marshal Lord Roberts, *Forty-One Years in India* (2 vols., 1897), II, p. 177.

14 *The Special Commission to inquire into the Organisation and Expenditure of the Army in India* (Simla 1879). It was referred to at the time as 'The Army Commission' or 'The Military Commission'; subsequently, as 'The Eden Commission' – see Brian Robson, 'The Eden Commission and the Reform of the Indian Army 1879–1893' *JSAHR*, LX (1979), pp. 4–13. Copies of its report are in the Ministry of Defence Central Library and in the IORL (reference L/MIL/17/5/1697).

15 The Kurram Valley, along with Pishin and Sibi, was quietly annexed to India in 1887.

16 Lytton to Cranbrook, 24 August 1879 (L P 218/21/p. 681). For Sandeman, see Biographical Notes.

I. January 1876 to August 1879

1 The post of Quartermaster-General India became vacant early in 1874 when the holder, Edwin Johnson, was appointed to the more senior post of Adjutant-General in India.

2 Sir Robert Henry Davies, Lieutenant-Governor of the Punjab.

3 Colonel O.T. Burne and Colonel George Colley respectively. Colley succeeded Burne early in 1878 and was succeeded in turn as Military Secretary by Colonel Thomas Baker – see Biographical Notes. The post of Military

Secretary to the Viceroy was essentially a social one, not concerned with military appointments; hence the resentment when Colley acted as Lytton's military adviser.

4   Sir Lewis Pelly had been chosen by Lytton to lead a mission to Kabul to discuss Anglo-Afghan relations, but the Amir, Sher Ali, declined to receive it. Early in 1877, Pelly conducted abortive talks at Peshawar with the Amir's envoy, Nur Mahomed Khan.

5   Colonel Allen Johnson, Secretary of the Military Department; Major-General Alexander Taylor, Deputy Inspector-General of Military Works; Thomas Henry Thornton, Secretary of the Civil Department of the Government of the Punjab; Major-General Sir Henry Norman, Military Member of the Viceroy's Council. Roberts, in his diary, records the attendance additionally of Donald Cameron McNabb, Commissioner of Peshawar, and Major-General Sir Peter Lumsden, Adjutant-General, India; but does not refer to Taylor or Johnson. He described the meeting as a 'very quaint affair' (RP 92–18, entry for 24 November 1876).

6   Lieutenant-Colonel Charles Metcalfe Macgregor, Assistant-Quartermaster-General, a passionate believer in the so-called 'Forward Policy' and in the inevitability of war with Russia; his Memorandum is in RP 227. Macgregor's name is sometimes spelled with a capital 'G', as in the biography produced by his wife, but he himself spells it with a small 'g' in his official papers and letters, and this is the form adopted here.

7   i.e. Basra.

8   The modern Cizre, on the Tigris, some 80 miles above Mosul.

9   Francis Rawdon Chesney (1789–1872), the originator of the 19th century overland route to India across what is now Iraq. He explored the Tigris in 1831 and again, with steamships, in 1835–7 – see H.L. Haskins, *British Routes to India* (1928), pp. 150–2, 160–71.

10   Colonel Henry Knightley Burne, Secretary to the Government of India in the Military Department.

11   Major-General Michael Biddulph, commanding the Quetta reinforcements; returned to India with surplus troops in March 1879 and did not serve in the second campaign.

12   Lieutenant-General Robert MacLagan RE, Chief Engineer of the Punjab, retired 1878.

13   Probably Henry Scott, Public Works Department, stationed at Rawalpindi.

14   Probably Captain Edward Harvey RE, Punjab Public Works Department, Kohat Division.

15   Colonel Thomas Harmer Sibley, Deputy Commissary General, Bengal Army.

16   Lieutenant-Colonel William Garrow Waterfield, Bengal Staff Corps, Commissioner of Peshawar, attached to the Kurram Column as Chief Political Adviser.

17   Colonel Samuel Black, Bengal Staff Corps.

18 The abbreviations used here and elsewhere are

Wing	a half-battalion of four companies
F/A, RHA	F Battery, A Brigade, Royal Horse Artillery
G/3, RA	G Battery, 3 Brigade, Royal Artillery
5th PC	5th Punjab Cavalry, Punjab Frontier Force
5th PI	5th Punjab Infantry, Punjab Frontier Force
21st PNI	21st Bengal (Punjab) Native Infantry
23rd Pioneers	23rd Bengal Native Infantry (Pioneers)
2/8th Foot	2nd Battalion, 8th Foot (British Army)

19 Colonel John James Hood Gordon, commanding 29th Bengal (Punjab) Native Infantry – see Document 43, Section 1 Note 55 and Biographical Notes.

20 The Turis occupied the Kurram Valley; as Shiah Muslims, they were at odds with the surrounding, predominantly Sunni tribes and had petitioned in 1860 to be taken under British protection. The Ghilzais are one of the two great Afghan confederations (the other being the Duranis, from whom the ruling house in Afghanistan came) – see Sir Olaf Caroe, *The Pathans* (London, 1958) and Vartan Gregorian, *The Emergence of Modern Afghanistan* (Stanford, 1969) pp. 25–45.

21 The Daur Wazirs lived south-west of Thal, in what is now Northern Waziristan; the Jajis occupied the area round Ali Khel, while the Chakmannis, Mangals and Maqbils lived to the west of the main Kurram Valley.

22 The Bangash inhabited the area between Kohat and Thal, including the southern extremity of the Kurram Valley.

23 A Sayid is a leader claiming descent from the Prophet Mahomed's grandson, Husain. The Shiahs are one of the two main divisions of Muslims; since the Turis were Shiahs and the surrounding tribes Sunnis, these Sayids were presumably Turis.

24 The Zaimukhts were a notoriously predatory tribe inhabiting the angle between the southern end of the Kurram Valley and the Miranzai Valley between Thal and Kohat.

25 Wali Mahomed, a half-brother of the Amir Sher Ali.

26 A jirga is a meeting of tribal leaders and elders.

27 Lieutenant-Colonel George Villiers, Grenadier Guards, one of Roberts' two Orderly Officers, and a cousin of Lady Lytton.

28 Brigadier-General John Bulkeley Thelwall, previously commanding the 21st BNI, now commanding one of the two infantry brigades in the Kurram Column. He returned to England, on sick leave, in February 1879. For Roberts' official assessment of him, see Document 42.

29 John Withers McQueen, see Biographical Notes and Document 263.

30 This is Kipling's famous 'screw gun', a jointed steel gun, with a rifled, muzzle-loading barrel, firing a 7 pound shell to a maximum range of 4,000 yards; it was introduced in 1878 and not widely used in the Second Afghan

War. For details, see Brigadier-General C.A.L. Graham, *The History of the Indian Mountain Artillery* (Aldershot, 1957).

31 Brigadier-General Alexander Hugh Cobbe, previously commanding the 17th (Leicestershire) Foot. For Roberts' official assessment, see Document 42.

32 Lieutenant-Colonel Francis Howell Jenkins, commanding the Queen's Own Corps of Guides.

33 Lieutenant-Colonel Henry James Buchanan, 9th Foot, then serving on the staff of South East District at Chatham.

34 Captain Louis Henry Emile Tucker, Bengal Infantry attached Political Service; Major Charles Edward Macaulay, Assistant Commissioner at Dera Ismail Khan; Captain Robert Warburton, Bengal Staff Corps.

35 Archibald Christie, Bengal Civil Service, attached to Political Service, Assistant Commissioner of Peshawar.

36 Captain Frederick Theophilus Goad, Bengal Staff Corps, attached to the Transport Department of the Kurram Column; Captain Charles Folliott Powell, 5th (Hazara) Gurkhas. See also Document 50.

37 Major George Nicolas Channer VC, 29th Bengal Native Infantry; Lieutenant Henry Philip Picot, 29th Bengal Native Infantry.

38 Lieutenant William Bernard Wilson, Bengal Staff Corps, attached 12th Bengal Cavalry.

39 The cutting which Lyall enclosed (Document 25) was from the *Bombay Gazette*; it is not clear whether Lyall made a mistake in his letter or whether the wrong cutting was enclosed but the former explanation is indicated.

40 Captain George Swinley, RA, commanding No. 2 (Derajat) Mountain Battery; Captain Harrison Ross Lewin Morgan, RA, commanding No. 1 (Kohat) Mountain Battery.

41 See Biographical Notes.

42 Major James Calder Stewart, Bengal Staff Corps; Major Thomas James Williams Bulkeley; Major Benjamin Williams, Bengal Staff Corps.

43 Captain Robert Henry Francis Rennick, Bengal Staff Corps, employed on political duties in first campaign.

44 Malcolm Macpherson – see Documents 37, 38, 39, 40, 41.

45 'Shahzada' is a Persian word meaning literally 'son of the King'; in practice, it had come to mean that the holder claimed descent from a royal house. The Shahzada Sultan Jan was a Muslim Extra Assistant Commissioner in the Punjab administration.

46 A number of the Sikh native states, such as Patiala, Nabha, Jhind and Kapurthala, volunteered contingents of their own state troops, who were employed subsequently on garrison duties in the Kurram Valley.

47 For Collett, see Biographical Notes. For Macpherson, see also Document 48.

48 Boyle was the Special Correspondent of the London newspaper *The Standard*, accompanying the Kandahar column; for Pretyman, see Biographical Notes.

49 Dillon was Assistant Military Secretary to the Commander-in-Chief in London, responsible for Indian matters; he had served with Roberts on the Abyssinian Expedition in 1867–8. See also Biographical Notes.

50 Lieutenant-Colonel William Stirling, RA; Major Sidney Parry, RA.

51 Alexander Hadden Lindsay, RA; did not serve in second campaign 1879–81.

52 Aeneas Perkins, RE. Despite his apparent poor health, he served as Roberts' Chief Engineer in the second campaign. Macgregor described him as 'about the worst tempered fellow I know' (Diary entry for 19th October 1879 – Trousdale, p. 111). Roberts, as C-in-C India, appointed Perkins to the Oudh Division; when he vacated the command, it was described as 'The Third Relief of Lucknow'.

53 Colonel F. Barry Drew, commanding 2/8th Foot.

54 Major, acting Lieutenant-Colonel, Augustus Arthur Currie, commanding the 23rd (Punjab) Bengal Native Infantry (Pioneers).

55 J.J.H. Gordon.

56 The reference is to the disaster at Isandlwhana, in Zululand, on 22 January 1879.

57 Padshah Khan was the leading Ghilzai chief and therefore a potential ally of great importance.

58 Captain Arthur Conolly, Bengal Staff Corps, attached to the Political Service.

59 Brigadier-General John Watson, commanding the Punjab Chiefs Contingent – see Biographical Notes. Commanded in Kurram 1879–80.

60 Lieutenant-General Sir Edward Hamley, the leading British academic strategist of his day, now best known for his textbook *The Operations of War*, first published in 1866.

61 Colonel Arthur Cory, Bengal Staff Corps (retired), employed as war correspondent.

62 Major Edmund Roche Elles, RA; probably Major Cecil James East, 57th Foot, employed in the Intelligence Branch of the Quartermaster-General India's Department until he retired in May 1879.

63 Captain Walter Andrew Wynter, 33rd (Duke of Wellington) Foot; Major Arthur Prior Palmer, Bengal Staff Corps (later C-in-C India 1900–02).

64 Possibly J.W.H. Hozier, a minor writer on cavalry reform but more likely H.M. Hozier, a correspondent with the Abyssinian Expedition and subsequently a military writer. I am indebted to Dr Beckett for this suggestion.

65 Lieutenant-Colonel Henry Tyndall, commanding 2nd Punjab Infantry, PFF; retired with honorary rank of Major-General 1883.

66 The distinction which Roberts is making is between the regular regiments of the Bengal Army, under the direct control of the Commander-in-Chief India, and the regiments of the Punjab Frontier Force (of which Roberts was still Commandant), which came under the direct control of the Lieutenant-Governor of the Punjab. Tyndall and his regiment accompanied Roberts to Kabul in the second campaign.

67 See Biographical Notes and Introduction to Section 4.

68 The Under-Secretary of State was Edward Stanhope – see Biographical Notes.

69 George Anderson, Liberal MP for Glasgow 1868–85; for Anderson's Question and Stanhope's Answer, see *Hansard*, Third Series, CCXLIII, cols. 1312–13; the Government was compelled to wait for a formal report from Roberts which he submitted on 21 March 1879 (Document 55).

70 The only cavalry involved were the 5th Punjab Cavalry.

71 See Biographical Notes.

72 Abdullah Jan was a younger son of the Amir Sher Ali and a half- brother of Yakub Khan.

73 Daud Shah was the Afghan Commander-in-Chief.

74 Secretary of State for India in succession to Salisbury.

75 Captain Robert Gossett Woodthorpe, RE, Superintendent of Surveying with the Kurram Column. He served in the same capacity with Roberts in the second campaign.

76 Roberts refers to the peace negotiations between Yakub and Cavagnari in the British camp at Gandamak which resulted in a treaty on the 26th May.

77 Captain O'Moore-Creagh, commanding the Mhairwarra Battalion, had fought a gallant action against Mohmand tribesmen at Kam Dakka, in the Khyber valley, on 22 April 1879, for which he received the VC – see Robson, op cit, pp. 108–10. He was C-in-C India 1909–14.

78 Probably the modern Pir Sarai, some 10 miles south-south-east of Ali Khel.

79 Not located.

80 Sir Bartle Frere (see Biographical Notes) was accused of deliberately precipitating the Zulu War by issuing an ultimatum to the Zulu king, Cetewayo, without the concurrence of the Cabinet in London.

81 This is the commission on Indian Army reform ultimately chaired by Sir Ashley Eden – see Documents 66, 68 and Introduction to Section 1, Note 14.

82 Charles Edward Bernard, Additional Financial Secretary to the Government of India, later Chief Commissioner in Burma; Lieutenant-Colonel Edward Ridley Colbourne Bradford, Bengal Staff Corps, Resident in Rajputana.

83 Brigadier-General Frederick William Jebb, 67th Foot, Adjutant-General of the Madras Army; Brigadier-General G.R.S. Burrows, Quartermaster-General of the Bombay Army and the defeated commander at Maiwand in July 1880 – see also Biographical Notes.

84 Colonel Thomas Baker, Military Secretary to the Viceroy – see Biographical Notes.

85 Major George Stewart, Guides, and Captain Charles Strahan, RE, both on the staff of Sir Sam Browne's Khyber Column, where Macgregor was serving as Chief of Staff.

86 i.e. the tribal elders of the Bakhakhel clan of the Khugiani tribe of Pathans.

87 An official escort of tribesmen guaranteeing safe conduct against attack by other tribesmen.

88 Lytton's very long letter of 11 June 1879, setting out his hopes and aims for the Commission, is RP 37/16.
89 Brigadier-General Hamilton Forbes, previously commanding the Bhopal Battalion.
90 Lieutenant-Colonel George Hubert Parker.
91 Captain Richard George Kennedy, Bengal Staff Corps, serving as DAQMG of the Kurram Column; Lieutenant Neville Chamberlain, Central India Horse, son of General Sir Neville Chamberlain (see Biographical Notes), serving as one of Roberts' Orderly Officers.
92 Major-General Alexander Fraser, RE, Secretary of Public Works Department, Government of India; Roberts had started the construction of a permanent cantonment at Shalozan, some ten miles east of the Peiwar Kotal.
93 Mahomed Hiyat Khan, a Muslim officer of the Punjab administration, serving as an Assistant Political Officer in the Kurram. He was to play a highly significant role at Kabul in the second campaign.
94 Brigadier-General William Godfrey Dunham Massy – see Biographical Notes. Known as 'Redan Massy', having led the assault on the Redan, at Sevastopol in September 1855.
95 Kushdil Khan, another half-brother, or possibly a cousin, of Yakub Khan.
96 Lieutenant-Governor of the Punjab.
97 The town of Tank, some forty miles north west of Dera Ismail Khan, was sacked by Mahsud tribesmen in 1879. The area, subsequently known as Waziristan, was claimed by the Amir but regarded by the Indian Government as semi-independent, under British protection. A punitive expedition was mounted against the Mahsuds in April 1881, with limited success. The opening up of the Gomal Pass in 1890 and the demarcation of the Indo-Afghan frontier (the Durand Line) in 1893 resulted in Waziristan becoming a formidable and intractable military problem which lasted down to 1947.
98 George Batten, Bengal Civil Service, Private Secretary to the Viceroy while Colley was serving in Zululand. For Batten's appointment, see Mary Lutyens *The Lyttons in India* (1979), pp. 154–5.
99 Captain John Francis James Miller, 23rd Bengal Native Infantry (Pioneers); Captain Frederick Thomas Nelson Spratt, RE.
100 Lieutenant Philip Thomas Buston, RE; Lieutenant Francis Bacon Longe, RE.
101 Lieutenant Suene Grant, RE, Assistant Field Engineer in the Kurram.
102 Captain Mark Henry Heathcote, Bengal Staff Corps.
103 Major Arthur Robert Chapman, 1st Bengal Cavalry; Captain Arthur Broome, Bengal Staff Corps, serving as a Transport officer with Roberts' force.
104 Mr S.J. Josephs, Public Works Department (Telegraph Department).
105 Not identified – presumably a local Jaji or Mangal chief.

II. September 1879 to October 1880 – Introduction

1 Sam Browne's Khyber force had been dispersed while Stewart's force at Kandahar had just started to retire to India and was in any case some 300 miles from Kabul. Haines does not seem to have suggested giving the Kurram force to a more senior commander.

2 The one major physical obstacle between the forward British post at Ali Khel and Kabul, the Shutargardan Pass, was occupied, on instructions from Simla, by Massy on 11 September. From Kushi, the road to Kabul was flat and easy, with one obstruction, the Sang-i-Nawishta defile, five miles south of Kabul.

3 The force which Roberts took forward from Kushi consisted of one cavalry and two infantry brigades, with 18 guns, about 6,500 men in all, with 6,000 followers and 4,000 animals.

4 Although officially called Charasia, Hanna shows convincingly that the correct name is Charasiab ('four watermills'). Because of a shortage of transport, Roberts had only the equivalent of a large brigade with him, opposed to thirteen Afghan regular regiments and several thousands of irregulars. For details, see Hanna, op cit, III, pp. 65–79, and Robson, op cit, pp. 126–33.

5 See Roberts to Lady Macgregor 21 February 1888 (NMS 886.1, 1955–675/6).

6 For a highly critical account of the proceedings of these two commissions, see Macgregor's diary (Trousdale, op cit, pp. 108, 111, 112–14 and passim). There is ample evidence that other officers, including Stewart at Kandahar, were uneasy about the executions. Lytton and Cranbrook were initially in favour of blowing up the Amir's palace, the Bala Hissar, in imitation of Pollock blowing up the main bazaar in 1842, but the idea was quietly abandoned.

7 Roberts, despite long service in the Quartermaster-General's Department, had no proper Intelligence Officer or Department ('Deane tells me that . . . your Intelligence Department has practically consisted of General Hills, who does not understand a word of the only language in which it is possible to communicate with Afghans.' Lytton to Roberts 25 January 1880 (LP 22/p. 62)). One motive for sending up Griffin was to improve intelligence ('Roberts greatly needs a stronger political staff, were it only to act as a sort of intelligence department.' Lytton to Cranbrook 13 January 1880 (LP 22/p. 30)). Throughout the war, British commanders lacked good information about the opposition, as Maiwand, Ahmed Khel and the events of December 1879 outside Kabul demonstrated.

8 For the Massy affair, see Hanna, III, pp. 175–193 and Robson, *The Road to Kabul*, pp. 151–4. Trousdale is certainly wrong in attributing this to Roberts' jealousy (Trousdale, op cit, p. 62); Massy was no kind of rival to Roberts. On returning to India, Massy received another brigade command and, in due course, promotion to major-general and the command in Ceylon.

9 'But privately my impression is that the Kabul executions were unwise and that they may have tended to precipitate the recent hostile combination.' Lytton to Cranbrook 31 December 1879 (LP 21/ p. 1143). 'You will have gathered from my last two or three letters to you that I share your anxiety about the consequences of some of Roberts' recent political and administrative proceedings. He is a splendid soldier; but his management of the political situation has not been altogether as judicious as I had hoped it would be; and, unfortunately, the strongest men about him have hitherto been officers destitute of political or administrative training, and incompetent to give him good advice or assistance in any but military matters.' Lytton to Cranbrook 28 January 1880 (LP 22/ p. 82).

10 'Roberts (entre nous) had been making a great mess of political affairs in Kabul. We are now sending up Griffin as Chief Political Officer, and although nominally subordinate to Roberts, he will virtually be the head. Something of this sort ought to have been done long ago. There is not a man of sense among Roberts' advisers and nothing can exceed the stupidity he has shown in all non-military matters. . . The belief in Roberts' strategical qualifications has evidently been terribly shaken!' Sir John Strachey to Sir Richard Strachey 28 January 1880 (IOR MSS Eur F 127/1).

11 The other parts of the plan, including a march by Roberts' troops through Bamian (west of Kabul), fell through. For details, see Abridged Official History, pp. 367.

12 For detailed accounts of Maiwand, see Leigh Maxwell, *My God – Maiwand* (1980), Robson, Ch. 12 and Hanna, III, pp. 403–28.

13 Roberts, op cit, II, p. 330.

14 Stewart's first reaction was unfavourable ('In my opinion the moving of troops from Kabul towards Kandahar is not sound in strategy or policy, and it is only the impossibility of sending a sufficient reinforcement from India by Sinde route that will justify it.' Stewart to Foreign Department 29 July 1880 (HP29/39), but he quickly accepted Roberts' view.

15 Wisely because, on his showing at Ahmed Khel, Stewart was not in the same class as a field commander. For the near disaster at Ahmed Khel, see Hanna, III, pp. 326–32, and Robson, ibid, pp. 192–6. It was Stewart's only action as a commander.

16 Phayre was delayed by transport problems and by hostile attacks from tribesmen. No one got a peerage. Roberts had to wait until 1892.

II. September 1879 to October 1880

1 The 44th BNI was composed of Gurkhas.

2 i.e. non-Muslims.

3 Lieutenant-Colonel Franklin Phillips Mignon and Captain William Luckhardt, both Bombay Staff Corps.

4   Captain Robert McGregor Stewart, RA; Major Henry Bathurst Hanna, Bengal Staff Corps (the subsequent historian of the Second Afghan War); Major George Edward Langham Somerset Sanford, RE.

5   Colonel Arthur Moffat Lang, RE; Captain James Dundas VC, RE (later killed in an explosion at Sherpur); Captain Arthur Thomas Preston, RE.

6   John Adam Tytler, Bengal Staff Corps; commanded brigade in Khyber in first campaign, and in Kurram in second campaign. Promoted to major-general but died at Thal in February 1880.

7   Henry Mortimer Durand – see Biographical Notes.

8   Nakhshband Khan, living on pension in Kabul, had warned Cavagnari about the danger from mutinous Afghan regiments – see his testimony in *Afghanistan (1880) No. 1*. After the massacre he fled from Kabul and joined Roberts.

9   Major-General James ('Jemmy') Hills (–Johnes) – see Biographical Notes.

10 The Nawab Ghulam Hussein Khan Alizai had been British vakil at Kabul, after long service as Native Commandant of the 15th Bengal Cavalry. He was appointed KCSI on 29 July 1879.

11 The Mustaufi (Habibullah Khan) was the Finance Minister; the Wazir (Shah Mahomed Khan) was the Chief Minister; Yahiya Khan was an uncle by marriage of the Amir Yakub Khan and was appointed Governor of Kabul in September 1879. He was deported to India in December 1879 with his brother, Zakariah Khan.

12 The ruler of Kashmir was suspected of a treacherous intrigue with the Russians – hence Lytton's keenness to locate incriminating evidence in Kabul. As punishment, the Kashmir ruler was deprived of territory which Lytton had earlier awarded him.

13 Bakhtiar Khan had been the British vakil in Kabul before the war and had died there while delivering a message from Lytton in April 1879. Lytton suspected that the Amir or his minions had had him poisoned. His body does not seem to have been recovered.

14 Major-General Robert Onesiphorus Bright, commanding the Khyber line of communication under Roberts – see Biographical Notes.

15 Surgeon-Major Henry Walter Bellew, Bengal Medical Department, attached Political Service. He had accompanied the mission to Afghanistan in 1857 – see Robson *The Road to Kabul*, p. 33 – as well as Forsyth's mission to Kashgar in 1873, and had travelled through Persia, Afghanistan and Baluchistan in 1872 – see his *Journal of a Political Mission to Afghanistan in 1857, From the Indus to the Tigris . . . in 1872* and *Kashmir and Kashgar . . . in 1873–74.*

16 Lieutenant-General John Luther Vaughan, on half pay – see Biographical Notes.

17 Not identified.

18 No signed Treaty was discovered and it is doubtful if one was ever signed. Roberts located an Afghan Foreign Office clerk who professed to be able to

remember the terms of such a treaty. These agree well with those given by Yavorski, the Russian mission's doctor, in his *Journal of the Russian Embassy through Afghanistan and the Khanate of Bukhara in 1878–79* (2 vols., Calcutta, 1885).

19 Mahomed Ayub Khan, the younger brother of Yakub, and Governor of Herat.

20 Major-General George Greaves – see Biographical Notes.

21 See Section 1, Note 10. Not to be confused with Colonel O.T. Burne – see Biographical Notes.

22 Surgeon-Major Isidore Bourke, Army Medical Department.

23 The reference to *The Standard* is an allusion to Roberts' earlier difficulties with Macpherson [see Documents 37, 39, 41].

24 Nek Mahomed, an uncle of the Amir Yakub Khan.

25 Major-General Sir William Nott had commanded the troops at Kandahar in the First Afghan War; Major Eldred Pottinger had helped the Afghans defend Herat in 1837–8.

26 Major-General Sir William Elphinstone had commanded the British army destroyed in the passes between Kabul and Jellalabad in the winter of 1841–2 – see J.A. Norris, *The First Afghan War 1838–42* (Cambridge, 1967) and Patrick Macrory, *Signal Catastrophe* (1966).

27 Mahomed Akbar Khan, son of the Amir Dost Mahomed, had led the Afghan forces in the attack on the British army at Kabul in the winter of 1841–2 – see Norris, op cit. pp. 378–81 and passim.

28 The Pathan code of conduct.

29 Yakub left Kabul, under escort, on 1 December 1879 and reached Peshawar on the 9th. He remained effectively a State prisoner in India, on a British pension, until his death at Mussoorie in 1923.

30 The village of Ben-i-Badam, in the Wardak Valley, south west of Kabul, had been burned by Baker on the 28th November, in reprisal for a British foraging party having been fired on – see Robson, op cit, p. 148. The telegram illustrates Roberts' lack of information on the strength and movements of the Afghan insurgents.

31 Brigadier-General Charles Gough, commanding the 1st Brigade of Major-General Bright's Khyber Lines of Communication force – see Biographical Notes.

32 Brigadier-General Charles George Arbuthnot, commanding the 2nd Brigade of Bright's force – see Biographical Notes. The brigade did not move to Kabul.

33 Lieutenant-Colonel John Hudson, commanding the 28th BNI at Lataband, some 20 miles east of Kabul. C-in-C Bombay in 1893.

34 Gough's brigade reached Sherpur on 24 December, the day after the great Afghan attack. Roberts and many of his officers believed that Gough could have moved sooner but the Commander-in-Chief subsequently commended Gough's performance.

35 i.e., Ghulam Hussein – see Note 10 above.

36 See Biographical Notes.

37 Roberts and Griffin had clashed before the war – see LP 22/1 – for reasons which have not been discovered; Roberts does not mention the matter in his *Forty-One Years in India*.

38 Haines and other members of the Army Headquarters Staff clearly resented, inter alia, Roberts' direct access to Lytton, via Colley, in securing what he wanted for his Kurram force (Document 12, for example). See also Lytton's warning (123).

39 Frederick Harrison, a well-known and respected journalist, published the first of his major articles attacking the executions at Kabul, in the *Fortnighty Review* on 1st December 1879, using information which could only have come from officers of Roberts' force. Communicating with the newspapers was not a military offence.

40 In fact, Gladstone's celebrated Midlothian by-election campaigns, in which he bitterly attacked, *inter alia*, the Afghan war, were a major factor in the Conservative defeat in the General Election of March 1880.

41 A yaboo (or yabu) was a native pony.

42 Probably Major Edward Samuells Cooke, Bengal Staff Corps.

43 For Hudson, see Note 33; Lieutenant-Colonel Francis Brownlow, commanding 72nd Highlanders (killed at battle of Kandahar on 1 September 1880); Lieutenant-Colonel Robert Cunliffe Low, 13th Bengal Cavalry; Major George White, 92nd Highlanders – see Biographical Notes.

44 The figure of 87 executions appears to represent the situation as at 26 December 1879 – see Lytton's letter to Frederick Harrison, 22 February 1880 (LYP 218/22/pp. 125–8) Lytton wrote to Egerton on 4 January 1880 saying that Roberts had hanged another 10 men since 26 December (LYP 218/22/p. 5), but Roberts subsequently claimed that there had been some double-counting. Macgregor, in his diary for 11 February 1880, wrote that Roberts had 'told deliberate falsehoods' in saying that so many men had suffered for being concerned in the attack on the Residency (Trousdale, op cit, p. 156).

45 Mir Bacha was the leading chief in Kohistan, the area north of Kabul, and a strong opponent of the British.

46 A misprint for Major-General *James* Hills – see Biographical Notes.

47 Lieutenant-Colonel Robert Stewart Cleland, commanding 9th Lancers; died of wounds at Murree on 7 August 1880.

48 Haines proposed to take direct command of operations in Afghanistan from Kabul. Stimulated by members of his staff, notably Greaves, he appears to have felt that Roberts and Stewart were getting all the credit and prestige from the war (Document 123).

49 Abdurrahman made it absolutely clear in negotiations that he claimed the full extent of the kingdom left by his grandfather, the Amir Dost Mahomed[137].

50 Major John Palmer Brabazon, 10th Hussars, a former ADC to Lytton and a member of the Prince of Wales' social circle.

51 Stewart marched from Kandahar with his troops, en route for Kabul, on 27 March 1880.

52 Pinjore, on the road from Kalki up to Simla, was the site of famous Mogul gardens.

53 Roberts received a GCB and a grant of £12,500 for his services in the second campaign but felt that he had been inadequately rewarded by comparison with Wolseley [189, 190].

54 Major-General George Pollock commanded the so-called Army of Retribution which occupied Kabul in September 1842 and blew up the main bazaar in retribution for the destruction of Elphinstone's army in the winter of 1841–2 – see Norris, op cit, passim. The 'Cabul' medal only was awarded to his troops.

55 A fresh medal was given for the Second Afghan War, with six clasps ('Ali Masjid', 'Peiwar Kotal', 'Charasia', 'Ahmed Khel', 'Kabul' and 'Kandahar').

56 For the Memorandum itself, which is very lengthy, see the annexure to RP 101/CCCLXIV.

57 Lieutenant-Colonel William Kidston Elles, Assistant Adjutant-General at the War Office, London.

58 News of Burrows' defeat at Maiwand on the 27th July reached Kabul on the 28th, within hours of the first survivors reaching Kandahar. The telegraph between Kandahar and Kabul was not cut for some days.

59 Major-General Charles Ash Windham was defeated outside Cawnpore on the 26th–27th November 1857 by a force under the rebel leader, Tantia Tope. The allusion was particularly apposite since Roberts had arrived at Cawnpore only three days after the defeat – see *Forty-One Years in India*, pp. 364–5.

60 Presumably so that he could check seniority dates and qualifications of officers in the Bombay and Madras Armies whom he did not know.

61 Lieutenant-General James Maurice Primrose – see Biographical Notes.

62 Major Oliver Beauchamp St John, Political Agent at Kandahar – see Biographical Notes.

63 A clear and significant reference to the allegations referred to in Documents 55 and 93.

64 Not identified. The letters, which dated from the autumn of 1879 and the spring of 1880, were part of Roberts' attempts to find a successor to Yakub.

65 Sher Ali Khan, an elderly uncle of the Amir Yakub Khan, had been formally recognised as the Wali (or Governor) of Kandahar province in March 1880. Ayub's success proved Sher Ali to be a man of straw and he retired to India in December 1880.

66 Captain Edward Straton, 22nd Foot, Roberts' Chief Signals Officer; Captain St John Thomas Frome; Captain Robert Hunter Murray; Lieutenant Seymour Charles Hale Monro; Lieutenant Stuart Alexander Menzies; Lieutenant Donald William Stewart (son of Sir Donald Stewart); Lieutenant-Colonel Arthur Battye and Major James Barry Slater, Bengal Staff Corps.

67 Maclaine, of E/B Battery, Royal Horse Artillery, had been captured during the retreat from Maiwand; efforts to secure his release had been unsuccessful. His throat was cut just before the British troops reached Ayub's camp. See also Documents 169 and 170.

68 Colonel Thomas Gilbert Kennedy, Bengal Staff Corps; he assumed command of the PFF on 7 September 1880.

69 Roberts had been in India continuously since 1869. It would appear that he was suffering from general debility, accentuated by nearly two years of heavy active service; he had also suffered from dysentery on the march down from Kabul. He recovered quickly in England.

70 Stewart assumed office as Military Member in September 1880, only to be appointed C-in-C India in succession to Haines, three months later.

71 Ross's suggestion, which would seem to have been derived from the example of the Victoria Cross, was acted upon.

72 The precise state of morale at Kandahar cannot now be determined. Roberts' assessment was vigorously denied by some of the Bombay officers there – see, for example, Major-General Sir John Hills, *The Bombay Field Force 1880* (1900). The sickness rate, always a good indicator of morale, was not particularly high. Roberts may have subconsciously exaggerated the matter in order to underline the quality of his own force. For the impressions of a relatively unbiased observer, see Brian Robson (ed) 'The Kandahar Letters of the Reverend Alfred Cane', *JSAHR*, LXIX, Nos. 279, 280 (Autumn, Winter 1991).

73 Roberts' assessment has to be seen in the light of his membership of the Bengal Army and of his belief in the superiority of the so-called 'martial races' – see Introduction to Section 4. Major-General Hume, a British Service officer, who succeeded Roberts in command at Kandahar, took a much more favourable view of the Bombay regiments under his command – see his detailed assessments in HP38/pp. 217–18. At Tofrek, in March 1885, the 17th BNI broke and fled while the 28th Bombay Native Infantry stood firm. On balance, the best regiments were probably as good as the mass of the Bengal infantry but not as good as the best, such as the PFF and Gurkha regiments.

74 Lieutenant-Colonel John Porter Malcolmson, commanding the 3rd Sind Horse, and Major Albert Purcell Currie, commanding the 3rd Bombay Light Cavalry, were court-martialled at Bombay in March–April 1881 on charges alleging misconduct at the battle of Maiwand and during the subsequent retreat, and acquitted. A copy of the proceedings of the preliminary Court of Enquiry held at Kandahar is in HP38/pp. 154–64; the courts martial proceedings are in IOR L/MIL/3/915.

75 This is the only personal letter to Roberts from Haines in either the Roberts or Haines archives.

76 The Marri and Achakzai tribes of Baluchis had created serious trouble in August 1880, following the news of the defeat at Maiwand, delaying Phayre's

efforts to relieve Kandahar. After Ayub's defeat, brigades under Baker and
Macgregor were despatched to punish them – see Robson, *The Road to
Kabul*, pp. 262–3.

77 Major Sir Robert Sandeman, Agent to the Governor-General in Baluchistan.

78 Major Charles Bean Euan Smith, Madras Infantry, employed on political
duties.

79 The Kizzilbash ('red heads') were a Persian-speaking people of Turcoman
origin descended from troops who had accompanied Nadir Shah, the founder
of modern Afghanistan, from Persia in 1747. The name refers to their tradi-
tional hats. They formed an élite within the Afghan army.

III. October 1880 to July 1885 – Introduction

1 For a typescript copy of this speech, see RP 163/1. Roberts' papers reveal no
trace of interest in British Army reform before this date. The presumption
must be that his interest was aroused by observing British troops during the
Second Afghan War, and then heightened post–1880 by the realisation that a
senior administrative post in the British Army was now a possibility.

2 Colley had been an original member of Wolseley's 'Ring'.

3 Timothy Michael Healy (1855–1931), MP for Wexford 1880–3, Governor-
General of the Irish Free State 1922–8.

4 The course of events can be traced in the Childers and Gladstone papers and
in *The Letters of Queen Victoria* (Third Series).

5 Roberts had been brought up in the Bengal Army. The Mutiny had brought
him into close contact with Sikh, Punjabi and Gurkha troops who had
formed the core of the native troops at the siege of Delhi and later. By 1903,
11 of the 43 Madras infantry regiments which had existed in 1881 had been
converted to Punjabi regiments and 6 disbanded.

6 Copies are in RP 95/II and IOR MSS Eur D734/7.

7 For a copy of this paper, see RP 162/14 and IOR MSS Eur D734/8.

8 Macgregor visited the site of Wolseley's victory at Tel-el-Kebir and wrote a
highly critical letter to Roberts – Macgregor to Roberts 19 April 1883 (RP 38/2).

9 This proposal appears to have been Roberts' main contribution to the work
of the Eden Commission since he was called away at a very early stage to lead
the march on Kabul.

10 Commander-in-Chief General Order No. 80 of 1 July 1881.

11 *Nineteenth Century*, XV, No. 88 (June 1884) pp. 1055–74. A copy of the
paper is in RP 139/5.

12 See Trousdale, op cit, p. 220.

13 Roberts may have met the Duke of Cambridge in 1859 when receiving his
VC from the Queen but there is no specific evidence of them meeting before
Roberts' return to England in 1880. The first letter from Roberts to the Duke
appears to be from Kabul dated 26 November 1879, referring to a letter from
the Duke of 24 October 1879 (RA Add MSS E/1/8961).

14 Winston Spencer Churchill, *The Life of Lord Randolph Churchill* (2 vols, 1906), II, pp. 490–1.

15 'We are not yet free from the peril of war. . . It will be a critical struggle: we ought not to throw away a single chance. Now Roberts, beyond comparison, is the man who knows most, & has done most in Afghan warfare . . . It is vital in this matter to have a man whose merit has been tried, & who thoroughly knows his work. I do not think this appointment will do any injustice to Lord Wolseley. I think that Roberts has been quite the equal of Wolseley in the brilliancy of his successes, as well as in the importance of the field upon which they have been won. There is a general impression in the Army that Wolseley has had much more than his share of opportunities of distinction'. Salisbury to Ponsonby (Private Secretary to the Queen) 25 July 1885 (RA Add MSS E/30/179).

III. October 1880 to July 1885

1 General Sir Charles Henry Ellice, Adjutant-General of British Army 1876–82.

2 Lieutenant-Colonel Gerald de Courcy Morton. Served on Roberts' staff throughout the Second Afghan War, Adjutant-General India 1895–8.

3 Toungoo, some 160 miles north of Rangoon.

4 Lieutenant-General Sir Arthur James Herbert was Quartermaster-General from 1882 to 1887.

5 Lieutenant-General William Payne; commanded Bangalore Division 1879–83.

6 Major-General Thomas Fourness Wilson, Military Member of the Viceroy's Council 1881–6.

7 i.e. Roberts' letter of 28 February 1882 (Document 180).

8 Childers had asked for Roberts' views – Childers to Roberts 17 March 1882 (RP 17/f4).

9 This is clearly a misprint for 'Prussians'.

10 Roberts wrote to Dillon in similar terms on 16 June 1882 (reference RP 97–1/XIV), giving him permission to show it to the Duke of Cambridge.

11 i.e. the 20th Bengal (Punjab) Native Infantry and the 45th Bengal Native Infantry (Rattray's Sikhs).

12 Stewart is using the term in the sense of those regiments recruited from 'Hindostan', the old term for India east and south of the Punjab.

13 Stewart's regiment was the pre-Mutiny 9th Bengal Native Infantry, in which he served from 1841 until it mutinied in May 1857. Matthew Coombs Paul was lieutenant-colonel in the regiment in 1838 and George Smith in 1848. Thomas Henry Paul, promoted to Major-General in 1841, served in Java but not apparently in the 9th.

14 Sir Edwin Norman, Sir Richard Strachey (brother of John) and Sir Ashley Eden were members of the Council of India in London.

15 This may be Robert Crozier, a clerk in the India Office, or possibly Lieutenant-Colonel Stanley Crozier, Oxfordshire Light Infantry.

16 Sir Archibald Alison (1826–1907). Commanded Aldershot Division 1883–8, retired as full general 1893.

17 Mr (later Sir) Courtenay Ilbert, the Law Member of the Viceroy's Council, introduced his Criminal Procedure Code (Amendment) Bill in 1883, which sought to extend the jurisdiction of Indian native judges to cover Europeans, who had hitherto had the privilege of being tried only by European judges. The Bill raised a violent storm among Europeans and there was even a plot to kidnap the Viceroy. For details of the affair, see S. Gopal, *British Policy in India 1858–1905* (Cambridge, 1965) and Edwin Alan Hirschman, *White Mutiny* (Delhi, 1980) p. 18.

18 The article was entitled 'The Present State of the Army' – see *Nineteenth Century*, LXIX (November 1882). Copy in RP 139/f3.

19 General (later Field Marshal) Sir John Lintorn Arabin Simmons (1821–1903). For the article, entitled 'The Critical Condition of the Army', see *Nineteenth Century* for March 1883.

20 Colonel David MacFarlan, Ordnance Consulting Officer to the India Office.

21 Australian horses (called 'walers', from the State of New South Wales), were extensively used by the Indian cavalry at this time because of their stamina – see Major G. Tylden, *Horses and Saddlery* (1965).

22 See Section 1, note 30. The screw gun was not replaced until 1900 when a jointed, breech-loading, 10-pounder was introduced – see Graham, op cit, pp. 101 and 444. M.L.R. signifies Muzzle Loading Rifled, B.L.R. is Breech Loading Rifled.

23 W.K. Elles (qv).

24 Colonel Paget Walter L'Estrange, RA, had written to Roberts, complaining about not getting a brigade command – see RP 97–2/LXV and LXX.

25 The paper– *Is an invasion of India by Russia possible?* – was not published but circulated to selected people. For a copy, see RP 95/II; for a convenient summary, see Document 199.

26 The Camp of Exercise, held near Bangalore, in January 1884; both Stewart and Hardinge were present.

27 See Biographical Notes.

28 G. de C. Morton (qv) and Lieutenant-Colonel William Forbes Gatacre.

29 W.K. Elles, commanding the Nagpore Force, and Edward George Dixon, commanding the 8th Madras Native Infantry.

30 Lieutenant-Colonel Alexander Macdonell Rawlins RA; Colonel George Stanley Hooper; Lieutenant-Colonel John Cecil Russell, 12th Lancers.

31 Major-General Sir Charles Patton Keyes, commanding the Hyderabad Contingent.

32 William Anthony Gib, commanding the Ceded District, had commanded a brigade under Bright in the Second Afghan War; Brigadier-General Harry Armstrong Brett, commanding 1st Battalion, Oxfordshire Light Infantry.

33 Major Robert Sandham; Major Augustus John Lavie; Captain Nugent Jonathan Nugent, commanding the depot at Wellington, in the Nilgiri Hills.

34 Lieutenant-Colonel George Swinley; Major Alex Dingwall Anderson; Major Archibald Broadfoot.

35 Lieutenant-Colonel Fitzmaurice Beauchamp.

36 Lieutenant-Colonel John Fletcher Caldwell.

37 Lieutenant-Colonel Humphrey Mangal Lamont Colquhoun.

38 Some foreign observers attended and Roberts, with his experience of the German Army manoeuvres in August 1881, paid particular attention to their treatment.

39 See Note 25 above.

40 An Anglo-Russian Boundary Commission delineated the northern boundary of Afghanistan in 1884–5. Sir Peter Lumsden was appointed Head of the British component. Roberts would almost certainly have been unacceptable to the Amir on account of the Kabul executions.

41 See Note 25.

42 i.e. the Gomal Pass.

43 *Free Trade in the Army* – see Introduction to this Section, Note 11.

44 Major-General Mikhail Dimitrievitch Skobolev (known as the 'White General' because of his uniform and horse) defeated the Tekke Turcoman tribes at Geok Tepe, some 40 miles north west of Askabad, in what is now Turkmenistan, on 24 January 1881 – see Fitzroy Maclean, *A Person from England* (1958) pp. 214–16.

45 The Thal Chotiali route from the Indus to Kandahar had been traversed by Biddulph in 1879 – see Robson *The Road to Kabul* p. 95.

46 John Gelson Gregson, Baptist minister and founder, in 1862, of the Soldiers' Total Abstinence Association. He had met Roberts at Kabul when serving as chaplain to the 72nd Highlanders – see his book *Through the Khyber Pass to Sherpore Camp, Cabul* (1883). For a sketch of the Temperance movement in the army in India, see Stephen Wood 'The Other Half: Further developments in recording the history of British Military temperance movements' *Army Museum '86*, (NAM, 1986).

47 Granville was Foreign Secretary and Kimberley Secretary of State for India.

48 Colonel James Keith Fraser, currently on half pay, late Life Guards.

49 i.e. during the Bangalore Camp of Exercise – see note 26.

50 This refers to Sir Gerald Graham's first expedition to Suakin against the Mahdiist leader, Uthman Digna, in February 1884, and particularly to the actions at El Teb and Tamai.

51 Lieutenant-General Sir Frederick Wellington John Fitzwygram, commanding the Cavalry Brigade at Aldershot and Inspector-General of Cavalry for Great Britain 1879–84.

52 Lieutenant-Colonel George Tyndal, Madras Staff Corps.

53 John Eldon Gorst (1835–1916), Solicitor General 1885–6, Under Secretary for India 1886–91 and Financial Secretary to the Treasury 1891–2.

54 The gun invented by Thorsten Nordenfeldt was not a true machine gun but rather a volley gun manually operated by a crank, thus allowing it to be made in different calibres without significant change. It was extensively used in the Royal Navy but not to any great extent in the British or Indian armies.

55 News of the fall of Khartoum reached Wolseley on the Nile at Korti on the 4th February, and London on the 5th, so Roberts was quick off the mark.

56 During Graham's second expedition against Uthman Digna, in 1885, a force under Sir John McNeil was attacked at Tofrek on 22 March. The 17th Bengal Native Infantry (BNI) broke and fled, the 15th BNI and the 28th Bombay Native Infantry (BoNI) stood firm. The classic account is William Galloway, *The Battle of Tofrek* (Edinburgh, 1887); for a good, short account, see Michael Barthorpe, 'The Battle of Tofrek 1885' *JSAHR*, LXIII, No. 253 (Spring 1985), pp. 1–10.

57 Abdurrahman did not die until 1901. The grim, gallows humour for which he was famous is conveyed in two poems by Kipling – *The Ballad of the King's Jest* and *The Ballad of the King's Mercy*, as well as in the short story *The Amir's Homily*. Kipling reported the Amir's visit for his newspaper *The Civil and Military Gazette* – see Thomas Pinney *Kipling's India; Uncollected Sketches 1884–88* (1986).

58 Russian troops occupied the Pendjeh oasis, 140 miles south of Merv, in territory claimed by the Afghans, on 30 March 1885. A compromise ultimately left the oasis in Russian hands but the crisis enabled Gladstone's Cabinet to liquidate its commitments in the Sudan.

59 Donald MacKenzie Wallace, successively Private Secretary to two Viceroys, Dufferin and Lansdowne. The paper was '*What are Russia's vulnerable points?*' – see Introduction to this Section.

60 A Guards Brigade and a New South Wales contingent had formed part of Graham's force at Suakin in 1885 – see note 56.

61 Charles Marvin, journalist, traveller and author of many books on the Russian conquest of Central Asia.

62 i.e. membership of the Council of India in London.

63 i.e. the Duke of Cambridge.

64 Hardinge, a Guardsman, was well-connected socially with the Royal family.

65 i.e. from his abortive expedition to the Sudan.

66 Lieutenant-General Lord Chelmsford had commanded the troops in the Zulu War until relieved by Wolseley after the disaster at Isandlwhana in January 1879.

67 i.e. Macpherson would join the Viceroy's Council as Military Member.

68 Lieutenant-General Sir Edmund Augustus Whitmore, Military Secretary to the Commander-in-Chief, the Duke of Cambridge. Brownlow, one of two Assistant Military Secretaries, was responsible for Indian matters and seems in practice to have worked directly to the C-in-C.

69 Stewart suffered from dyspepsia, for which Lady Roberts had prescribed a milk diet.

IV. December 1885 to April 1893 – Introduction

1 Only the Earl of Moira, C-in-C India from 1813 to 1823, held the post for longer.

2 For the printed minutes etc., see Roberts' printed *Minutes, notes etc. Part I 1877–December 1889, Part II January 1890–April 1893, with Index* (Calcutta, 1891 and 1893); copies in RP 96 and IOR L/MIL/17/5/1615. For the list of decisions see *Short Report on important questions dealt with during the tenure of command of the Army in India by General Lord Roberts* (Simla, 1893).

3 Kipling got no closer to the war than a fleeting visit to Rangoon in March 1889 but see his poem *The Ballad of Boh Dah Thone* (published in 1888) and his short stories 'The Taking of Lungtungpen' (in the collection *Plain Tales from the Hills*, published in 1888) and 'A Conference of the Powers' (in the collection *Many Inventions*, published in 1893). For the outbreak of the war, see A.T.Q. Stewart *The Pagoda War* (1972).

4 See Biographical Notes. White, an unknown major at 37, commanded a brigade under Prendergast and when the latter was relieved in March 1886, took over the chief operational command, in Upper Burma (the former kingdom of Ava), in the rank of local major-general, a command which he held until 1889.

5 For details of the construction of these lines, see P.S. Berridge *Couplings to the Khyber* (Newton Abbott, 1969). For details of the other road and rail improvements undertaken during Roberts' tenure, see *Short Report*, pp. 49–54.

6 Between 1884 and 1893, there were six major expeditions on the north west and northern frontiers (Zhob Valley 1884 and 1890, Black Mountain 1888 and 1891, Hunza-Nagar 1891, Miranzai 1891).

7 By the late 1890s, the balance had swung back as the tribes obtained modern, high velocity, magazine rifles. The most critical campaigns fought on the North-West Frontier were those in 1919–20 (see *Operations in Waziristan 1919–1920*, Confidential, Calcutta, 1921).

8 See Brian Robson, 'Changes in the Indian Army', *JSAHR* Vol. LXX (1992), pp.126-7.

9 Memorandum no. 54/Cavalry/430 of 10 March 1903 laid it down that henceforth the rifle would be the primary weapon of the cavalry. See also Edward Spiers, 'The British Cavalry 1902–1914', *JSAHR* LVII (1979) pp. 71–9.

10 Copy in RP 96-2/CCXXII.

11 Drunkenness, debt and embezzlement were the commonest reasons in India for officers being required to resign their commissions or dismissed; Roberts' correspondence contains many such cases. There are relatively few instances of officers being asked to resign on grounds of professional incompetence.

12 *Short Report*, p. 3.

13 Ibid, p. 6.

14 For details of unification and centralisation under Roberts see Robson *Eden Commission*. For the proposal to use common files, see Roberts' official Note *On the relations of the Commander-in-Chief in India with the Military Department of Government*, dated 5 August 1889 (copy in RP 96–1/CVII). The system then remained basically unchanged until Kitchener amalgamated the post of Military Member with that of Commander-in-Chief in 1905.

15 With few exceptions, senior appointments in India could be held by British or Indian Army officers. There was thus a constant tug-of-war between the two Commanders-in-Chief to ensure a fair distribution of such posts. Close acquaintance with Roberts' papers suggests that, while he tried hard to give proper weight to merit and competence, the Duke was apt to attach more weight to social factors. But both laid stress on appearance and gentlemanliness.

IV. December 1885 to April 1893

1 George Earle Buckle, editor of *The Times* 1884–1912, the co-biographer of Disraeli and editor of Queen Victoria's letters. RP 100–1/II has the initials inverted, presumably a printer's or copyist's error.

2 The first paper was presumably *Is an invasion of India by Russia possible?*, dated 31 December 1883 – see Section 3, note 25; Russia occupied Merv in February 1884. The second paper was clearly *What are Russia's vulnerable points ?*, dated 22 May 1885 – see Introduction Section 3, note 6.

3 A clear reference to Wolseley's plans – see Preston *Frustrated Great Gamesmanship*.

4 The Anglo-Russian Boundary Commission – see Section 3, note 40.

5 Major-General Sir George Byng Harman, Military Secretary at the Horse Guards 1885–92.

6 Colonel Richard Blundell-Hollinshead-Blundell, Assistant Adjutant-General at the War Office.

7 Probably Colonel Sir Baker Creed Russell, 13th Hussars.

8 Colonel George Benjamin Wolseley, Assistant Adjutant-General, Lahore Division (brother of Garnet Wolseley); Colonel Robert Grahame Elphinstone Dalrymple, 19th Hussars; Colonel Henry Augustus Bushman, 9th Lancers; Colonel John Henry Alexander, RA.

9 The Khojak route, tunnelling under the Khwaja Amran range, was chosen but the line never went beyond the Anglo-Afghan border, at Chaman. A branch line, via Nushki, along the southern border of Afghanistan, as far as the Persian border, was built in 1916–18 to support operations in South Persia – see *History of the Great War: Operations in Persia 1914–1919*, edited by Brigadier-General F.J. Moberley (1929, reprinted 1991) pp. 192–3, 253.

10 I.e. Sir Donald Stewart, Lieutenant-General Wilson, Military Member, and Theodore Cracroft Hope, Ordinary Member, of the Viceroy's Council, Brigadier-General James Browne, Chief Engineer of the Sind-Pishin Railway.

11 In January 1876 – see Roberts, op cit, II, pp. 83–4.

12 Lieutenant-General Sir Charles Reid, then commanding the Lahore Division; like Roberts a survivor of the siege and capture of Delhi in the summer of 1857.

13 Brigadier-General Richard Campbell Stewart, Madras Staff Corps; Colonel George Luck, 15th Hussars; Brigadier-General Richard James Combe Marter, commanding the Gwalior District.

14 Donald James Mackay, 11th Baron Reay, Governor of Bombay 1885–90; Sir Charles Aitchison, Lieutenant-Governor of the Punjab 1882–7.

15 Commander-in-Chief, East Indies Station 1885–8, and later First Sea Lord 1893–9.

16 Colonel Charles Knowles, Hampshire Regiment.

17 Brigadier-General Alured Clark Johnson, RA, commanding Eastern District of the Madras Army; Colonel Malcolm Charles Farrington.

18 Lieutenant Reginald Wilton Hugh Macdonald was court-martialled and dismissed the service.

19 Lieutenant-Colonel James Graham Robert Douglas Macneill, Madras Staff Corps.

20 At Minhla, on 17 November 1885, the 12th Madras Native Infantry refused to advance against some Burmese, thus confirming the low opinion of Madras troops held by Roberts – see Roberts to Brownlow, 28 December 1885 (RP 100–1/XI).

21 Sir Henry Rawlinson (1810–95). Soldier, explorer, diplomat, scholar. Member of the Council of India 1858–9, 1868–95. His book *England and Russia in the East* (1875) was very influential in calling attention to the Russian expansion towards India.

22 Colonel Sir Joseph West Ridgeway, Lumsden's successor as Chief British Commissioner on the Anglo-Russian Boundary Commission.

23 Major-General Thomas Elliott Hughes, Military Member of the Viceroy's Council 1885–6.

24 Lieutenant-Colonel Willoughby Wallace Hooper, the Provost Marshal with Prendergast's force, was a keen amateur photographer and was accused by Moylan of having delayed executions of dacoits in order to take photographs and to extract confessions – see Stewart, op cit, p. 126.

25 Brigadier-General Sir Oriel Viveash Tanner; he had commanded the 29th Bombay Native Infantry and the garrison at Khelat-i-Ghilzai in the Second Afghan War.

26 These papers are *Notes on 'Proposals for the defence of the North-West Frontier*, dated 22 June 1886 (RP 96–1/XIV), *Memorandum on a proposal of the Government of India to appoint Native gentlemen to the commissioned ranks of the Army in the same grades as European officers*, dated 29 July 1886 (RP 96–1/XVII), and *Memorandum on the desirability of making a military road through the Kohat Pass*, dated 17 August 1886 (RP 96–1/XVIII).

27 The second battalions of the 1st, 2nd, 3rd and 5th Gurkhas and the 39th

(Garwhali) Bengal Native Infantry were all formed in 1886. By the time Roberts left India in 1893, two more battalions had been formed, making 7 out of the 9 battalions authorised in 1885.

28   I.e., the army of the Sikh kingdom of the Punjab before 1849.

29   Roberts' views here are in contrast to his later position – see Document 265 and Introduction.

30   Major-General Robert Rollo Gillespie, commanding the Mhow Division of the Madras Army; a descendant of Sir Rollo Gillespie, the hero of the Vellore mutiny in 1806.

31   Colonel William Galbraith; Colonel Frederick John Keen.

32   Colonel Charles Smith Maclean, Bengal Staff Corps.

33   Colonel George Robertson Hennessey, Bengal Staff Corps.

34   Major-General David Macfarlan, commanding the Sirhind Division of the Bengal Army.

35   Colonel Alfred Robert Davidson Mackenzie, 3rd Bengal Cavalry; Colonel Henry Marsh Pratt, Bengal Staff Corps.

36   Lieutenant Lord Clandeboye, 17th Lancers, son of the Viceroy.

37   Lepel Griffin (qv), against whom Lytton clearly still had some animus as a result of a clash over the recognition of Abdurrahman in 1880.

38   Sir William Gull, the most fashionable physician of the day and doctor to the Royal family.

39   Lord Randolph Churchill resigned as Chancellor of the Exchequer in December 1886 over economies on the Army Budget. He never regained office and died of syphilis in January 1895 – see Winston Churchill, *Lord Randolph Churchill* (1906).

40   Lieutenant-General Sir James Outram (1803–63), the 'Bayard of India' and one of the heroes of the Indian Mutiny. Military Member of the Viceroy's Council 1858–60.

41   Colonel George Bruce Malleson, the historian of the Indian Mutiny, and writer on military subjects. His book, *The Russo-Afghan Question and the Invasion of India*, was published in 1885.

42   Presumably another reference to Wolseley and his circle.

43   The Right Reverend Edward Ralph Johnson, Bishop of Calcutta 1876–98.

44   The Maharajah Dhulip Singh, last ruler of the kingdom of the Punjab. Deposed after the Second Sikh War in 1849 and died in England in 1893.

45   Major David Keith Barr, late Bombay Staff Corps but transferred to the Political Service; Agent at Baghelkhund in Central India.

46   Major (later Colonel Sir) Howard Melliss, Bombay Staff Corps.

47   Captain James David Barry, RA.

48   Lieutenant Bryan Thomas Mahon, 8th Hussars. Later, a full General and Commander in Salonika 1915–6. In the upshot Barry did not resign, although he lost a year's leave, and left India on medical grounds in 1888 (see RP 100–2/LV).

49   All, significantly, members of Wolseley's 'Ring'.

50 Commanding a brigade under McQueen in the Hazara Field Force against the Black Mountain tribes.

51 An entanglement of branches or wood.

52 The Black Mountain is on the left bank of the Indus, some 60 miles due north of Rawalpindi. It is exceptionally rugged country and the tribes there gave trouble to the British throughout the nineteenth century. Roberts had some knowledge of the area from his part in the Ambeyla expedition of 1863 – see Roberts, op cit, II, pp. 1–22.

53 Colonel Edward Lacon Ommaney, late Bengal Staff Corps, Commissioner of Peshawar and attached to McQueen as Political Officer.

54 'What part should India take in the event of war between England and Russia?', dated 22 August 1888 (RP 95/XXIII).

55 Major-General Sir John Hudson, commanding a division of the Bengal Army. He had commanded the Indian Contingent at Suakin in 1885 which had included a company of Madras Sappers and Miners.

56 The Moplahs are a fanatical class of South Indian Muslims; the Kukas ('Shouters') were an extreme Sikh sect; the Wahabis an extreme Muslim sect originating in Arabia in the middle of the 19th century which had spread to India.

57 A clear misprint or error of copying for 'Hartington'.

58 Wolseley was Adjutant-General from 1882 to 1890. Despite the Hartington Committee report, no substantial change was made to the position of the Adjutant-General until 1904, following the Esher Committee's report, which brought into being a true General Staff and an Army Board.

59 A War Office civil servant acting as Stanhope's Private Secretary.

60 Friction with Portugal had arisen over rival claims to Nyasaland and Mashonaland in East Africa. The crisis subsided with the conclusion of an Anglo-Portugese Convention in August 1890 and concluded with a further Convention in June 1891 – see E.A. Axelson, *Portugal and the Scramble for Africa* (Johannesburg, 1967).

61 Some 30 miles east of Goa.

62 The difficulty was that the Queen and the Duke of Cambridge wanted the Duke of Connaught to succeed Roberts as C-in-C India, which Salisbury and the rest of the Cabinet were determined to resist, one Royal C-in-C having proved enough. The only way out was to persuade Roberts to extend his tour pro tem. Roberts himself was in favour of the Duke succeeding him.

63 Wolseley.

64 See RP 99/CCXLVIII; also RP 95/XXXIX.

65 See RP 99/CLXXIX; also RP 95/XLV.

66 Roberts believed that in the Black Mountain expedition of 1888 McQueen had failed to achieve his military objectives through excessive deference to the political views of the Punjab Government, and despite Roberts' 'prodding'. For the military details of the expedition see *Frontier and Overseas Expeditions*, I, pp. 145–167.

67 Brackenbury succeeded Chesney as Military Member of the Viceroy's Council in 1890. An original member of Wolseley's 'Ring', he was extremely clever but had little experience of India. Roberts clearly regarded some of his views as unsound and found him less congenial than Chesney and his predecessors.

68 Wolseley was widely believed to favour a Continental strategy for reasons of military ambition.

69 For the Wantage Committee of 1890, see A.R. Skelley, *The Victorian Army at Home* (1977).

70 J.J.H. Gordon, who was now Assistant Military Secretary at the War Office.

71 Sir Redvers Henry Buller (1839–1908), Adjutant-General 1890–7; Sir Henry Evelyn Wood (1838–1919), commanded the Aldershot Division 1889–93. Both former members of the 'Ring'.

72 Strachey did not live to complete the work and it was completed by Lady Betty Balfour – see Lady Betty Balfour, *The History of Lord Lytton's Indian Administration 1876–1880* (London, 1899).

73 Colonel Yanov, of the Imperial Russian Army, had arrived on the Pamirs in July 1891, with an escort of Cossacks. In August 1891 he forcibly expelled Captain Francis Younghusband, 1st King's Dragoon Guards, who was exploring there on behalf of the Indian Government. Yanov's activities led directly to the Hunza-Nagar expedition of November 1891 which extended a British protectorate over these two hitherto independent states. For a detailed, scholarly survey of events in this area, see G.J. Alder, *British India's Northern Frontier 1865–1895* (1963); for more popular treatments, see Peter Hopkirk, *The Great Game* (1990), which also has a useful bibliography on Anglo-Russo-Afghan relations in the 19th century, and John Keay, *The Gilgit Game* (1979).

74 The Mehtar (or ruler) of Chitral, Aman-ul-mulk, died in August 1892 and it is not clear whether Roberts is referring to him or to his successor, his son Afzul. Afzul was soon murdered by his uncle, setting off a bloody succession struggle. Surgeon-Major George Robertson, Political Agent at Gilgit, moved to Chitral early in 1895 to control events there and was promptly besieged until relieved on 20 April 1895. For details of the siege and its background, see, in addition to Alder, Hopkirk and Keay, Robertson's own account, *Chitral: The Story of a Minor Siege* (1898, reprinted 1991) and John Harris, *Much Sounding of Bugles: The Siege of Chitral 1895* (1975).

75 N.K. Giers, the Russian Foreign Minister.

76 The Hazaras, a people of possibly Mongol origin living in Central Afghanistan, had been in rebellion against the Amir for several years. There may have been Russian involvement but it seems unlikely.

77 Roberts succeeded Wolseley as Commander-in-Chief in Ireland in 1895, a congenial post in view of his ancestry although a backwater militarily.

Biographical Notes

Other persons mentioned in the transcripts are identified in the Notes.

Abdurrahman, the Amir (1844–1901). Son of Sher Ali's half-brother, Afzal. Fought against Sher Ali 1864–8, then exiled in Russia until 1880. Ascended throne 1880.

Ali, the Amir Sher (1820–79). Fifth son and heir of the Amir Dost Mahomed. After a bitter struggle with his half-brothers Afzal and Azim, succeeded in establishing himself as Amir in 1868. Died at Mazar-i-Sharif in February 1879, en route for Russian territory.

Arbuthnot, Charles George (1824–99). Commissioned Royal Artillery 1843. Service in Crimea 1856, Afghanistan 1879–80, Burma 1886–7. Inspector-General of Artillery, India 1878–80, Inspector General of Artillery, War Office 1883–5, President of Ordnance Committee 1885–6, C-in-C Madras Army 1886–91. Major-General 1881, KCB 1881, General 1890.

Baker, Thomas Durand (1837–93). Commissioned 18th Foot 1854. Service in Crimea 1854–6, Mutiny 1857–8, New Zealand 1864–6, Afghanistan 1879–80, Burma 1886–7. Adjutant-General India 1884–8, Allahabad Division 1887–90, Quartermaster-General War Office 1890–3. Major-General and KCB 1879.

Brackenbury, Henry (1837–1914). Commissioned Royal Artillery 1856. Service in Mutiny 1857–8, Franco-Prussian War 1870–1, Ashanti 1873–4, Zululand 1879, Sudan 1884–5. Private Secretary to Viceroy 1880, Director of Military Intelligence, War Office 1886–91, Military Member of Viceroy's Council 1891–6, President of Ordnance Board 1896–9, Director General of Ordnance 1899–1902. Major-General 1885, KCB 1894.

Bright, Robert Onesiphorus (1823–96). Commissioned 19th Foot 1843. Service in Crimea 1854–6, Hazara Expedition 1868, Afghanistan 1879–80. Meerut Division 1878–83. Major-General 1868, KCB 1881, General 1887.

Browne, Samuel James (1824–1901). Commissioned Bengal Cavalry 1840. Service in Second Sikh War 1848–9, Mutiny 1858 (VC), Afghanistan 1878–9. Military Member of Viceroy's Council 1878, Lahore Division 1879. Major-General 1870, KCSI 1876, KCB 1879, General 1888.

Brownlow, Charles Henry (1831–1916). Commissioned Bengal Infantry 1847. Service in Second Sikh War 1848–9, China 1860, Ambeyla Expedition 1863, Hazara Expedition 1868, Lushai Expedition 1871–2. Rawalpindi Brigade 1872–7, Assistant Military Secretary, War Office 1879–89. Major-General 1881, KCB 1872, General 1889, Field Marshal 1908.

Burne, Owen Tudor (1837–1909). Commissioned 20th Foot 1855. Service in Crimea 1855–6, Mutiny 1857–8. Private Secretary to Viceroy 1868–72 (Mayo) and 1876–8 (Lytton), Secretary of Political Department of India Office 1874–87, Council of India 1887–97. KCSI 1879.

Burrows, George Reynolds Scott (1827–1917). Commissioned Bombay Infantry 1844. Service in Afghanistan 1879–80. Quartermaster-General Bombay Army 1871–9.

Cambridge, George William Frederick Charles, 2nd Duke of (1819–1904). Entered British Army 1837. Service in Crimea 1854. Commander-in-Chief of British Army 1856–95. Major-General 1845, General 1856, Field Marshal 1862.

Cavagnari, Louis Napoleon (1841–1879). Commissioned Bengal Infantry 1858. Service in Mutiny 1857–9, Afghanistan 1878–9. Joined Political Service 1861, Deputy Commissioner at Kohat 1866–77, at Peshawar 1877–9, Resident at Kabul 1879. Killed at Kabul 3 September 1879.

Cecil, Robert Arthur Talbot Gascoyne, 3rd Marquess of Salisbury (1830–1903). Conservative MP for Stamford 1853–68, Under-Secretary of State for India 1866–7, Secretary of State for India 1874–8, for Foreign Affairs 1878–80, Prime Minister and Foreign Secretary 1885–6, 1886–92 (Foreign Secretary 1887–92), Prime Minister 1895–1902 (and Foreign Secretary 1895–1900, Lord Privy Seal 1900–02).

Chamberlain, Neville Bowles (1820–1902). Commissioned Bengal Infantry 1837. Service in First Afghan War 1839–42, Gwalior 1843, Second Sikh War 1848–9, Mutiny 1857–8, Ambeyla Expedition 1863. C-in-C Madras Army 1876–81. Major-General 1864, KCB 1863, General 1877, Field Marshal 1900.

Chamberlain, Neville Francis Fitzgerald (1856–1944). Commissioned 11th Foot 1873. Service in Afghanistan 1878–80, Burma 1886–7, South Africa 1899–1900, KCB 1903. Inspector-General, Royal Irish Constabulary 1900–16.

Chapman, Edward Francis (1840–1926). Commissioned Royal Artillery 1858. Service in Abyssinia 1867–8, Afghanistan 1880, Burma 1885–6. Military Secretary to C-in-C India 1881–5, Quartermaster-General India 1885–9, Director of Military Intelligence, War Office 1891–6, GOC Scotland 1896–1901. Major-General 1889, KCB 1905, General 1896.

Chesney, George Tomkyns (1830–1905). Commissioned Bengal Engineers 1848. Service in Mutiny 1857. Secretary of Military Department, India 1880–6, Military Member of Viceroy's Council 1886–91. Major-General 1886, KCB 1890, General 1893.

Childers, Hugh Culling Eardley (1827–96). Liberal MP for Pontefract 1860–85, for South Edinburgh 1886–92. First Lord of Admiralty 1868–71, Chancellor of Duchy of Lancaster 1872–3, Secretary of State for War 1880–2, Chancellor of Exchequer 1882–5, Home Secretary 1886.

Churchill, Lord Randolph (1849–95). Conservative MP for Woodstock 1874–85, for South Paddington 1885–95. Secretary of State for India 1885–6,

Chancellor of the Exchequer and Leader of the House 1886–7. Father of Sir Winston Churchill.

Collen, Edwin Henry Hayter (1843–1911). Commissioned Royal Artillery 1863. Service in Abyssinia 1867–8, Sudan 1885. Secretary of Military Department, India 1887–96, Military Member of Viceroy's Council 1896–1901. Major-General 1900. KCIE 1893.

Collett, Henry (1836–1901). Commissioned Bengal Infantry 1855. Service in Mutiny 1858–9, Assam 1862–3, Abyssinia 1867–8 Afghanistan 1878–80, Burma 1886–7, Lushai Expedition 1889–90, Manipur 1891. GOC Peshawar District 1892–3. Major-General 1892, KCB 1891.

Colley, George Pomeroy (1835–1881). Commissioned 2nd Foot 1852. Service in China 1860, Ashanti 1873–4, Zululand 1879, South Africa 1881. Professor at Staff College 1868–73, Military, and then Private, Secretary to Viceroy 1876–80, GOC Natal 1881. Major-General 1880, KCSI 1879. Killed at Majuba Hill 1881.

Connaught and Strathearn, Arthur William Patrick Albert, Duke of, (1850–1942). Commissioned Royal Engineers 1868. Service in Egypt 1882. Rawalpindi Division 1883–6, C-in-C Bombay Army 1886–90, Southern Command England 1890–3, Aldershot Command 1893–8, Irish Command 1900–4, Inspector-General of Forces 1904–7, Mediterranean Command 1907–09, Governor-General of Canada 1911–16. Major-General 1880, General 1893, Field Marshal 1902.

Cross, Richard Assheton, 1st Viscount (1823–1914). Conservative MP for Preston 1857–62, for South West Lancashire 1868–85, for Newton 1885–6. Home Secretary 1874–80 and 1885–6, Secretary of State for India 1886–92, Lord Privy Seal 1895–1900. Viscount 1886.

Dillon, Martin Andrew (1826–1913). Commissioned 98th Foot 1843. Service in Second Sikh War 1848–9, Crimea 1856, China 1860, Abyssinia 1867–8. Secretary of Military Department, India 1870–6, Assistant Military Secretary, War Office 1878–83, Lucknow, Rawalpindi Divisions 1884–8. Major-General 1878, KCB 1887, General 1892.

Dufferin and Ava, Frederick Temple-Hamilton-Temple Blackwood, 1st Marquess of, (1826–1902). Under Secretary for India 1864–6, for War 1866, Governor-General of Canada 1872–8, Ambassador to Russia 1879–81, to Turkey 1881–3, Viceroy of India 1884–8, Ambassador to Italy 1889–91, to France 1891–6. Marquess 1888.

Durand, Henry Mortimer (1850–1924). Joined Bengal Civil Service 1878. Political staff in Afghanistan 1879–80, Secretary of Foreign Department, India 1888–94, Mission to Kabul 1893, Minister at Teheran 1894–1900, Ambassador to Spain 1900–3, to USA 1903–6. KCIE 1884.

Fergusson, James, 6th Baronet (1832–1907). Commissioned Grenadier Guards 1851. Service in Crimea 1854–6. Liberal MP for Ayrshire 1857–68. Governor of South Australia 1868–73, of New Zealand 1873–5, of Bombay 1880–5,

Under Secretary for India 1860–7, for Home Affairs 1867–8, for Foreign Affairs 1886–91, Postmaster-General 1891–2.

Frere, Henry Bartle Edward (1815–84). Joined Bombay Civil Service 1834. Chief Commissioner, Sind 1850–9, Member of Viceroy's Council 1859–62, Governor of Bombay 1862–7, of the Cape 1877–80. KCB 1859.

Gordon, John James Hood (1832–1908). Commissioned 29th Foot. Service in Mutiny 1857–9, Afghanistan 1879–80, Burma 1886–7. Assistant Military Secretary, War Office 1891–6. Major-General 1886, KCB 1898. General 1898.

Gordon, Thomas Edward (1832–1914). Commissioned 4th Foot 1849. Service in Mutiny 1857–8, Afghanistan 1879. Rohilkund Brigade 1882–7, Secretary and Military Attaché, Teheran 1889–93. Major-General 1886, KCIE 1893, General 1894.

Gough, Charles John Stanley 1832–1912). Commissioned Bengal Cavalry 1848. Service in Second Sikh War 1848–9, Mutiny 1857–8 (VC), Bhutan 1864–5, Afghanistan 1879–80. Hyderabad Contingent 1881–5, Oudh Division 1885–90. KCB 1881, Major-General 1885, General 1894. Father of Sir Hubert Gough who commanded the Fifth Army in France 1916–18.

Gough, Hugh Henry (1833–1909) Commissioned Bengal Cavalry 1853. Service in Mutiny 1857–8 (VC), Abyssinia 1868, Afghanistan 1878–80. Lahore Division 1887–92. Major-General 1887, KCB 1880, General 1894.

Grant Duff, Mountstuart Elphinstone (1829–1906). Liberal MP for Elgin 1857–81. Under Secretary for India 1868–74, for Colonies 1880–1, Governor of Madras 1881–6. GCSI 1886.

Greaves, George Richards (1831–1922). Commissioned 70th Foot 1849. Service in Mutiny 1857–8, New Zealand 1860–6, Ashanti 1874. Sudan 1885. Chief Secretary, Cyprus 1878, Adjutant-General India 1879–84, Meerut Division 1885–90, C-in-C Bombay Army 1890–6. KCMG 1881, Major-General 1882, General 1896.

Griffin, Lepel Henry (1838–1908). Joined Bengal Civil Service 1860. Chief Secretary, Punjab 1870, Political Chief of Staff at Kabul, 1880, Agent to Governor-General in Central India 1881–89. KCSI 1881.

Haines, Frederick Paul (1819–1909). Commissioned 4th Foot 1839 . Service in First Sikh War 1845–6, Second Sikh War 1848–9, Crimea, 1854–6. Mysore Division 1865–70, C-in-C Madras Army 1871–5, C-in-C India 1876–81. Major-General 1864, KCB 1871, General 1877, Field Marshal 1890.

Hamilton, Ian Standish Monteith (1853–1947). Commissioned 12th Foot 1872. Service in Natal 1881, Sudan 1884–5, Burma 1886–7, South Africa 1899–1901. Southern Command UK 1905–9, Adjutant-General, War Office 1909–10, Mediterranean Command 1910–15, Gallipoli Expedition 1915. Major-General 1899, KCB 1900, General 1907.

Hardinge, Arthur Edward (1828–1892). Commissioned 41st Foot 1844. Service in First Sikh War 1845–6, Crimea 1854–5. Allahabad Division 1873, Meerut Division 1873–8, C-in-C Bombay Army 1881–5, Governor of Gibraltar 1886–90. Major-General 1871, KCB 1886, General 1883.

Hills(-Johnes), James ('Jemmy') (1833–1901). Commissioned Bengal Artillery
1853. Service in Mutiny 1857–8 (VC), Abyssinia 1868, Lushai Expedition
1871–2, Afghanistan 1878–80, Major-General 1879, KCB 1881.

Johnson, Allen Bayard (1829–1907). Commissioned Bengal Infantry 1846.
Service in Second Burma War 1853, Mutiny 1857–8. Military Secretary,
India Office 1877–89. Major-General 1888, KCB 1889, General 1892.
Brother of C.C. Johnson (q.v.)

Johnson, Charles Cooper (1829–1907). Commissioned Bengal Infantry 1844.
Service in First Sikh War 1846, Mutiny 1857–8, Hazara Expedition 1868.
Quartermaster-General India 1878–80. Major-General 1878, KCB 1881.

Johnson, Edwin Beaumont (1825–93). Brother of Allen and Charles Johnson
(qv). Commissioned Bengal Artillery 1842. Service in First Sikh War 1845–6,
Mutiny 1857–8. Quartermaster-General India 1873–4, Adjutant-General
India 1874–7, Member of Council of India 1874–7, Military Member of
Viceroy's Council 1877–80. Director General Army Education at War Office
1884–6. Major-General 1868, KCB 1875, General 1877.

Khan, Ayub (1855–1914). Fourth son of the Amir Sher Ali. Appointed Governor
of Herat by his brother, the Amir Yakub Khan (q.v.), in 1879. Marched on
Kandahar in June 1880, defeated British brigade at Maiwand and besieged
Kandahar. Defeated by Roberts on 1 September 1880 and retired to Herat.
Occupied Kandahar in July 1881 but defeated by Abdurrahman in September
1881. Pensioner in India from 1884 to 1914, dying at Lahore.

Khan, the Amir Yakub (1849–1923). Third son of the Amir Sher Ali. Succeeded
as Amir in February 1879 and abdicated in October the same year. State prisoner in India until his death at Mussoorie in 1923.

Lansdowne, Henry Charles Keith Petty Fitzmaurice, 5th Marquess of, (1845–
1927). Under Secretary of War 1872–4, of India 1880, Governor-General of
Canada 1883–8, Viceroy of India 1888–94, Secretary of State for War
1895–1900, for Foreign Affairs 1900–5.

Lumsden, Peter Stark (1829–1918). Commissioned Bengal Infantry 1847.
Service in Mutiny 1857–8, China 1860, Bhutan 1865. Quartermaster-General
India 1868–73, Adjutant-General India 1874–9, Chief of Staff India 1879,
British Head of Afghan Boundary Commission 1884–5, Member of Council
of India 1883–93. Major-General 1881, KCB 1879, General 1890.

Lyall, Alfred Comyn (1835–1911). Joined Bengal Civil Service 1856. Service in
Mutiny 1857–8. Agent to Governor-General in Rajputana 1874–8,
Secretary in Foreign Department 1878–81, Lieutenant-Governor of North
West Provinces 1882–7, Member of Council of India 1887–1902. KCB
1881.

Lytton, Edward Robert Bulwer, 1st Earl of, (1831–91). Diplomatic Service
1849–72, Minister to Portugal 1872–76, Viceroy of India 1876–80,
Ambassador to France 1887–91. Earl 1880.

Macgregor, Charles Metcalfe (1840–87). Commissioned Bengal Infantry 1857.
Service in Mutiny 1857–9, China 1860, Bhutan 1864–5, Abyssinia 1878–80.

Quartermaster-General India 1881–85, Punjab Frontier Force 1885–87. KCB 1880, Major-General 1881.

Macpherson, Herbert Taylor (1827–86). Commissioned Bombay Infantry 1845. Service in Persia 1856, Mutiny 1857–8 (VC), Lushai Expedition 1871–2, Afghanistan 1879–80, Egypt 1882, Burma 1886. C-in-C Madras Army 1885–6. Major-General 1882, KCB 1880, General 1885.

Massy, William Godfrey Dunham Massy (1838–1906). Commissioned 19th Foot 1854. Service in Crimea 1854–6 (VC), Afghanistan 1879–80, Gwalior Brigade 1879–84, GOC Ceylon 1888–93. Major-General 1886.

McQueen, John Withers (1836–1909). Commissioned Bengal Infantry 1854. Service in Mutiny 1857–8, Jowaki Expedition 1877–8, Second Afghan War, Black Mountain Expedition 1888. Commanded Hyderabad Contingent 1885–6, PFF 1886–90. KCB 1888, Major-General 1891, Lieutenant-General 1895.

Napier, Robert Cornelis, 1st Baron Napier of Magdala, (1810–1890). Commissioned Bengal Engineers 1826. Service in First Sikh War 1845–6, Second Sikh War 1848–9, Mutiny 1857–9, China 1860, Abyssinia 1867–8. Military Member of Viceroy's Council 1861–5, C-in-C Bombay Army 1865–8, C-in-C India 1870–6, Governor of Gibraltar 1876–83. Major-General 1861, KCB 1859, General 1874, Field Marshal 1883. Baron 1868.

Newmarch, Oliver Richardson (1834–1920). Commissioned Bengal Infantry 1855. Service in Mutiny 1857–8. Accountant-General Military Department India 1878–86, Secretary in Military Department 1886–7, Military Secretary, India Office 1889–99. Major-General 1887, KCSI 1894.

Norman, Henry Wylie (1826–1904). Commissioned Bengal Infantry 1844. Service in Second Sikh War 1848–9, Mutiny 1857–9. Military Member of Viceroy's Council 1870–7, Member of Council of India 1880–3, Governor of Jamaica 1883–9, of Queensland 1889–95. Major-General 1869, KCB 1873, General 1882, Field Marshal 1902.

Phayre, Robert (1820–97). Commissioned Bombay Infantry 1839. Service in First Afghan War 1839–42, Sind 1844, Persia 1856, Mutiny 1857–8, Afghanistan 1879–80. Mhow Division 1881–6. Major-General 1879, KCB 1880, General 1889.

Pretyman, George Tindal (1845–1917). Commissioned Royal Artillery 1865. Service in Afghanistan 1878–80, South Africa 1899–1900. Military Secretary, Madras 1881–4, Military Secretary, Bloemfontein 1900, of Kimberley District 1901, GOC Secunderabad District 1902–3, Commander of Forces in Madras 1904, Burma Division 1906–7. Major-General 1897, KCMG 1900.

Primrose, James Maurice (1819–92). Commissioned 43rd Foot 1837. Service in South Africa 1851–2, Mutiny 1858, Afghanistan 1879–80. Poona Division 1878–80. Major-General 1868.

Ripon, George Frederick Samuel Robinson, 1st Marquess of, (1827–1909). MP 1852–9. Under Secretary of State for War 1859–61, for India 1866–8, Lord President of Council 1868–73, Viceroy of India 1880–6, First Lord of

Admiralty 1886, Secretary of State for Colonies 1894–5, Lord Privy Seal 1905–8.

Roberts, Abraham (1784–1873). Commissioned Waterford Militia 1801, 48th Foot 1803, Bengal Infantry 1804. Service in Second Maratha War 1805, First Afghan War 1838–40. Punjab, and then Peshawar, Division 1852–4. Major-General 1852, KCB 1865, General 1864.

Roberts, Ada Edwina Stewart, 3rd Countess (1875–1955). Second daughter of Frederick Sleigh Roberts (qv). Married Henry Lewin (later Brigadier-General, Royal Artillery) 1913. One child, Frederick, killed in Norway 1940.

Roberts, Aileen Mary, 2nd Countess (1870–1944). Elder daughter of Frederick Sleigh Roberts. Unmarried.

Roberts, Frederick Sleigh, 1st Earl, of Kandahar (1832–1914). Commissioned Bengal Artillery 1851. Service in Mutiny 1857–8 (VC), Ambeyla Expedition 1863, Abyssinia 1867–8, Lushai Expedition 1871–2, Afghanistan 1878–80, Burma 1886–7, South Africa 1899–1900. C-in-C Madras Army 1881–5, C-in-C India 1885–93, Irish Command 1895–9, C-in-C South Africa 1899–1900, C-in-C British Army 1901–04. Major-General 1878, KCB 1879, General 1885, Field Marshal 1895, Baron 1892, Earl 1901.

Ross, John (1829–1905). Commissioned Rifle Brigade 1846. Service in Mutiny 1857–8, Perak 1875–6, Afghanistan 1879–80. Poona Division 1881–6, GOC Canada 1888–93. Major-General 1877, KCB 1881, General 1891.

St John, Oliver Beauchamp Coventry (1837–91). Commissioned Bengal Engineers 1856. Service in Abyssinia 1867–8, Afghanistan 1878–80. Political Officer at Kandahar 1878–80, Resident in Kashmir 1883–6, in Baroda 1887–91, Agent to Governor-General in Baluchistan 1891. KCSI 1882.

Sandeman, Robert Groves (1835–92). Commissioned Bengal Infantry 1856. Service in Mutiny 1857–8. Civil employment in Punjab 1859–77, Agent to Governor-General in Baluchistan 1877–92. KCSI 1879.

Stanhope, Edward (1840–93). Conservative MP for Mid-Lincolnshire 1874–85, for Horncastle Division 1885–93. Under-Secretary of State for India 1878–80, President of Board of Trade 1885, Secretary of State for Colonies 1886–7, Secretary of State for War 1887–92.

Stewart, Donald Martin (1824–1900). Commissioned Bengal Infantry 1840. Service in Mutiny 1857–8, Abyssinia 1867–8, Afghanistan 1878–80. Chief Commissioner, Andaman Islands 1871–5, GOC Lahore Division 1875–8, C-in-C India 1881–5, Member of Council of India 1885–1900. Major-General 1876, KCB 1879, General 1881, Field Marshal 1894.

Thibaw (?1858–1916). Ruler of the Kingdom of Ava and Lord of the White Elephants 1878–85. Deposed by British and died in exile in India.

Vaughan, John Luther (1820–1911). Commissioned Bengal Infantry 1840. Service in Gwalior 1843, Crimea 1855–6, Mutiny 1857–8, Ambeyla Campaign 1863, Afghanistan (as war correspondent) 1879–80. Major-General 1870, KCB 1884.

Watson, John (1829–1919). Commissioned Bombay Infantry 1848. Service in

Second Sikh War 1848–9, Mutiny 1857–8, Afghanistan 1879–80. Commanded Indian Contingent in Malta 1878, Resident at Baroda 1882–8. Major-General 1881, KCB 1886. General 1891.

White, George Stuart (1835–1912). Commissioned 27th Foot 1853. Service in Mutiny 1857–8, Afghanistan (VC) 1878–80, Egypt 1884–5, Burma 1885–9, South Africa 1899–1900. C-in-C India 1893–7, Quartermaster-General War Office 1897–9, GOC Natal 1899–1900, Governor of Gibraltar 1901–5. Major-General 1889, KCB 1886, General 1893, Field Marshal 1902.

Wolseley, Garnet Joseph, 1st Viscount (1833–1913). Commissioned 12th Foot 1852. Service in Second Burma War 1852–3, Crimea 1854–6, Mutiny 1857–8, China 1860, Red River Expedition 1870, Ashanti 1873–4, Zululand 1879–80. Egypt 1882, Sudan 1884–5. Quartermaster-General War Office 1881–2, Adjutant-General 1882–90, Irish Command 1890–5, C-in-C British Army 1895–9. Major-General 1874, KCB 1874, General 1882, Viscount 1885, Field Marshal 1885.

Bibliography

1 Manuscript sources

Centre for Kentish Studies, Maidstone
U 1590/0305/1–2 papers of Edward Stanhope.

Duke University, North Carolina, William R. Perkins Library
7–21–72 letters from Roberts to publishers.
7–1–61 two letters, to Charles Macgregor and Sir John Strachey.

India Office Library and Records
MSS Eur D 567 papers of Sir Thomas Baker.
　　　　　D 727 papers of Sir Henry Mortimer Durand.
　　　　　D 734 papers of Sir Denis Fitzpatrick.
　　　　　D 951 papers of Sir Owen Tudor Burne.
　　　　　D 958 papers of 5th Marquess of Lansdowne.
　　　　　E 218/1–174 papers of 1st Earl of Lytton.
　　　　　E 243 papers of 1st Viscount Cross.
　　　　　F 108 papers of Field Marshal Sir George White.
　　　　　F 114 papers of 1st Baron Napier of Magdala.
　　　　　F 127 papers of the Strachey family.
　　　　　F 130 printed copies of papers of 1st Marquess of Dufferin and Ava.
　　　　　F 132 papers of Sir Alfred and Sir John Lyall.

National Army Museum
(Roberts papers) 7101–23/7, 10, 12, 14, 15, 26, 31, 34, 37, 38, 44, 46, 49, 51, 57,
　　　　　63, 65, 78, 80, 82, 84, 90, 92, 95, 96, 97, 98, 99, 100, 101, 103,
　　　　　139, 148, 149, 150, 154, 158, 160, 161, 162, 163, 164, 167, 168,
　　　　　225, 227
(Haines papers) 8108–9/1, 29, 34, 38
(Baker papers) 7804–76

National Museum of Scotland
I.A. 886.1 letters from Roberts to Macgregor and Lady Macgregor 1885–1891.

Royal Archives, Windsor
Add MSS E/1 letters from Roberts to Duke of Cambridge 1879–93.

Royal Commonwealth Society Library
Childers MSS 5/1–228

2 Official publications and works of reference

Army Lists 1876–93.

Bengal Army Lists 1876–93.

Buckland, C.E., *Dictionary of Indian Biography* (1906).

Cardew, Lieutenant F.G (ed.), *The Second Afghan War.* Compiled by and under the orders of Major-General Sir C.M. MacGregor. Abridged and re-edited in the Intelligence Branch of the Quartermaster-General's Branch, Simla. (2 vols., Calcutta, 1897).

[*Eden Commission*] Report of the Special Commission appointed by His Excellency the Governor-General in Council to enquire into the Organisation and Expenditure of the Army in India (1 vol. and 4 vols. of appendices, Simla, 1879).

History of the Third Burmese War (6 vols. and 3 vols. of indices, Calcutta and Simla, 1887–94).

Leverson, Lieutenant J.J. (trans.), *The Siege and Assault of Denghil-Tepe – General Skoboleff's report* (War Office, 1887).

Mason, Captain A.H., *Expedition against the Black Mountain tribes under Major General John Withers McQueen in 1888* (Simla, 1889).

Farrington, Anthony, *Guide to the records of the India Office Military Department* (1982).

Frontier and Overseas Expeditions from India
 I Tribes north of the Kabul River (Simla, 1907)
 II North West Frontier Tribes between the Kabul and Gumal Rivers (Simla, 1908)
 V Burma (Simla, 1907).

[*Hartington Committee*] Report of the Royal Commission on the Civil and Professional Administration of the Naval and Military Departments (C5979, 1890).

Hodgson, Major V.C.P., *List of the officers of the Bengal Army 1758– 1834* (4 vols., 1927–47).

Indian Army List (New Series) 1891–94.

India Office List, The, 1876–1893.

MacGregor, Major-General Sir Charles, *The Second Afghan War.*
 Compiled and Collated by and under the Orders of Major-General Sir C.M. MacGregor, KCB, CSI., CIE., Quartermaster-General in India (6 vols., Simla, 1885).

Madras Army Lists 1882–85.

Oliver, S.P. (ed.) *The Second Afghan War 1878–80.* Abridged. *Official History* (1908)

Parliamentary Papers

1878/9, LVI, Copy of the report of Major-General Roberts on the operations in the Khost Valley in January 1879.

1878/9, LVI (East India (Khost Valley)) Copy of papers relating to the proceedings of Major General Roberts in the Khost Valley on the 7th and 8th days of January 1879.

1878/9, LVI Address of Major-General Roberts to the chiefs of Kurram on the 26th December 1878.

1878/9, LVI Despatch from the Government of India, No. 136 of 1879, forwarding treaty of peace (C2362).

1880, LIII Afghanistan (1880) No. 1 Correspondence relative to the affairs of Afghanistan (C2457).

1880, LIII Despatch from the Government of India (with report from Lieutenant-General Sir F.S. Roberts (C2523).

1880, LIII Afghanistan (1880) No. 2 Papers relating to the advance of Ayoob Khan on Kandahar (C2690).

Short report on the important questions dealt with during the tenure of command of the Army in India by General Lord Roberts 1885–1893 (Simla, 1893)

[*Wantage Committee*] Report of the Committee appointed by the Secretary of State to consider the Terms and Conditions of Service in the Army (C5979, 1892).

3 Biographies and memoirs

(all books published in London unless noted otherwise)

Balfour, Countess of (ed), *Personal and Literary Letters of Robert, First Earl of Lytton* (2 vols., 1906)

Cecil, Lady Gwendolen, *The Life of Robert, Marquis of Salisbury 1830–1902* (4 vols., 1921–32).

Durand, Sir H.M., *Alfred Lyall* (Edinburgh and London, 1913);
– *The Life of Field Marshal Sir George White VC* (2 vols., 1915).

Edwards-Stuart, Ivor, *A John Company General. The Life of Sir Abraham Roberts* (Bognor Regis, 1983)

Elsmie, G.R., *Field Marshal Sir Donald Stewart, G.C.B., G.C.S.I. C.I.E. An Account of His Life, Mainly in His Own Words* (1903)

Gordon, T.E., *A Varied Life* (1906).

James, David, *Lord Roberts* (1954).

Khan, Sultan Mahomed, *The Life of Abdur Rahman* (2 vols., 1900).

Lehman, Joseph E., *All Sir Garnet. A life of Field Marshal Lord Wolseley* (1964)

Lutyens, Mary, *The Lyttons in India. An Account of Lord Lytton's Viceroyalty 1876–1880* (1979).

Lyall, Sir A., *The Life of the Marquis of Dufferin and Ava* (2 vols., 1905).

MacGregor, Lady(ed), *The Life and Opinions of Major-General Sir Charles Metcalfe MacGregor, K.C.B., C.S.I., C.I.E., Quartermaster-General in India* (2 vols., Edinburgh and London, 1888).

Roberts, Field Marshal Earl, *Forty-One Years in India, from Subaltern to Commander-in-Chief* (2 vols., 1897).

Trousdale, W. (ed), *War in Afghanistan: The Personal Diary of Major-General Sir Charles Metcalfe MacGregor* (Detroit, 1985).

Vibart, H.M., *The life of General Sir Harry N.D. Prendergast (The Happy Warrior)* (1914).

Wolf, Lucien, *The Marquess of Ripon* (2 vols., 1921).

4 Secondary works

Afghan Committee. The Causes of the Afghan War, being a selection of the papers laid before Parliament, with a connecting narrative and commentary (1879).

Alder, G.J., *British India's Northern Frontier 1865–95* (1963).

Anglesey, Marquess of, *A History of the British Cavalry 1816–1919 Vol. 4 (1899–1913)* (1986).

Balfour, Countess of, *The History of Lord Lytton's Indian Administration 1876–1880* (1899).

Becker, S., *Russia's Protectorates in Central Asia. Bokhara and Khiva, 1865–1942* (Cambridge, Mass., 1968).

Bence-Jones, Mark, *Palaces of the Raj* (1973).

Berridge, P.S.A., *Couplings to the Khyber* (Newton Abbott, 1969).

Bonarjee, P, *History of the Military Department of the Government of India* (Calcutta, 1905).

Caroe, Sir Olaf, *The Pathans 550 BC – 1957 AD* (1958).

Chakravarty, S., *From Khyber to Oxus. A Study of Imperial Expansion* (New Delhi, 1976).

Chavda, V.K., *India, Britain, Russia. A Study in British Opinion 1838–1878* (New Delhi, 1967).

Coen, Terence Creagh, *The Indian Political Service. A Study in Indirect Rule* (1971).

Collen, Lieutenant-General Sir Edward, *The Indian Army; a sketch of its history and organisation* (Oxford, 1907).

Crosthwaite, C.E., The Pacification of Burma (1968).

Curzon, George, Marquess, of Kedleston, *Tales of Travel* (1923).

Davies, C.C., *The Problem of the North West Frontier 1890–1908. With a Survey of Policy since 1849* (Cambridge, 1932).

Edwards, H. Sutherland, *Russian Projects against India, from Czar Peter to General Skoboleff* (1885).

Elliott, Major-General J.G., *The Frontier 1839–1947* (1968).

Geyer, Dietrich, *Russian Imperialism. The Interaction of Domestic and Foreign Policy 1860–1913* (Leamington Spa, 1987).

Gopal, S., *The Viceroyalty of Lord Ripon 1880–84* (Cambridge, 1963).

– *British Policy in India 1858–1905* (1965).

Graham, Brigadier-General C.A.L., *The History of the Indian Mountain Artillery* (Aldershot, 1957).

Greaves, R.L., *Persia and the Defence of India 1884–1892* (1959).

Gregson, the Reverend J.G., *Through the Khyber Pass to Sherpore Camp, Cabul. An Account of Temperance Work among our Soldiers in the Cabul Field Force* (1883).

Gregorian, Vartan, *The Emergence of Modern Afghanistan: Politics of Reform and Modernisation* (Stanford, Ca., 1969).

Hanna, Colonel H.B., *The Second Afghan War 1878–1879–1880* (3 vols., 1899–1910).

Harris, John, *Much Blowing of Bugles. The Siege of Chitral 1895* (1975).

Harrison, Frederick, *Martial Law at Kabul* (1880).

Heathcote, T.A., *The Indian Army: The garrison of British Imperial India 1822–1922* (1979).

Hirschman, Edwin Alan, *White Mutiny* (New Delhi, 1980).

Holdich, Sir Thomas, *The Indian Borderland 1880–1900* (1901).

Hopkirk, Peter, *The Great Game. On Secret Service in High Asia* (1990).

Hoskins, H.L., *British Routes to India* (New York, 1928).

Keay, John, *The Gilgit Game* (1979).

Kennedy, A.L.. *Salisbury 1830–1903. Portrait of a Statesman* (1953).

MacGregor, Sir Charles, *The Defence of India* (Simla, 1884).

Malleson, Colonel George Bruce, *The Russo-Afghan Question and the Invasion of India* (1885).

Marvin, Charles, *The Railway Route to Herat* (1885).

Mason, Philip, *A Matter of Honour. An Account of the Indian Army* (1974).

Maxwell, Leigh, *My God – Maiwand! Operations of the South Afghanistan Field Force 1878–80* (1979).

Misra, B.B., *The Administrative History of India 1834–1947. General Administration* (Bombay, 1970).

– *The Bureaucracy in India. An Historical Analysis of Development up to 1947* (New Delhi, 1977).

Morgan, Gerald, *Ney Elias. Explorer and Envoy Extraordinary* (1971).

Moulton, E.C., *Lord Northbrook's Indian Administration 1872–1876* (1968).

Norris, J.A., *The First Afghan War 1838–1842* (Cambridge, 1967).

Phillips, C.H. (ed.), *Handbook of Oriental History* (1951).

Robertson, Sir George, *Chitral, The Story of a Minor Siege* (1898).

Robson, Brian, *The Road to Kabul. The Second Afghan War 1878–1881* (1986).

Seton-Watson, Hugh *The Russian Empire 1801–1917* (Oxford, 1967).

Shadbolt, S.H., *The Afghan Campaigns of 1878–80. Compiled from Official and Private Sources* (2 vols. 1882).

Sidebottom, J.K., *The Overland Mail. A Postal Historical Study of the Mail Route to India* (1948).

Singhal, D.P., *India and Afghanistan 1876–1907* (Queensland, 1963).

Skelly, A.R., *The Victorian Army at Home* (1977).

Skennerton, Ian, *The Service Lee: the Lee-Metford and Lee-Enfield rifles and carbines 1880–1980* (1980).

Spiers, Edward, *Army and Society 1815–1914* (1980).

– *The Late Victorian Army* (Manchester, 1992)

Stewart, A.T.Q., *The Pagoda War. Lord Dufferin and the fall of the Kingdom of Ava 1885–6* (1972).

Tylden, Major G., *Horses and Saddlery: an account of the animals used by the British and Commonwealth armies from the 17th century to the present, with a description of their equipment* (1961).

Wheeler, Geoffrey, *The Modern History of Soviet Central Asia* (1964).

Yapp, Michael, *Strategies of British India. Britain, Iran and Afghanistan* (Oxford, 1980).

Yavorski, Dr I.L., *Journey of the Russian Embassy through Afghanistan and the Khanate of Bukhara in 1878–79* (trans. Calcutta, 1885).

5 Articles

Bulletin of the Institute for Historical Research
Beckett, Ian, 'The Stanhope Memorandum of 1888: a Reinterpretation' (LVII (1984) pp. 240–7).

English Historical Review
Cowling, Maurice, 'Lytton, the Cabinet and the Russians, August to November 1878' (LXXVI (1961) pp. 59–79).

Historical Journal
Preston, Adrian 'Sir Charles MacGregor and the Defence of India' (XII (1969) pp. 58–77).

International History Review
Preston, Adrian 'Frustrated Great Gamesmanship: Sir Garnet Wolseley's Plans for War against Russia 1873–1880' (II (1980) pp. 239–65).

Williams, Beryl 'Approach to the Second Afghan War: Central Asia during the Great Eastern Crisis 1875–78' (II (1980) pp. 216–38).

Journal of Asian History
Klein, Ira, 'Who Made the Second Afghan War?' (VIII (1974) pp. 97–121).

Journal of Imperial and Commonwealth History
Preston, Adrian 'Wolseley, the Khartoum Relief Expedition and the Defence of India 1885–1900' (VI (1977–8) pp. 254–80).

Journal of the Society for Army Historical Research
Barthorpe, Michael, 'The Battle of Tofrek 1885' (Vol. LXIII (1985) pp. 1–10).

Robson, Brian 'The Eden Commission and the reform of the Indian Army 1879–95 (LX (1982) pp. 4–13).
– 'Changes in the Indian Army 1882–93' (LXX (1992) pp. 126–7
– 'The Kandahar Letters of the Reverend Alfred Cane' (LXIX (1991) pp. 146–60, 206–20).
Spiers, Edward, 'The British Cavalry 1902–1914 (LVI (1979) pp. 71–79).
National Army Museum Annual Reports
Rice, Elizabeth Talbot, 'Imperial Service Troops 1888–1920' (1979–80).
Wood, Stephen, 'The Other Half: further developments in the history of British military temperance movements' (1986).
Victorian Studies
Bond, Brian, 'Recruiting the Victorian Armies 1870–92' (V (1962) pp. 331– 38).

Index

(Ranks are those held on last mention)

Monro, Lt. S.C.H., 212, 436 n.66
Moplahs, 393, 447 n.56
Morale
  at Kandahar, 220–2, 437 n.72
  affected by active service, 261
Morgan, Capt. H.R.L., 51, 427 n.40
Morton, Col. G. de C., 287, 439 n.2
Mounted Infantry
  R. forms corps at Kabul, 161–2
  role of cavalry as, 329, 332, 443 n.9
Mulk, Aman-ul-, 448 n.74
Mullahs, 60, 68, 90
Murray, Capt. A.R., 212, 436 n.66
Muserzais (tribe), 96, 103
Musketry
  need to improve, 230, 313
  new syllabus for, 403
Mustaufi, the (see Khan, Habibullah)

Napier, Fd. Marshal Lord, of Magdala, 6, 58, 169, 231, 246, 253, 309, 326, 412, 454
Newspapers
  Bombay Gazette, 49
  Civil and Military Gazette, 76, 136, 172
  Daily News, 157
  Daily Telegraph, 93
  Englishman, 71
  Pall Mall Gazette, 317
  Pioneer, 172
  Standard, 58, 61, 64, 76, 81, 92, 137, 434 n.23
  Times, 85, 93, 95, 133, 331
  Times of India, 47
Newspaper correspondents, 18
  instructions for, 17
  R.'s use of, xix, 284–5, 331–2, 384
Nordenfeldt (see under Guns)
Norman, Brig.-Gen. F., 355
Norman, General Sir H., 8, 182, 267, 425 n.5, 439 n.14, 454
Northbrook, 1st Earl of, 2, 300
Nott, Maj.-Gen. Sir W., 140, 434 n.25
Nugent, Capt. N.J.N., 287, 441 n.33
Nushki, 335, 444 n.9
Nuttall, Brig.-Gen. T., 222

Ommaney, Col. E.L., 391, 447 n.53
Ootacamund, 225
  R. moves HQ to, 231, 301–4, 309
Outram, Lt.-Gen. Sir J., 372, 446 n.40
Oudh, 364
Oxus (Amu-Darya) River, xv, 1

Palmer, Maj. A.P., 78, 428 n.63
Pamirs, xvi, 328, 416–18
Parker, Lt.-Col. G.H., 104, 430 n.90
Parry, Maj. S., 68, 428 n.50
Passes
  Altamur, 102
  Bolan, xviii, 344
  Darwazgai, 52
  Gomal, xviii, 328, 441 n.42
  Khyber, 111
  Khojak, 15, 334
  Kohat, 347
  Lakarai, 101
  Spingawi, 41
  Zurmat, 21
Pathans (race), 34, 36, 41–2, 197
Paul, Lt.-Col. M.C., 266, 439 n.13
Paul, Maj.-Gen. T.H., 266, 439 n.13
Payn, Lt.-Gen. W., 241, 439 n.5
Peiwar Kotal (pass), 4, 65
Pelly, Sir L., 3, 8, 425 n.4
Perkins, Maj.-Gen. Aeneas, 69, 428 n.52
Persia, 11–13, 392, 444 n.9
Peshawar, 8, 183
Phayre, Maj.-Gen. R., 115, 223, 226, 432 n.16, 454
Picot, Lt. H.P., 42, 427 n.37
Pinjore, gardens at, 184, 436 n.52
Pir, Hazar, 39, 47, 52–3, 55, 59
Pishin, 75, 217, 296, 323, 339, 424 n.15
Pollock, Maj.-Gen. G., 196, 436 n.54
Portugal, friction with, 396, 447 n.60
Pottinger, Maj. Eldred, 140, 434 n.25

Powell, Capt. C.G., 39, 427 n.36
Pratt, Col. H.M., 356, 446 n.35
Prendergast, Maj.-Gen. H.N., 286,
327, 339, 341
occupies Mandalay 1885, 343
R.'s assessment of, 343
Preston, Capt. A.T., 119, 433 n.5
Pretyman, Lt.-Col. G.A., 64, 92–3, 454
Primrose, Lt.-Gen. J.M., 208, 210,
220–2, 226, 454
Punjab
Frontier Force, xiv, 3, 213
Maharaja of, 378, 446 n.44
Sikh Kingdom of, 349

Quartermaster-General (British Army),
xix, 230, 234–8, 239–41
Quartermaster-General India, xii, 4, 76
Quetta, 16, 75, 218, 296, 339, 344

Races, martial, xvii, 258–9, 263–6, 328,
352–3, 437 n.73
Radical Party, 158, 339, 341, 353, 369,
408
Railways
to Kandahar, xviii, 296, 323, 328,
334, 344–6, 444 n.9
through Khyber, xviii
on NW Frontier, xviii, 422 n.14, 443
n.5
Rawalpindi, 104
Rawlins, Lt.-Col. A.M., 287, 440 n.30
Rawlinson, Sir H., 300, 445 n.21
Reay, 11th Baron, 336, 445 n.14
Reid, Lt.-Gen. Sir C., 335, 445 n.12
Rennick, Capt. R.H.F, 54, 71, 76, 81,
84, 104, 106, 427 n.43.
Reviews
Fortnightly, 164, 181, 375
Nineteenth Century, 284, 307, 415
Quarterly, 284
World, 384
Richards, Admiral Sir F., 337, 445
n.15

Ridgeway, Col. Sir J., 290, 340, 445
n.22
Ripon, Marquess of, 193, 213, 226,
296, 326, 454
Robat, 220
Roberts, Gen. Sir Abraham, xii
Roberts Gen. Lord (Frederick Sleigh),
455; early career, xi–xii; Lytton's
patronage, 1, 2, 3, 413; takes
command of Kurram force, 20;
occupies Kurram, 4; leads expedition to Khost, 79, 85; accusa-
tions of cruelty against, 50, 55,
82, 86, 230; expels war correspondent, 61–4; appointed to
Eden Commission, 102, 242;
takes command of Kabul force,
111; receives Lytton's instructions, 112, 119, 123, 127, 131;
occupies Kabul, 112, 128–9; sets
up Military Commission, 112–13,
133, 166; views on political scene,
144, 154–6, 202; besieged but
defeats attackers, 112, 147, 156;
secures Massy's removal, 169–70;
170; attacked over executions,
148, 154, 432 n.9, 435 n.39; relations with Griffin, 114, 151, 182;
resents Stewart's role, 114,
186–7, 191–2, 195, 202; appointed to Kandahar relief force, 115,
205–06; defeats Ayub, 212, 216,
219; on morale at Kandahar,
220–2, 437 n.72; made C-in-C
Madras, 115, 217, 225; speech on
Army reform, 229, 279, 409, 438
n.1; views on short-service, xix,
229, 232–3, 277–9, 295–6,
408–10, 413–16; rivalry with
Wolseley, xviii, 229, 284, 409–10,
422 n.17; appointed to
Transvaal, 229; offered post of
Quartermaster-General, 230,
234–8, 240–1; views on Madras

Singh, the Maharaja Dhulip, 378, 446 n.44
Skobolev, Maj.-Gen. M.K., xvi, 298, 441 n.44
Slater, Maj. J.B., 212, 436 n.66
Smith, Lt. Manners, 118, 126
Smith, Lt.-Col. G., 266, 439 n.13
Smith, Maj. C.B. Euan, 227, 438 n.78
Spratt, Capt. F.J.N., 109, 430 n.99
Spingawi (Kotal, pass), 41
Stanhope, Edward, MP, 82, 152, 180–1, 277, 301, 394, 398, 402, 413, 419–20, 429 n.68, 455
Stewart, Fd. Marshal Sir D., 100, 103, 114, 179, 181–2, 185, 195, 202, 205, 217, 226, 233, 246, 254, 284, 300, 324–5, 335, 349, 432 n.15, 455
Stewart, Lt. Donald, 212, 436 n.66
Stewart, Maj.G., 101, 429 n.85
Stewart, Maj.J.C., 51, 86, 427 n.42
Stewart, Brig.-Gen. R.C., 336, 355, 445 n.13
Stewart, Capt. R.M., 118, 433 n.4
Stirling, Lt.-Col. W., 68, 428 n.50
Strachey, Sir J., 412
Strachey, Maj.-Gen. Sir R., 267, 439 n.14
Strahan, Capt. C., 101, 429 n.85
Straton, Capt. E., 212, 436 n.66
Sudan, 297
  Graham's expeditions 1884, 296, 307, 441 n.50
  1885, 232
  Wolseley's expedition 1884–5, 316
Suez Canal, 11, 259, 262
Suiya, 96
Suzeereh (see Cizre)
Swinley, Lt.-Col. G., 51, 287, 427 n.40, 441 n.34

Tank (place), 108, 430 n.97
Tanner, Brig.-Gen. Sir O.V., 344, 445 n.25

Taylor, Maj.-Gen. A., 8, 425 n.5
Tehsildar, xxvi, 38
Telegraph, electric, 50, 109
Tel-el-Kebir, action at, 1882, 232, 438 n.8
Temperance, 233, 299–300, 329, 376
Tepe, Geok, 298, 441 n.44
Tezin, 94
Thal, 6
Thelwall, Brig.-Gen J.B., 35, 37–8, 42, 52, 55, 65, 69, 426 n.28
Thornton, T.H., 8, 425 n.5
Tigris, River, 9
Tofrek, action at, 1885, 232, 317, 442 n.56
Toungoo, 238, 439 n.3
Transvaal, 229
Tribes
  Achakzais, 224, 437 n.76
  Bangash, 33, 426 n.22
  Chakmannis , 33, 426 n.21
  Hazaras, 448 n.76
  Jadrans, 60, 99
  Jajis, 21, 33, 54, 91, 95, 99–100, 110, 426 n.21
  Kizzilbash, 228, 438 n.79
  Kohistanis, 145, 149
  Mangals, 33, 39, 50, 52, 54, 60, 74, 99, 102, 426 n.21
  Maqbils, 33, 426 n.21
  Marris, 224, 437 n.76
  Muserzais, 96, 103
  Pathans, 34, 36, 41–2, 197
  Turis, 21, 32, 56, 426 n.20
  Wazirs, 108, 426 n.21
  Zaimuhkts, 21, 33, 426 n.24
Tucker, Capt. L.H.E., 38, 427 n.34
Tunnel, Channel, 232, 254–6, 439 n.8
Turkestan, Russian, 12
Turkey, 11
Tyndal, Lt.-Col. G., 308, 441 n.52
Tyndal, Lt.-Col. H., 80, 428 n.65
Tytler, Maj.-Gen. J.A., 119, 433 n.6

ROBERTS IN INDIA

ARMY RECORDS SOCIETY
(FOUNDED 1984)

Members of the Society are entitled to purchase back
volumes at reduced prices.
Orders should be sent to the Hon. Treasurer, Army Records Society,
c/o National Army Museum,
Royal Hospital Road,
London SW3 4HT

The Society has already issued:

Vol. I:
The Military Correspondence of
Field Marshal Sir Henry Wilson 1918–1922
Edited by Dr Keith Jeffery

Vol. II:
The Army and the
Curragh Incident, 1914
Edited by Dr Ian F.W. Beckett

Vol. III:
The Napoleonic War Journal of
Captain Thomas Henry Browne, 1807–1816
Edited by Roger Norman Buckley

Vol. IV:
An Eighteenth-Century Secretary at War
The Papers of William, Viscount Barrington
Edited by Dr Tony Hayter

Vol. V:
The Military Correspondence of
Field Marshal Sir William Robertson 1915–1918
Edited by David R. Woodward

Vol. VI:
*Colonel Samuel Bagshawe and the
Army of George II, 1731–1762*
Edited by Dr Alan J. Guy

Vol. VII:
Montgomery and the Eighth Army
Edited by Stephen Brooks

Vol. VIII:
*The British Army and Signals Intelligence
during the First World War*
Edited by John Ferris